"BEST OF *LOTUS*"

REPRINT SERIES

LOTUS
Magazine

THE
MACRO BOOK

.

Expert Advice for *1-2-3* and *Symphony* Users

DANIEL GASTEIGER

with

Paula Dempsey, Robert Quinn, Donald E. Klamon
Timothy Berry, Chris Brown

Series Editor: Steven E. Miller
LOTUS PUBLISHING CORPORATION

ADDISON-WESLEY PUBLISHING COMPANY, INC.
Reading, Massachusetts ▲▼ Menlo Park, California
New York   Don Mills, Ontario   Wokingham, England   Amsterdam
Bonn   Sydney   Singapore   Tokyo   Madrid   San Juan

Library of Congress Cataloging-in-Publication Data

Lotus magazine, the macro book.

("Best of Lotus" reprint series)
Includes index.
1. Lotus 1-2-3 (Computer program)
2. Symphony (Computer program) 3. Macro
instructions (Electronic computers) 4. Business
—Data processing. I. Lotus (Cambridge, Mass.)
II. Title. III. Title: Lotus magazine.
HF5548.4.L67G37 1988   005.36'9   88–933
ISBN 0–201–15665–6

Cover illustration by Philippe Weisbecker.

ISBN 0-201-15665-6

ABCDEFGHIJ–A L–898
Second Printing, May, 1988

ACKNOWLEDGMENTS

This book would not be possible without the staff of *LOTUS* magazine: Carolyn L.Adams, Suki Adams, Claudia Basso, Mary Ellen Bittel, Lisa Boyd, Chris Brown, Paula Dempsey, Cynthia G. Fitzgerald, Deborah Flynn-Hanrahan, Elisabeth Folsom, Rich Friedman, Daniel Gasteiger, Linda J. Gill, Christopher J. Gowland, Phyliss L. Greenberg, William H. Gregory, Ruth Hawryluk, Kathy Heaton, Robert Hildebrand, Elizabeth Jensen, Sue Ellen Kelly, Katherine Koerner, Alice H. Mangum, Subhadra Mattai, Eleanor M. McCarthy, Janet H. Meacham, Nancy E. Miller, Steven E. Miller, Kathy Minnix, Mary Jean Mockler, Christopher Morgan, Jeanne Nisbet, Madonna O'Brien, James R. Pierce, Stacy M. Pierce, Carol Recchino, Richard W. Ridington Jr., Phyllis A. Sharon, Jennifer Smith, Jan Souza, Carrie Thomas, Julie E. Tuton, Regina L. Twiss, Jill Winitzer.

In addition, we acknowledge the staff of the Lotus Development Graphic Services department: Helen Betz, Andy Hollinger, Bonnie McCoy, Henry Nigro, Judy Riessle, and Andrea Soule.

CONTENTS

SECTION 7   Letters to the Macro Editor, Questions,
             and Advice   355

Welcome to the

"BEST OF *LOTUS*"

The job of *LOTUS* magazine is to give you access to the experts. We solicit the best authors and trainers. We present articles and technical advice from the people at Lotus Development Corporation. And we provide a forum for all of you to talk to each other in your efforts to apply computer skills to solving everyday business problems.

Monthly magazines are typically treated as disposable. You get them in the mail, scan the table of contents, read a bit, then throw them out. That's what we expected to happen to *LOTUS* magazine. But we were wrong.

From the earliest issues you let us know that you were saving your back copies and filling in gaps in your collection. (For those of you still wishing to do this, we have limited numbers of back issues at $5 each. Mail your check, address, and list of desired issues to *LOTUS*, P.O. BOX 9160, Cambridge, MA 02139-9160.)

It became obvious that you were archiving *LOTUS* to use as a reference source and a training tool. But as the pile of old issues climbed higher and higher, you began having problems finding the specific articles you dimly remembered reading sometime ago. Our semiannual indexes helped, but that wasn't enough.

As a way to meet this need and to make our old material available to new subscribers, we are offering a reprint series in book form. It will include *LOTUS* articles from all of our back issues and will be organized around such focused themes as macros, good ideas, worksheet skills, and business applications.

Our reasons for publishing *LOTUS* magazine are the same now as when we started. We believe *1-2-3* and *Symphony* users need straightforward, practical instruction on how to get the most from their computers and their software. Our research tells us that *1-2-3* and *Symphony* users are part of a special group of people who are using computers not only to automate manual tasks but also to create new ways of doing business. These people aren't computer experts. They occupy all levels of their organizations and hold all kinds of titles. What unites them is their desire to use the computer as an efficient tool.

Our ongoing challenge is to invent a new kind of magazine, suitable for both beginners and experts, written in ordinary language, that starts from the software you use and works through to the solutions you need. We are inspired by the growing network of local user groups, in which people come together to share their knowledge, listen to news announcements, attend a featured presentation, break up into special interest groups, and enjoy one another's company.

LOTUS, we believe, has to act and feel like a "user group in print." There has to be lots of room for reader feedback and contributions. In order to keep in front of such a rapidly changing industry, we have to stay in constant contact with our readers through mail-in cards, telephone surveys, focus groups, questionnaires, and direct phone calls. As it has turned out, we get hundreds of letters from you each month, and a good percentage of the material in every issue of *LOTUS* starts as a reader contribution.

We also know that *LOTUS* has to look good. We use high-quality paper, solicit illustrations from the best artists, and make sure our layout is clean, clear, and worth looking at. We feel we can't ask people to pay for something that looks second rate.

Finally, *LOTUS* can't be a textbook or a specifications sheet. This is not a techie magazine. Our readers are busy people who need to get their jobs done. Everything we publish has to immediately help someone accomplish something. Because you are busy people, our articles have to be relatively short, our illustrations instructive, our models effective.

Since the first issue of *LOTUS* reached readers in May 1985, the magazine's list of paid subscribers has grown faster than that of any other magazine in the history of United States publishing. We're very proud of that fact, primarily because it says we've stayed in touch with you, and are continuing to serve your needs. While we don't expect that growth rate to continue, we do intend to remain as closely connected to our readership as possible as the magazine continues to evolve and grow.

LOTUS was just the first venture of Lotus Publishing Corporation. We have worked with other publishers to create international editions of the magazine, the first appearing in the United Kingdom. We've published a special insert about engineering and scientific computing, called ESC. We've created a catalog sales operation called Lotus Selects. This reprint series signals our entrance into book publishing.

But in all our efforts, we know we will succeed only if we maintain an interactive relationship with our readers. Please let us know what you think of this book series and of our other endeavors. Our address is Lotus Publishing Corporation, P.O. Box 9160, Cambridge, MA 02139-9160.

Steven E. Miller
Series Editor
Director of New Product Development
Lotus Publishing Corporation

Introduction to

THE MACRO BOOK

One of the reasons for *1-2-3*'s rapid rise to spreadsheet dominance was macros. Macros transformed *1-2-3*, and then *Symphony*, from merely an excellent applications package into an interactive programming environment. That concept seems rather intimidating so macros acquired a reputation as an expert-level skill. And that's a shame because macros can also be very simple. This book is intended for beginners as well as advanced users.

It's true that you can use *1-2-3* and *Symphony* without ever creating a macro. In fact, whenever possible, it is best to accomplish a task without using macros. But once you've discovered how helpful macros can be, you'll be amazed that you ever got along without them. And helping you learn how to use macros to increase your productivity is the goal of this book.

Macros are most immediately useful as a way to speed up repetitive tasks. At their simplest, macros are a form of automatic typing. Instead of having to enter manually a series of frequently used keystrokes, you just press two keys, and the macro enters the series for you. You can make these macros do even more by including keystrokes that issue regular *1-2-3* or *Symphony* commands. For example, a simple macro of this type might send the keystrokes needed to widen a spreadsheet column. None of this involves any programming expertise or advanced knowledge of *1-2-3* or *Symphony*.

When you've mastered the basic skills, you can begin placing "flow-of-control" commands in your macros. These commands let your macros perform tasks such as examining cell contents in your worksheet and then, depending on the result of the examination, perform one or another series of actions. If you're really confident of your technique you can create totally automated applications ready for use by other people.

This book comprises selected articles and columns that appeared in *LOTUS* from May 1985 through October 1987. Obviously, most of the chapters are reprints of Daniel Gasteiger's popular *1-2-3* and *Symphony* Macros columns. Along with these are some of Paula Dempsey's Macro Basics columns, Bob Quinn's and Donald Klamon's For Developers columns, and a couple of macro-oriented feature articles, including Chris Brown's "Write Your First *1-2-3* Macro."

In this book, we have maintained the various conventions used in *LOTUS* magazine. For example, we use uppercase letters for macro commands, program commands, and @functions. We use lowercase letters for range names and cell addresses used by macros, and each macro's name appears to the left of its first cell.

Remember that all lines of macro code must be entered as labels. When you copy macro code into your own worksheets, make sure to place an apostrophe (a left-justifying label prefix) before any line of code that begins with a number, an arithmetic operator (+ , −, *, and so on), or any other label prefix, such as a slash (/), backslash (\), or caret (^). If you don't, you may get unexpected results. Remember, when you're copying macro code into your own worksheet, for any line that visibly begins with a slash (/), a label prefix character such as a caret (^) or a backslash (\), a value (3), or any arithmetic operator (+ , −, *, etc.), you must place an apostrophe (') which serves as a left-justifying label prefix before the entry or you may get unexpected results. In addition, whenever possible, we have followed the practice of referring to worksheet ranges using range names (*total*) rather than cell addresses (A2..B4). This makes the macros easier to understand and reduces the chance of error as your worksheet evolves and the desired range shifts location.

The Macro Book is for users of all releases of *1-2-3* and *Symphony*. Some articles are written for users of a particular program or release. In almost all cases, however, the general techniques used in the articles are relevant for all users. In fact, most of the macros written for one version of a product can be used in other versions and, with some simple changes, even in other products. For example, all releases of *1-2-3* support the /X macro commands, so macros that rely on these "flow-of-control" methods will work in all versions of that product. In addition, *1-2-3* Releases 2, 2.01, and all versions of *Symphony* share a similar macro language, so macros written for any one of these products often work in the others.

To let you know immediately what product or release an article is most relevant for, we have placed the following symbol on the first page of each chapter and letter:

| A | 2 | S |

This symbol has three parts which stand for *1-2-3* Release 1A, *1-2-3* Release 2/2.01, and *Symphony* respectively. If all three parts are visible, the article is immediately relevant for users of all three categories of products and releases. If only one or two parts are visible, the article is most relevant to users of the products and releases included in those categories.

Inevitably, there are some limits to the use of macros across products and versions. *1-2-3* and *Symphony* have different menu structures and occasionally use different menu commands for the same function. Therefore, if you are translating macros between *1-2-3* and *Symphony* you must usually rewrite any lines that issue menu commands. Similarly, *1-2-3* lacks *Symphony*'s multiple environments, so any *Symphony* macros that use windowing, communications, form entry, or word processing capabilities cannot be carried over into *1-2-3*. In addition, while *1-2-3* uses the slash key (/) to access the main menu, *Symphony* divides the task between the SERVICES and the MENU keys. To complicate things a bit more, when Symphony is in SHEET mode you can also use the slash key to access the main spreadsheet menu and in *1-2-3* Release 2/2.01 you can use the macro keyword {MENU} to press the slash key.

Finally, since *1-2-3* Release 2 was a major upgrade of the old Release 1A, it often takes tricky techniques and hard work to make the older release accomplish what can be done rather easily in later releases. Therefore, even though Release 1A macros often contain good examples of macro methodology, the specific macros may not be relevant for other releases of *1-2-3* or *Symphony*. On the other hand, since many *1-2-3* clones use Release 1A as their starting point these macros might be useful in those products.

There are seven sections in *The Macro Book*. The first section, "Getting Started: Not Only for Beginners," explains what macros are, provides some short but useful macros, then explains differences between macros written for the various releases of *1-2-3* and *Symphony*. The second section, "Macro Techniques," shows you how to make your macros more powerful and effective. The third section, "Using Data," presents ways to use macros to enter, compute, and rearrange data, including methods for creating mailing labels. The fourth section, "For *Symphony*, but Not Exclusively," is intended specifically for *Symphony* users, although users of *1-2-3* Release 2/2.01 might find some of these techniques helpful as well. The fifth section, "More Power for *1-2-3* Release 1A," is focused on people still using that early release of *1-2-3*. You can use most of the macros presented in this section in Release 2/2.01, although there may be more efficient methods of accomplishing the same tasks in the later releases. The sixth section, "For Advanced Users" will help more-experienced macro programmers develop worksheets to be used by others. And the seventh section, "Letters to the Macro Editor," is a compilation of letters to the *LOTUS* macro editor, and the editor's response. Most of these letters and the replies were edited by Paula Dempsey.

We hope you enjoy this book. And if you have discovered your own techniques for getting the most out of your macros, please share them with the rest of us. Every issue of *LOTUS* magazine includes macro letters and good ideas — all of which come from people like you. Just because you think something is obvious doesn't mean it isn't news to someone else. So keep those letters coming to the Macros Editor, *LOTUS* Magazine, P.O. Box 9123, Cambridge, MA., 02139-9123.

A NOTE ON THE AUTHORS

Daniel Gasteiger is the Macro Department Editor for *LOTUS* magazine.

Paula Dempsey started at Lotus Development in the Product Support Department, came to *LOTUS* Magazine as an Assistant Technical Editor, and is now back at Lotus Development Corporation as a Technical Writer.

Chris Brown is the Senior Editor for Features and Departments at *LOTUS* magazine.

Donald E. Klamon is Assistant Vice President and Manager of End-User Computing for the Hibernia Bank in San Francisco.

Robert Quinn founded the New Jersey Lotus Users' Group and then his own company, Q-Soft. He now works as the Symphony Product Marketing manager for Lotus Development Corporation.

Tim Berry is the President of Infoplan, a Palo Alto, California developer of custom templates. He is the author of *Working Smart with Electronic Spreadsheets* published by Hayden Books.

SECTION

1

GETTING STARTED:
Not Only for Beginners

Getting started can be the most difficult part of using macros. Perhaps you've done fine without them. Perhaps you just haven't had time to learn. The good news is that, like pushing a stalled car, once you overcome the initial inertia, moving forward doesn't require much effort.

In fact, with macros, even the first couple of steps are no big deal once you know some simple facts. And that's exactly what you'll get from this section of the book. The first chapter, "Write Your First *1-2-3* Macro," will help both *1-2-3* and *Symphony* beginners realize it's not as bad as they thought.

However, the real point of learning macros is to increase your computer productivity. So the following four chapters describe how to create everyday utilities — short, simple macros that help automate repetitive tasks. These are among the most valuable chapters in this whole book.

The last three articles in this section help overcome the upgrade blues by showing *1-2-3* Release 2/2.01 users how to translate macros that were written for Release 1A, and helping *Symphony* users adapt macros written for *1-2-3*.

If you are a *Symphony* user, you should not automatically skip over the *1-2-3* chapters in this book. Similarly, *1-2-3* users should not assume that a *Symphony*-oriented chapter won't contain valuable tips. The principles behind most good macro code are most often transferable.

1

Write Your First 1-2-3 Macro

Spend 20 minutes with this low-intensity tutorial
and you'll be well on your way to macro literacy.

BY CHRIS BROWN

Stop everything. Clear your worksheet and move the pointer to cell B1. Now type *Today I am going to write my first macro* ~. Congratulations, you've just written your first macro. That's all there is to it, and if you think that the entry in cell B1 looks suspiciously like a label, you've gleaned a fundamental principle of macro lore. Macros are really labels entered into worksheet cells. In the macro you've just written, the text is followed by a tilde (~). A tilde is a special macro symbol that tells *1-2-3* to press the Return key.

At this point, your first macro won't do much since you can't invoke it. (*Invoking* a macro is a high-tech way of saying *starting* a macro.) To invoke this macro, you must first name it. No problem. Press the slash key and select Range Name Create, then enter \a when prompted for the name, and press Return twice to enter the name and specify B1 as the range. So you won't forget the name you've given this macro, move the pointer to A1 and enter '\a. (Don't forget to precede the backslash with a label prefix such as the apostrophe.) You have now named your first macro by providing a range name for the cell in which it resides (B1), and you've also documented your first macro by placing its name immediately to the left in cell A1. Nice going, you're showing excellent technique.

You can use any letter of the alphabet to name a macro. Whatever letter you use must be preceded by the backslash. You can also name a *1-2-3* macro \∅. With this special name, the macro automatically executes when you load the worksheet

	A	B	C	D	E	F
1	\a	Today I am going to write my first macro.~				
2						
3						
4						
5	Today I am going to write my first macro.					

FIGURE 1. Believe it or not, this is a simple *1-2-3* macro. The keystrokes contained in B1 can be duplicated in cell A5 (or any other cell) by merely invoking the macro. Pressing MACRO-A instructs *1-2-3* to type the contents of B1 as though you were pressing the keys yourself. The label entry in A1 documents the macro by reminding you that the macro is named *\a*. The macro has been given this name because you assigned *\a* as the range name of cell B1. The tilde following the text in B1 represents a press of the Return key. This tells *1-2-3* to place the label in the cell currently occupied by the pointer, in this case A5.

containing it. A macro named \∅ is the *1-2-3* equivalent of a DOS AUTOEXEC.BAT file.

Run your first macro and see what happens. Move the pointer to A5. Now hold down the MACRO key (Alt on most computers) and press A (if your computer lacks an Alt key, consult your *1-2-3* documentation for invoking macros). Voila. Your macro executes and automatically retypes the keystrokes you entered in cell B1, then presses the Return key (remember the tilde?). This illustrates a second principle of macro lore. A macro is really nothing more than an automatic typing machine that will duplicate any keystrokes you specify. Keystrokes, such as the ones used so far, can represent letters that form words. They can also specify *1-2-3* command sequences by mimicking the menu choices you make while issuing *1-2-3* commands. Your worksheet should look like the one in figure 1.

SEE, IT'S EASY

So it's safe to put aside all your preconceptions about *1-2-3* macros. You don't have to be a spreadsheet guru or computer overachiever to devise and write simple macros. Sure, you can use advanced macros to automate large, complex applications, and watching *1-2-3* step through such applications while seemingly on autopilot is certainly impressive. Macros, however, are just as useful for simplifying routine operations. Saving and retrieving files, placing labels or values in cells, and naming ranges are just a few examples. Using macros to perform these everyday operations is the first step toward macro fluency.

Let's write another macro. Move the pointer to cell B7, enter '/RNC, and press Return. Be sure to begin this entry with a label prefix. If you do not, *1-2-3* assumes that you are trying to name a range rather than specify a macro command sequence.

	A	B	C
7	\r	/RNC	
8			
9			
10			

FIGURE 2. This macro duplicates the *1-2-3* command sequence required to assign a range name. Cell A7 documents the macro by letting you know the range name assigned to cell B7. Cell B7 contains a label entry that calls up the *1-2-3* command menu and then chooses Range Name Create from it.

To use this macro, you must first assign a range name to the cell in which it resides. Select /Range Name Create, and when prompted for a name, type \r and press Return. Press Return a second time to specify cell B7 as the range to name. Document this macro by positioning the pointer in A7 and entering '\r into this cell. Once again, be sure to initiate this entry with a label prefix. If you don't, you'll end up with more r than you bargained for in A7. (The label prefix tells *1-2-3* that you're entering a label rather than activating the repeating label function.) Your worksheet should look like figure 2.

Will the macro work? Of course. Move to cell B10 and invoke the macro by holding down the Alt key and pressing R. Your screen flickers briefly as *1-2-3* steps with lightning speed through the commands you've specified. Before you know it, the control panel displays the *Enter name:* prompt. Since you'll be using cell B10 for your third macro, give it a range name now. In response to the prompt, enter \w and press Return twice. Hot stuff. You've just used a macro to name another macro. Document this new macro by moving the pointer to cell A10 and entering '\w.

A COLUMN-WIDTH MACRO

Although cell B10 is blank, you've given it a range name. Now you must devise a macro to put in it. This new macro will help you speed up the setting of worksheet column widths. Move to B10 and enter the keystrokes required to adjust a column's width. Remember, the first character you enter will not be the slash (/). Every macro is a label and must be preceded by a label prefix. So enter the following in B10: '/WCS. Test this macro by holding down the Alt key and pressing W. You are quickly prompted to enter a column width. For now, simply press Return to accept the default width of 9.

You can make this macro a bit more useful. Suppose your worksheet layout requires that several columns have widths of 15 characters. If you specify this width in the macro you've just created, *1-2-3* will automatically perform the entire width-setting operation for each column. In B11 enter '15~. Be sure to begin the

	A	B	C	D	
10	\w	/WCS			
11		15~			
12					
13					

FIGURE 3. This two-cell macro allows you to set column widths to 15 characters by pressing two keys — MACRO and W. The macro name appears in A10. In B10 a Worksheet Column-Width Set command (in Release 2, Worksheet Column Set-Width) is issued. In B11 a column width of 15 is supplied in response to the command prompt, and a tilde completes the entry by indicating a press of the Return key.

entry with the label prefix and to end it with the tilde. Your macro should look like the one in figure 3. Position the cell pointer in column A and watch the action.

Hold down the MACRO key and press W. When the macro executes, column A automatically expands to a width of 15 characters, and column B instantly shifts to the right. Now anytime you need to set column widths to 15 characters, position the cell pointer in the appropriate column and press MACRO-W.

This macro also illustrates a third piece of macro lore. A macro can occupy more than one cell on the worksheet. Multicell macros are in fact desirable since individual cells can be used to hold related groups of instructions or commands. In the column-width macro, the first cell (B10) holds the initial *1-2-3* command sequence /WCS. The second macro cell (B11) specifies the column width (15) and presses the Return key (~), which completes the width-setting operation.

This macro illustrates some other important characteristics of *1-2-3* macros. Although a macro can occupy any number of vertically adjacent cells in a worksheet column, only the top cell need be given a range name; *1-2-3* assumes that cell entries below the top cell are part of the same macro. *1-2-3* reads down a macro cell group and executes all instructions specified until it encounters a blank or nonlabel cell. Once *1-2-3* discovers a blank or nonlabel cell, it assumes that it has reached the end of the macro.

What happens when the last cell of a macro bumps up against another cell containing an entry? That depends on the entry. If the entry is a number or numeric formula, *1-2-3* ignores it since no label prefix is detected. If the entry is a label, *1-2-3* attempts to read it as part of the macro. When this occurs, two things can happen. At worst, *1-2-3* executes an unexpected command that alters worksheet contents. At best, *1-2-3* types the label into the control panel. In general, it's wise to give macros a wide berth on your worksheet. Put your macros in the upper-left or upper-right portion of the worksheet, where they are easy to find and safe from harm. Remember, inserting a blank cell in the middle of a macro brings the macro to a crashing halt. If you place macros to the right of your active worksheet area and then insert a row in your worksheet, you may interrupt a macro's instruction flow.

TABLE 1: SPECIAL-KEY INDICATORS

Key Indicator	Function	Key Indicator	Function
~	Return (referred to as tilde)	{ABS}	ABS
{DOWN}	DownArrow	{GOTO}	GOTO
{UP}	UpArrow	{WINDOW}	WINDOW
{LEFT}	LeftArrow	{QUERY}	QUERY
{RIGHT}	RightArrow	{TABLE}	TABLE
{HOME}	Home	{CALC}	CALC
{END}	End	{GRAPH}	GRAPH
{PGUP}	PageUp	{ESC}	Escape
{PGDN}	PageDown	{BS}	Backspace
{BIGLEFT}*	Move left one screen	{DEL}	Delete (use only in Edit mode)
{BIGRIGHT}*	Move right one screen	{~}*	To have tilde appear as ~
{EDIT}	EDIT	{{} and {}}*	To have braces appear as { and }
{NAME}	NAME		

*Available in *1-2-3* Release 2.

EDIT THAT MACRO

Since macros are merely labels, you can edit them with ease. Consider the preceding macro. Suppose you want to set the column width to 40, rather than 15, characters. Move the pointer to cell B11 and press the EDIT key. Now press the LeftArrow key three times to position the cursor under the 1. Press Delete twice to delete 15, then type *40* and press Return. Note the entry in B11. The macro has been edited to set column widths to 40 characters.

Let's continue our editing to encompass another concept of macro lore — the special-key indicator. Special-key indicators are macro commands that duplicate the functions of several special keys on your keyboard. Those keys control cursor movement, provide special *1-2-3* functions such as WINDOW and EDIT, and allow you to insert, delete, backspace, escape, and more (see table 1). You can include these special keys in any macro you write; the only catch is that you must enclose the names used to represent them in braces ({ }). We'll include some of these special keys in our \w macro.

	A	B	C
10	\W	/WCS	
11		40~	
12		{DOWN 4}{RIGHT}	
13			

FIGURE 4. We've edited the macro in figure 3 to do a bit more. Cell B12 now holds special-key indicators enclosed in braces. These tell *1-2-3* Release 2/2.01 to move the pointer down four rows and right one column after resetting the column width. You can use numbers in conjunction with certain keywords in *1-2-3* Release 2/2.01.

Move the pointer to cell B12 and enter *{DOWN} {RIGHT}*. Place the pointer in column A and invoke the macro by pressing MACRO-W. Note the pointer movement. After *1-2-3* executes the macro keystrokes required to reset the column width in cells B10 and B11, it executes the instructions in cell B12 and moves the pointer down one cell, then right one cell. If you use Release 2/2.01, move back to B12 and edit the entry to read *{DOWN 4}{RIGHT}*. Your macro should now look like the one in figure 4. Move the pointer to A12, invoke the macro, and note the new position of the pointer. It is in cell B16. In Release 2/2.01, you can add numbers to certain special-key indicators to specify repetitions of those instructions.

AT LAST—A WORD-WRAP MACRO

While you're at it, why not write one last macro — the denouement of this first encounter with *1-2-3* macros. This macro will allow you to use *1-2-3* to write memos on your worksheets. It will automatically wrap text from one row to the next in a worksheet column. You're getting pretty fancy now, and in addition to using a few macro key indicators, you'll be using a macro /X command. What, you ask, are /X commands? These special commands control the instruction flow within macros. Using the various /X commands (see table 2), you can create looping or branching macros or macros that present users with various prompts and menus. We'll start by creating a macro that loops back on itself.

First, document the macro by entering the following into cell A16: *'\t Text Processing Macro*. Move the pointer to B16, assign \t as the range name of this cell, and begin entering the macro exactly as it appears in figure 5. Don't leave anything out, and be sure to place a label prefix before all cell entries beginning with a slash. Once you've entered the macro, move the pointer to cell A21. Invoke the macro by pressing MACRO-T; note that the command (CMD) indicator appears, which means that a macro is in operation. (You didn't notice this indicator before because the previous macros executed so quickly.)

	A	B
16	\t Text Processing Macro	{EDIT}{?}~
17		/RJ~
18		{END}{DOWN}
19		/XG\t~
20		
21	The creation and use of macros is	
22	really a simple matter. However, the	
23	macro I'm in the midst of now is a bit	
24	of a mystery to me.	

FIGURE 5. This *1-2-3* word-wrap macro isn't as complicated as it looks. It has been assigned the range name \t and is documented in cell A16. The first instruction it executes is a special-key indicator that places *1-2-3* in Edit mode. The next special-key function ({?}) instructs *1-2-3* to pause until you press Return. The tilde that completes this entry tells *1-2-3* to escape from the Edit mode. Range Justify command keystrokes are executed in B17, and the special-key indicators in B18 place the pointer at the end of the text segment. The /XG command in B19 tells the macro to go to the cell named \t (B16) and to begin executing the instructions found there. This loops the macro back on itself where it again waits to accept input. Stop this macro by pressing Control-Break.

Now type the following memo: *The creation and use of macros is really a simple matter. However, the macro I'm in the midst of now is a bit of a mystery to me.* As you type, the control panel fills with text that eventually scrolls off the screen to the left. When you finish typing, press Return. You have just typed a long label entry into cell A21.

HOW IT WORKS

The first instruction in cell B16 is {EDIT}. This special-key indicator places *1-2-3* in the Edit mode. The next instruction is {?}. This tells *1-2-3* to pause until you press Return. You can do virtually anything during a {?} command, but all you should do with this macro is type text and then press Return. (Once you press Return, *1-2-3* processes the next command.) The tilde completes this cell entry by telling *1-2-3* that you have finished entering text and are ready to leave the Edit mode.

When you finish typing and press Return, *1-2-3* continues on, reading the keystrokes in cell B17. Here it executes a Range Justify command. Since you set the width of column A to 40 characters, the sentences you typed are broken into blocks of text as close to 40 characters in length as possible. Words extending beyond that limit are not split because the *1-2-3* Range Justify command is designed to break a label at the blank space prior to a word exceeding the column-width limit. If the text label you typed isn't 40 characters wide, the cell pointer ends up at the bottom of the worksheet. If this happens, press UpArrow End UpArrow EDIT. Start a new paragraph by pressing DownArrow twice, then continue typing.

TABLE 2: THE /X COMMANDS

Command	Function
/X*Icondition*~...	If-then
/XG*location*~	Continue reading keystrokes at location
/XC*location*~	Call a subroutine
/XR	Return from subroutine
/XQ	Quit macro execution
/XL*message*~ *location*~	Display a message in the control panel, prompting user to input label to be stored in location
/XN*message*~ *location*~	Display a message in the control panel, prompting user to input a number to be stored in location
/XM*location*~	Process a user-defined menu

Instructions in cell B18 move the pointer to the end of the paragraph or text block. The /XG command in cell B19 tells the macro to execute the commands found in the cell named \t. The net effect is that the macro loops back to the instructions in cell B16. When this happens, *1-2-3* once again returns to Edit mode and waits placidly for your keyboard input.

After you invoke this macro, you may not know how to turn it off. Since it is an endless loop, it is always waiting for more input. Not to worry. You can stop almost any macro dead in its tracks by holding down the Control key and pressing Break. Try it. If you're using *1-2-3* Release 1A, you are immediately returned to the Ready mode. In Release 2/2.01, *1-2-3* beeps and flashes the ERROR indicator, which means that you've stopped a macro in midstream. Press the Escape key to clear the error, and resume your spreadsheet work. (If the Break key had been disabled, this method of halting a macro would not have worked. In such a case, you must let a macro run its course or shut off and restart your computer.)

There you have it: a first encounter with macros. The ones you have written so far are rudimentary and provide just a glimpse of what you can do with this powerful programming technique. It's a beginning, however, and your future macros are limited only by your own ingenuity and increasing skill. Remember, in the ongoing battle for primacy that we all fight with our computers, macros are valuable weapons. Using them, it's easy to make your machine sit up and bark like a dog.

2

Introductory Macros

How to create a simple macro that enters text and formula.

BY PAULA DEMPSEY

If you find yourself doing the same thing over and over again, think macros. Macros are short computer programs that automate your spreadsheet work. You write the macro once and can then perform the task as often as you want with only two keystrokes. But don't worry, you don't have to be a programmer to write them.

Many *1-2-3* and *Symphony* users have told us that they don't use macros. Their reasons range from "I haven't had time to learn about them" to "I already know enough about spreadsheets to get my work done. Why complicate matters?" Admittedly, macros aren't appropriate for all spreadsheet tasks, but if you invest a little time in learning how and when to write macros, you can reap the benefits of time saved.

Macros can perform such time-consuming procedures as printing multiple ranges while you're away from the computer. Macros are also handy if you prepare worksheets that other people use. You can create worksheets that run with a series of prompts and menus so that even someone with no knowledge of *1-2-3* or *Symphony* can use them. But macros are most commonly used to perform short, routine tasks. This type of macro is called a utility macro.

A UTILITY MACRO

Let's say that each time you use the worksheet to type a business letter, you must enter your company's address. The following macro enters an address for you with just two keystrokes:

	A	B
1	\a	P.O. Box 9123~{DOWN}
2		Cambridge, MA 02139~

In a new worksheet, enter in cells B1 and B2 the labels shown in the figure. These two cells contain the macro. You may not have used the tilde character (~) before. On an IBM keyboard, it is found on the same key as the single open-quotation mark.

Before you can run a macro, you must assign a range name to the first cell in the macro. In *1-2-3* this range name must be a backslash followed by a single letter, *a* to *z*. (In *Symphony* you can use any range name for a macro.) It is a good practice to enter a macro's name in the cell to the left of the macro's first cell and then assign the name. Enter \a in cell A1. Be sure to type an apostrophe before \a so that your entry will be treated as an ordinary label, not as a repeating label. Now name the macro by placing your cell pointer in cell A1 and selecting /Range Name Labels Right. Press Return to accept cell A1 as the specified range. This assigns the range name \a to cell B1, the macro's first cell.

You're now ready to run your first macro. Move the pointer to a blank area of the worksheet. (In *Symphony* make sure you're running this macro in a SHEET window. Although you can run macros in any *Symphony* environment, you would have to modify this particular macro to make it work properly in a DOC window.) To start the macro, hold down the MACRO key and press *A*, the single letter specified in the macro's name. If your computer doesn't have a MACRO key, consult your *1-2-3* or *Symphony* documentation for instructions on invoking macros. The macro enters the address into the worksheet automatically.

Most of the characters in the macro represent the keystrokes you would type if entering the address manually. Let's examine how *1-2-3* and *Symphony* interpret each macro instruction.

P.O. Box 9123~{DOWN}   The program begins by typing *P.O. Box 9123* into the edit line in the top-left corner of your screen. It is exactly as if you had just typed the phrase yourself from the keyboard. The tilde that follows this phrase is used in macros to indicate the Return key. When the program encounters the tilde, it "presses" the Return key, which enters the contents of the edit line into the current cell, that is, the cell containing the pointer. Next in the macro is the keyword {DOWN}. In macros all special keys, such as pointer-movement keys and function keys, are indicated with characters enclosed by braces (except the Return key, which is represented by a tilde). All of the special-key indicators are listed in your *1-2-3* or *Symphony* documentation. {DOWN} represents the DownArrow key. When the macro encounters {DOWN}, it moves the cell pointer down one cell. After processing all the macro code in cell B1, the macro looks to the next cell down, B2, for more instructions, which it then processes.

Cambridge, MA 02139~ The macro types the phrase *Cambridge, MA 02139* into the edit line. The tilde enters the contents of the edit line into the current cell. After processing all the macro code in cell B2, the macro looks to the next cell down, B3. When it finds that this cell is blank, it stops processing.

Cells B1 and B2 both contain labels. In fact, macros always consist entirely of labels arranged in contiguous cells in a column (*1-2-3* Release 2/2.01 and *Symphony* macros can also contain string formulas). When the macro finishes processing keystrokes in the first cell of the macro, it looks to the cell below to continue reading keystrokes. When the macro encounters another label or string, it continues processing. When it encounters a blank or numeric cell, it stops processing. To ensure that your macro stops after it processes the last line, leave the cell below your macro blank. Otherwise, the macro would try to process the characters in the cell below the macro, causing unintended results.

Neither line in this macro is very long. We could have entered the entire macro into one cell rather than two. In fact, it's possible to enter up to 240 characters of macro instructions in one cell, but editing a label this long is no easy task. It's generally a good practice to break your macros into short labels.

Now let's go one step further and add a line to our macro that enters the current date below the city, state, and zip code. In cell B3, enter the label *{DOWN}@TODAY~/RFD2~* (in *Symphony*, *{DOWN}@NOW~{MENU}FD2~*). Go to a blank part of the worksheet and press MACRO-A to start the revised macro. Here's what the new line does:

{DOWN} Causes the pointer to move down one cell from where the city, state and zip code are entered.

@TODAY~ (in *Symphony* **@NOW~**) Enters the current date into this cell. The function @TODAY is unique to *1-2-3* Release 1A, but it can be interpreted by Release 2/2.01. If you run this macro in *1-2-3* Release 2/2.01, the program automatically converts the cell entry @TODAY to @NOW.

/RFD2~ (in *Symphony* **{MENU}FD2~**) Tells the program to give the cell the Date 2 format. These are the same keystrokes you'd use to change the format manually.

You can see how easy it is to create macros that enter text and formulas and issue commands. Add some instructions of your own to this macro. You'll be surprised at what you can do.

OCTOBER 1986

3

A Worksheet Adding Machine

With simple macros, you can enter and sum numbers
in a worksheet column as easily as you can
on an adding machine.

BY PAULA DEMPSEY

Entering numbers down a worksheet column requires two repetitive steps. First you type a number, then you press the DownArrow key to enter the number into the current cell and move the pointer down. If your keyboard has separate numeric and pointer-movement keypads, you can use keypads to enter numbers quickly. If your pointer-movement keys double as a numeric keypad, you must disable the pointer-movement keys in order to use the keypad for numeric data entry. This process is cumbersome, but you can make it significantly easier by using a macro to move the cell pointer.

The following *1-2-3* macro pauses so that you can enter a number, then moves the pointer to the next cell down the column. The macro automatically restarts, pauses so that you can enter the next number, moves the cell pointer down, and so on.

	A	B
1	\a	{?}{DOWN}
2		/XG\a~

Although this macro works in all releases of *1-2-3*, users of Release 2/2.01 may wish to use the following macro, which uses Release 2/2.01's advanced macro commands. This macro will also work in *Symphony*.

To try the macro, start with a blank worksheet and enter the labels as shown.

	A	B
1	\a	{?}{DOWN}
2		{BRANCH \a}

When you enter a label that begins with a backslash, slash, or arithmetic operator (such as *, −, +, @, and so on), start with a label prefix (an apostrophe). Assign the label in cell A1 as the range name for cell B1; position the pointer in cell A1, press slash (in *Symphony*, MENU), and select Range Name Labels Right. Then press Return. You're ready to run the macro.

Move the pointer to cell G1, press the NumberLock key to enable the numeric keys on the auxiliary keypad, hold down the MACRO key (Alt on most computers — your documentation includes instructions on invoking macros) and press A. Type any number and press Return. The macro enters the number into cell G1 and automatically moves the pointer to cell G2. Each time you enter a number, the macro moves the pointer down one row and restarts. When you've finished entering numbers, stop the macro by pressing the Break key (on most computers hold down Control and press Break). Stopping a macro this way may produce a beep and an ERROR indicator. Press Escape to clear the error and continue work on the worksheet.

Here's a line-by-line description of how the macro works:

{?}{DOWN}   The keyword {?} tells the macro to pause until you press Return. Whatever you type before pressing Return appears in the control panel at the top of your screen. When you press Return, the macro continues processing commands — in this case, the {DOWN} keyword. This enters into the current cell whatever you just typed, then moves the pointer to the next row.

/XG\a~   The \XG command tells *1-2-3* to continue reading macro instructions in the cell name before the tilde that finishes the command. In this case, that cell is named \a. The command means "continue processing macro commands in the cell named \a." It does not move the pointer to \a. This procedure is called branching. The equivalent *Symphony* command for branching is {BRANCH \a}. A macro that branches back on itself in this manner and that has no provision for stopping itself (other than intervention by a user) is called an infinite loop macro.

THE DECIMAL FEATURE

You can modify this macro to include the decimal feature of an adding machine. Change the first line of your macro, contained in cell B1, to read {?}*.01 {CALC}{DOWN}. Now without you typing a decimal point, the number you enter will have two decimal places. The macro automatically places a decimal point before the last two digits. For example, when you enter the number 6342, the macro stores the number as 63.42. Here's how it works:

{?}*.01{CALC}{DOWN}   The {?} command causes the macro to pause. You type a number, which appears in the control panel, and press Return. When you press Return, the macro types the characters *.01, which turns your entry into a formula. The {CALC} command converts the formula to the formula's value (in this sequence, {CALC} does not recalculate the worksheet). Finally, the keyword {DOWN} enters the value and moves the pointer to the next row.

SUMMING THE COLUMN

After entering a column of numbers, you can use the following macro to enter a formula at the bottom of the column to sum the numbers:

	A	B	C	D	E
5	\s	\-{DOWN}			
6		@SUM({UP}.{END}{UP})~			

To run the macro, enter the labels as shown. Use the Range Name Labels Right command to assign \s as the name of the first cell of the macro (cell B5). Put the cell pointer in the first blank cell below the column of numbers you wish to sum. Hold down the MACRO key and press S. The sum appears below a dashed line, and the macro stops. Here's how the macro works:

\-{DOWN}   Types a repeating label prefix (\) and a dash. The {DOWN} command then moves the pointer to the next row, leaving the previous cell filled with dashes.

@SUM({UP}.{END}{UP}) ~   Enters the @SUM formula into the cell below the dashed line. This step begins by typing the characters *@SUM(*. Then the sequence {UP}.{END}{UP} begins indicating the range to sum. It points to the cell containing the dashed line and anchors the cell pointer. The {END}{UP} sequence completes the range designation by expanding the pointer to include all contiguous entries in the column. The ending parenthesis completes the @SUM formula, and the tilde enters the formula into the current cell.

This macro can sum only contiguous entries in a column. For example, if there is a blank cell halfway up the column of numbers you wish to sum, the {END}{UP} sequence will expand the pointer only to the last filled cell before the blank. Half the numbers in the column will not be included in the sum.

DECEMBER 1986

4

Utilities

These short macros, submitted by our readers, can reduce your effort in building worksheets and performing regular maintenance tasks.

BY DANIEL GASTEIGER

To use any of these utilities, enter them into your worksheet as shown in the illustrations, then use the /Range Name Labels Right command to assign range names associated with the macros. You can place the macros anywhere on your worksheet as long as you assign range names to the appropriate cells (see the Conventions box for further explanation).

DATE MACROS

To enter dates in a format that *1-2-3* recognizes, you use the @DATE function. This takes the form @DATE *(year, month, date)*, where *year* is a number having up to three digits (85 equals 1985, 185 equals 2085) and *month* and *day* can have up to two digits each. It evaluates to a serial number for the date you enter. The serial numbers start with 1, which represents January 1, 1900, and run to 73050, which represents December 31, 2099.

If you use many dates in your worksheet, the @DATE function quickly becomes tedious. Several readers have recommended the following macro to speed up the process:

	A	B	C	D	E
1	\d	@DATE({?},{?},{?})~			
2					

It simply starts entering the @DATE function into the current cell, pauses for you to type the year and press Return, types a comma and pauses for you to enter the month, types another comma and pauses once more for you to enter the day, then finishes the @DATE function and enters it into the cell. Since this produces only the serial number for the date, other readers have suggested combining it with the command sequences /Range Format Date 1 Return and /Worksheet Column-Width Set 10 Return, which give the cell a date format and widen the column so the date becomes visible:

	A	B	C	D	E
1	\d	@DATE({?},{?},{?})~			
2		/RFD1~			
3		/WCS10~			
4					

Once you enter a date, you usually move to another cell to continue your work with the worksheet. Your macro can move the cell pointer along the current row with the {RIGHT} command or down the current column using the {DOWN} command.

	A	B	C	D	E
1	\d	@DATE({?},{?},{?})~			
2		/RFD1~			
3		/WCS10~			
4		{DOWN}			

A few readers use a macro that lets them enter dates in the familiar month/day/-year format rather than *1-2-3*'s year/month/day format:

	A	B	C	D	E
1	\d	/XNMonth (MM)? ~month~			
2		/XNDay (DD)? ~day~			
3		/XNYear (YY)? ~year~			
4		/RFD1~/WCS10~			
5		@DATE(year,month,day){CALC}~			
6					
7	month				
8	day				
9	year				

Here's how it works:

/XNMonth (MM)? ~month~ Displays the prompt *Month (MM)?* in the control panel and places the number you enter into the cell names *month*.

/XNDay (DD)? ~day~   Displays the prompt *Day (DD)?* and places your entry into the cell named *day*.

/XNYEAR (YY)? ~year~   Displays the prompt *Year (YY)?* and places your response into the cell name *year*.

/RFD1~/WCS10~   Gives the current cell the format Date 1 and sets the column width to 10.

@DATE (year,month,day){CALC}~   Calculates the serial number of the date you entered based on the values stored in the cells *year, month,* and *day*, then enters the value into the current cell.

Some readers want to know on what day of the week a date falls. They have devised the following macro, which enters a date's day into the cell to the right of the date:

	A	B	C	D	E
11	\f	/RNCdate~~{RIGHT}			
12		/XI(@MOD(date,7)=0)~Saturday~			
13		/XI(@MOD(date,7)=1)~Sunday~			
14		/XI(@MOD(date,7)=2)~Monday~			
15		/XI(@MOD(date,7)=3)~Tuesday~			
16		/XI(@MOD(date,7)=4)~Wednesday~			
17		/XI(@MOD(date,7)=5)~Thursday~			
18		/XI(@MOD(date,7)=6)~Friday~			
19		/RNDdate~{DOWN}{LEFT}			
20		/XG\f~			

Point to the cell whose weekday you want to know. Be sure the cell to the right is empty, since the macro writes the weekday in it. Then start the macro. Here's what happens:

/RNCdate~ ~{RIGHT}   Assigns the range name *date* to the current cell, then moves the cell pointer to the right.

/XI(@MOD(date,7) = 0)~Saturday~   Enters the label *Saturday* into the cell if the remainder of the equation *date* divided by 7 (date/7) equals 0. For all dates after March 1, 1900, *1-2-3* counts Saturday as the first day of the week. If the remainder of date/7 does not equal 0, *1-2-3* skips to the next command.

/XI(@MOD(date,7) = 1)~Sunday~   Enters the label *Sunday* into the cell if the remainder of date/7 equals 1.

The macro uses the same logic in each step containing a /XI statement to determine what label it should enter into the cell. When it has processed the last /XI command, it deletes the range name *date*, so you can use the macro again. By appending the commands {DOWN}{LEFT}/XG\f~ to the original macro, you can use it to place weekdays next to every date in a column. However, be sure to stop the macro when it reaches the last entry or you'll end up with a column of *Saturdays* running to the bottom of your worksheet.

POSITIONING CELL ENTRIES

Labels in a worksheet can be right-aligned, centered, left-aligned, and repeated through the width of the cell (in Release 2/2.01 and *Symphony*, labels can also be given a nonprinting left-aligned format). Once you have entered labels into the worksheet, you can change their alignment by issuing the /Range Label-Prefix command. This lets you realign entire ranges of labels with one command sequence.

Values are always right-aligned in the worksheet. This helps to distinguish them from labels but limits your freedom in designing worksheet models. Several readers have submitted macros that insert label-prefix characters in front of values, turning the values into labels. These modified cell entries are more flexible for visual presentation, but because all labels in *1-2-3* Release 1A have a value of zero, they are useless in formulas. (Release 2/2.01 users can reference labels that resemble numbers in formulas by using the @VALUE function.) If you aren't using the numbers on your worksheet for arithmetic operations, try this macro to center them in the column:

	A	B	C	D	E
22	\c	{EDIT}{HOME}^{DOWN}			
23		/XG\c~			
24					

Place the cell pointer on the first cell of the column of numbers you want centered before you start the macro. Stop it by holding down the Control key and pressing Break when the cell pointer reaches the end of your data.

Release 2/2.01 users can convert numbers to centered labels without a macro. Though the steps may seem complex, for long columns of numbers the process is considerably faster than using a macro. It works like this: Move the cell pointer to an empty column on either side of the column you want to convert. If there is no empty column, insert one on the right side using the /Worksheet Insert Column command. Assume the column of numbers you're converting runs from A1 to an undetermined row. Go to B1 and enter the formula @STRING(A1,0). Copy this down column B to the same row as the last entry in Column A — the fastest technique I know is to press slash and select Copy, then press Return period Left End Down Right Return.

With the cell pointer still in cell B1, press slash and select Range Values, then press End Down Return Left Return. The formulas in column B will display ERR;

erase them by pressing slash and selecting Range Erase End Down Return. Finally, move to A1 and press slash, select Range Label Center, press End Down, and finish with Return. If you inserted a column at the beginning of the process, delete it.

DIVIDING LINES

Many readers use macros that create dividing lines on the worksheet. Some of the macros insert rows or columns in which to draw lines; others create the lines in the current row or column. Use the following macro to create dividers in the current row:

	A	B	C	D	E
25	\r	/XLDividing Line character? ~~			
26		{EDIT}{HOME}{DEL}\~			
27		/C~.			

When the macro prompts with *Dividing line character:* in the control panel, enter the character you want repeated across the row. A common choice is the equal sign (=). Press Return, then use the Left- and RightArrow keys to highlight the part of the row that should contain the divider. Finally, press Return.

Use the following macro to produce vertical dividers in the current column:

	A	B	C	D	E
29	\v	/XLDividing Line character: ~~			
30		{EDIT}{HOME}{DEL}^~			
31		/C~.			

It is similar to the previous macro except that the preferred character to enter at the prompt is the split vertical bar ¦. Also, use the Up- and DownArrow keys to highlight the area in the column where you want the divider. Some readers suggest that you set the width of a column holding the divider to 1, thereby eliminating large gaps in your data.

COLUMN WIDTHS AND OTHER QUICKIES

If you've written macros, you've probably written one that sets column widths. Many readers recommend the following macro to help you set all your column widths efficiently:

	A	B	C	D	E
33	\w	/WCS{?}~{RIGHT}/XG\w~			
34					

The macro starts the /Worksheet Column-Width Set procedure, pausing so that you can adjust widths with the arrow keys or enter them numerically. It then moves the cell pointer to the right and starts again. You stop the macro by pressing the Break key.

A reader offered a macro to reset all columns to the default column width (9):

	A	B	C	D	E
36	\n	/WCR{RIGHT}/XG\n~			
37					

When all the column widths have been reset, stop the macro by pressing the Break key.

Here are a few short macros to split the window horizontally or vertically and to clear the second window from the screen:

	A	B	C	D	E
38	\h	/WWH~			
39					
40	\l	/WWV~			
41					
42	\x	/WWC			

To use them, place the cell pointer where you want the window to split, then invoke the appropriate macro. There is no need to position the pointer to clear windows.

The following macros turn worksheet protection on and off:

	A	B	C	D	E
44	\p	/WGPE			
45					
46	\u	/WGPD			

You needn't worry about where the cell pointer is when you use either of these macros.

One of the simplest utilities I've seen was created in response to the criticism that

1-2-3 takes four keystrokes to erase the contents of the current cell. The following utility cuts that number in half:

	A	B	C	D	E
54	\e	/RE˜			
55					

Though *1-2-3* is designed to process numbers rather than words, many readers use it to do both. As a result, they need to reset document spacing from single to double and back. You can do this by using printer setup strings, but the varied spacing this creates appears in margins as well as text and often gives unsatisfying results.

Here's a reader-generated macro that double-spaces worksheets before printing:

	A	B	C	D	E
48	\s	{DOWN}/WIR˜			
49		{DOWN}/XG\s˜			

If you think you'll need a single-spaced copy of the file later on, save it once before using the macro. Then put the cell pointer on the first row of the range you want double-spaced. Stop the macro by pressing the Break key when it has finished spacing the entire active area. To revert back to single spacing, retrieve the earlier version of the file or use the following macro:

	A	B	C	D	E
51	\q	/WDR˜{DOWN}			
52		/XG\q˜			

Be sure the cell pointer starts on the first blank line of the worksheet with this macro.

THE ULTIMATE UTILITY

Utilities are popular for obvious reasons. Most users have a few macros that speed their work, and there are plenty of tasks to optimize. When you've decided what utilities are most useful to you, put them in a single file and save the file with a distinctive file name (LIBRARY is a good choice). Retrieve this file whenever you start a new worksheet, and immediately resave it with a new file name. Now all your utilities are at your fingertips as you build your model.

5

Graphing Utilities

Simple macros can speed up your work with graphics and even control a graphics slide show.

BY DANIEL GASTEIGER

1-2-3 lets you create several different types of graphs to represent data stored on the worksheet. The number of graphs you can create with each worksheet is limited only by the amount of RAM you have available. But the more graphs you create, the more difficult it becomes to manage the graphs. This month we'll look at a few macros to use when you work with *1-2-3*'s graphics capabilities.

SOME GENERIC DATA

Many business worksheet applications lend themselves well to presenting graphic data. Quarterly sales projections, earnings statements, hiring trends, questionnaire results, stock prices, and technical research all involve data you can graph to augment your reports. Rather than focus on a particular application, we'll create some meaningless data to use throughout this discussion. When we're finished, you can apply to your own data the techniques we've explored.

Enter the labels in row 14, then enter the formula @DATE(87,3,8) into cell A15. In cell A16, enter the formula +A15+1, then assign a date format to cells A15 and A16: Press slash, select Range Format Date 1, indicate range A15..A16, and press Return. Cells A15 and A16 should contain asterisks indicating that the cells' format can't display all the data the cells contain. Widen column A: Press slash, select Worksheet Column Set-Width (Worksheet Column-Width Set in Release 1A), press RightArrow, and press Return. Dates should appear in the formatted cells. Copy cell A16 to range A16..A20.

Use the Data Fill command to enter data in column B: press slash, select Data Fill, indicate range B15..B20, and press Return. *1-2-3* prompts for a Start value; press Return to accept the default (0). *1-2-3* prompts for a Step value; enter 0.3. 1-2-3 prompts for a Stop value; simply press Return.

In cell C15 enter the formula @SIN(B15), and in cell D15 enter the formula @COS(B15). Copy these formulas as follows: Press slash, select Copy, indicate range C15..D15 as the range to copy from and press Return, then indicate range C15..C20 as the range to copy to and press Return. Finally, enter labels in row 14 to identify each column. Your worksheet should look like the following:

	A	B	C	D
14	Date	Value	Sine	Cosine
15	08-Mar-87	0	0	1
16	09-Mar-87	0.3	0.295520	0.955336
17	10-Mar-87	0.6	0.564642	0.825335
18	11-Mar-87	0.9	0.783326	0.621609
19	12-Mar-87	1.2	0.932039	0.362357
20	13-Mar-87	1.5	0.997494	0.070737

GRAPHING THE DATA

To create a graph in *1-2-3*, you must identify the data to be graphed. *1-2-3* automatically creates a line graph of the data unless you indicate otherwise. Once you've created a graph, you can assign it a name, preserving the graph's settings within the worksheet. You can then create a new graph representing different data and name the new graph to preserve its settings. When you've created several named graphs, you can view each in turn by selecting the graph's name from a menu. Let's create several graphs (their content is unimportant) and see how all this works.

Press slash and select Graph X. Indicate range A15..A20 and press Return. Select B, indicate range C15..C20, and press Return. Now select View to see the graph you've just created. Because this is a line graph of sine values, we'll name the graph SINELINE. Press the Spacebar (or almost any other key) to return to the Graph menu, then select Name Create, and enter *sineline*. *1-2-3* returns you to the Graph menu.

View the sine data as a bar graph by selecting Type Bar View from the Graph menu. Press the Spacebar to return to the Graph menu, then preserve this new graph as SINEBAR by selecting Name Create and entering *sinebar*. Create two graphs of the cosine data as follows:

Select Reset B Quit to cancel the setting for the sine data. This cancels the setting for the current graph only, not for the two named graphs. Now select C, indicate range D15..D20, and press Return. When you select View, *1-2-3* displays a bar graph of the cosine data. Press the Spacebar, then preserve the settings by selecting Name

Create and entering *cosbar*. Select Type Line and then View (you needn't view every graph before naming it, but it's often encouraging to see that your menu choices have indeed altered a graph's appearance). Name this graph COSLINE: Select Name Create and enter *cosline*.

So far you've preserved four different graphs: two graphs of the sine data and two of the cosine data within the worksheet. Create two more graphs that display all of the data: Select A, indicate range B15..B20, and press Return. Select B, indicate range C15..C20, and press Return. Name this graph ALLLINE (view it first, if you wish). Then select Type Bar and name the new graph ALLBAR (again, you can view it first if you wish).

NAMING AND RENAMING

As you create several graphs in a single worksheet, you may begin to modify the graphs, adding titles and legends or changing display formats to make the graphs more comprehensive. When you wish to modify a graph, you first use the Graph Name Use command in order to select the graph. Then you make changes and preserve the changes in the worksheet by once again using the Graph Name Create command.

Because you repeat the graph-naming process so often as you create and modify graphs, the procedure is ideally suited to be implemented as a macro. The following is a macro that speeds up the graph-naming and renaming processes:

	A	B	C	D	E
11	\p	{ESC}{ESC}{ESC}{ESC}{ESC}{ESC}			
12		/GVNC			

To create the macro, enter the labels in our sample worksheet as shown. Then assign \p as the range name for the macro's first cell (cell B11): Press slash, select Range Name Labels Right, indicate cell A11, and press Return. To run the macro, hold down the MACRO key (Alt on most computers) and press P. Here's what happens:

{ESC}{ESC}{ESC}{ESC}{ESC}{ESC}   Presses the Escape key six times (Release 2/2.01 users can rewrite this line to read {ESC 6}). This step ensures that 1-2-3 is in Ready mode before the macro begins the name-creation process. You may be modifying a graph, working within the menus when you decide to preserve your work. The multiple {ESC} sequence will back *1-2-3* out of the menus from almost any point.

/GVNC   Presses slash and selects Graph View Name Create. When *1-2-3* processes the Graph View commands in this step, the current graph appears on your monitor. This provides an opportunity for you to check your work before preserving your changes to the graph. The graph displays until you press a key, then *1-2-3* processes the Name Create commands and the macro stops. If you are satisfied with the graph as you viewed it, type a name or point to an existing name in the menu in the control panel, and press Return. If you wish to modify the graph further, press Escape twice and return to the Graph menu.

MACRO DESIGN

This graph-naming macro is by no means the only graph-naming macro in the world, and it may not satisfy people who've already written similar macros. The macro is representative of graph-naming macros. As with all the macros we present, you should modify this macro to suit your working style.

You may not care to view your graphs before naming them. If this is the case, eliminate the V in the second line of the macro. You may want the macro to finish with *1-2-3* in Ready mode, in which case you should modify the last line of the macro to read /GVNC{?}~Q. Note, however, that when you rewrite the macro this way, if you wish not to preserve the graph settings after viewing the graph, you must stop the macro by pressing the Break key (on most computers, hold down the Control key and press Break). If this results in an error condition, simply press Return or Escape to clear the error.

Keep in mind as we continue that the techniques we present are representative of a much greater collection of macros, many of which can perform identical tasks.

RESELECTING GRAPHS

Often while modifying one of several graphs, you realize that you'd like to make a change in other graphs. It's common to switch from one graph to another throughout a work session.

The following one-line macro can speed up this process:

	A	B	C
1	\c	/GNU{?}~Q	

To use this macro, enter it as shown and assign the name *\c* to cell B1. Then, assuming *1-2-3* is in Ready mode when you start the macro (hold down the MACRO key and press C), here's what happens:

/GNU{?}~Q Presses slash, selects Graph Name Use, and pauses until you press Return. The macro pauses while *1-2-3* is displaying a menu of existing graph names from which you can choose. When you point to a name and press Return, the macro presses Return, and *1-2-3* displays the selected graph. When you press a key to clear the graph display (as before, any key will do), the macro selects Quit from the Graph menu, returning *1-2-3* to Ready mode.

Release 2/2.01 users can modify the macro to read /GNU{NAME}{?}~Q. Including the {NAME} command causes *1-2-3* Releases 2 and 2.01 to display all the graph names at once, rather than just the few that would normally appear in the control panel.

You might find it easier to keep track of the different graphs you create if you enter the name of each graph as a label in the worksheet. Then you can refer to the names quickly as long as they are visible when you first access the menus.

Listing graph names on the worksheet has another advantage. You can use a list of graph names in creating macros that manage the graph-selection process. Enter the following macro on the worksheet you've created to follow this discussion:

	A	B	C
1	select	/C~usename~	
2		/GNU	
3	usename		
4		~Q/XR	
5			
6	\u	/XCselect~	

Assign the labels shown in column A as range names for the adjacent cells of column B: Select /Range Name Labels Right, indicate range A1..A6, and press Return. Now enter the following list of labels beginning in cell E1. Note that each label represents a graph for which we've already created a name:

	E
1	sineline
2	sinebar
3	cosline
4	cosbar
5	allline
6	allbar

This macro performs the same task as the previous macro: It speeds the graph-selection process. To use the macro, start in Ready mode and point to the name of the graph you wish to make current. Then start the macro by pressing MACRO-U. Here's what happens:

/XCselect~ Calls the subroutine named *select*. The macro continues processing commands found in the cell named *select*. We wrote the graph-selection macro as a subroutine so that we could use the routine as part of another macro. We'll take a look at that in a moment.

/C~usename~   Copies the current cell to the cell named *usename*. This places a copy of the highlighted graph name into a cell within the macro (cell B3).

/GNU   Presses slash and selects Graph Name Use. By now the next cell (B3) contains the name of the graph you wish to use. The macro types that name in response to the prompt that *1-2-3* displays, albeit so quickly that you might not see it happen.

~Q/XR   Presses Return, entering the name just typed. *1-2-3* displays the selected graph and the macro pauses. When you clear the graph by pressing a key, the macro selects Quit and *1-2-3* returns to Ready mode. Then the subroutine ends, and the macro continues processing immediately after the /XC command that started the subroutine. In this case, there are no commands following the /XCselect~ statement, so the macro stops.

To get the real benefit from this macro, whenever you create a new graph, make sure you add the graph's name to the list in column E. Better still, consider using the macro's subroutine to create graphics slide shows.

SLIDE SHOWS

You've done almost all the work needed to create graphics slide shows. A graphics slide show is a presentation of a sequence of graphs. You preprogram *1-2-3* to display each graph in the sequence automatically. You might use such a show as a part of almost any business presentation. Enter the following macro steps into your worksheet:

	A	B	C
8	/s	/XCselect~	
9		{DOWN}/XG\s~	

Assign \s as the name for cell B8. Your slide show is ready to run. Place the cell pointer in the first cell of the list of graph names (cell E1) and press MACRO-S. Here's what happens:

/XCselect~   Calls the subroutine named *select*. As explained earlier, the subroutine makes current the graph whose name you've highlighted with the cell pointer. *1-2-3* displays the graph and the macro pauses. When you (and whoever is viewing your slide show) are finished examining the graph, press any key. The subroutine finishes processing and control of the macro passes to the commands in cell B9.

{DOWN}/XG\s~   Moves the cell pointer down to the next graph name in the list and restarts the macro. The subroutine processes again, displaying the graph associated with this new name. Each graph displays in turn until *1-2-3* has displayed all the graphs in the list. After the last graph displays, the macro stops running automatically. *1-2-3* will be part way through a menu sequence (or in an error condition, depending on which release of *1-2-3* you're using). Press Escape until *1-2-3* returns to Ready mode.

In Releases 2 and 2.01 edit the fourth line of the subroutine, cell B4, to read {WINDOWSOFF}~Q/XR and edit cell B8 to read {PANELOFF}/XCselect~. With these changes, the slide show will proceed from one graph to the next without displaying the worksheet. However, if you wish to interrupt this macro, simply pressing the Break key (Control-Break) may not suffice. To interrupt the macro, press Break several times quickly.

MARCH 1987

6

Symphony Demo Graphics

With these techniques you can write
a graphics slide show or even a self-running demo
including text, worksheet data, and graphs.

BY DANIEL GASTEIGER

Symphony lets you create several different graphs from data contained in a worksheet. One way to do this is first to establish a collection of settings on a named settings sheet. You can then name a new settings sheet and establish a second collection of settings that identify a different graph. You can name as many settings sheets as memory will allow, and each settings sheet can identify and define a unique graph.

Symphony also provides you with several different ways to keep track of the graphs that you create in a worksheet. You can work with a single window and attach a desired graph to that window when you wish to view or modify the graph. Or you can attach each graph to its own window and make a particular graph's window current when you wish to view or modify the graph. Let's create a few macros that exploit *Symphony*'s windowing capability to manage and display your graphs.

A FEW GRAPHS

Before we can write macros to manage our graphs, we should create some graphs for our macros to manage. For this discussion it's not important what the graphs represent, so we'll create some arbitrary data to work with.

Make sure that your computer has a graphics board and that you've installed a graphics driver in your *Symphony* driver set. Then, starting in a new worksheet, press MENU, select Range Fill, indicate range A17..A47, press Return twice, type 2, and press Return twice. *Symphony* fills the range beginning with zero and increasing by 2 with each cell in the range. Enter the following formulas in cells B17, C17, and D17, as indicated:

B17:@SIN(A17)
C17:@COS(A17)
D17: + B17*C17

Copy range B17..D17 to range B17..B47: press MENU, select Copy, indicate range B17..D17 and press Return, then indicate range B17..B47 and press Return. We're ready to create some graphs.

Before generating a graph from this data, we'll create a window to hold the graph. Although from within a single window you can create as many graphs as memory allows, we'll create one window for each graph and thereby provide a simple mechanism for browsing through the finished graphs.

To create a new window, press SERVICES and select Window Create. *Symphony* prompts you to enter a name for the window. Type *sinecurve* and press Return. From the resulting menu, select GRAPH to indicate that this should be a GRAPH window. *Symphony* highlights the current window and prompts you to indicate the window area; press Return to accept the highlighted area as the area for the new window. Select Quit from the resulting menu and *Symphony* presents a blank, or nearly blank, GRAPH window, depending on which release of *Symphony* you're using.

Press MENU and select 1st-Settings Range X. Indicate range A17..A47 and press Return. Select A, indicate range B17..B47, and press Return. Select Quit, then select Name Create and enter *sinecurve*. Select Quit and *Symphony* displays a line graph of the data.

The name of the graph appears in the bottom-left border of the window (the window's name appears in the bottom-right corner). In most releases of *Symphony,* the graph name will be MAIN — not the intended name, SINECURVE. To make the proper graph appear in this window, use the Attach command: press MENU, select Attach, highlight the name SINECURVE, and press Return. The resulting display will appear unchanged from the previous graph, except that the graph name on the bottom left of the window will match the window name on the bottom right.

This completes the procedure to follow in creating each graph in its own window: create a new window, generate a new graph, and attach the new graph to the new window. Let's do another.

To create a new window, press SERVICES, select Window Create, and enter *circle*. Select GRAPH, press Return, and select Quit. The new graph window, called CIRCLE, displays the graph you generated a moment ago (SINECURVE).

To create a new graph, select MENU 1st-Settings Name Create, and enter *circle*. Then select Type XY. Select Range X, press Backspace, and indicate range B17..B47. Select A, press Backspace, and indicate range C17..C47. Select Quit Quit.

Finally, to attach the new graph to the new window, press MENU, select Attach, indicate the new graph name, and press Return.

Repeat these steps to create the following graphs:

Window	Graph	Type	X Range	A Range
HEXAGON	hexagon	XY	B17..B47	D17..D47
VERTSIN	vertsin	XY	B17..B47	A17..A47
BARGRAF	bargraf	Bar	B17..B47	C17..C47

A SLIDE SHOW

By now you've generated six graphs — five that you named and one that *Symphony* named automatically. With practice, creating windows and attaching graphs becomes second nature. A collection of graphs created this way is particularly interesting when you use it in making presentations. As you discuss the month's sales figures or the next quarter's projected expenditures, you can page through a collection of graphs simply by pressing the WINDOW key.

Symphony keeps the windows you create in a stack, with the current window on top. When you press the WINDOW key, *Symphony* pulls the bottom window out from under the stack and places it on top. This becomes the current window. All you need do to prepare a slide show of the graphs you've created is to put the windows in an appropriate order. Here's a short macro to help put your windows in order:

	A	B	C
1	\s	{SERVICES}WU{MENU}	

To create the macro, return to the first window, MAIN, and enter labels in the worksheet as shown in the illustration. Assign the label in cell A1 as the range name for cell B1: press MENU, select Range Name Labels Right, indicate cell A1, and press Return. Start the macro by holding down the MACRO key (Alt on most computers) and pressing S. Here's what happens:

{SERVICES}WU{MENU} Presses SERVICES, selects Window Use, and presses MENU. This produces a full-screen menu of window names. Use the Arrow keys to select the window that should come next in sequence in your slide show. When you use the Window Use command to select a window, *Symphony* pulls the window out of the stack and puts it on top.

After you run this macro for the first time, isolate the window you've made current; press SERVICES and select Window Isolate. This hides all the other windows so that you can't access them by pressing the WINDOW key. Now whatever other windows you add to the sequence will be the only windows that appear in your slide show.

AUTO-GRAPHICS

You can write a macro that presents slide shows automatically for such purposes as self-running demonstrations of templates or instructional material. The following macro lets you program a different time delay between each slide to synchronize the slide show with a prerecorded narration:

```
        A       B        C        D        E
1  secs
2  name
3
4  wind     {DEFINE name:string,secs:value}
5           {SERVICES}WU{name}~
6           {WAIT @NOW+@TIME(0,0,secs)}
7
8  \d       {PANELOFF}{wind sinecurve,4}
9           {wind circle,3}
10          {wind hexagon,10}
11          {wind vertsin,3}
12          {wind bargraf,0}
```

To use the macro, enter it as shown and assign the labels in column A as range names for the adjacent cells of column B: Press MENU, select Range Name Labels Right, indicate range A1..A8, and press Return. The macro contains a subroutine named *wind*. When you start the macro, *Symphony* performs the subroutine repeatedly as indicated by the commands that begin in cell B8. When you start the macro by pressing MACRO-D, here's what happens:

{PANELOFF}{wind sinecurve,4}   Disables redisplay of the control panel, calls the subroutine named *wind*, then passes the variables *sinecurve* and *4* to the subroutine. *Sinecurve* is the name of the window to display, and *4* is the number of seconds for which the window should display. The subroutine contains a command that stores the variables on the worksheet; it works as follows:

{DEFINE name:string,secs:value}   Tells *Symphony* to store a string in the cell named *name* and a value in the cell named *secs*. The string and value that *Symphony* stores are described in the command that calls the subroutine.

{SERVICES}WU{name}~   Presses SERVICES, selects Window Use, calls *name* as a subroutine, and presses Return. This is the step that displays the window described in the subroutine call.

{**WAIT @NOW + @TIME(0,0,secs)**} Causes *Symphony* to pause until the computer's clock equals the current time plus the number of seconds indicated in the cell named *secs*. When the number of seconds has elapsed, control of the macro shifts back to the command immediately following the subroutine.

{**wind circle,3**} Calls the subroutine named *wind*, passing along the variables *circle* and *3*. This causes *Symphony* to display the window named CIRCLE for three seconds.

{**wind hexagon,10**} Causes *Symphony* to display the window named HEXAGON for 10 seconds. The macro continues in this manner, displaying the window named VERTSIN for three seconds and displaying the window named BARGRAF for 0 seconds (since BARGRAF is the final window, it remains on-screen after the macro stops).

This self-running demo isn't limited to a graphics presentation. It can include subroutine calls that display any *Symphony* window. By combining windows that contain descriptive text, worksheet data, and graphs, you can produce a comprehensive instructional program or demonstration. Play around with these for a while, and then create a self-running demo of your own.

MARCH 1987

7

Upward Compatibility, Part 1

Some observations for people who upgrade from *1-2-3* Releases 1A or 2 to 2.01.

BY DANIEL GASTEIGER

This column has been dedicated from its inception to presenting techniques that help *1-2-3* users push their software beyond its documented functionality. We've looked at ways to perform label arithmetic, to find and edit records in databases, and to create such advanced programming tools as For loops and assignment statements. We've shown that, for the most part, there are few sophisticated tools *1-2-3* Release 1A can't provide.

Then Lotus Development Corp. created *1-2-3* Release 2, a product that virtually eliminates the need to write clever macros to perform some of these feats. It was expected that worksheets created in *1-2-3* Release 1A would be entirely compatible with *1-2-3* Release 2, and at first glance, it appeared that *1-2-3* Release 1A macros would work just as well in Release 2.

Time has shown, however, that Release 1A macros do not necessarily perform as intended in *1-2-3* Release 2. Enter Release 2.01, which is more likely to interpret Release 1A macros as you'd expect. This chapter begins a two-part exploration of upward compatibility problems between the three releases of *1-2-3*.

MENU STRUCTURE

1-2-3 Release 2 recognized all Release 1A commands and formulas. In fact, Release 2 lets you make all the menu selections that you can make in Release 1A. This doesn't mean, however, that your macros will make the right menu selections.

1-2-3 Release 2 contains several menu items that Release 1A does not. Each of these was added at the right end of its respective menu but to the left of any Quit command on the menu. For example, the System command in Release 2 falls between the original Quit and Data commands on the main menu.

The arrangement of new menu items is for the benefit of people who customarily select the right-most items of a menu by pressing End Return. The new menu items had to go somewhere. They'll invalidate your macros only if your macros make menu selections by moving the menu pointer and pressing Return. In Release 1A, the two macros in the following illustration perform the same task:

	A	B	C	D
1	\m	/DSG		
2				
3	\s	/{LEFT}{LEFT}~{RIGHT}		
4		{RIGHT}~{LEFT}{LEFT}~		

Each macro presses slash and selects Data Sort Go. When you run the first macro (named \m) in *1-2-3* Release 2, the macro also presses slash and selects Data Sort Go. The second macro, when run in Release 2, presses slash and selects System, returning you to DOS command level (or resulting in an error condition). People who have written Release 1A macros that select menu items by the point-and-press method are likely to be disappointed when they run their macros in Release 2.

/DATA FILL

The Data Fill command lets you fill a worksheet range with a sequence of numbers. You select /Data Fill and *1-2-3* prompts you to indicate the range to fill. Generally, you indicate a range containing many cells. *1-2-3* then prompts you to indicate the first number to enter into the range, the Start value. When you enter a value, *1-2-3* prompts for the Step value, the interval that *1-2-3* should use to calculate the next number in the sequence. After you enter a Step value, *1-2-3* prompts for the highest number to enter into the range, the Stop value.

1-2-3 enters the Start value into the top-left cell of the indicated range, then adds the Step value to the Start value and enters the result in the next cell in the range. For each cell in the range, *1-2-3* adds the Step value to the value in the last filled cell and stores the result. *1-2-3* continues filling cells until every cell in the range is filled or until the latest fill value exceeds the Stop value. For a one-cell range, *1-2-3* Release 1A ignores the Step and Stop values and simply stores the Start value in the target cell.

The Data Fill command emerged as one of the most useful macro tools in *1-2-3* Release 1A. Because the command accepts numbers, cell references, formulas, and range names for any of the Start, Step, and Stop values, the command lets Release 1A macro writers alter the value of any cell on the worksheet without actually moving the cell pointer to the cell and editing its contents. For example, a Release 1A macro can use the command /DFtarg~targ+4~ ~ ~ to increase the value in the cell named *targ* by 4.

In the past, this column has presented several macros that exploit the Data Fill command, one of the most popular being a macro that date-stamps worksheets. This macro enters the value of the serial number for the current day into a cell named *date*:

	A	B	C
1	date		
2			
3	\m	/DFdate~@TODAY~~~	

The macro doesn't work in Releases 2 and 2.01.

There is a Data Fill command in *1-2-3* Release 2, but the command works differently from the way it works in Release 1A. If the Stop value you specify does not equal or exceed the Start value (except when you specify a negative Step value), Release 2 makes no entry into the target cell. The date-stamp macro fails in Releases 2 and 2.01 because today's date serial number is greater than the default Stop value that *1-2-3* provides (that is, 8192).

To use the Data Fill command in your Release 2 and 2.01 macros as you did in 1A, you must anticipate the greatest number your Data Fill commands will process and include a greater number as the Stop value in your macros. Many existing Release 1A macros that use the Data Fill command will need modification before they'll work in Releases 2 and 2.01. The remainder of this column deals with some of them.

DATES

Release 1A introduced the @TODAY function, which gave us a taste of date arithmetic. The @TODAY function generates an integer representing the day's date. The number represents how many days have passed since January 1, 1900.

Release 2 went beyond @TODAY by providing the @NOW function. The @NOW function provides information about how many days have passed since the turn of the century and how many seconds have passed since the day started. The @NOW function generates a date serial number that includes decimal values representing the time of day.

Release 1A macros that use the @TODAY function in date arithmetic may not function properly in Release 2. Release 2 automatically translates @TODAY to @NOW, attaching several decimal places of digits to the original integer value. If your macros perform calculations on these values to determine equality, you may be disappointed with the results in Release 2.

Release 2.01 takes the translation of @TODAY to @NOW even further. When you or your macros enter @TODAY into the worksheet, Release 2.01 translates the entry to @INT(@NOW), eliminating the decimal portion of the date and time serial number. In Release 2.01, your 1A date arithmetic should function as intended.

PRINTING RANGES

One bothersome change in Releases 2 and 2.01 of *1-2-3* is the method by which you indicate a Print range. In Release 1A, you merely indicate the column that contains labels you wish to print. If a label extends over adjacent columns, *1-2-3* Release 1A still prints the entire label. Your macros can easily assign Print ranges to print documents composed of text.

The newer releases of *1-2-3* work differently. They require that you indicate a Print range encompassing all the characters you wish to print. If your Release 1A macro uses an {END}{DOWN} sequence to indicate a range to print, the same macro in Releases 2 and 2.01 may not print all of the intended text. You must modify the Release 1A macro before it will function properly in Releases 2 and 2.01.

DATA FILL WITH ERR

Someplace on the planet someone has probably written a Release 1A macro that uses the Data Fill command to enter ERR into a cell. If you're that person, beware. Releases 2 and 2.01 won't necessarily process your 1A macro properly. The following macro works differently in 1A from the way it works in Releases 2 and 2.01:

	A	B	C	D
1	marker			
2				
3	\m	/DFmarker~@ERR~~~		

In Release 1A, the macro enters ERR into the cell named *marker*. However, in Releases 2 and 2.01 the macro leaves *marker* blank. The Data Fill command in Release 2 will enter ERR into *marker* if you adjust and revise the macro code to read /DFmarker~ @ERR~ ~ @ERR~ .

Let's suppose your macro uses the Data Fill command to copy a value from one cell to another, then tests whether the copied value is ERR. The following macro steps perform this task, with quite different results in 1A from those in Releases 2 and 2.01.

	A	B	C	D
1	test			
2	marker	ERR		
3				
4	\m	/DFtest~marker~~~		
5		/XI@ISERR(test)~/XGsort~		
6		/REtest~/XGstart~		

Here's how the macro works in Release 1A:

/DFtest~marker~ ~ ~   Places the value of *marker* into the cell named *test*. Since *marker* evaluates to ERR, *test* also evaluates to ERR.

/XI@ISERR(test)~/XGsort~   Determines whether or not *test* contains ERR. If *test* contains ERR, control of the macro passes to the cell named *sort*; otherwise, the macro continues processing in the next cell (B6). In this example, the macro branches to *sort*.

/REtest~/XGstart~   Erases *test* and transfers control to the cell named *start*. In this example, *1-2-3* doesn't process this step because the last macro command transferred control to a different routine.

Here's how the macro steps work in Releases 2 and 2.01:

/DFtest~marker~ ~ ~   Places the value of *marker* into the cell named *test*. Because the value of *marker* is ERR, this step leaves *test* blank.

/XI@ISERR(test)~/XGsort~   As in Release 1A, determines whether or not *test* contains ERR. In this example, *test* doesn't contain ERR, so the macro continues processing commands in the next cell (B6). Those commands erase *test* and transfer control of the macro to the cell named *start*.

If you've written Release 1A macros that exploit this unorthodox application of the Data Fill command, you may have to modify your macros before they'll work in *1-2-3* Releases 2 and 2.01.

NOW WHAT?

In view of the differences we've described so far, switching from *1-2-3* Release 1A to Release 2.01 might require some changes to your worksheet. Depending on the types of macros you've written, reworking large Release 1A applications for use in Releases 2 and 2.01 might prove time-consuming.

So far we've explored some of the changes to *1-2-3*'s functionality. We've avoided discussing label arithmetic and the advanced macro commands because these topics deserve a column of their own. In the next chapter we'll explore these more advanced topics.

8

Upward Compatibility, Part 2

More observations for people who upgrade from *1-2-3* Releases 1A or 2 to 2.01.

BY DANIEL GASTEIGER

If you upgrade from Release 1A or Release 2 of *1-2-3*, you might expect your macros to make the transition with you, and for the most part, Release 1A macros do work in later releases. However, there are several differences between releases that might cause macro failure for people who upgrade without guidance.

In the previous chapter we explored a few features of *1-2-3* Releases 2 and 2.01 that can affect macros written in Release 1A. In this chapter we continue the exploration.

/XL AND /XN

When *1-2-3* Release 1A processes a /XL or /XN command, the worksheet does not recalculate, even if you have set recalculation to automatic. Releases 2 and 2.01, however, *do* recalculate the worksheet when they process either of these commands if you have set recalculation to automatic.

This difference is more likely to slow down your data-entry macros than to cause macro failure. But aside from being slower, certain Release 1A macros could behave differently in Release 2. As a case in point, take a Release 1A macro I wrote that names the current cell, moves the cell pointer, accepts data input, and finally tests the value of the named cell. If the named cell had somehow relied on the cell into which I entered data, the macro would not work as intended in Release 2. If your data-entry macros don't contain such unlikely steps but are running noticeably slower, try setting recalculation to manual (/Worksheet Global Recalculation Manual).

LABELS AREN'T NUMBERS

The most problematic difference between *1-2-3* Releases 1A and 2 is the ability of Release 2 to perform label (string) arithmetic. If you switched from Release 1A to Release 2, you quickly learned that labels no longer evaluated to 0. (In Release 2.01 labels again evaluate to 0, a change that can affect macros created in any earlier release of *1-2-3* — we'll see how in a minute.) The illustrations at the bottom of the page show a single worksheet retrieved in Release 1A on the top and in Release 2 on the bottom. Cell A4 contains the formula + A1 + A2.

The difference in the way Releases 1A and 2 evaluate labels affects the calculation of formulas in the worksheet, the calculation of formulas in /X commands, and the function of the Data Fill command. The effect of label arithmetic on worksheet formulas is obvious: When you retrieve a Release 1A worksheet in Release 2, ERR appears wherever a formula references a cell containing a label (certain @functions allow references to a range containing a label). The other effects of label arithmetic are more subtle. Let's take another look at the /XN command.

When a macro processes a /XN command, *1-2-3* displays a prompt in the control panel and pauses to accept your input. *1-2-3* stores your entry as a number in a prespecified cell. If you enter a label — or more likely, a formula reference to a label (such as + B1, where cell B1 contains a label) — in response to a /XN command in Release 1A, the macro stores 0 in the target cell. In Release 2, as you'd expect, *1-2-3* stores ERR when you make a label entry.

	A	B
1	This is a label	
2	8	
3		
4	8	

	A	B
1	This is a label	
2	8	
3		
4	ERR	

To review, Release 1A evaluates labels numerically as 0, Release 2 evaluates labels as ERR, and Release 2.01 evaluates labels as 0. So you'd expect to see problems when you switch from Release 2 to Release 2.01, but not when you switch from Release 1A to Release 2.01. Unfortunately, Release 2.01 doesn't always evaluate labels as 0. If you make a label entry in response to a /XN command, *1-2-3* Release 2.01 stores the entry as ERR instead of 0.

These observations are especially important to people who've written data-entry macros that verify user entries. Your macro might test to determine whether an entry falls within a specific numeric range. While a Release 1A macro need test only for values that fall within the desired range, Release 2 and 2.01 macros must also test for the expression ERR. Without the added test, a macro's /XN commands might accept label entries and store them as ERR, even though the macro is designed to allow only entries falling between 500 and 1000.

The following illustrations show a Release 1A (top) and a Release 2/2.01 macro that successfully verifies user entries:

	A	B	C	D	E
1	\e	/XNNumber between 500 and 1000: ~test~			
2		/XI500<test#AND#test<1000~/XGskip~			
3		/XG\e~			
4	skip	/XN.....			
5					
6	test				

	A	B	C	D	E
1	\e	/XNNumber between 500 and 1000: ~test~			
2		/XI@ISERR(test=0)~/XG\e~			
3		/XI500<test#AND#test<1000~/XGskip~			
4		/XG\e~			
5	skip	/XN.....			
6					
7	test				

The point of instruction is not how to write data-entry macros that verify user entries (neither macro is well written). But rather, if you've already written Release 1A macros in a particular way, those macros will not work as you intend when you retrieve them in Release 2 or 2.01.

DATA FILL

In a previous chapter we discussed the Data Fill command, exploring the different ways the command handles such expressions as @ERR and @NA. Admittedly, not many people use the Data Fill command to assign ERR and NA expressions to worksheet cells. Another unlikely use of the Data Fill command is to assign a label's value to a worksheet cell. Still, it's interesting to note the difference in the Data Fill command's behavior for the various releases of *1-2-3*:

	A	B	C	D
1	\m	/DFtarg~source~~~		
2				
3	source	test		
4	targ			

The preceding macro simply places the value of the cell named *source* into the cell named *targ*. *Source* contains the label *test*. In Release 1A the macro enters the value $\emptyset$ into the cell names *targ*. In Releases 2 and 2.01, the macro leaves *targ* blank.

THE /XI COMMAND

The /XI command is a conditional branching statement. As written in the following illustration, the command means, "If the value of *test* equals 3, process commands starting in the cell named *rout*; otherwise, process commands in the cell directly below this one (B2)":

	A	B	C
1	\t	/XItest=3~/XGrout~	
2		{UP}{LEFT}	
3			
4	rout	{DOWN}{RIGHT}	
5			
6	test		

If *test* contains a label, *1-2-3* Release 1A determines that *test* doesn't equal 3, and the macro continues processing commands in cell B2. Under the same circumstances, *1-2-3* Release 2 compares the label with the value 3. In Boolean logic, anything that is not zero evaluates to true; since the value of *test* is ERR — @VALUE(test) = ERR — the macro branches to the cell named *rout*. Release 2.01 behaves identically to Release 1A in this application.

SOME RELATED OBSERVATIONS

That exhausts what we know of how older macros might misbehave when run in a later release of *1-2-3*. But the discussion brings to mind some thoughts about the features of Releases 2 and 2.01 that don't exist in Release 1A. If you make the transition from Release 1A to Release 2 or 2.01, there are several points to keep in mind.

For example, the Release 2 advanced macro command {IF} doesn't behave like the /XI command. The {IF} and /XI commands are similar in that they evaluate an equation and branch according to the result (∅ equals false, and not ∅ equals true) — *1-2-3* either performs the remainder of the commands in the cell being processed (true) or skips those commands and continues processing commands in the next cell (false).

The /XI command interprets ERR and NA as true. If an equation used in the command evaluates to ERR, the macro will continue processing in the cell containing the /XI command. The {IF} command, however, interprets ERR and NA as false. Keep this in mind as you build your macros. One command might prove more useful than the other for certain applications.

Another feature of Releases 2 and 2.01 that you might overlook is the ability of their command keywords to accept arguments. Your macros need no longer contain long sequences of {UP}, {RIGHT}, {PGDN}, {ESC}, or other commands. If the command should repeat four times, simply enter {RIGHT 4}. If the command should repeat as many times as is recorded in the cell named *count*, use the instruction {DOWN count}.

Learn the advanced macro commands. The Data Fill command was a great tool for Release 1A macro designers, but it's clunky when compared to Release 2's {LET} and {PUT} commands. Also learn the new menu sequences. Many of Release 2's menu selections eliminate the need for some of the more popular Release 1A macros.

If you're making the change from Release 1A to Release 2 or 2.01, go all the way. Most of your Release 1A macros will work as intended in the later releases, and with editing, all your macros will work. But if you rework the macros completely, the speed and power of your new macros will quickly recoup the time you expend in writing them.

FEBRUARY 1987

9

Macro Extras

The Macro Conversion Aid and Range Input add-ins can help you move your macros from *1-2-3* into *Symphony*.

BY DANIEL GASTEIGER

A *1-2-3* file that you retrieve in *Symphony* may not perform just as you'd like. The formulas and some of the settings will be intact, but many of the macros will behave as collections of random keystrokes. The menu structures of *Symphony* and *1-2-3* are sufficiently different that most keystroke macros won't work when moved between products.

For those who want to bring their macros over from *1-2-3*, rewriting each macro to work in *Symphony* appears a daunting task. However, if you're not interested in redesigning and rewriting your macros to take advantage of *Symphony*'s broader capabilities, you'll probably get a kick out of the Macro Conversion Aid.

MCA.APP

The Macro Conversion Aid (MCA) is an add-in created by Lotus Development Corp. MCA has been available for about two years, but unless you're a CompuServe subscriber, or you've called Lotus and asked specifically for such a tool, you probably have not heard of the add-in.

Once attached to *Symphony*, MCA can translate *1-2-3* macro code into *Symphony* macro code. The add-in changes *1-2-3* menu sequences into *Symphony* menu sequences so that the effects approximate those of the original *1-2-3* keystrokes. MCA also translates /X commands into equivalent *Symphony* Command Language commands.

You use MCA as you use any other add-in. To attach MCA to *Symphony*, select SERVICES Application Attach, enter the full path name of the directory containing the add-in (if the file named MCA.APP is on a disk in the B drive, enter *b:*; if the file is in a directory named \ADDINS on your C drive, enter *c:\add- ins*), then point to the file named MCA.APP and press Return. Select Quit to leave the menu.

To translate a macro, retrieve into *Symphony* the file that contains the macro. Then press SERVICES, select Application Invoke, indicate MCA, and press Return. *Symphony* prompts for the range to translate. Indicate the range that contains the macro code you wish to translate and press Return. The conversion is almost instantaneous, though long macros take longer to translate than short ones. The moment MCA finishes its translation, your converted macro is ready to run.

SOME CAVEATS

MCA translates almost every *1-2-3* command and menu sequence into *Symphony* equivalents, but there are some things that just won't convert. For example, *1-2-3*'s Range Justify command doesn't exist per se in *Symphony*. You can approximate the Range Justify command by switching the window type to DOC (or creating a separate DOC window), resetting the margins, and returning to a SHEET window—but MCA doesn't attempt to re-create these steps. Rather, MCA replaces every occurrence of the Range Justify command with the message {∗∗*'RJ' COMMAND DOESN'T EXIST IN SYMPHONY*∗∗}.

There are other *1-2-3* commands that simply don't have *Symphony* equivalents. *1-2-3*'s /Range Input and /Worksheet Window Synch commands have no *Symphony* counterparts (MCA doesn't recognize the Range Input add-in, which we'll discuss in a moment), and *Symphony* lacks TABLE and QUERY keys. During a translation, MCA replaces each of these *1-2-3* commands with a message that indicates translation isn't possible.

Even with an accurate translation, some of the macros that result from MCA won't work in *Symphony*. The most common problems arise in *1-2-3* macros that contain /XL and /XN commands. MCA translates these commands flawlessly when they contain a cell or range-name reference to the target cell, such as the following:

/XLEnter first name: ~first~

However, when the original /XL or /XN commands don't specify target cells, the resulting translations are meaningless in *Symphony*. The following is a legitimate *1-2-3* /XN command followed by MCA's nonfunctional *Symphony* equivalent. In *1-2-3* the command accepts numeric input to the current cell. In *Symphony* the translated command causes a macro to bomb:

1-2-3:   /XNEnter number of years: ~ ~

Symphony: {GETNUMBER "Enter number of years: ",}

MCA doesn't seem to know that *Symphony* and *1-2-3* handle sorting in different ways. *1-2-3* expects that the range of data to be sorted will not include database field headers. *Symphony* expects the sort range to have field headers at the top of each column. If your *1-2-3* macro uses the /Data Sort Data-Range command to indicate sort data, MCA's resulting *Symphony* macro will not indicate the correct sort data.

There seems to be a relationship between a macro's complexity and MCA's ability to translate the macro successfully. The most complex *1-2-3* macros arise in Release 1A, where you must create peculiar kludges to overcome the product's limitations. The greater the limitation that the macro overcomes, the less likely the macro is to work in *Symphony* after the translation.

We haven't tried to illuminate all of MCA.APP's shortcomings. Rather, we've presented a sampling of the types of problems to expect when using the MCA add-in. Generally, MCA will translate your macros adequately, leaving you to make a few corrections. On the other hand, your translated macros won't take advantage of any of *Symphony*'s added utility (*1-2-3* Release 2 and 2.01 macros generally do much better in *Symphony* after a quick transformation by MCA than do *1-2-3* Release 1A macros). If you're interested only in instant gratification, then try MCA.APP to convert macros from *1-2-3* into *Symphony*. If you're interested also in elegance, rewrite your translated macros to exploit some of *Symphony*'s worksheet alternatives.

INPUT.APP

1-2-3's Range Input command provides a means to create data-entry forms on the worksheet. Early releases of *Symphony* lacked a Range Input command, perhaps because the FORM window offers a powerful alternative. In fact, there has been a Range Input add-in as long as there has been MCA.

If you're making the transition from *1-2-3* to *Symphony*, INPUT.APP can extend the lives of your *1-2-3* macros. And even if you started spreadsheeting with *Symphony*, you might find use for this utility.

To use INPUT.APP, attach it as follows: Press SERVICES, select Application Attach, press Escape twice, and enter the full path name of the directory that contains the add-in (if the add-in is in the B drive, enter *b:*; if the add-in resides in the SYMPHONY directory of your C drive, enter *c:\symphony*). Then point to INPUT.APP, press Return, and select Quit to leave the menu.

As stated earlier, you use the Range Input command to create data-entry input forms on the worksheet. To create such a form, begin in a blank worksheet and set column widths as follows: A–1, B–14, C–2, D–1, E–5, F–2, and G–1. For example, to set the width of column A, point to cell A1, press MENU, select Width Set, and enter 1.

Enter labels into the following cells as listed:

Cell	Label
A1	First name:
D1	Last name:
A4	Street:
A7	City:
D7	St:
G7	Zip:

Then enter the characters \ = into each cell of the following ranges: A3..B3, D3..H3, A6..H6, A9..B9, D9..E9, and G9..H9. Unprotect cells A2, D2, A5, A8, D8, and G8. For example, point to cell A2, press MENU, select Range Protect Allow-Changes, and press Return. Your data-entry form is ready to fly.

Assuming you've already attached INPUT.APP, press MENU and select Range Input. Indicate range A1..H9 and press Return. The cell pointer jumps to cell A2 and *Symphony* displays the words *Range Input* in the bottom-left corner of your screen. Make an entry (type a label and press Return), then move the cell pointer by pressing the RightArrow key. The pointer moves to cell D2, skipping over the protected cells B2 and C2. Make another entry and press RightArrow; the cell pointer jumps to cell A5. Each time you press an Arrow key, the cell pointer moves to a different unprotected cell in the data input range. You deactivate the Range Input operation by pressing Escape, or by pressing Return without making an entry.

When *Symphony* processes a Range Input command in a macro, the macro pauses until you deactivate the Range Input operation. Then the macro reassumes control and continues processing with the command immediately following the Range Input command.

Generally, once a user has filled a Range Input data-entry form, the associated macro copies the data out of the form into a database. Then the macro erases the entries in the form and recycles, letting the user fill the form with new entries.

If you're moving your *1-2-3* macros into *Symphony*, try using MCA to translate the macros. Then replace any messages that read {**'*RI*' *COMMAND DOESN'T EXIST IN SYMPHONY***} with the commands {*MENU*} *RI*. Attach INPUT.APP, and give the macros a whirl. If the translated macros feel clunky, perhaps it's time to start fresh. If you're a seasoned *Symphony* user, play around with INPUT.APP. It offers an interesting alternative to *Symphony*'s FORM window.

GETTING INVOLVED

If you have *Symphony* Release 1.2, you already own INPUT.APP. The add-in resides on your Help and Tutorial Disk. If you have Release 1, 1.01, or 1.1, you can find INPUT.APP in CompuServe's World Of Lotus. MCA.APP is also available in the World of Lotus.

If you don't have access to CompuServe, contact a local software distributor or a user group. The add-ins aren't copy-protected, and you shouldn't be charged for copies. You may be charged for the floppy disk, but a distributor or user group should offer to copy the add-ins onto your disks free of charge.

If all else fails, write directly to Information and Warranty, Dept. M, Lotus Development Corp., 55 Cambridge Pkwy., Cambridge, MA 02142

MAY 1987

SECTION
2

MACRO TECHNIQUES

Once you've written your first macro and developed your own set of utilities, the next step is to make sure those macros are as efficient as possible. You're also going to want to use macros to do more than simply enter labels and widen columns—you'll want to expand your repertoire of macro techniques. This section starts on a seemingly simple level by showing you how to move the cell pointer and highlight ranges. You are also introduced to the simplest of macro commands, the /X commands found in all versions of *1-2-3*. Release 2 can (and *Symphony* users must) translate these into the basically equivalent command keywords.

While all this seems simple, these techniques unlock the power of macros by giving you control over a macro's "flow-of-control." That is, they let you control which set of instructions the macro will execute and direct the macro from one set of instructions to another. For example, you can automatically change the format of every cell in a column or double every value in a range by having your macro loop through the same set of instructions until the repetitive task is done. You can even create *1-2-3-* and *Symphony*-like menus, complete with prompts that let you select which tasks the macro will execute.

At this stage, you've moved beyond beginner status and have begun macro programming. This is real programming, worthy of subtle bragging at your next party. Actually, an argument can be made that creating a worksheet model is also a kind of entry level programming. So macro programming is a step beyond that—at least, intermediate level!

1

Specifying Ranges with Pointer-Movement Commands

Here's how to specify a range within a macro without using cell addresses.

BY PAULA DEMPSEY

Writing macros that are generic enough to specify any range of cells can be tricky. For example, suppose you often copy a formula down a column, and you want to create a macro that will perform this task automatically. The following techniques will come in handy.

The *1-2-3* macro in cell B1 of the following figure copies the contents of the current cell to the row below.

	A	B
1	\a	/C~{DOWN}~
2		

To create this simple macro, first enter the labels shown in range A1..B1. If you're using *Symphony*, replace the entry in cell B1 with {MENU}C~{DOWN}~. Next you must name the macro by assigning the label in cell A1 as a range name for the first line of the macro: With the pointer in cell A1, press slash (in *Symphony*, MENU), select Range Name Labels Right, and press Return to indicate cell A1 as the range of label entries. In *1-2-3* the macro name must consist of a backslash followed by a single letter, but in *Symphony* you can use almost any range name (see the *Symphony* documentation for details on naming macros). Before you use the macro, enter the labels and numbers as shown in the following figure.

	A	B
6	AMOUNT	DISCOUNT
7	25.06	
8	19.16	
9		

Enter the formula +A7*0.15 in cell B7 and use the macro to copy this formula to cell B8: Position the pointer in cell B7 and start the macro by holding down the MACRO key (Alt on most computers) and pressing A. The program processes the keyboard instructions too quickly to follow, but here's what happens. The macro presses slash (in *Symphony*, MENU) and types C to select Copy from the menu. When the program prompts for the range to copy from, the tilde (~) presses Return to accept the current cell. When the program prompts for the range to copy to, {DOWN} presses the DownArrow key to move the pointer to the row below, and the tilde presses Return to accept the new current cell.

Now suppose that there are six numbers in range A7..A12. In order to copy the formula from cell B7 to the appropriate cells in column B, the macro must be able to point to range B8..B12. The following macro does the trick:

	A	B
1	\a	/C~
2		{DOWN}.{DOWN}{DOWN}{DOWN}{DOWN}~
3		

If you want to try this macro, simply overwrite the label in cell B1 with the new sequence of commands (in *Symphony* replace the slash with {MENU}). Enter the second line of code in cell B2 as shown. You need not include the second cell of the macro within range \a. You need assign a range name only to the first cell of the macro. Also, erase the formula in cell B8 and enter a number in each cell of range A9..A12.

Position the pointer in cell B7 and start the macro. Your software processes all the macro commands in the first line of macro code, then looks to the cell below for further commands to process. The macro processes all contiguous labels in the column as commands and stops running when it encounters a blank or nonlabel cell. Here's what this macro does:

/C~   Presses slash (MENU in *Symphony*) and selects Copy, then presses Return to accept the current cell as the source range from which to copy.

{DOWN}.{DOWN}{DOWN}{DOWN}{DOWN} ~   Moves the cell pointer down one row, presses the period key to anchor the cell pointer, extends the highlight four more rows downward, and presses Return to indicate the target range for the Copy command.

If the desired To range is very long, including a {DOWN} command for every cell makes for an unnecessarily large and slow macro. In *1-2-3* Release 2/2.01 and *Symphony*, you are able to specify the DownArrow key any number of times within one command. For example, you can shorten the command sequence {DOWN}{DOWN}{DOWN}{DOWN} to {DOWN 4}.

This may seem like a practical approach for designating small ranges; however, processing the command {DOWN 50} takes the program the same amount of time as processing 50 {DOWN} commands. Another approach is to use the {PGDN} command. This macro command moves the pointer down 20 rows at once. To expand a highlight down a column of 42 cells, use the command sequence {PGDN 2}{DOWN 2} (in 1-2-3 Release 1A, {PGDN}{PGDN}{DOWN}{DOWN}).

Often, however, a macro that specifies a range of a predetermined size isn't useful — you may need a macro that can copy a formula to a range that will vary from use to use. With our example, suppose that column A contains anywhere from 20 to 350 numbers. You wish to enter a formula in every cell of column B to the right of these numbers. The following macro solves the problem (in *Symphony* replace the slash with {MENU}):

	A	B
1	\a	/C~
2		{DOWN}.{LEFT}{END}{DOWN}{RIGHT}~
3		

Here's how the macro works. When the program prompts for a To range, {DOWN} moves the pointer to the cell below, and the period key anchors the highlight. {LEFT} expands the highlight to the adjacent cell in column A, and {END}{DOWN} expands the highlight to include all of the numbers below, up to the first blank row, as well as the adjacent cells in column B. {RIGHT} shrinks the highlight so that it includes only the cells in column B that are adjacent to the numbers in column A. The tilde presses Return to accept the highlighted area as the To range.

The disadvantage of using {END}{DOWN} is that it will expand the highlight only to the last filled cell before a blank cell. The preceding macro won't be able to copy the formula down 300 cells if column A contains entries in ranges A8..A150 and A152..A307 but cell A151 is blank. It will copy the formula only to range B8..B150. In this example, using {PGDN 15} to expand the highlight down 300 rows is appropriate. But there is a more efficient approach:

	A	B	C	D	E	
1	\a	/C~				
2		{DOWN}.{END}{DOWN}				
3		{LEFT}{END}{UP}{RIGHT}~				
4						

This macro is similar to the previous one. Enter it as shown (*Symphony* users should substitute the command {MENU} for the slash shown in cell B1), and assign \a as the name for cell B1: Press slash (MENU in *Symphony*), select Range Name Labels Right, indicate cell A1, and press Return.

To run the macro, point to the cell that contains the formula you wish to copy (B7 in this example), hold down the MACRO key (Alt on most computers), and press A. Here's what happens:

/C~   Presses slash and selects Copy, then presses Return to accept the current cell as the source range.

{DOWN}.{END}{DOWN}   Moves the cell pointer down, then anchors the pointer and extends the highlight to the bottom of the worksheet.

{LEFT}{END}{UP}{RIGHT}~   Extends the highlight to the left so that it covers columns A and B; presses End UpArrow, which shrinks the highlight to encompass the last entry in column A; then shrinks the highlight to cover only column B and presses Return to accept the highlighted range as the target for the Copy command.

The success of this macro relies on there being no entries in the worksheet below the ranges involved in the copying procedure.

JUNE 1987

2

Flow Control

Presenting *1-2-3*'s /X commands you can use to direct the flow of your macros.

BY DANIEL GASTEIGER

Macros are labels in vertically adjacent cells. The labels represent keystrokes you might use to perform a task. When you give the range containing these labels a two-character name—a backslash and single-letter combination such as \m—you can "play back" the keystrokes as needed. *1-2-3* runs through them automatically as though you are typing them.

If *1-2-3* macros were merely automatic typing, they would save you hours of monotony. But *1-2-3* includes a collection of commands that work only while a macro is running. These are called the slash X (/X) commands, and the control they give you over the flow of your macros turns *1-2-3*'s macro facility into a simple programming language.

THE ONE-WAY BRANCH

A branch command, as the term suggests, reroutes a macro from its normal course. By definition, a macro processes keystrokes stored as labels in vertically adjacent cells. A branch is any diversion from this flow. The /XG command performs the simplest branch in *1-2-3* macros.

This column has previously covered several macros that use the /XG command. I usually use it to create looping macros. For example, the infinite loop macro in the following illustration lets you use the numeric keypad for data entry. It moves the cell pointer down each time you press Return:

	A	B	C	D
1	\m	{?}{DOWN}		
2		/XG\m~		

To use the macro, enter it as shown and assign the range name \m to cell B1 by placing the cell pointer in cell A1, issuing the /Range Name Labels Right command, and pressing Return. Move the cell pointer to the top of the column in which you wish to enter data, press the NumberLock key, and start the macro by holding down the MACRO key and pressing M (Alt on most computers). If your computer lacks an Alt key, consult your *1-2-3* documentation for instructions on invoking macros.

The macro pauses until you press Return, then moves the cell pointer down. You can press any keys while the macro pauses at a {?} command, but the moment you press Return, *1-2-3* processes the next macro step — in this case {DOWN}. Once you've pressed the NumberLock key, the NUM indicator appears in the bottom-right corner of your screen. This tells you that the numeric keypad will produce numbers rather than cursor movement. You can type a number, press Return, and so on until you finish entering data in the current column. Then hold down the Shift key and use the Arrow keys to move the cell pointer to the top of the next column. Once there, release the Shift key and you're ready to enter another column of data.

This is called an infinite loop because the command /XG\m~ sends the macro to process keystrokes in the cell named *\m*, looping back to the beginning. The macro continues running until you stop it by holding down the Control key and pressing Break. After you stop the macro, remember to turn off the NUM indicator by pressing the NumberLock key. Doing so frees the numeric keypad for pointer movement.

The /XG command can pass control of a macro to any cell. This alone is not particularly useful, but combined with the /XI command, /XG becomes an indispensable tool.

CONDITIONAL BRANCHING

The /XI command also redirects the flow of a macro. This command determines whether or not an indicated value equals zero. If so, the macro skips other commands in the cell and continues processing in the next cell. If the indicated value does not equal zero, the macro continues processing in the same cell. This is called conditional branching. The following illustration shows a /XI command:

	A	B	C	D
1	\i	/XIvalue>5~{DOWN}		
2				
3	value	8		

The command means "If the value of the cell named *value* is greater than 5, move the cell pointer down. Otherwise, do nothing." In this example, as with most /XI applications, *1-2-3* uses Boolean algebra to determine which commands to process.

A Boolean expression in *1-2-3* is a statement that is either true or false. If the statement is true, its value is 1; but if the statement is false, it equals 0. The comparison $3 = 3$ is true; therefore, it equals 1. The opposite comparison, $3 < > 3$ (3 does not equal 3), is false; therefore, it equals 0.

In the example, the Boolean expression is *value* > 5. This equals 1 because the cell named *value* contains an 8. The macro processes the {DOWN} command that is in the same cell as the /XI command. If *value* equals 5 or less, the expression equals 0. The macro then ignores the {DOWN} command and instead processes whatever command appears in the next cell. If *value* is not greater than 5, the macro does nothing since the next cell is empty.

The following macro combines a /XI command with a /XG command. This macro moves the cell pointer to the right whatever number of times you indicate:

	A	B	C	D
	A	B	C	D
1	\m	/DFcounter~0~~~		
2	loop	/DFcounter~counter+1~~~		
3	value	{RIGHT}		
4		/XIcounter<number~/XGloop~		
5				
6	number			
7	counter			

Enter the macro and its associated labels. Then assign range names by placing the cell pointer in cell A1, issuing the /Range Name Labels Right command, then pressing End Down End Down Down Return. To run the macro, place a value in the cell named *number*, then press MACRO-M. Here's what happens:

/DFcounter~0~ ~ ~   Sets the value of the cell named *counter* to zero. The Data Fill command places a sequence of numbers into a specified worksheet range. In this case, the range specified is a single cell named *counter*. The sequence of numbers specified begins with zero, and since the target range contains only one cell, the Step and Stop values that delimit the numeric sequence are not relevant. The extra tildes in the command account for these.

/DFcounter~counter + 1~ ~ ~   Increases the value of the cell named *counter* by one.

{RIGHT}   Moves the cell pointer one cell to the right.

/XIcounter<number~/XGloop~   Branches to the cell named *loop* if the value of the cell named *counter* is less than that of the cell named *number*. If *counter* is equal to or greater than *number*, the macro looks for keystrokes in the next cell. Since it finds none, the macro stops.

The macro compares *counter* with *number*, branches back to *loop*, increases the value of *counter*, moves the cell pointer, and compares *counter* and *number* again, until *counter* equals *number*. Obviously, this isn't the fastest way to move across the worksheet, but it illustrates conditional branching.

THE BOOMERANG BRANCH

The /XG command sends a macro on a one-way trip from one macro routine to another. A similar command, /XC, sends a macro on a round trip. The latter process is known as calling a subroutine. When a macro processes a /XC command, it jumps to the location named in the command and processes code until it encounters a /XR command. It then returns to the command immediately after the /XC command. The following illustration shows the flow of a macro containing a subroutine call:

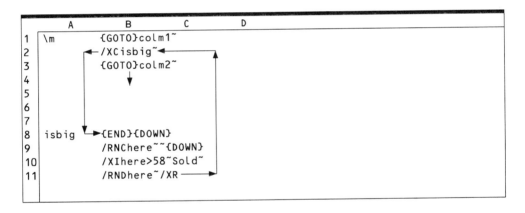

The following illustration shows the same macro with a few added steps:

	A	B	C	D
1	\m	{GOTO}colm1~		
2		/XCisbig~		
3		{GOTO}colm2~		
4		/XCisbig~		
5		{GOTO}colm3~		
6		/XCisbig~		
7				
8	isbig	{END}{DOWN}		
9		/RNChere~~{DOWN}		
10		/XIhere>58~Sold~		
11		/RNDhere~/XR		

This macro sends the cell pointer to a cell named *colm1*, then calls the subroutine named *isbig*. *Isbig* moves the cell pointer to the last contiguous cell of data in the column, and if the value of that cell is greater than 58, it enters the word *sold* in the cell directly below it. Otherwise, it does not alter the worksheet. In either case, it returns from the subroutine. The macro moves the cell pointer to *colm2* and calls the subroutine again to perform the same set of instructions on this second column of data. Finally, the macro moves the pointer to *colm3* and calls the subroutine once more.

You could write a macro that performs the same task without subroutine calls, but it would be twice as long since you would have to include three copies of the subroutine within the body of the macro. Subroutines make it easy to reuse collections of commands within a macro. They also make it easy to decipher macro code. With subroutines set apart on the worksheet, each is easy to distinguish from the other. Take *isbig*, for example. This name suggests that the subroutine determines whether or not a value is large. When you create subroutines for your own applications, give them appropriate names and your macros will be easier to understand.

A subroutine called from within another subroutine is called a nested subroutine. When you nest subroutines, a /XR command returns control of the macro to the command after the last /XC command processed. If your macro calls more than 16 (31 in Release 2/2.01) subroutines before processing a /XR command, it fails and presents the error message *Too many nesting levels in macro calls*. Keep this in mind while building intricate macro applications.

LETTING YOU DECIDE

When you press the slash key, *1-2-3* presents the first menu in its menu tree. When you make a selection from the menu, you move along a branch of the tree. It is easy to become accustomed to this simple method of directing *1-2-3*'s activity.

Using the /XM command, your macros can present customized menus that appear in the control panel and look like the ones you access via the slash key. These menus let your macros branch in any of eight different directions.

The /XM command tells *1-2-3* where to find instructions for creating a menu. It takes the form /XMmenu~, where *menu* can be any range whose top-left corner contains the first cell of menu instructions. Menu instructions comprise an area of two rows by up to eight columns. The first row contains the menu choices; the second row contains associated long prompts. The following excerpt from a macro named *m* creates a three-choice menu in the control panel:

	A	B	C	D	E
26	\s	/XMsavemen~			
27		/XG\m~			
28					
29	savemen	Same	New	Cancel	
30		Use current name	Use new name	Don't save the file	
31		/FS~R	/XGrename~	/XG\m~	
32					

When the macro processes the command /XMsavemen~ in cell \s, it creates a menu based on the instructions starting in the cell named *savemen*. The menu appears below:

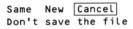

```
Same  New  [Cancel]
Don't save the file
```

	A	B	C
1			
2			

You determine which branch the macro takes either by highlighting the desired choice and pressing Return or by pressing the first letter of a menu item. The macro continues processing in the cell directly under a choice's corresponding long prompt in the menu instructions. If you select New from the menu shown above, the macro processes the command /XGrename~, which causes the macro to branch to the *rename* routine elsewhere on the worksheet.

Unlike standard *1-2-3* menus, customized menus can contain more than one choice starting with the same letter. If this is the case, when you make a selection by pressing a letter key, the macro processes the leftmost selection starting with that letter. You can select any item by pointing with the Arrow keys and pressing Return, but you will avoid trouble by using items with discrete first letters.

Notice in the illustration that the cell following the /XM command contains a command. If you press Escape in response to the menu, *1-2-3* processes this command. Whenever you press Escape while using a customized menu, the macro looks for instructions immediately after the /XM command that generated the menu. If you have not included instructions after the /XM command, the macro stops running.

STOPPING A MACRO

Sometimes you simply want your macro to stop. The /XQ command stops a macro and returns the worksheet to command mode. You will find this useful in conditional branching if you want a macro to stop under certain conditions. For example, if you want the macro to stop when your sales amount is larger than your payment amount, use the command:

/XIsales > payments ~ /XQ.

As you learn to use the /X commands, you will discover that *1-2-3* presents few obstacles a macro can't overcome. From two-step utilities to 300-line commercial template applications, /X commands hold the true power of *1-2-3* macros.

NOTES FOR *1-2-3* RELEASE 2/2.01 USERS

1-2-3 Release 2 contains the /X commands found in Release 1A, and they work as described in this column. In addition, each /X command is complemented by an advanced macro command that performs nearly the same function. The following is a table of the /X commands discussed in this article and their analogous advanced macro commands:

/XGaddress ~	{BRANCH address}
/XIcondition ~	{IF condition}
/XCroutine ~	{routine}
/XR	{RETURN}
/XMmenu1 ~	{MENUBRANCH menu1}
/XQ	{QUIT}

The advanced macro commands differ in several ways from their corresponding /X commands. For instance, you can use /X commands only at places in a macro where the worksheet is in Ready mode. A /X command accesses an invisible choice from the main *1-2-3* menu. If your macro is doing something that would normally preclude using the menu, /X commands are not valid.

Bracketed macro commands are valid any place in a macro except within other bracketed commands. You can use them at points where the worksheet is in Ready mode, where the macro is partway through a menu sequence, or even where the macro is entering data into a cell. This makes the advanced macro commands more powerful than the /X commands.

The {IF} command is quite different from the /XI command. As mentioned in the article, /XI interprets zero as false and interprets anything not equal to zero as true. This means the values ERR and NA equal true in the /XI command. The {IF} command considers zero, ERR, and NA to be false. Keep this in mind when deciding which conditional statement to use.

To call a subroutine with the advanced macro commands, simply enclose its name in braces. Subroutine calls have no associated command words.

JANUARY 1986

3

Moving the Cell Pointer

These techniques might help you reduce the number
of movement commands in your macros.

BY DANIEL GASTEIGER

You can use many different keystroke sequences to get around in *1-2-3*. The Home, PageUp, PageDown, Tab, Shift-Tab, GOTO, and Arrow keys all move the cell pointer, and several of these keys in combination with the End key provide even more navigation commands. If you're typical of our readers, you use combinations of all these keystrokes while creating and using worksheet models.

Macros are simply collections of keystrokes stored as labels, so they can move the cell pointer almost as effectively as you can. Unfortunately, there are several movement tasks that macros don't perform efficiently. When your macros must move the cell pointer to the left or right within a single row or up and down in a single column, you must often write long sequences of {LEFT} or {RIGHT} commands. If you were doing the tasks manually, you could rely on sight to determine when you had moved the cell pointer to its destination; your macros must rely on other information.

THE MODEL

Let's assume that you need to keep track of your company's expenditures and that you create a table that spans 30 columns of a worksheet. The first column holds check numbers, the second describes the checks' recipients, and each of the remaining columns represents a different account number from which the checks were drawn. The illustration in the adjacent column shows the first few columns of such a table.

Your goal is to be able to enter the appropriate information for each check without looking up at your computer screen. This could be as simple as typing four pieces of information for each check: number, payee, account number, and amount. If you start the macro with the cell pointer in the *Chknum* column, the macro accepts the check number, then moves the cell pointer to the right. The macro then accepts the check's description and account number. Based on the account number, the macro determines which column in this row should receive the check's amount. To save space, the remainder of this discussion applies to a table containing only 11 columns.

BRUTE STRENGTH

Many "brute strength" solutions to this problem use a collection of {RIGHT} commands arranged so that the user can select the number of RightArrow keystrokes needed to reach the appropriate column. These solutions require the user to remember each account's distance (in columns) from the *Description* column. The macro would be more useful if it kept track of how many {RIGHT}s to process; the user shouldn't have to bother.

You can devise many schemes for your macros to keep track of how many {RIGHT}s to process. The one we'll discuss requires that you add two extra rows to your table and that you arrange the account numbers in your table in ascending numerical order. This lets you use the @HLOOKUP function to calculate the number of {RIGHT} commands your macro should process.

	A	B	C	D	E	F
40	Chknum	Description	100	115	230	233
41	3435	Sales Luncheon			$97.35	
42	3436	On-site seminar				$325.00
43	3437	Slide Service		$25.12		
44	3438	Equipment	$983.20			
45	3439	Client Lunch			$35.49	

Copy the row of your table's column headers into the second row above the table. To do this, press slash, select Copy, indicate A40..K40 (assuming 11 columns of data), press Return, indicate A38, and press Return. Then number the cells of range B39..K39 from 0 to 9; to do this, select /Data Fill, indicate B39..K39, and press Return four times. The range A38..K39 will serve as a lookup table. Assign it the name *heads*. The following is a macro that exploits this arrangement:

	A	B	C	D	E	F
1	\i	/XNEnter check number ~~{RIGHT}				
2		/XLEnter description of charges ~~				
3	bck	/XNEnter account number ~act~				
4		/XI@HLOOKUP(act,heads,0)<>act~/BBB{ESC}/XGbck~				
5		/XCmvrght~				
6		/XNEnter amount ~~/RFC~~				
7		{DOWN}{END}{LEFT}/XG\i~				
8						
9	act					
10	col		0			
11						
12	mvrght	/Ccol~col~				
13		/XIcol>=1~{RIGHT}				
14		/XIcol>=2~{RIGHT}				
15		/XIcol>=3~{RIGHT}				
16		/XIcol>=4~{RIGHT}				
17		/XIcol>=5~{RIGHT}				
18		/XIcol>=6~{RIGHT}				
19		/XIcol>=7~{RIGHT}				
20		/XIcol>=8~{RIGHT}				
21		/XIcol>=9~{RIGHT}				
22		/XR				

Enter the macro as shown and assign the labels in column A as range names for the adjacent cells in column B: select /Range Name Labels Right, indicate A1..A12, and press Return. Enter the formula @HLOOKUP(act,heads,1) into the cell named *col* (cell B10).

To use the macro, point to the cell below the last entry of column A in the table, then hold down the MACRO key (Alt on most computers) and press I. If your computer lacks an Alt key, consult your *1-2-3* documentation for information on invoking macros. Here's what happens:

/XNEnter check number ~ ~{RIGHT}   Displays the prompt *Enter check number*. When you enter the check number and press Return, the macro stores your entry in the current cell, then moves the cell pointer to the right.

/XLEnter description of charges ~ ~   Displays the prompt *Enter description of charges*. When you enter the description and press Return, the macro stores your entry in the current cell.

/XNEnter account number ~act~   Displays the prompt *Enter account number*. When you enter the account number and press Return, the macro stores your entry in the cell named *act*.

/XI@HLOOKUP(act,heads,0)< >act~/BBB{ESC}/XGbck~   Determines whether the account number you entered in response to the last prompt is valid. If the account number is invalid, *1-2-3* beeps and recycles to the previous command, giving you an opportunity to reenter the account number; otherwise, control of the macro passes directly to the next step (cell B5). The formula in the /XI command simply compares the value in *act* with the value of the formula @HLOOKUP(act,heads,∅). This equals 1 if *act* is a valid account number, and ∅ if *act* is not valid.

/XCmvrght~   Calls the subroutine named *mvrght. Mvrght* moves the cell pointer to the column whose account number now appears in the cell named *act.* We'll see how this works in a moment.

/XNEnter amount ~ ~/RFC~ ~   Displays the prompt *Enter amount,* places your entry in the current cell, selects /Range Format Currency, and indicates two decimal places as the desired display format for the current cell.

{DOWN}{END}{LEFT}/XG\i~   Moves the cell pointer down and back to the left border of the worksheet, then restarts the macro. Note that the macro relies on your table beginning in column A. If your table doesn't begin in column A, the {END}{LEFT} command sequence will overshoot the first column of the table.

Here's how the *mvrght* routine moves the cell pointer:

/Ccol~col~   Copies the cell named *col* onto itself. This updates the formula in *col. Col*'s formula determines the offset from the current column of the column containing the account number that you indicated. Updating *col* in this step ensures that the subroutine will move the cell pointer to the proper column.

/XIcol > = 1 ~ {RIGHT}   Determines whether *col* is greater than or equal to 1. If *col* is greater or equal, the cell pointer moves right. If *col* isn't greater, the cell pointer doesn't move. In either case, control of the macro passes to the next step.

/XIcol > = 2 ~ {RIGHT}   Determines whether the column offset value (*col*) is greater than or equal to 2 and either moves the cell pointer or leaves the cell pointer in place.

Each of these steps follows the same logic for each line of code in the subroutine. The cell pointer moves right once for each line until the comparison number of one of the /XI statements is greater than *col.* The pointer then stops while *1-2-3* continues processing the /XI commands. When *1-2-3* finally processes the /XR statement in cell B22, control of the macro returns to the command immediately following the /XC command that called the subroutine. In this example the macro continues processing in cell B6. Because this is an infinite loop macro, you must stop it by pressing the Break key (Control-Break on most PCs) when you've finished entering data.

LIMITATIONS

There are several variations on this macro technique, each of which uses the /XI command and a series of movement commands to move the cell pointer. The macro shown is one of the more efficient variations, but it suffers from a few limitations.

The routine takes up a lot of space to accomplish what ought to be a simple task. It is particularly cumbersome when your table occupies several tens or hundreds of worksheet columns; the *mvrght* subroutine will extend deep into the worksheet. Who wants to edit so many lines of code?

The routine is also very slow. For small tables like the one described, the cell pointer moves quickly enough. But no one wants to wait for a macro to process 30 or more {RIGHT} commands between each check entry. Unfortunately, most movement macros suffer from this problem. Worse still, there are no entirely satisfactory solutions.

A SHORTER SUBROUTINE

The following is a short, simple approach to the movement macro problem described above:

	A	B	C	D	E	F
1	\i	/XNEnter check number ~~{RIGHT}				
2		/XLEnter description of charges ~~				
3	bck	/XNEnter account number ~act~				
4		/XI@HLOOKUP(act,heads,0)<>act~/BBB{ESC}/XGbck~				
5		/XCmvrght~				
6		/XNEnter amount ~~/RFC~~				
7		{DOWN}{END}{LEFT}/XG\i~				
8						
9	act					
10	col		0			
11						
12	mvrght	/Ccol~col~				
13		/WIR~/DF{BS}.{END}{RIGHT}~				
14		0~1~col~{END}{RIGHT}/WDR~				
15		/XR				

Notice that the only difference between this and the previous macro is the length and functioning of the subroutine named *mvrght*. The routine still moves the cell pointer to the appropriate column in the table, but it uses a completely different set of commands. The main macro works as described earlier. Here's how the new subroutine works:

/Ccol~col~   Copies *col* onto itself, updating the formula that calculates the account number's column offset from the current column.

/WIR~/DF{BS}.{END}{RIGHT}~   Inserts a row directly above the current row. The cell pointer remains in the new, empty row. Then the macro begins issuing a Data Fill command, pressing the Backspace key to cancel the previous fill range, anchoring the cell pointer, and highlighting the entire row from the current cell to column IV as the new fill range.

0~1~col~{END}{RIGHT}/WDR~   Continues issuing the Data Fill command by indicating ∅ as the start value, 1 as the step value, and *col* as the stop value. *1-2-3* fills the row with incremental numbers starting in the current cell and continuing to the column containing the selected account number. The macro then presses End RightArrow, which moves the cell pointer to the last cell containing data in the current row. Finally, the macro presses slash and selects Worksheet Delete Row, which removes the newly created row from the worksheet. The cell pointer is left in the desired cell.

/XR   Transfers control of the macro back to the command immediately following the /XC command that called the subroutine.

Brevity is the advantage of this movement subroutine. No matter how many columns your table occupies, the subroutine as written can accommodate it. However, because the subroutine inserts and deletes a row, the routine becomes slower and slower as you increase the amount of data in your worksheet.

You can improve the routine's performance a tad by setting worksheet recalculation to manual. Also, if you design your worksheets carefully, you can write a more efficient routine by omitting the /WIR~ and /WDR~ commands. The modified routine might appear as follows:

	A	B	C	D	E	F
12	mvrght	/Ccol~col~				
13		{RIGHT}/DF{BS}.{END}{RIGHT}~				
14		1~1~col~{LEFT}{END}				
15		{RIGHT}/RE{END}{LEFT}{RIGHT}{RIGHT}~/XR				

This routine requires that there be nothing in the table to the right of the entry you are making when the routine runs and that there be nothing in the first column located to the right of the table. It also assumes that it should preserve the two leftmost entries in each row that receives an entry. If you use this technique in tables having different numbers of columns leading into the *mvrght* routine (for example, columns A, B, C, D, and E all receive entries before the macro calls *mvrght*), change the number of {RIGHT}s in the Range Erase command in the last line of the routine to accommodate the difference. This routine will also benefit from having recalculation set to manual. Here's how the routine works:

/Ccol~col~   Copies *col* onto itself.

{RIGHT}/DF{BS}.{END}{RIGHT}~   Moves the cell pointer to the right and starts a Data Fill command, canceling the previous Fill range and indicating a new Fill range that extends to the first nonblank cell in the current row (or to column IV if the row is empty).

1~1~col~{LEFT}{END}   Fills the Fill range with numbers from 1 to the offset number calculated in *col*, then moves the cell pointer left (in case the offset number equals 1), and presses the End key.

{RIGHT}/RE{END}{LEFT}{RIGHT}{RIGHT}~/XR Presses the Right key, sending the cell pointer to the last filled cell in the range. Then the routine selects /Range Erase, presses End LeftArrow RightArrow RightArrow (highlighting the entire row of entries, then backing up two columns to preserve columns A and B), and presses Return. Finally, the routine finishes with the /XR command.

1-2-3 Release 1A macros that move the cell pointer can be tedious to write and use. For the type of problem presented, there is no clean and simple approach. Every technique has drawbacks, but some are better suited to particular applications than others.

NOTES FOR RELEASE 2/2.01 USERS

1-2-3 Release 2/2.01 accepts arguments in many of its movement keywords. To move the cell pointer right six columns, you can use the command {RIGHT 6}. The argument can also be the address or name of a cell that contains a value. Rather than write a subroutine to move the cell pointer, replace the subroutine call in the original macro (the /XCmvrght~ command in B5) with the commands {RECALC col} {RIGHT col}. These update the formula in *col* and move the cell pointer to the appropriate column, respectively.

With this arrangement you still must wait while the cell pointer moves cell by cell across the worksheet. Alternatively, you can write a string formula that calculates the address of the target cell and accepts your entry without even moving the cell pointer.

First, remodify the table, replacing the numbers in row 39 with the letters that identify each column. For example, enter *C* in cell C39, *D* in cell D39, and so on. For large tables, do this quickly by entering the following formula into cell C39 and copying it across the row:

$$@MID(@CELL(``address",C36..C36),1,$$
$$(@MID(@CELL(``address",$$
$$C36..C36),2,1)< >``\$")+1)$$

Once copied, use the Range Values command to convert the formulas in row 39 to values. Then replace the formula in *col* with the following:

$$@HLOOKUP(act,heads,1)\&@STRING$$
$$(@CELLPOINTER(``row"),\emptyset)$$

The modified macro appears at the top of the next page.

The commands in cells B1 through B4 are identical to those in the macros in the main article. Things are a little different starting in cell B5:

{RECALC col}   Recalculates the formula in *col*. The new value will equal the

```
      A            B            C         D        E        F
 1  \i        /XNEnter check number ~~{RIGHT}
 2            /XLEnter description of charges  ~~
 3  bck       /XNEnter account number ~act~
 4            /XI@HLOOKUP(act,heads,0)<>act~/BBB{ESC}/XGbck
 5            {RECALC col}
 6            /XNEnter amount ~{col}~/RFC~{col}~
 7            {DOWN}{END}{LEFT}/XG\i~
 8
 9  act
10  col                    ERR
```

address of the cell that should contain the check's amount.

/XNEnter amount ~{**col**}~/**RFC**~{**col**}~ Displays the prompt *Enter amount* and places your entry in the cell named in *col*. This happens because the {col} command calls *col* as a subroutine, processing all the keystrokes that it contains. The macro then assigns a currency format with two decimal places to the cell named in *col*.

{**DOWN**}{**END**}{**LEFT**}/**XG**\i~ Moves the cell pointer down and back to column A, then restarts the macro. Stop the macro by pressing the Break key when you've finished entering data.

JULY 1986

4

Loops and Counters

Use these techniques to create shorter, more efficient macros that automate repetitious code.

BY PAULA DEMPSEY

A macro is a list of keyboard instructions that causes *1-2-3* or *Symphony* to perform a worksheet task automatically. Range B1..B5 in the following figure contains a macro that converts a series of numbers into centered labels.

```
      A        B
1  \a    {EDIT}{HOME}^~{DOWN}
2        {EDIT}{HOME}^~{DOWN}
3        {EDIT}{HOME}^~{DOWN}
4        {EDIT}{HOME}^~{DOWN}
5        {EDIT}{HOME}^~{DOWN}
```

The instructions in each cell of the macro are identical because the macro performs the same task on five adjacent cells in a column.

To create this macro, start with a blank worksheet and enter the label {EDIT}{HOME}^~{DOWN} in cell B1. (Remember to type a label-prefix character, such as an apostrophe, before the label itself). Copy the contents of cell B1 to range B2..B5. Press slash (in *Symphony*, MENU, select Copy, indicate cell B1 as the range to copy from and B2..B5 as the range to copy to. To name the macro, enter the label \a in cell A1, press slash (in *Symphony*, MENU), select Range Name Labels Right, indicate cell A1, and press Return. In *1-2-3* the macro name must consist of a backslash followed by a single letter. In *Symphony* you can use any range name (see the documentation for more details).

You're now ready to run the macro. Enter five numbers in a column as shown in the following figure, then position the pointer in cell D1.

	D	E
1	2	
2	4	
3	16	
4	8	
5	10	

Since the entries are values, they are right-justified in the cell. When the macro adds the centering label prefix (^), it converts the numbers into labels. (If you want to refer to the numeric value of a label in a *1-2-3* Release 2 or 2.01 or a *Symphony* formula, enclose the cell reference within the @VALUE function. In *1-2-3* Release 1A numeric labels have a value of zero when you use them in formulas).

To start the macro, hold down the MACRO key (Alt on most computers) and press A. The keyword {EDIT} puts the contents of the current cell into Edit mode. {HOME} positions the cursor under the first character of the entry and then the program types the centering label prefix. The tilde (~) enters the edited entry into the cell, and {DOWN} moves the pointer to the next row down.

When the program finishes processing keystrokes in the first line of the macro, it looks to the cell below for more instructions. Since the instructions in cell B2 are the same, the program will edit the next number in the column in exactly the same way. *1-2-3* and *Symphony* will process the remaining lines in the macro and then look to cell B6 for more instructions. When the program determines that cell B6 is blank, the macro stops.

When you want to perform a repetitive task on a series of cells, it's easy to write the instructions once, then copy them down the column so that the instructions are repeated as many times as you specify. However, if you want to conserve worksheet space, or if the number of repetitions will vary, create a loop. A loop tells the macro to process the same instructions repeatedly so that you have to write the instructions only once. The looping macro in the following figure will center numbers in a column in a *1-2-3* Release 2 or 2.01 or a *Symphony* worksheet. (This macro will not work in *1-2-3* Release 1A since it uses advanced commands that will work only in *Symphony* and later releases of *1-2-3*.)

	A	B
1	\b	{EDIT}{HOME}^~{DOWN}
2		{BRANCH \b}

The statement {BRANCH \b} tells the program to continue processing commands in the cell named *\b*. (In *1-2-3* Release 1A replace the command {BRANCH \b} with /XG\b~.) Unlike the first macro, the task will not be repeated a specified number of times. The macro will continue to loop back to cell B1 and start over until you stop the macro by pressing the Break key (on most computers, hold down Control and press Break). Stopping a macro this way may produce a beep and an ERROR indicator. Press Escape to clear the error.

There are a number of ways to make the macro stop running automatically after looping a specified number of times. *1-2-3* users can use the following technique:

	A	B
1	\c	{EDIT}{HOME}^~{DOWN}
2		/DFcounter~counter+1~~~
3		/XIcounter=5~/REcounter~/XQ
4		/XG\c~
5		
6	counter	

Enter all the labels as shown. Then assign the labels in column A as range names for the adjacent cells in column B. Press slash, select Range Name Labels Right, and indicate range A1..A6. To run the macro, position the pointer over the first cell in the column of numbers, hold down the MACRO key, and press Return. Here's how the macro works:

{EDIT}{HOME}^~{DOWN}   Adds the centering label to the contents of the current cell and moves the pointer to the next row down.

/DFcounter~counter + 1 ~ ~ ~   Presses slash, selects Data Fill, and specifies *counter* as the Fill range. When *1-2-3* prompts for a Start value, the tilde presses Return to enter the result of *counter + 1*. The remaining two tildes accept the default Step and Stop values. This line of the macro increases *counter* by 1.

/XIcounter = 5 ~ /REcounter ~ /XQ   Tests whether *counter* equals 5. If so, *1-2-3* will process the instructions following the first tilde. */REcounter~* erases the contents of *counter* so that the next time you run the macro, *counter* will be blank. /XQ tells *1-2-3* to stop processing the macro.

If *counter* does not equal 5, *1-2-3* will ignore the instructions following the tilde and continue processing commands in the next line of the macro.

/XG\c~   Tells *1-2-3* to continue processing commands in *\c*.

1-2-3 Release 2/2.01 and *Symphony* offer a more efficient loop and counter routine. The following figure shows the same application, but it uses the {FOR} command.

	A	B
1	\f	{FOR counter,1,5,1,sub}
2		
3	sub	{EDIT}{HOME}^~{DOWN}
4		
5	counter	

The {FOR} command tells the program to process instructions at a specific location a designated number of times. This command takes five arguments in the form {FOR *counter-location,start-number,stop-number,step-number, starting-location*}. When the program processes the {FOR} command, it enters the Start number in the counter location, which in this example is *counter*. Then it compares the value in *counter* to the Stop value. If *counter* is less than or equal to the Stop value, the program will process the instructions, or subroutine, at the starting location. The program then increases *counter* by the Step value, compares *counter* to the Stop value, and so on. When *counter* exceeds the Stop value, the program stops processing the {FOR} command.

To use this macro, enter all the labels as shown, assign the labels in column A as range names for the adjacent cells in column B, position the pointer in the first cell in the column of numbers, hold down the MACRO key, and press F. To alter the number of times the program processes the subroutine, make the Stop number equal to the number of iterations. It's not necessary to include instructions to erase the contents of *counter* since the program will enter a Start number in *counter* when it begins to process the {FOR} command.

FEBRUARY 1987

5

Looping Macros

A collection of observations and techniques
to help control your looping macros.

BY DANIEL GASTEIGER

The more you get to know macros, the more it seems they can do almost anything. Judging from the mail we receive at *LOTUS*, it's apparent that your macros are doing a lot of looping. In this article we'll explore looping macros, review some tips from past columns, and present some new tidbits about these popular macro techniques.

A SIMPLE LOOP

The following macro converts a column of formulas into their current values:

	A	B	C	D
1	\a	{EDIT}{CALC}		
2		{DOWN}/XG\a~		

To create the macro, enter the labels shown and assign \a as the name for cell B1; point to cell A1, press slash, select Range Name Labels Right, and press Return. Convert a column of formulas by pointing to the first entry in the column and starting the macro. Here's what happens:

{EDIT}{CALC} Presses the EDIT key followed by the CALC key. *1-2-3* calculates the current value of the contents of the cell and displays that value in the control panel.

{DOWN}/XG\a ~ Moves the cell pointer down, thereby entering the newly calculated value into the cell, then restarts the macro. The /XG command, used in almost every looping macro, directs *1-2-3* to look at the cell named before the tilde where, in this case, it will find more macro commands to process. In this step, the named cell is \a; *1-2-3* loops to the macro's first step and continues converting formulas to values.

This is called an infinite-loop macro because there are no commands in the macro to make it stop processing. Left unattended, *1-2-3* will repeat the macro again and again, ultimately moving the cell pointer to the bottom of the worksheet. The pointer will try to continue its downward motion, bouncing off the bottom border of the worksheet with each attempt.

You can stop an infinite loop (or almost any other macro) by pressing the Break key (done on most computers by holding down the Control key and pressing Break). Normally, this results in an error indication, which you clear by pressing Escape or the Return key.

A SIMPLE LOOP STOPPER

The most common question we receive about looping macros is "How can I get the macro to stop itself?" In past columns we've presented several ways to stop looping macros. Let's review.

Perhaps the simplest approach to stopping a loop is to place a particular value in the cell after the last cell the macro should process. The following is a macro that tests each cell and stops when it finds the designated value:

	A	B	C
1	\a	{EDIT}{CALC}{DOWN}	
2		/C~test~	
3		/XItest=9999~/XQ	
4		/XG\a~	
5			
6	test		

Enter the macro as shown and assign the labels \a and *test* as names for the cells to their right. Before you run the macro, enter the value 9999 into the cell at the end of the column of formulas you want to process. Point to the first formula in the column and start the macro. Here's what happens:

{EDIT}{CALC}{DOWN}   Calculates the current value of the cell and moves the cell pointer down, entering the just-calculated value into the cell.

/C~test~   Copies the new current cell to the cell named *test*.

/XItest=9999~/XQ   Tests the value of the cell named *test*. If that value equals 9999, the macro stops. If *test* doesn't equal 9999, the macro continues processing in the next cell. The /XI command is called a conditional statement. This simply means that it directs *1-2-3* to do one thing if a particular condition is met; otherwise, *1-2-3* does something else. The condition tested in this macro is "Does *test* equal 9999?" If the condition is met, *1-2-3* continues processing commands in the cell containing the /XI command. If the condition is not met, *1-2-3* immediately starts processing commands in the cell directly below the /XI command. Consequently, when *1-2-3* processes this step, if *test* equals 9999, *1-2-3* encounters the /XQ command, which stops the macro; otherwise, *1-2-3* executes the next line of code:

/XG\a~   Restarts the macro.

This loop-stopping technique is limited because it also stops the macro if one of the cells you want it to process coincidentally contains the chosen test value. In addition, you may run into trouble when processing a column of formulas. When the macro copies a formula to the cell named *test*, adjusted relative cell references in the formula refer to new cells. The adjusted formula might equal the test value, causing the macro to stop.

STOPPING ON EMPTY

Another good way to stop a macro is to use an empty cell. If your macro can recognize an empty cell, it can stop when it has finished processing a column of data. The following macro tests each cell for the presence of data and stops when the tested cell is empty:

	A	B	C	D
1	\a	{EDIT}{CALC}{DOWN}		
2		/C~test~		
3		/XI@COUNT(test)=0~/XQ		
4		/XG\a~		
5	test			
6				

Test must be a two-cell range (range B5..B6 is a good choice in this example). The first two steps of the macro are identical to the first two steps of the previous macro. They convert the contents of a cell into its current value, move the cell pointer down, and copy the new cell to the range named *test*. Now the macros differ. Since *test* is a two-cell range, the Copy command generates two copies of its source cell. Then *1-2-3* processes the following command:

/XI@COUNT(test) = 0 ~/XQ   Determines whether *test* contains data. If *test* contains no data, the macro stops; otherwise, it continues processing in the next cell. The @COUNT function equals the number of cells in a specified range that contain either labels, values, or formulas. However, @COUNT of a single cell equals 1 whether or not the cell contains data, so you must use a range of at least two cells when doing this kind of test.

XG\a~   Restarts the macro.

THE EFFICIENCY FACTOR

It's important to consider how quickly your macros complete their tasks. Macros that do a day's work in three hours aren't as valuable as ones that do the work in 20 minutes. The last two macros we've presented are rather inefficient because they recalculate the worksheet twice per cell processed — once when the cell pointer moves down after recalculating a cell and again as a result of the Copy command.

You can speed up the macros simply by setting recalculation to manual (/Worksheet Global Recalculation Manual). Unfortunately, since many applications require that worksheet values remain current while the macro is running, setting recalculation to manual is not always an option.

For macros that require constant updating of the worksheet, use techniques that reduce the number of times *1-2-3* recalculates. The most effective (and, incidentally, the most popular) approach is to use moving range names.

A moving range name is one that the macro assigns to the first test cell, then to the next test cell, and so on until it encounters the value or condition for which the macro is testing. The following macro relies on a moving range name to determine when it should stop looping:

	A	B	C	D
1	\a	{EDIT}{CALC}{DOWN}		
2		/RNCtest~{BS}~		
3		/XItest=9999~/XQ		
4		/XG\a~		

Once you've entered and named the macro, create the table shown below to see how the macro works. (There's a hidden agenda in this suggestion. Give it a try and see what happens.) The entries in column B are values; the entries in columns C and D are formulas. Enter the values in column B, then enter +B9*5% in cell C9 and +B9+C9 in cell D9. Copy range C9..D9 to range C9..C11, then give the range B9..D11 a currency format with two decimal places:

	A	B	C	D
8		Price	Tax	Total
9	Brush	$8.79	$0.44	$9.23
10	Scraper	$1.75	$0.09	$1.84
11	Razor	$2.59	$0.13	$2.72

Before you run the macro, enter the value 9999 into cell C12, then put the cell pointer in C9. Here's what happens:

{EDIT}{CALC}{DOWN}   Converts the cell contents from a formula to a value and moves the cell pointer down.

/RNCtest~{BS}~   Assigns *test* as the name for the current cell. The {BS} command cancels any previous assignment of the range name, letting *1-2-3* reassign it with each loop of the macro.

/XItest = 9999~/XQ   Determines whether *test* equals 9999. If *test* equals 9999, the macro stops; otherwise, the macro continues processing in the next cell.

/XG\a~   Restarts the macro.

After you run the macro, you may notice a problem: the formulas in column D now refer to the wrong cells. This is because when you assign a range name to a cell, the references to that cell in other formulas become "attached" to the range name. Reassigning such a name without first deleting it drags the attached references along to the new cell.

Rewrite your way around this situation as follows:

	A	B	C	D
1	\a	{EDIT}{CALC}{DOWN}		
2		/RNCtest~~		
3		/XItest=9999~/RNDtest~/XQ		
4		/RNDtest~		
5		/XG\a~		

Before you run the macro, enter 9999 into the cell at the end of the column you're converting to values. Also, make sure that the range name *test* doesn't exist on the worksheet. Here's how the macro works:

{EDIT}{CALC}{DOWN}   Converts the cell's contents to a value and moves the cell pointer down.

/RNCtest~ ~   Assigns *test* as the range name to the current cell.

/XI(test) = 9999~/RNDtest~/XQ   Determines whether *test* equals 9999. If *test* equals 9999, the macro deletes the range name *test* (so you can run the macro again without fail) and stops; otherwise, it continues processing in the next cell.

/RNDtest~   Deletes the range name *test*. This "detaches" any formulaic references to the current cell, freeing *test* for use on the macro's next loop.

/XG\a~   Restarts the macro.

If you prefer that your macro stop when it encounters an empty cell, rewrite the macro as follows:

	A	B	C	D
1	\a	{EDIT}{CALC}{DOWN}		
2		/RNCtest~{UP}~		
3		/XI@COUNT(test)=1~/RNDtest~/XQ		
4		/RNDtest~		
5		/XG\a~		

This assigns *test* as a two-cell range encompassing the current cell and the cell above the current cell. @COUNT of *test* will equal 1 when the cell pointer reaches a data-free cell. If the column adjacent to the one you're converting doesn't contain entries, your macro can create a two-cell range across two columns and test for @COUNT(test) = 0.

FOR LOOPS

No discussion of looping would be complete without mentioning FOR loops. FOR loops are standard in most programming languages, though they're noticeably lacking in *1-2-3*. A FOR loop processes a sequence of commands a specific number of times. In most cases you supply a number at which the loop should start counting, a number by which the loop should count, and a number at which the loop should stop. For example, you could instruct a FOR loop to start counting at 3, to count by twos, and to stop when it reaches 11. The loop would run five times.

You can simulate a FOR loop in *1-2-3* by creating a counter that increases (or decreases) in value each time the macro processes the loop. The following macro demonstrates such a loop. It assumes that the column segment of data it is processing contains entries in every cell and that there are at least two entries in the column:

	A	B	C	D
1	\a	/RNCcolumn~{END}{DOWN}~		
2		/DFtarg~@COUNT(column)~~~		
3	loop	{EDIT}{CALC}{DOWN}		
4		/DFtarg~targ-1~~~		
5		/XItarg=0~/RNDcolumn~/XQ		
6		/XGloop~		
7				
8	targ			

This loop counts down starting from the number of entries in the column. It stops when the counter equals 0. Assign the labels in column A as names for the adjacent cells of column B. Then start the macro with the cell pointer on the first entry in the column to convert. Here's what happens:

/RNCcolumn~{END}{DOWN}~   Assigns the name *column* to the entire column of entries. Note that there can be no blank cells in the column or the macro will not name the entire column of entries.

/DFtarg~@COUNT(column)~~~   Places the value of @COUNT(column) into the cell named *targ*. This seems like an odd application of the Data Fill command, but it provides a convenient way to put information into cell *targ*. @COUNT(column) equals the number of entries the macro will process.

{EDIT}{CALC}{DOWN} Converts the cell's contents to a value and moves the cell pointer down.

/DFtarg~targ–1~ ~ ~ Decreases by one the value of the cell named *targ*.

/XItarg = 0 ~/RNDcolumn~/XQ Tests the value of *targ*. If *targ* equals 0, the macro deletes the range name *column* and stops. Otherwise the macro processes commands in the next cell.

/XGloop~ Transfers control to the cell named *loop*. The macro continues looping, subtracting 1 from *targ* on each pass, until *targ* equals 0.

There are many ways to create FOR loops in *1-2-3*. Each relies on some type of counter that keeps track of the number of iterations of the loop. Use the example shown above as a starting point for designing your own FOR loops, or apply any one of the other loop-stopping techniques presented in this article. Once you've learned to design loops that stop themselves, you may never again press the Break key.

NOTES FOR RELEASE 2/2.01 USERS

1-2-3 Release 2/2.01 includes a command that converts entire ranges of formulas into values. This feature makes obsolete the macros described in the main article, although the techniques they employ work in *1-2-3* Release 2/2.01 as they do in Release 1A.

But Release 2/2.01 users have more commands available to help control looping macros. For example, rather than copying a cell to a named range or creating and deleting a range name for each cell you wish to test, refer to the current cell using the @CELLPOINTER command. Rewrite the original macro as follows so that it stops when it encounters a blank cell:

	A	B	C	D	E
1	\a	{EDIT} {CALC} {DOWN}			
2		/XI@CELLPOINTER("type")<>"b"~/XG\a~			

The expression @CELLPOINTER("type") can equal b, l, or v, depending on whether the current cell is blank, contains a label, or contains a numeric value, respectively. Similarly, the expression @CELLPOINTER("contents") equals the value (numeric or string) of the current cell. If you write the macro as follows, it will stop when it encounters a cell containing the value 9999:

	A	B	C	D	E
1	\a	{EDIT}{CALC}{DOWN}			
2		/XI@CELLPOINTER("contents")<>9999~/XG\a~			

1-2-3 Release 2/2.01's {FOR} command lets you create true FOR loops. The following macro uses such a loop to duplicate the one presented under the FOR LOOPS subheading in the main article:

	A	B	C	D	E
1	\a	/RNCcolumn~{END}{DOWN}~			
2		{FOR count,@COUNT(column),1,-1,rout}			
3		/RNDcolumn~			
4					
5	rout	{EDIT}{CALC}{DOWN}			
6	count	0			

Here's how the macro works:

/RNCcolumn~{END}{DOWN}~ Assigns the name *column* to the entire column of entries. This fails if any cell within the data range is blank.

{FOR count,@COUNT(column),1,-1,rout} Starts a FOR loop. The loop starts by placing the value of the command's second argument, @COUNT(column), into the cell named in the first argument, *count*. It determines from the fourth argument, -1, whether to increase or decrease the counter on each pass, then compares the first and third arguments. In this case, if the first is smaller than the third, the loop stops and the macro proceeds to the next step. Otherwise, the macro continues processing commands in the cell named in the fifth argument, *rout*. When the subroutine *rout* is finished, the value of the first argument, *count*, decreases. *1-2-3* compares the values of the first and third arguments once again, processing the subroutine, and so on, until the value of the first argument equals the value of the third.

/RNDcolumn~ Deletes the range named *column*.

These are just a few of the variations available to you in Release 2/2.01. If you prefer not to use the {FOR} command to create FOR loops, explore the {LET} statement. The {LET} command can replace the Data Fill command for assigning and updating values in counters. Your macros will be more efficient if you use the {FOR} and {LET} commands in place of the more familiar Data Fill, /XG, and /XI commands.

6

Macros Within Macros

Using subroutines to modularize your macros can save hours of editing and rewriting.

BY DANIEL GASTEIGER

Just as you invoke macros to perform repetitive tasks for you, the macros you create can invoke subroutines. A subroutine can be a single macro command, or it can be several commands strung together.

A macro usually consists of a main set of commands that direct the macro's overall operation. This main set can contain subroutine calls that temporarily transfer control to a different set of commands. When the macro processes a {RETURN} command or runs out of steps to perform in the subroutine, control transfers back to the step immediately following the subroutine call in the main set of commands.

A macro subroutine call is simply the name of the desired subroutine (assigned with the MENU Range Name Create command) enclosed in braces. For example, to call the subroutine named *edrout*, your macro uses the command {edrout}. Although you can use lowercase or uppercase letters for subroutine names, our examples use lowercase letters so that subroutine calls are clearly distinguished from command keywords:

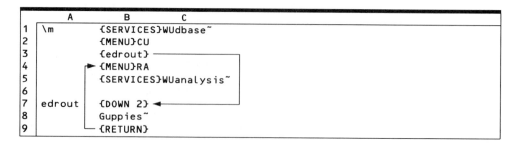

SUBROUTINES FOR SIMPLIFICATION

There are several good reasons to use subroutines. Subroutines add structure to your macros. If you write a separate subroutine for each of five operations — data entry, sorting, formatting, reviewing, and printing, for example — you can write a macro consisting of a main routine that calls each subroutine when needed. If you name each subroutine according to its function, you can quickly determine the macro's use. Also, rather than having one hard-to-read lump of macro code on your worksheet, you'll have several smaller and more manageable routines.

Subroutines also reduce the amount of typing that you must do to create macros. If you need a macro that repeatedly performs the same task, you can write a single subroutine for the task and have the main routine call it when needed. This saves you from repeating the macro steps again and again throughout the macro.

If you create macros containing subroutines, you can easily restructure your macros. When all the macro commands are lumped together, it is difficult to move collections of related commands from one part of the macro to another. If a macro consists solely of subroutine calls, you can restructure it by simply moving the calls themselves. In fact, if you have several applications macros on a worksheet, each can call the same subroutines. *Symphony* 1.1/1.2 users can even use the *Symphony* Macro Library Manager Add-In to create subroutine libraries that worksheet-dependent macros can call.

Another advantage to subroutine calls is that they let you easily edit your macros. While building an application, you may occasionally realize that you have left out a vital piece of a macro. Rather than restructure and rewrite the macro to accommodate the missing code (the preferred approach), you can simply drop a subroutine call wherever needed and write a subroutine consisting of the appropriate steps. The resulting macro is messy and difficult to follow, but it works.

BRINGING ALONG DATA

Symphony's subroutine calls let you transfer, or pass, data to a subroutine along with control of the macro. Within a subroutine call, you can specify values — numbers, cell addresses, range names, labels, or formulas — to be stored on the worksheet for use by the subroutine during its current run. Such a subroutine call might look like this:

{move 4,2}

In this example, 4 and 2 are values that the subroutine named *move* will use.

To pass data to a subroutine, you must include a {DEFINE} statement as the first step of the routine. The {DEFINE} statement tells *Symphony* what to do with values being passed to the subroutine. In the statement you specify the cell or cells that will receive the values and the way that the data should be treated. A {DEFINE} statement that accepts data from the previous subroutine call might look like this:

{DEFINE down:value,right:value}

This statement tells *Symphony* to evaluate the first argument of the subroutine call and place the result in the cell named *down*, then evaluate the second argument and place the result in the cell named *right*. When you use the value option in a {DEFINE} statement, *Symphony* attempts to evaluate the arguments being passed to the subroutine. If the arguments are formulas, *Symphony* stores only their current values. If the arguments are range names, *Symphony* stores the values contained in the named ranges.

The {DEFINE} statement also has a string option:

{DEFINE down:value,right:string}

This statement tells *Symphony* to evaluate the first argument of the subroutine call and place the result in the cell named *down*, then place a label copy of the second argument into the cell named *right*.

Values passed to a subroutine are stored in cells on the worksheet. Commands and formulas within the subroutine can refer to these cells, giving different results for each value passed from the subroutine call. The following subroutine sets a specified column to a specified width. It is a variation on an idea presented by John Posner in the book *The Lotus Guide to the Symphony Command Language* (Addison-Wesley, 1985).

	A	B	C	D	E
7	assign	{DEFINE col:string,width:string}			
8		{GOTO}			
9	col				
10		1~{MENU}WS			
11	width				
12		~{RETURN}			

If the macro calls this subroutine with the command {assign c,25}, the subroutine sets the width of column C to 25. If the command reads {assign z,40}, the subroutine assigns a width of 40 to column Z.

Here's how it works:

{assign c,25}   Calls the subroutine named *assign*, passing along the values c and 25.

{DEFINE col:string,width:string}   Treats the first argument of the subroutine call as a label and places it into the cell named *col*; then treats the second argument of the call as a label and places it into the cell named *width*.

{**GOTO**}   Presses the GOTO key. Since there is no cell address immediately following the {GOTO} command in this cell, the macro continues in the new cell — the cell named *col*, which now contains the letter that was passed to the subroutine, in this case, the letter C, the column address.

1~{MENU}WS   Finishes the {GOTO} command that started two lines earlier. The macro processes the 1 as the second part of a cell address — that is, the row number — and the tilde (~) presses Return. The cell pointer moves to cell C1. Then the macro starts the column width set process by pressing MENU Width Set. By now the next line of the macro, named *width*, contains the number passed by the subroutine call (in this case, 25), and the macro types this in response to the MENU Width Set prompt.

~{RETURN}   The tilde ends the MENU Width Set command by entering the column width. The {RETURN} command ends the subroutine.

OTHER USEFUL SUBROUTINES

When you create applications for other people, there are several processes that you use repeatedly. Applications run faster and are less confusing when your macro includes the {WINDOWSOFF} and {PANELOFF} commands, which suppress screen updating. If you often call on these commands, try the following subroutine named *wof*:

	A	B	C	D
4	wof	{WINDOWSOFF}{PANELOFF}		
5				

Of course, the macro sometimes needs to redraw the screen to present information to the user. Here's a subroutine called *won* that does this:

	A	B	C	D
6	won	{WINDOWSON}{PANELON}		
7				

If your macro offers the user several different windows in which to work or displays messages, such as help screens or error messages, contained in different windows, you may frequently use the following command sequence: {SERVICES}WUwindowname~ (that is, SERVICES Window Use windowname Return). To shorten the command, abbreviate {SERVICES} to {S}, a convention that *Symphony* allows. Take the abbreviation process a step further by writing the following subroutine and naming it *w*:

	A	B	C	D
8	w	{SERVICES}WU		
9				

Now to make a different window current, your macro can use the commands {w}windowname~.

Sometimes you want your macro to display a message on the screen before continuing. The following subroutine, named *ps*, generates a pause of whatever length you specify in the subroutine call:

	A	B	C	D
10	ps	{DEFINE delay:value}		
11		{WAIT @NOW+TIME(0,0,delay)}		
12		{RETURN}		
13				
14	delay			

Using the command {ps 6}, here's what happens:

{DEFINE delay:value}   Evaluates the argument of the subroutine call and stores the result in the cell named *delay*. In this case, the value is 6.

{WAIT @NOW + @TIME(0,0,delay)}   Causes the macro to pause the number of seconds specified in the cell named *delay* (in this case, six seconds). The {WAIT} command causes a macro to pause until the computer's clock time is equal to or greater than the value specified in the command.

{RETURN}   Ends the subroutine. The macro continues with the step after the subroutine call.

A WORD OF CAUTION

Symphony does not distinguish reserved keywords from subroutine calls. If you name a subroutine or any other range on the worksheet with a reserved keyword, such as MENU or EDIT, when you use the keyword in a macro, the macro treats the keyword as a subroutine call. For example, if you create the range name *menu* on your worksheet, *Symphony* processes that range as a subroutine whenever it encounters a {MENU} command. Keep this in mind when you assign range names for your macro applications.

As you create applications, watch for certain command sequences that recur throughout your macros and create subroutines to perform the repetitive tasks. If you are using *Symphony* Release 1.1/1.2, place your favorite subroutines into a macro library and load the library before you run your applications.

7

Writing Conditional Statements

Use the {IF} command to evaluate user responses to macro prompts.

BY PAULA DEMPSEY

A macro is a short program that you can write to automate spreadsheet routines. For example, a macro might compute year-to-date sales totals and then print out a report. You can make it easier for others to use your macros by creating them with menus and prompts that guide users through the process. This article shows you how to create prompts and use {IF} commands to evaluate user responses to those prompts.

The macro below uses the {GETLABEL} and {GETNUMBER} commands to ask questions and store responses. It also uses the {IF} command to evaluate answers. These commands are available only in *1-2-3* Releases 2 and 2.01 and *Symphony*. Similar commands are available in *1-2-3* Release 1A; however, the command that corresponds to {IF}, /XI, cannot evaluate labels.

```
     A         B
1  fb
2
3  \f   {GETLABEL "John Hannah played for the New England Patriots for 12 seasons? (T or F) ",fb}
4       {IF fb="F"}{GETLABEL "Correct! Press Return to continue.",fb}
5       {IF fb="T"}{GETLABEL "Incorrect. Press Return to continue.",fb}
6  loop {GETNUMBER "How many seasons did John Hannah play for the Patriots? ",fb}
7       {IF fb=13}{GETLABEL "Correct! Press Return to quit.",fb}{QUIT}
8       {GETLABEL "Incorrect. Press Return to try again.",fb}{BRANCH loop}
```

To use this macro, start with an empty worksheet and enter the labels shown in rows 1 through 5. Leave rows 6 through 8 blank for now. Assign the labels in cells A1 and A3 as range names for the adjacent cells in column B: Press slash (in *Symphony*, MENU), select Range Names Labels Right, and specify range A1..A3.

In *1-2-3* the range name you assign to the first cell of the macro must consist of a backslash followed by a single letter (in this example, we used \f). In *Symphony* you can enter practically any combination of alphanumeric characters as a range name — see your documentation for details.

To start the macro, hold down the MACRO key (Alt on most computers) and press F. Here's what happens when *1-2-3* or *Symphony* begins to process the commands in the macro:

{GETLABEL "John Hannah played for the New England Patriots for 12 seasons? (T or F) ",fb}   Has the form {GETLABEL *"prompt",location*}. The program displays the prompt in the edit line of the worksheet and pauses for your response. Your answer is stored as a label in the cell named *fb*. After the program processes the commands in cell B3, it looks to the cell below for further instructions.

{IF fb = "F"}{GETLABEL "Correct! Press Return to continue.",fb}   Evaluates your response and displays a message accordingly. In this example, {IF} determines whether the cell named *fb* contains the label F. If it does, the program processes the {GETLABEL} command, which displays the specified prompt and pauses for a response. Pressing Return causes the program to enter an apostrophe label prefix in *fb*.

If *fb* does not contain F, the program ignores the remaining commands in cell B4 and looks to the cell below for further instructions.

{IF fb = "T"}{GETLABEL "Incorrect. Press Return to continue.",fb} Evaluates whether your response was true and displays an appropriate prompt if so. The program processes these commands in a fashion similar to the line above, then looks to the cell below for further instructions. When it finds that the cell below is blank, the macro stops and the program returns to Ready mode.

If cell B6 were not blank and contained a label that did not consist of macro commands, the program would try to process the characters, causing unintended results. Remember to leave the cell below the last line of the macro blank.

If you're using *1-2-3* Release 2.01 with the ASCII collating driver, which determines sort order, then the {IF} command is case-sensitive. (*1-2-3* Release 2 and *Symphony* users needn't worry about case-sensitivity.) Replace the {IF} command in cell B4 with {IF @UPPER(fb) = "F"} and in cell B5 with {IF @UPPER(fb) = "T"}. The string function @UPPER reads all of the letters in the label in *fb* as uppercase letters, so you may enter your responses in uppercase or lowercase letters.

Now return to the worksheet and enter the labels in rows 6 through 8 of the figure. Assign the label in cell A6 as the range name for the adjacent cell in column B:

Press slash (in *Symphony*, MENU), select Range Name Labels Right, and specify cell A6. Restart the macro by holding down the MACRO key and pressing F. Here's what happens when the program processes the commands starting in cell B6:

{GETNUMBER "How many seasons did John Hannah play for the Patriots? ",fb}   Displays the specified prompt and pauses for you to enter a number. The program stores the number in *fb*.

{IF fb = 13}{GETLABEL "Correct! Press Return to quit.",fb}{QUIT} Evaluates whether your response equals 13. If so, the program displays a congratulatory prompt, pauses for you to press Return, and quits.

{GETLABEL "Incorrect. Press Return to try again.",fb}{BRANCH loop}   Displays the prompt in the {GETLABEL} command and pauses for you to press Return. When you press Return, the program processes the BRANCH statement, which instructs it to process the commands in the subroutine named *loop*. This set of instructions creates a loop that continues until your response equals 13.

AUGUST 1987

8

Creating Customized Menus

Write a simple macro to create your own menus
in *1-2-3* or *Symphony*.

BY PAULA DEMPSEY

1-2-3 and *Symphony* use menus to guide you through such worksheet tasks as saving worksheets or printing ranges. Menu-driven programs are easy to learn because you don't have to memorize commands and their syntaxes. Instead, you select the commands from a menu.

You can make your worksheets easier for others to use by creating customized menu options that incorporate macros   short programs that automate specific worksheet tasks. For example, suppose the worksheet you've created for novice *1-2-3* or *Symphony* users requires them to enter information on the worksheet, save the worksheet into a file named REPORT, then print the information contained in the range named *print*. Let's assume that the first step, entering information, is clearly defined by instructions on the worksheet. To help users save the worksheet and print the report, you can write a macro that creates the following menu:

```
G1:'\m
Save  Print  Quit
Save worksheet
```

The Save and Print menu options automate the procedures for saving a worksheet and printing a range, respectively. The following macro creates the Save and Print menu:

```
       G        H                I              J        K
1  \m      {MENUBRANCH menu1}
2
3  menu1 Save             Print             Quit
4        Save worksheet Print report      Quit menu
5        /FSreport~R    /PPRprint~AGPX   {QUIT}
```

This macro is designed for *1-2-3* Releases 2 and 2.01 — it contains commands unavailable in *1-2-3* Release 1A. To make the macro work in the earlier release, replace the command {MENUBRANCH menu1} in cell H1 with */XMmenu1~*, and replace the command {QUIT} in cell J5 with */XQ*. The latter command works in any release of *1-2-3*. If you're using *Symphony*, modify the keystroke sequences to accommodate the different menu structure: Replace the contents of cell H5 with {SERVICES}FSi{ESC}report~Y, and replace the contents of cell I5 with {SERVICES}PSSRprint~QAGPQ.

Each line of the macro is a label, so in *1-2-3*, type an apostrophe label prefix at the beginning of each line that starts with a slash; otherwise, the command menu will appear when you type a slash. Next, assign a range name to the first cell of the macro. In *1-2-3* you must assign a name that consists of a backslash followed by a single letter, in this case \m (in *Symphony* you can use any range name — see your documentation for more details). For this macro, also assign the range name *menu1* to cell H3. If you haven't already done so, enter the labels \m and *menu1* in the column to the left of the macro as shown in the figure. To assign these labels as range names for the adjacent cells to the right, position the pointer in cell G1, press slash (in *Symphony*, MENU), select Range Name Labels Right, and indicate range G1..G3 by pressing End DownArrow Return.

Save this worksheet by pressing slash (in *Symphony*, SERVICES), selecting File Save, and entering *report*. The program saves the worksheet in a file named REPORT in the current directory. Next assign the name *print* to range A1..E45, the area of the worksheet where the report will be located: Press slash (in *Symphony*, MENU), select Range Name Create, enter *print*, and indicate range A1..E45.

To start the macro, hold down the MACRO key (Alt on most computers) and press M. (For the benefit of your worksheet users, be sure to put instructions for starting the macro on the worksheet.) The program begins processing the first line of code in the range named \m. The command {MENUBRANCH menu1} (in *1-2-3* Release 1A, /XMmenu1~) displays the contents of *menu1* and the adjacent cells to its right in a menu format in the control panel. Use the pointer-movement keys to move the pointer over each item. Note that a description of the highlighted item appears in the edit line (in *Symphony* the description appears above the customized menu). The program uses the descriptions you entered under the menu items on the worksheet.

In our example, we entered the menu items in range H3..J3 and the corresponding descriptions in the adjacent cells in the row below.

Select a menu item just as you would in *1-2-3* or *Symphony* — either by pointing to it and pressing Return or by typing the first letter. If you use menu choices that begin with different letters, your users can make a selection by typing the first letter of the item. Once you make a selection, the program processes the commands in the cell under the description that corresponds to that selection. For example, if you select Save, the program processes the keystrokes in cell H5. These keystrokes press slash (in the *Symphony* macro, SERVICES) and select File Save from the command menu. When the program prompts for a file name, the macro types *report* (in *Symphony* the macro clears any existing file name and then types *report*). The tilde (~) presses Return to enter the file name. The macro assumes that you've already saved this worksheet in a file in the current directory at least once before. When the program asks if you want to replace the current version of the file, the macro types R (in the *Symphony* macro, Y) to replace the file. When the program finishes processing the keystrokes in this cell, it looks to the cell below for more commands to process. Since the cell below is blank, the macro stops.

If you select Print, the macro enters *print* as the print range, then selects Align Go Page Quit to print the report. Since there are no instructions in the cell below these keystrokes, the macro ends. If you want the macro to redisplay the menu after selecting Save or Print, add the branching statement {*BRANCH \m*} (in *1-2-3* Release 1A, */XM\m~*) in cells H6 and I6. This command tells the program to continue processing commands at *\m*. The command in *\m* tells *1-2-3* or *Symphony* to redisplay the menu so that you can make another selection.

If you choose the last menu item, Quit, the program processes the {QUIT} command (in *1-2-3* Release 1A, /XQ) and leaves the macro, returning to Ready mode. It's a good idea to include Quit as a menu item, as the user might otherwise press Escape to try to leave the menu, causing unintended results.

Keep these rules in mind when you create your own menus: The program allows a maximum of eight items per menu. Enter the items in adjacent cells in a row, one item per cell, leaving the cell to the right of the last item blank. You need to assign a range name only to the leftmost item in the row. The program will automatically include the contents of this cell in the menu, as well as each cell to its right up to the first blank cell. Finally, enter a brief description for each menu choice in the cell below the item. Leaving this cell blank causes an error. If you prefer to omit a description, enter a space in the description cell.

9

Making Menus with Symphony

Techniques you can use to let other users decide which path your macro should follow.

BY DANIEL GASTEIGER

When you create applications, there may be times when you want your macros to give you, or whoever is using them, a choice from a list of options — the same sort of options you have when you press the MENU or SERVICES key. This list of options is called a menu. In this article we'll look at some of the ways you can use macros to create custom menus.

The *Symphony* Command Language {MENUBRANCH} and {MENUCALL} commands allow you to create *Symphony*-like menus. These commands work similarly in that each displays a menu in the control panel. The following macro displays a menu that lets you choose whether or not to save the current worksheet as a file named EXAMPLE, even if you have already saved the worksheet using a different file name.

```
Don't save
No  Yes
```

```
        A          B             C
1   \e         {MENUBRANCH menu1}
2
3   menu1      No            Yes
4              Don't save    Save the worksheet
5                            {SERVICES}FS{ESC}example~Y{ESC}
```

Name cell B1 \e and cell B3 *menu1* by issuing the MENU Range Name Labels

Right command. When you press MACRO-E, here's what happens:

{MENUBRANCH menu1}   Causes the macro to create a menu based upon the instructions contained in the range named *menu1*. The macro uses the first row of labels in the range (cells B3 and C3) as the menu choices. It uses the second row of labels (cells B4 and C4) as long prompts for the menu. These are descriptive phrases that appear in the control panel when you use the menu pointer to highlight a selection.

In this example, the long prompt for No is *Don't save* and the long prompt for Yes is *Save the worksheet*. When you make a selection, either by pointing and pressing Return or by typing the first letter of the menu choice, the macro processes commands found in the cell directly under the label containing the long prompt for that choice. If you select No from the menu in this example, the macro stops because there are no macro commands in cell B5. If you select Yes, the macro processes the following commands, which are in cell C5.

{SERVICES}FS{ESC}example~Y{ESC}   Selects SERVICES File Save and assigns the file name EXAMPLE. If the disk already contains a file with this name, the current worksheet overwrites the one on the disk. Although this is not a particularly useful macro, it does illustrate the {MENUBRANCH} command.

Using the {MENUBRANCH} command, you may create a menu containing several choices that begin with the same letter:

```
Replace contents of the current cell
Replace  Search  Save  Quit
```

	A	B	C	D	E
1					

However, if you type an *S* to make your selection from the menu, *Symphony* assumes that you selected Search. When you make a selection from a user-defined menu by typing the first letter of the menu choice, *Symphony* uses the leftmost choice that begins with that letter. The only way to select Save from the menu shown is to use the arrow keys or Spacebar to point to the choice and then press Return. To ensure that your menus work as *Symphony's* menus do, avoid using the same letter to begin two or more choices.

With one exception, the {MENUCALL} command is identical to the {MENUBRANCH} command. When *Symphony* encounters a {MENUBRANCH} command, it processes the menu instructions and follows the path the user selects until it encounters the first cell that does not contain a label; then the macro stops. After processing a {MENUCALL} menu, *Symphony* follows the selected path until it encounters a cell that does not contain a label. It then returns to the command following the {MENUCALL} to continue processing keystrokes.

A BIT OF ETIQUETTE

The structure of {MENUBRANCH} and {MENUCALL} menus can lead to some very confusing worksheets. The worksheet below contains one {MENUBRANCH} statement, the instructions for creating the menu, and some of the macro steps associated with each menu choice. This is only an illustration; it is not a complete macro:

	A	B	C	D
1	\m	{MENUBRANCH choices}		
2				
3	choices	Input	Copy	Reset
4		Enter datPut data Clear all variables		
5		{BLANK co{MENU}IRa{BLANK var1}		
6		{GOTO}col{MENU}RNL{LET count,1}		
7		{DOWN} {MENU}Cin{IF dat>10}{BRANCH skip}		

Even on the worksheet, this can be difficult to decipher. Instead of writing all the steps for each menu choice directly under the corresponding long prompt, use {BRANCH} statements to make the macro easier to read. The following is the same menu using {BRANCH} statements to direct the macro to appropriate routines on the worksheet. (This example isn't complete. I have omitted several lines of macro instructions within each *rout* routine.)

	A	B	C	D
1	\m	{MENUBRANCH choices}		
2				
3	choices	Input	Copy	Reset
4		Enter data intPut data into Clear variables		
5		{BRANCH rout1}{BRANCH rout2}{BRANCH rout3}		
6				
7	rout1	{BLANK colm1}		
8		{GOTO}colm1~		
9		{DOWN}		
18	rout2	{MENU}IRabove~		
19		{MENU}RNLUabove~		
20		{MENU}Cinputrow~above~		
35	rout 3	{BLANK var1}		
36		{LET count,1}		
37		{IF dat>10}{BRANCH skip}		

The command after each long prompt in the menu instructions is a {BRANCH} statement. If you select Input from the menu that this macro generates, the macro looks for instructions in the cell named *rout1*. If you select Copy, the macro processes instructions in the cell named *rout2*, and if you select Reset, the macro continues with *rout3*. Laying out your macros like this makes them easier to read because long commands don't get buried behind commands in adjacent cells. This layout also enables you to identify named cells quickly. For more thoughts on this approach, take a look at "Writing Structured Macros," on page 287.

HANDLING ESCAPE IN MENUS

When you press the Escape key in response to a regular *Symphony* menu, you move one step back along the command sequence you followed to arrive at the menu. If you had pressed only the SERVICES key and then pressed Escape, *Symphony* would return to Ready mode. If you have selected SERVICES File and then pressed Escape, *Symphony* would return you to the SERVICES menu; pressing Escape again would return *Symphony* to Ready mode.

If you press Escape in response to a user-defined menu, the macro continues processing the command found immediately after the {MENUBRANCH} or {MENUCALL} command. This feature lets you create layered menu systems like those of *Symphony*.

The following is an incomplete macro, part of which illustrates a two-level menu.

	A	B	C
1	\m	{MENUBRANCH menmn}	
2			
3	menmn	Print	Save
4		Create report	Save the worksheet
5		{BRANCH print}	{BRANCH save}
6			
7	print	{MENUBRANCH prnmenu}	
8		{BRANCH \m}	
9			
10	prnmenu	Pause	No pause
11		Pause for new pages	Continuous feed

So far, this macro does nothing but generate menus. The range names *\m, menmn, print,* and *prnmenu* are assigned to cells B1, B3, B7, and B10, respectively. When you press MACRO-M, you are presented with the menu named *menmn:*

```
Create report
Print  Save
```

	A	B	C
1	\m	{MENUBRANCH menmn}	

If you press the Escape key in response to this menu, the macro stops running because there are no further macro instructions following the first {MENUBRANCH} command. Selecting Print causes *Symphony* to display the menu named *prnmenu:*

```
Pause for new pages
Pause   No pause
```

	A	B	C
1	\m	{MENUBRANCH menmn}	

If you press Escape in response to this second menu, the macro processes the command after the second {MENUBRANCH} statement. That command, in cell B8, is {BRANCH \m}. This sends the macro looking for keystrokes to the cell named *\m* — the first {MENUBRANCH} command. *Symphony* once again displays the first menu. You have backed up one level. Pressing Escape a second time stops the macro.

Be careful when designing macros that contain user-defined menus. If your macro uses the {BREAKOFF} command to keep users from "exploring" the worksheet, a {MENUBRANCH} or {MENUCALL} statement can help them beat that protection. If you don't include a command to reroute the macro, pressing Escape at a menu turns the user loose on your worksheet.

IS THIS THE ONLY WAY?

The *Symphony* {MENUBRANCH} and {MENUCALL} commands let you create powerful *Symphony*-like menus. With a little care, you can use them to lead other users through applications you develop. Although powerful, these menus are not appropriate for every application. They are limited to eight selections per menu, and they aren't easily adapted for selecting items from lists that vary in length from day to day.

10

Alternative Menus

An exploration of alternatives to the {MENUBRANCH} and {MENUCALL} commands.

BY DANIEL GASTEIGER

Symphony offers two macro commands you can use to create your own menus: {MENUBRANCH} and {MENUCALL}. They create *Symphony*-like menus in the control panel and give users control over the flow of your macro. Because {MENUBRANCH} and {MENUCALL} menus can display only up to eight choices, they are cumbersome when you are dealing with large numbers of selections. Let's explore some techniques that can help you create more versatile menus within your macro applications.

WHAT'S THE ADVANTAGE?

There are several common uses for large menus. Your macro may need to determine who is using it so that it can present data of interest to that person. Or you may wish to offer more than eight different ways of examining data on the worksheet. Alternate menus can handle both of these situations.

When you create an application that 10 people will be using and data of interest to each of them resides in separate files, you can create a full-screen menu to steer the users to their own data. This illustration shows a simple full-screen menu:

	A	B	C	D
1				
2	Type the number next to your			
3	name and press Return			
4				
5	1. Lisa	6. Mary		
6	2. Eric	7. Connie		
7	3. Joyce	8. Arturo		
8	4. Kristen	9. George		
9	5. Matt	10. Ally		

The macro that uses this menu sends the cell pointer to the top-left corner of the menu (cell A1 — in this example, named *topleft*) and prompts the user to enter a number. Based on the number the user enters, the macro calls a subroutine to combine the appropriate data into the worksheet. The main body of the macro appears below.

	H	I	J	K	L
1	\m	{GOTO}topleft~			
2		{GETNUMBER "Enter your number",num}			
3		{GOTO}datarange~			
4		{BLANK datarange}			
5		{IF num<1#OR#num>11}{BRANCH \m}			
6		{IF @INT(num)=1}{lisa}			
7		{IF @INT(num)=2}{eric}			
8		{IF @INT(num)=3}{joyce}			
9		{IF @INT(num)=4}{kristen}			
10		{IF @INT(num)=5}{matt}			
11		{IF @INT(num)=6}{mary}			
12		{IF @INT(num)=7}{connie}			
13		{IF @INT(num)=8}{arturo}			
14		{IF @INT(num)=9}{george}			
15		{15 @INT(num)=10}{ally}			
16		{BRANCH mainrout}			
17					
18	num				
19					
20	lisa	{SERVICES}FCCEIFlisa~			
21					
22	eric	{SERVICES}FCCEIFeric~			

The illustration shows only two of the subroutines, one named *lisa* and the other named *eric*. Here's how the macro works.

{GOTO}topleft~   Makes the custom menu visible. *Topleft* is the name of the cell at the top-left corner of the area on the worksheet that contains the menu (in this case, cell A1).

{**GETNUMBER "Enter your number",num**}   Displays the prompt *Enter your number* in the control panel and places the number you type into the cell named *num*.

{**GOTO**}datarange~   Sends the cell pointer to the top-left corner of the range named *datarange*. This range should be large enough to contain each worksheet that the macro will combine into it. Establish *datarange* when you create the macro.

{**BLANK datarange**}   Erases *datarange* to prepare it for incoming data.

{**IF num < 1#OR#num > = 11**}{**BRANCH \m**}   Assures that the number you entered at the prompt is a valid menu choice. If the number is less than 1 or greater than or equal to 11, the macro starts over and gives you a chance to make a valid selection.

{**IF @INT(num) = 1**}{**lisa**}   Calls the routine named *lisa* if the value you entered is 1. Notice that if the number you entered is greater than 1 but less than 2, the macro still processes the *lisa* subroutine.

The precautionary use of the @INT function and the {IF} statement in the previous step prevents users from disabling the macro.

The *lisa* subroutine consists of the commands {SERVICES}FCCEIFlisa~. This means "Press the SERVICES key and select File Combine Copy Entire-File Ignore Formulas, type *lisa*, and press Return." It combines the file named *lisa* into the current worksheet. Once the file is combined, the macro returns to the command following the {lisa} subroutine call in the main body of the macro (cell K7).

{**IF @INT(num) = 2**}{**eric**}   Calls the routine named *eric* if the value you entered is 2. The *eric* subroutine works like the *lisa* subroutine, except that it combines a file named *eric* into the worksheet. After combining the file, the macro returns to the cell after the {eric} subroutine call (cell K8).

With each {IF} statement, the macro calls a different subroutine, combines a file into the worksheet, and returns to the command following the subroutine call. The macro skims over {IF} statements that don't produce matches. After the correct subroutine has run, the macro processes the command in cell K16.

{**BRANCH mainrout**}   Sends the macro looking for keystrokes to the cell named *mainrout*. *Mainrout* can be a routine that analyzes the data combined by the *lisa, eric*, and so forth, subroutines, prints a report, or performs any other tasks necessary for the person using the application.

STREAMLINED MENUS

You can shorten this menu routine considerably by replacing each subroutine call with the commands contained within the subroutines themselves. For example, the command that reads

{IF @INT(num) = 1}{lisa}

can be rewritten to read

$$\{IF \ @INT(num) = 1\}\{SERVICES\}FCCEIFlisa\sim$$

You can then omit the subroutine named *lisa* from the worksheet.

Although the resulting macro is shorter, it is not the shortest macro possible. In fact, while this approach requires one extra statement for every menu choice, you can write a macro that requires only a few statements to combine the correct file, even though there are 10 names on the menu. The macro looks like this:

	H	I	J	K	L	M
1	\m	{GOTO}topleft~				
2		{GETNUMBER "Enter your number",num}				
3		{GOTO}datarange~				
4		{BLANK datarange}				
5		{RECALC form}				
6		{IF num<1#OR#num>=11}{BRANCH \m}				
7	form	{SERVICES}FCCEIFlisa~				
8		{BRANCH mainrout}				
9						
10	num					

Notice that the only {IF} statement in the new macro is the one that restarts the macro when you enter a selection that is not on the menu:

$$\{IF \ num < 1\#or\#num > = 11\}\{BRANCH \ \backslash m\}$$

Also notice the {RECALC form} command in cell I5. This command causes *Symphony* to recalculate the cell named *form* (cell I7) because, though that cell seems to contain a label entry, it actually contains the following formula:

$$+ \text{``}\{SERVICES\}FCCEIF\text{''}\&@CHOOSE(num-1,\text{``lisa''},\text{``eric''},\text{``joyce''},$$
$$\text{``kristin''},\text{``matt''},\text{``mary''},\text{``connie''},\text{``arturo''},\text{``george''},\text{``ally''})\&\text{`` \sim ''}$$

The formula evaluates to a different label for each change in the value of the cell named *num* located below the macro. When *num* equals 1, the formula evaluates to {SERVICES}FCCEIFlisa~, and when *num* equals 5, the formula becomes {SERVICES}FCCEIFmatt~.

DEALING WITH SUBROUTINES

For short command sequences that differ only slightly from menu choice to menu choice, this type of macro is useful. However, if your macro needs to offer several entirely unrelated menu choices, it must rely heavily on subroutines.

Using the menu shown below, your macro could offer to display historical data, print reports, run what-if tables, allow for data entry, and so on. In any case, a user's menu selection determines which subroutine the macro runs:

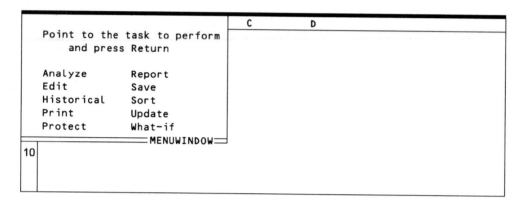

Rather than selecting a number corresponding to a menu choice, the user of this menu simply points to the desired choice and presses Return. The menu resides in its own window, which appears superimposed on whatever is already on the screen — *Symphony's* equivalent to the pull-down or pop-up menu. The macro that uses this menu calls subroutines that have the same names as the menu choices. For example, when you select Sort, the macro calls the subroutine named *sort*.

For this discussion, prepare your worksheet as outlined in the following instructions. As with most macros, you can build this application anywhere on your worksheet as long as you adjust the commands and windows accordingly.

Type the labels that constitute the menu into columns A and B of the worksheet and make sure that the first valid menu selection is in row 5. Type the instructions for using the menu into rows 2 and 3. Finally, use these keystrokes to create a window around the menu:

Press SERVICES and select Window Create. Type *menuwindow* and press Return. Select SHEET and use the arrow keys to adjust the window size; it should be large enough to surround only the menu and its instruction. Press Return and select Restrict Range, then press the Backspace key and move the cell pointer to cell A2. Anchor the pointer by pressing the Tab key, highlight cells A2..B9, and press Return. Select Borders Line and Quit. The macro is on the next page.

I've shown only the first few steps of a few of the subroutines to give an idea of how you might design your macro. Before you run this macro, create subroutines for each of the menu choices. You can replace the selections I've suggested with others more appropriate to your application. Place each subroutine in column K, below the

```
         J           K         L         M         N
 1  \m            {SERVICES}WUmenuwindow~
 2  back          {?}
 3                {IF @CELLPOINTER("row")<5}{BRANCH back}
 4                {DISPATCH @CELLPOINTER("contents")}
 5
 6  analyze       {SERVICES}WH~
 7                {GOTO}results~
──────────────────────────────────────────────────────────
15  edit          {SERVICES}WUdbase~
16                {SERVICES}WI
17
──────────────────────────────────────────────────────────
21  historical  {SERVICES}WH~
22                {GOTO}datarange~
```

main body of the macro, and type names of the subroutines into column J, adjacent to the first cell of each subroutine. Then assign all the subroutine names at once by putting the cell pointer in cell J1 and issuing the MENU Range Name Labels Right command sequence.

Here's how the macro works:

{SERVICES}WUmenuwindow~ Brings the window named *menuwindow* "to the top," making it appear as a pop-up menu.

{?} Causes the macro to pause until the user presses Return. The user can move the cell pointer anywhere within the *menuwindow* window.

{IF @CELLPOINTER("row")<5}{BRANCH back} Checks to determine the row in which the cell pointer rests. If the row number is less than 5, the macro loops to the cell named *back* (cell K2); to the user, it looks as though nothing has happened. This prevents the user from making invalid menu choices. When you build applications, you can place your pop-up menus in any row of the worksheet as long as you adjust this statement to match the position of the menu.

{DISPATCH @CELLPOINTER("contents")} Sends the macro looking for commands to process in the cell whose name is contained in the current cell — the cell the user has highlighted with the cell pointer.

Each subroutine should contain a statement such as {SERVICES}WH~ or {SERVICES}WUdbase~. These commands clear the screen and allow the subroutine to process without having the menu window active.

These are just a few techniques for creating your own menus. Experiment to determine which are best suited to the applications you write. Above all, have fun.

SEPTEMBER 1985

11

Command Contrasts, Part 1

We compare analogous commands and functions and discuss which to use when.

BY DANIEL GASTEIGER

I received the following request from Steven Breth of the Arlington, Va., office of Winrock International:

1-2-3 has many commands that can perform the same actions when used in macros under certain circumstances. For example, the Copy command is analogous to the {LET} command, and the @CHOOSE function is similar to the @VLOOKUP function.

It would be helpful to have an article that compares similar macro commands. This article should focus on which commands are fastest and should illuminate other comparative advantages.

That's a big article. This is part one.

ASSIGNMENT COMMANDS

The single largest collection of analogous macro commands in *1-2-3* is assignment commands. An assignment command places a value or values into the worksheet. The most familiar assignment command includes typing something (number, label, or formula) and pressing Return. This effectively assigns the entry to the current cell.

A macro can send the cell pointer to a destination cell, type something, and press Return. More often, you design a macro that simply types something and presses Return, for example, a particular word or phrase (such as your company's name) that arises often in your worksheet.

This approach to assigning a cell's contents is clear and straightforward. Its benefit over other assignment commands is that it can generate exact duplicates of a formula in any worksheet cell. Suppose you've used relative cell references to write a complex formula that you wish to replicate in several places on the worksheet. You want every copy to duplicate the original formula and not to adjust cell references.

Rather than edit the original formula and change its references to absolute, simply turn the formula into a macro: Point to the formula, press EDIT, type a tilde, press Home, type an apostrophe, and press Return. Copy the resulting label to an out-of-the-way cell, then assign a macro name to that cell. Renew the original formula by pointing to the cell holding it and running the new macro. From here on, to replicate the formula, point to the cell in which the copy should appear, and run the macro.

A related macro assignment technique is that of editing a cell's contents. For example, if a cell (or a column of cells) contains a value you wish to increase by 5%, you can edit the cell's contents to show the increase. The following illustration shows some data and a macro that increases each value by 5%:

	A	B	C	D
1	\c	{EDIT}*1.05{CALC}{DOWN}		
2		/XG\c~		
3				
4		4		
5		3		
6		8		
7		4		
8		9		

To create the macro, enter it as shown and assign its name by pressing slash, selecting Range Name Labels Right, indicating cell A1, and pressing Return. To run the macro, point to the first cell in the column of data you wish to convert (cell B4 in this example), hold down the MACRO key (Alt on most computers), and press C. The macro converts the data cell by cell. Stop the macro by pressing Control-Break after it processes the last value.

Like typing and pressing Return, the editing procedure can create identical copies of a single formula. A greater advantage of the procedure is its ability to modify a sequence of formulas or values in a uniform manner.

The two assignment techniques described so far are the most efficient macro approaches to manipulating formulas under most circumstances. If the specific formulas are important, you'll find no better way to deal with them. However, if you're interested more in the formulas' values or in the relationships described in the formulas, several other macro procedures are more efficient than the ones described so far.

ASSIGNING VIA MENUS

To type or edit an entry and press Return, a macro must first move the cell pointer to the cell that will receive the entry. The Data Fill command can make an assignment without moving the cell pointer, which makes this command convenient for applications that rely heavily on cell-pointer movement.

For example, suppose you use the previous macro, but you want it to stop when it finishes converting the data. Your macro can increase the value of a counter cell by one each time it makes a conversion. When the value of the counter matches a preset Stop value, the macro will stop. If the cell pointer must move to the counter cell after each conversion, the macro will be cumbersome and slow. But the Data Fill command lets your macro increase the counter without moving the cell pointer to it. The following is a modification of the first macro:

	A	B	C	D
1	\c	{EDIT}*1.05{CALC}{DOWN}		
2		/DFcounter~counter+1~~~		
3		/XIcounter=stop~/XQ		
4		/XG\c~		
5				
6	stop			
7	counter			
8				
9		4		
10		3		
11		8		
12		4		
13		9		

To modify your macro, insert two rows above row 2: Press slash, select Worksheet Insert Row, indicate range B2..B3, and press Return. Enter the labels shown in cells B2 and B3. Then insert three rows above row 6 and enter the labels shown in cells A6 and A7. Assign range names to cells B6 and B7: Press slash, select Range Name Labels Right, indicate range A6..A7, and press Return. If you wish, reenter the data starting in cell B9 to appear as it does in the illustration. Because there are five entries to convert, enter the number 5 into the cell named *stop* (B6). Then move the pointer to cell B9 and start the macro.

SUMMARY TABLE

Procedure	Advantages	Limitations
Type entry and press Return	Generates exact duplicates of formulas that contain relative cell references	Cell pointer must move to target cell
Edit entry	Can modify several formulas in a uniform manner	Cell pointer must move to target cell
/Data Fill	Can manipulate data during assignment process without moving the cell pointer; can fill a range with sequential values; available to Release 1A users	Slower than other alternatives; cannot manipulate labels
/Copy	Recreates relationally identical formulas; can assign identical values to every cell in a range	Cannot manipulate data during the assignment procedure
/Range Value	Assigns a formula's value to a cell; can assign a range of data in a single operation	Slow for single-cell assignments; cannot manipulate data during the assignment procedure
{LET}	Assigns a formula's value to a cell; fast; can manipulate data during assignment; can assign numeric and string values	Can make only one assignment per operation; may not update worksheet
{PUT}	Same advantages as {LET} command; lets you identify target cell indirectly	Same limitations as {LET} command

The macro uses one of the techniques described earlier to assign a new value to each cell in the column. It also uses a different assignment command, the Data Fill command, to stop itself when it has altered five cells' worth of data. Here's how the macro works:

{EDIT}∗1.Ø5{CALC}{DOWN}   Presses EDIT, types ∗1.Ø5, then presses CALC DownArrow. This is one of the two assignment procedures already described.

/DFcounter~counter + 1 ~ ~ ~   Selects /Data Fill, enters *counter* as the range to fill and *counter + 1* as the Start value, then accepts the default Step and Stop values to finish the command. This increases the value of *counter* by one.

/XIcounter = stop~/XQ   Determines whether the value of *counter* equals the value of *stop*. If the values are equal, the macro stops; otherwise, control of the macro passes to the following cell.

/XG\c~   Passes control of the macro to the cell named \c and restarts the macro. The macro continues this looping process until stopped by the /XI command in the previous step. Reset the value of *counter* to Ø if you wish to run the macro a second time. If you don't reset *counter*, the macro will keep running until you stop it by pressing the Break key.

The Data Fill command is intended to fill ranges of cells with sequential numbers. For example, you can generate a list of numbers from 1 to 25 by selecting /Data Fill, indicating range C11..C36 (or any range of column C that begins with C11 and ends after C36), and pressing Return. Then enter 1 as the Start value, 1 as the Step value, and 25 as the Stop value. There is no faster way to assign long sequences of values.

The Data Fill command has another edge over other menu-accessed assignment statements. The command can actually manipulate values during the assignment process. In the example, the Data Fill command assigns the value of the formula *counter + 1* to the target cell. Other assignment statements that you access via menus can assign only information that already exists in the worksheet.

For single-cell assignments, however, the Data Fill command is slow. It is also limited by the fact that it can assign only numeric values. We occasionally publish a macro that uses the Data Fill command as an assignment statement. This is primarily so users of *1-2-3* Release 1A will be able to use the macro. But if you're using *1-2-3* Release 2 or 2.01, you can often speed things up by replacing Data Fill assignment statements with {LET} or {PUT} commands. I'll discuss these commands further in a bit.

The Copy command is another assignment statement that your macros access from the menus. This command provides the most efficient way to duplicate a cell's contents or to perform a large number of relationally identical calculations. The Copy command copies literally; it cannot manipulate the data or formulas as it copies them. And anything the Copy command assigns must originate from some other cell or range on the worksheet.

For re-creating formulas whose references should adjust, the Copy command is unequaled in speed. You can create a formula once, name the cell that contains it, and write a macro that copies the formula from the named cell to the current cell — or to a specified range. Equally important, your macros can use the Copy command to assign large ranges of formulas, values, or labels in a single operation.

Often you wish your macro to assign a formula's current value to a particular cell. One simple way to do this is to use the Range Value command. For example, the cell named *source* (B3) in the following worksheet contains the formula +B1 + C1−A1. The macro in cell B5 assigns the value of that formula to the cell named *target* (B7):

The primary advantage of the Range Value command is its ability to assign values from a large range of data in a single operation. When assigning a single cell's value to another cell (as in the example), the Range Value command is not the fastest alternative. The Range Value command is also limited by its inability to manipulate the data that it assigns. As shown earlier, the Data Fill command can perform calculations on data and assign the result of those calculations to the target cell. The

```
          A           B           C           D
1         2           3           7
2
3  source             8
4
5  \v          /RVsource~target~
6
7  target
```

Range Value command can assign only values that already exist in the worksheet.

KEYWORD ASSIGNMENTS

There are several assignment statements among *1-2-3*'s advanced macro commands. Each of them can assign only values (numeric or string), so in spite of their superior speed, they cannot fulfill all of your macros' assignment needs.

The {LET} command serves almost the same purpose as the Range Value command. It can assign only values (numeric and string), and it can make only one assignment per operation. But the {LET} command makes an assignment far faster than does the Range Value or Data Fill command. Like the Data Fill command, the {LET} command can assign the result of a calculation to its target cell and thereby generate information that does not already exist on the worksheet.

For example, the {LET} command in the following macro combines labels from two different cells and assigns the resulting label, *two words*, to the cell named *target*:

```
          A           B           C           D
1  \c          {LET target,+two&" "&words}
2
3  two         two
4  words       words
5
6  target
```

As you can see, unlike the Data Fill command, the {LET} command can manipulate labels as well as numeric values.

1-2-3 doesn't necessarily update the worksheet after processing a {LET} command, so formulas or macro procedures that rely on the assigned value may not be accurate while the macro is running. It is good practice to have your macros recalculate such formulas before using them for output or for conditional branching operations.

The {PUT} command is similar to the {LET} command in that it will assign numeric or label values, and it can manipulate data during the assignment process. With the {PUT} command, however, you specify a range, a column, and a row offset to identify the target cell for the assignment. For example, in the following macro, *1-2-3* assigns the label *XXX* to the cell that is two columns to the right and three rows down from the top-left corner of the range named *block* (A4..D9):

	A	B	C	D
1	\p	{PUT block,2,3,"XXX"}~		
2				
3				
4	0	6	12	18
5	1	7	13	19
6	2	8	14	20
7	3	9	15	21
8	4	10	16	22
9	5	11	17	23

The {PUT} command is fast and very powerful for particular applications.

NO END IN SIGHT?

This topic is nasty. There are many ways to assign data and formulas to cells, and it's impossible to do them justice in an article of this length. You can argue that the Range Erase command assigns zero values to whatever cells it erases, as does the {BLANK} command. By way of comparison, the Range Erase command is slower than the {BLANK} command. But the {BLANK} command doesn't update the worksheet and the Range Erase command does.

You can also argue that {GETNUMBER} and {GETLABEL} commands assign input values to worksheet cells and that {READ}, {READLN}, and File Import operations make assignments as well. Many menu and macro commands are variously useful as assignment statements but probably won't be put into service as often as any of the commands I've described so far.

AUGUST 1987

12

Command Contrasts, Part 2

Which commands and functions are most appropriate for the macros you're writing?

BY DANIEL GASTEIGER

There is rarely just one way to write a macro. Many macro commands perform tasks that are analogous to tasks you can perform through menus. Several commands seem to duplicate @functions. Some @functions seem even to duplicate other @functions.

Although there may be several ways to write a particular macro, all those ways may not be equal. We've previously compared several common techniques that your macros can use to assign contents to cells. This time we compare other macro commands and @functions and discuss the benefits and limitations of more or less analogous macro techniques.

BRANCHING

1-2-3 processes macro commands from left to right in a cell and then looks for more commands to process in the next cell down the column. When a command or situation alters this flow of control, the macro is said to branch. In Release 1A, the /XG command provides this capability, while in Releases 2 and 2.01 you can use either the /XG or the {BRANCH} command.

The /XG command is limited in that it works only when a macro could normally access the menu. The {BRANCH} command can redirect macro flow at any point except from within the braces of another macro command. For example, the following figure shows two macros, one that misuses the /XG command and another that properly uses the {BRANCH} command:

	A	B	C	D
1	\m	This is a /XGskip~		
2				
3	\t	This is a {BRANCH skip}		
4				
5	skip	simple sentence.~		

To create those macros (and all the macros that appear in this chapter), enter labels as shown in the illustration. Then assign the labels in column A as range names for the adjacent cells of column B: Press slash, select Range Name Labels Right, indicate range A1..A5 (or the range appropriate for your situation), and press Return.

When you run the first macro, *1-2-3* enters the sentence *This is a /XGskip* into the current cell. Assuming you're using Release 2 or 2.01, when you run the second macro (named *\t*), *1-2-3* enters *This is a simple sentence* into the current cell.

One common use of branching is to make a macro restart itself and thereby repeat a series of commands indefinitely. But this is a rather limited capability. You realize the true power of branching commands when your macros can branch to different locations, depending on a set of conditions that exists in the worksheet.

CONDITIONAL BRANCHING

If your macro needs to make a decision, use a conditional statement. *1-2-3* Release 1A users can use the /XI command to conditionally redirect the flow of a macro. Release 2 and 2.01 users can use both the /XI and the {IF} commands.

Like the /XG command, the /XI command works only in situations where your macro might access *1-2-3*'s menu. The {IF} command, however, will work anywhere in a macro as long as it doesn't occur within the braces of another macro command. In addition, Release 2/2.01 users will find that the {IF} command processes more quickly than the /XI command.

Both commands redirect flow of a macro in the same way: If a value or condition in the worksheet evaluates to 0, control of the macro passes directly to the cell following the conditional statement. If the value or condition is not 0, the macro processes whatever commands follow the conditional statement in the current cell.

The /XI and {IF} commands actually don't evaluate conditional statements in the same way. When a conditional statement evaluates to 0, the statement is considered false. If the statement evaluates to 1 (or any other number but 0), it is considered true. For all intents and purposes, the value 0 is false, and the value not 0 is true.

But the /XI command interprets ERR and NA as being true (not 0). This is the opposite of the {IF} command, which considers ERR and NA to be false. If any of your conditional branching operations might involve ERR or NA values, be sure to pick the conditional statement that provides the results you desire.

The simplest applications of a conditional branching statement might offer users an opportunity to stop a looping macro. For example, the Release 2/2.01 macro in the following illustration uses a /XI command to determine whether you have finished entering data:

	A	B	C	D
1	\s	{?}~{DOWN}		
2		/XLAnother entry? (y or n)~test~		
3		/XItest="Y"~/XG\s~		
4				
5	test			

This isn't meant to be an example of superior macro design; it merely illustrates a common format of a conditional branch. Here's how it works:

{?}~{DOWN}   Causes the macro to pause until you press Return, then presses Return and moves the cell pointer down. While the macro pauses, you can type any characters, access the menus, or edit a cell's contents. You would most likely type an entry for the current cell. When you press Return, you signal *1-2-3* that you've finished making your entry.

/XLAnother entry? (y or n)~test~   Displays the prompt *Another entry? (y or n)* and places your response in the cell named *test*.

/XItest = "Y"~/XG\s~   Determines whether or not *test* contains the letter Y. If *test* contains a Y, the command /XG\s~ transfers control of the macro to the cell named \s. If *test* doesn't contain a Y, control of the macro passes directly to the next cell in column B (cell B4), which is blank, and the macro stops.

Situations often arise that demand several conditional branching statements to work together. For example, suppose you want your macro to let you select what the macro does next.

MULTIPLE BRANCHES

There are several techniques you can apply to have your macros offer options to their users. For example, the following illustration shows a macro that lets you select one of three options from a list that appears on the worksheet:

	A	B	C	D	E
1	\m	{PGDN}{GOTO}list~			
2		/XNEnter the number of your choice. ~test~			
3		/XItest=1~/XGfiles~			
4		/XItest=2~/XGprint~			
5		/XItest=3~/XGstop~			
6		/XG\m~			
7					
8	test				
9					
10	List	1. Files			
11		2. Print			
12		3. Quit			

This macro is not complete. It lacks the subroutines named *files*, *print*, and *stop*; therefore, it will fail if you run it and make a selection. Once again, the intent is to show only how such a macro might be constructed.

The macro starts by displaying the list of numbered entries in range B10..B12. Then it displays the prompt *Enter the number of your choice* and stores the number you enter in the cell named *test*. If you enter 1, control of the macro passes to the routine named *files*. If you enter 2, the macro processes commands beginning in the cell named *print*. If you enter 3, control passes to the cell named *stop*. If your entry is neither 1, 2, nor 3, macro control passes to the cell named \m, and you get another chance to make a selection.

As we'll see in a moment, this technique isn't particularly elegant, but it solves the problem. By using numbers to make selections, the macro will work in all releases of *1-2-3*. Also, the number of selections the macro can offer is limited only by the amount of space on the display.

Release 2/2.01 users can create a more sophisticated macro simply by listing the subroutine names in the worksheet and letting users point to the routine name they wish to select:

	A	B	C	D	E
1	\m	{PGDN}{GOTO}list~{?}			
2		{DISPATCH @CELLPOINTER("contents")}			
3					
4					
5	List	Files		Move the cell pointer	
6		Print		to your selection and	
7		Quit		press Return.	

The command statement {DISPATCH @CELLPOINTER("contents")} means "Transfer control of the macro to the cell whose name appears in the current cell." Hence, when you point to the cell that contains the label *Files* and press Return, control of the macro shifts to the routine named *files*. (Once again, this example is not complete. In reality the macro will fail if you make a selection.)

The benefit of the {DISPATCH} command is that it can make a macro branch dynamically; a single command has the power of several conditional statements. The {DISPATCH} command responds more rapidly than a sequence of conditional statements, and often the worksheet structures that support a {DISPATCH} command require less space and preparation than those that support a series of /XI or {IF} commands.

The disadvantage of both multiple conditional statements and the {DISPATCH} command is that the format of the selection process is unfamiliar to many users. The selection procedure most intuitive to a *1-2-3* user is one that involves moving a pointer through a menu in the control panel.

MENU BRANCHING

The /XM and {MENUBRANCH} commands provide a simple means by which your macros can branch to any one of eight different routines. These commands display *1-2-3* like menus based on a set of menu instructions stored on the worksheet. This illustration shows a macro that creates a three-choice menu:

	A	B	C	D	E
1	\k	/XMmenu1~			
2		/XG\k~			
3					
4	menu1	Files	Print	Quit	
5		Save, CombinReport, LStop the macro			
6		/XGfiles~	/XGprint~		

The contents of cells B5, C5, and D5 are *Save, Combine*; *Report, Letters, Envelopes*; and *Stop the macro*, respectively. Note that we've adjusted some of the column widths to clarify the display. You do not need to change these widths. Once again, this is not a complete macro. It simply shows the structure of a single set of menu instructions.

Menu instructions take up two rows of the worksheet. The first row (in this case, range B4..D4) contains labels that *1-2-3* will display as menu prompts. The second row of menu instructions (range B5..D5) contains labels that *1-2-3* will use as long menu prompts. One long prompt appears, depending on which menu item is highlighted by the menu pointer. The cells that follow each long prompt contain commands that *1-2-3* will process when you make a selection from the menu. Note that, as with other /X commands, your macro will process the /XM command correctly only if *1-2-3* can access its own menu when it encounters the command. The {MENUBRANCH} command can appear at any point in a macro except within the braces of another macro command.

For providing users with control over a macro's processing, there is no better branching mechanism than the /XM and {MENUBRANCH} commands. Menu instructions are quite easy to create, and the macro-generated menus are familiar to all *1-2-3* users. On the other hand, these menus are limited to no more than eight selections in any single menu. (There is always one more option than what appears on a menu — you can press Escape. When you press Escape in response to a menu, the macro continues processing commands directly after the /XM or {MENUBRANCH} command that created the menu.) As general branching statements, the /XM and {MENUBRANCH} commands are useless. These commands can redirect the flow of the macro only through user intervention. The sequential conditional statements and the {DISPATCH} commands can operate independent of interaction from a user.

MORE ON INTERACTION

Just as the menu-creation commands let users direct the flow of a macro while it runs, there are several commands that let users pass information to the worksheet during macro processing. As stated earlier, when *1-2-3* processes the {?} command, the macro pauses until someone presses Return. While the macro pauses, you can perform menu sequences, make cell entries, display graphs, and so on. But when you press Return, the macro continues processing with the command that directly follows the {?} command.

The {?} command is appropriate for quick-and-dirty macro development, particularly when you're the only one who's going to use the macros. But unless you plan otherwise (as shown in the earlier example), when a macro pauses at a {?} command, there are no instructions that direct a user what to do next. A user might damage the model you've created.

To account for these limitations, you can use the /XL and /XN commands or the {GETLABEL} and {GETNUMBER} commands. The /XL command displays a prompt in the control panel and makes the macro pause until you press Return. While the macro pauses, you may type any characters, but you can neither access the menus nor use the function keys. Whatever you enter in response to the prompt is stored in a predesignated cell as a label (/XL and {GETLABEL}) or as a number (/XN and {GETNUMBER}).

The /XL and /XN commands are significantly different from their advanced macro command equivalents. For one, as you must expect by now, the /XL and /XN commands are available only at times when your macro could access the menu. The {GETLABEL} and {GETNUMBER} commands are always available except within the braces of other macro commands. Also, the {GETLABEL} and {GETNUMBER} commands can display much longer prompts than can the /XL and /XN commands. But there are times when the /XL and /XN commands are more useful than their advanced macro command counterparts.

The {GETLABEL} and {GETNUMBER} commands accept input only into pre-designated cells. For example, the command {GETLABEL "Enter your name ",name} accepts input to the cell named *name*. To get these commands to accept input into the current cell requires writing extra steps in the macro or using dynamic macro code (code that rewrites itself depending on changing conditions in the worksheet). The /XL and /XN commands can quite easily accept input into the current cell. Simply omit a destination cell when you enter the command in your macro, and your entry will have nowhere else to go. For example, the command /XLEnter your name~ ~ accepts a label entry into the current cell.

MAKING CHOICES

This doesn't cover all the macro commands and techniques that have analogous approaches. You could study for years and never learn all of them. If nothing else, I hope this material provides a sense of what you're up against when you start to design and build macros.

The key to selecting an appropriate command or technique is to determine what works most efficiently in the situation you've created. What works best in one model won't necessarily work well in another. Thoroughly exploring all of *1-2-3*'s capabilities, whether or not you think you'll need them, will improve the chances that you'll find the best solution to your macro problems.

SEPTEMBER 1987

SECTION
3

USING DATA

An empty spreadsheet is useless. But when you fill it with data, it becomes a vital business tool. The first step is entering the data. Then come the formulas that establish the already known relationships among the data. Finally, you analyze the data to discover new relationships. In the process you will also do a lot of moving, calculating, editing, reformatting, and erasing of data. Macros can help you do all this faster and more efficiently.

The macros in this chapter help you place data in your worksheet, manipulate the data, build formulas, and perform calculations. Most of this work is done with numeric data, but tasks such as creating mailing labels are done with words.

Perhaps the most interesting articles in this section show you how to create macro-driven one-way, two-way, and three-way data tables. But, you jump to point out, *1-2-3* and *Symphony* already contain data-table (What-if) commands. Why reinvent the wheel? In this case, the reason is speed. When you select the data-table commands, *1-2-3* and *Symphony* have to recalculate the entire worksheet one time for each set of alternative values in the table. The bigger your worksheet and the more values in your table, the longer this process will take. And the rate of increase is geometric, so it doesn't take much to push the recalculation time past lunch.

However, the {PUT} command and the @INDEX function introduced in this section allow you to recalculate only those parts of the worksheet that directly affect the results of the table. This can significantly reduce the time it takes to run a complex data table. And since data tables are one of the most powerful what-if tools *1-2-3* and *Symphony* offer, these techniques are well worth the time it takes to learn them.

1

Data-Entry Routines, Part 1

This collection of *1-2-3* macro techniques can help you put data into your worksheet.

BY DANIEL GASTEIGER

Most of your work with *1-2-3* probably involves putting data into the worksheet, manipulating and comparing data, and getting data out of the worksheet. In this article we'll talk about ways that macros can ease the data-entry process.

A simple data-entry macro looks like this:

	A	B	C	D	E	F
1	\m	{?}				
2		{DOWN}				
3		/XG\m~				

You enter the label *\m* into cell A1 by pointing to that cell and typing '*\m*. Without the apostrophe, *1-2-3* displays the letter *m* repeated across the width of the cell. Assign \m as the macro name by pointing to cell A1, issuing the /Range Name Labels Right command, and pressing Return.

This macro is indispensable for entering long columns of data. Press MACRO-M, and move to the top of the column that you want to fill. Then start typing, and press Return after each entry. The cell pointer moves down automatically. If you wish to move around on the worksheet (to the top of the next column, for instance), simply press the appropriate arrow keys. The macro continues working until you stop it by holding down the Control key and pressing Break.

If you replace the {DOWN} command with the {RIGHT} command, the macro automatically moves the cell pointer to the right after you make each entry:

```
      A          B          C        D        E        F
1 | \m        {?}
2 |           {RIGHT}
3 |           /XG\m~
```

DATA ENTRY ON A STRUCTURED WORKSHEET

Some worksheets contain hundreds of values and formulas tied together to produce a collection of results. You can make the results rely on data in just a few cells of the worksheet and vary the values in those cells to compare the outcome of different scenarios.

Below is a worksheet that calculates the duration of a trip and the amount of gas a car will use based on the distance you enter in the cell named *distance* (B1):

```
       A          B        C        D        E        F
1 | distance
2 |
3 | mph          55
4 | mpg          26.5
5 |
6 | duration +distance/mph
7 | gas      +distance/mpg
```

Ordinarily, I wouldn't write a macro to control data entry for this tiny model, but you can apply the technique to larger models that require the input of several variables. With recalculation set to manual (/Worksheet Global Recalculation Manual), a data-entry macro might look like this:

```
        A          B        C        D        E        F
9  | \m        /XNHow far are you traveling? ~distance~
10 |           {CALC}
```

When you run the macro by pressing MACRO-M, here's what happens:

/XNHow far are you traveling? ~distance~   Causes *1-2-3* to display the prompt *How far are you traveling?* in the command panel. Enter the number of miles, and press Return; the number appears in the cell named *distance*. If you enter a label, *1-2-3* displays the error message *Illegal number input* in the lower-left corner of your screen. Clear the error by pressing Escape, and reenter the value. Be aware that if you enter a cell address, *1-2-3* places the value of that cell into the target cell.

{**CALC**} Causes *1-2-3* to recalculate the worksheet and, therefore, to update the values of the cells named *duration* and *gas*.

If you want to enter label entries, such as a person's name or a street address, you can write a macro using the /XL command:

	A	B	C	D	E	F
1	\m	/XLEnter name ~name~				
2		/XLEnter street ~street~				

The /XL command works like the /XN command, except that it places a label-prefix character in front of whatever you enter in response to the prompt it displays. Words, numbers, and number-letter combinations are stored as labels in the target cell exactly as you type them. The macro shown consists of two steps excerpted from a longer macro. Remember to assign the range names *name* and *street* to cells elsewhere on the worksheet before running the macro. Here's how the macro works:

/XLEnter name~name~ Displays the prompt *Enter name* in the control panel. When you type something and press Return, the characters you type are stored in the cell named *name*. If you respond to the prompt by pressing Escape, your macro stops running.

/XLEnter street~street~ Displays the prompt *Enter street* and places your response into the cell named *street*.

FILL-IN-THE-BLANKS DATA-ENTRY FORMS

Another way to expedite data entry is to create fill-in-the-blanks entry forms. The /Range Input command in *1-2-3* is ideal for this purpose. While /Range Input is active, you can move the cell pointer only to unprotected cells within a specified range.

Create the following worksheet, then unprotect cells B1..B5 by placing the cell pointer on cell B1 and pressing slash, selecting Range Unprotect, and pressing the DownArrow key four times, finishing with Return.

	A	B	C	D	E	F
1	Name:					
2	Street:					
3	City:					
4	State:					
5	Zip:					

Press slash, select Range Input, and indicate the range A1..D6. When you press Return, the cell pointer jumps to the first unprotected cell in the range (cell B1). When you repeatedly press the DownArrow key, the cell pointer moves to cells, B2, B3, B4, and B5 as usual, but then it jumps back to B1 instead of moving into cell B6. Pressing the RightArrow key repeatedly produces similar results. Pressing the UpArrow or LeftArrow key reverses the action. You are locked into the unprotected cells. Within these cells, *1-2-3* allows you to use only Arrow keys and the standard typewriter keys to enter data and edit entries; you cannot access the menu or use the function keys, with the exception of EDIT and HELP. To break out of Range Input, first be sure you have not previously typed something that has yet to be entered into the current cell, then press Escape or Return.

Range Input works even if the unprotected cells in the input range are not adjacent to each other. In the following worksheet, cells A2, A4, A6, B6, and C6 are unprotected. Using a Range Input command identical to the one used above restricts movement of the cell pointer to these cells:

	A	B	C	D	E	F
1	Name					
2						
3	Street					
4						
5	City	State	Zip			
6						

When a macro reaches a Range Input command, it locks you into the Input range until you break out of Range Input by pressing Return or Escape. Once you do this, the macro processes any commands that follow the Range Input command.

WHAT HAPPENS TO THE DATA?

A data-entry routine often needs to do more than let you enter values or labels into the worksheet. In many cases, a fill-in-the-blanks form like the one shown above represents a single record in a database. Ideally, your macro allows you to enter a record, places the data into a database, and lets you enter a new record, ad infinitum.

As with most macros, there are many possible methods of accomplishing this. One simple approach is to set up your database as follows, assigning the range name *dbase* (using the Range Name Create command) to the row containing column headers (G1..K1) and the range name *bottom* to the cell containing the label "bottom" (G2).

	G	H	I	J	K	L
1	Name	Street	City	State	Zip	
2	bottom					

Create a fill-in-the-blanks form as follows:

	A	B	C	D	E	F
1	Name	Street	City	State	Zip	
2						

Adjust the column widths to accommodate the largest entries you are likely to make. We've reduced the widths in this illustration to fit the page. Assign the name *inprange* to cells A2..E2 and unprotect that range by selecting /Range Unprotect, typing *inprange*, and pressing Return. Assign the name *form* to the range A1..E2. Now enter the following macro:

	A	B	C	D	E	F
9	\i	/RIform~				
10		{GOTO}bottom~				
11		/M~{DOWN}~				
12		/Cinprange~~				
13		/RNCdbase~{DOWN}~				
14		/RPdbase~				
15		/REinprange~				
16		/XG\i~				

Finally, assign the database Input range by issuing the /Data Query Input command, and entering *dbase*. Elsewhere on the worksheet, you can create Criterion and Output ranges for use in Data Query Find, Extract, Unique, and Delete operations.

Assign \i as the macro name by going to cell A9, selecting /Range Name Labels Right, and pressing Return. This allows you to start the macro by pressing MACRO-I. Here's what happens:

/RIform~ Activates Range Input, locking you into the unprotected cells in the range named *form*. You enter data, using the Arrow keys to navigate between cells, and press Return twice when you finish typing your last entry. The first Return enters data into the cell; the second ends the Range Input command, allowing the macro to continue with the commands that follow.

{GOTO}bottom~ Sends the cell pointer to the cell named *bottom* — the cell at the bottom of your database.

/M~{DOWN}~   Moves the contents of the current cell *(bottom)* down to make room for the new data.

/Cinprange~ ~   Copies the entries you have just typed from *inprange* to the current row.

/RNCdbase~{DOWN}~   Expands the range named *dbase* downward one row to include the new row of data. This automatically adjusts the Data Query Input range to include the entire database.

/RPdbase~   Protects the range named *dbase*. This step is included because the macro copies unprotected cells into the database. If you use this data-entry routine as part of a larger macro application, this step lets you include the Worksheet Global Protection Enable and Disable commands in the macro to protect the data in the database.

/REinprange~   Erases the range named *inprange* so the cells are empty when you start the next Range Input command.

/XG\i~   Sends the macro to process keystrokes in the cell named *i*, which is the first cell of the macro. You are ready to enter the next record of your database. Because this is an infinite loop macro, it will continue running until you stop it by holding down the Control key and pressing Break.

You can use these techniques to create data-entry routines for any *1-2-3* application. Decide what approach best suits your own work habits and put together an appropriate macro. You'll discover how these techniques speed up your data-entry chores.

AUGUST 1985

2

Data-Entry Routines, Part 2

These techniques will help you design data-entry routines appropriate to your own applications.

BY DANIEL GASTEIGER

A worksheet isn't particularly useful without data, but getting data into a worksheet isn't always as straightforward as it ought to be. More often than not you type a number or a label, then press an Arrow key to move the cell pointer to the next blank cell and make another entry. This technique is simple and practical, but it rarely satisfies all your data-entry needs.

This chapter begins a discussion about data entry in *1-2-3* and *Symphony*. We'll put together some macros and macro routines that can help to speed up your data-entry tasks, and we'll look at some techniques that you can apply when you create data-entry macros for use by other people.

COLUMNWISE DATA

A simple macro that speeds up columnwise data entry uses the {?} command to make the macro pause while a user types an entry. Though the technique is effective for many applications, it is risky to use in more involved macros written for less experienced users. When a macro pauses at a {?} command, the user can press any keys, access menus, change windows, move from cell to cell, and so on. A careless user might accidentally damage a model or lose data that took hours to compile.

1-2-3 Release 2/2.01 and *Symphony* contain several command keywords in addition to the {?} command that you can use in writing data-entry routines. Though none of these keywords is as versatile as the {?} command, you can use them creatively to design similar, but safer, routines.

The {GETNUMBER} and {GETLABEL} commands cause a macro to display a prompt in the control panel and accept input from a user. The {GETNUMBER} command evaluates the entry numerically and stores the result in a prespecified target cell; {GETLABEL} stores the user's entry as a label in the target cell.

Both commands take the following form:

{GETLABEL This is a prompt,*target*}

The first argument, *This is a prompt*, is the user-defined prompt that *Symphony* displays; the second argument, *target*, is the address or name of the cell in which *Symphony* stores the user's entry. While *Symphony* processes a {GETLABEL} or {GETNUMBER} command, users can neither access menus nor move around on the worksheet. They must either type a value or label and press Return, just press Return, or press Escape (the {GETLABEL} command stores a label prefix when a user presses only Return or Escape; the {GETNUMBER} command stores the value ERR).

Unfortunately, the {GETLABEL} and {GETNUMBER} commands are not designed to refer to the current cell. There is no argument specifying *this cell* that you can use in either command to channel a user's entry to the cell holding the cell pointer. There are, however, several techniques for adapting the {GETLABEL} and {GETNUMBER} commands to this data-entry task.

{GETLABEL} AND {MENU} COMMANDS

The following macro locks users into the current column. The macro accepts an entry into a prenamed cell, copies the entry to the current cell, then moves the pointer to the next cell down the column:

	A	B	C	D	E
1	\m	{GETLABEL "Enter a label ",temp}			
2		{MENU}Ctemp~~			
3		{DOWN}{BRANCH \m}			
4					
5	temp				

Enter the macro as shown and assign the labels in column A as names for the adjacent cells of column B; move the cell pointer to cell A1, press MENU, select Range Name Labels Right, and press End DownArrow Return. To use the macro, move the cell pointer to the first cell of the column that will receive entries and press MACRO-M (the *Symphony* documentation identifies the MACRO key for your computer). Here's what happens:

{GETLABEL "Enter a label ",temp} Displays the prompt *Enter a label* in control panel, and stores your entry in the cell named *temp*.

   {MENU}Ctemp~ ~   Copies the new contents of *temp* to the current cell.

   {DOWN}{BRANCH \m}   Moves the cell pointer down and transfers control
of the macro to the cell named *\m*; the first cell of the macro. The macro repeats itself
for each entry until you stop it by pressing Break (Control-Break on most computers).

DYNAMIC MACRO KEYWORDS

Using the Copy command is just one way to adapt the {GETLABEL} and
{GETNUMBER} commands to direct input to the current cell. Another technique
involves creating a string formula that changes dynamically, based on the location of
the cell pointer.

   We usually think of *Symphony* macro commands as labels, but a formula can also
be a macro command. The formula need only look like macro instructions for
Symphony to interpret it as such. For example, in the following illustration, cell B2
contains the formula + *\d*. To the *Symphony* macro processor, it appears as though
the commands of cell B1 are repeated in cell B2. When you run the macro, *Symphony*
moves the cell pointer down four times.

	A	B	C
1	\d	{DOWN 2}	
2		{DOWN 2}	

   By writing a formula that combines the @CELLPOINTER function with the
{GETNUMBER} command, you can make the {GETNUMBER} command accept
input directly to the current cell.

   The @CELLPOINTER function determines the status of any one of many
attributes that a cell can have. For example, the formula @CELLPOINTER ("width")
evaluates to a number representing the width of the current cell. The formula
@CELLPOINTER ("address") returns a string that represents the absolute address of
the current cell.

   Cell B2 of the macro in the figure below contains the following formula:

   + "{GETNUMBER Enter a value,"&@CELLPOINTER("address")&"}"

	A	B	C	D
1	\i	{RECALC next}		
2	next	{GETNUMBER Enter a value ,B4}		
3		{DOWN}		
4		{BRANCH \i}		

The formula currently displays as {GETNUMBER Enter a value ,B4} because *Symphony* has recalculated the worksheet since the cell pointer came to rest in cell B4. Cells B1 and B2 are named \i and *next* respectively.

To use the macro, place the cell pointer in the first cell of the column in which you wish to enter data. For this example, move the cell pointer to cell A6. Then press MACRO-I. Here's what happens:

{RECALC next}   Forces *Symphony* to recalculate the formula in the cell named *next* (on the first pass of the macro, however, you will not see the cell reference change). The @CELLPOINTER function doesn't update automatically when the cell pointer moves, so this step is necessary to ensure that the formula refers to the correct cell.

{GETNUMBER Enter a value ,A6}   Displays the prompt *Enter a value* , then stores your entry in cell A6.

{DOWN}   Moves the cell pointer to the next cell down the column.

{BRANCH \i}   Transfers control to the cell named \i and restarts the macro. The macro recalculated cell B4, updating it to read {*GETNUMBER Enter a value , A7*}, accepts input to cell A7, moves the cell pointer down, and so on, looping until you stop it by pressing the Break key.

SELF-BELAYING LOOPS

When you write data-entry macros for other people, it's best to supply a method by which users can stop the looping without creating an error condition. So far, we've presented only data-entry macros that loop interminably until you disrupt them. If the goal is to keep your users under macro direction, this kind of loop isn't appropriate.

One simple way to keep users under macro direction is to build an interrupt flag into the macro. This flag is a signal for which *Symphony* tests on each pass through the loop. If the flag is present, *Symphony* transfers macro control to a new macro routine; otherwise, the macro continues looping.

When you create a macro, choose an interrupt flag that is both uncommon and easy to remember. Your users should be able to accomplish their data-entry chores unfettered and still be able to quit the data-entry routine easily. We'll use the at sign (@) for our examples because it's easy to see in print. In normal practice I'd choose the period as my interrupt flag because it's easy to type.

The following macro accepts label entries into a cell named *temp*, determines whether the entry is a single @ sign, and branches accordingly. If the user types an @ sign, the macro stops:

```
         A          B          C          D          E
1  \m           {GETLABEL "Enter a label ",temp}
2               {IF temp="@"}{BRANCH start}
3               {MENU}Ctemp~~
4               {DOWN}{BRANCH \m}
5  temp
```

This is identical to the first macro presented, except for the second line of code. Here's how the macro works:

{GETLABEL "Enter a label ",temp} Displays the prompt *Enter a label*, then stores your entry in the cell named *temp*. For each pass of the loop, enter whatever label you desire. When you wish to stop entering data, enter an @ sign.

{IF temp = "@"}{BRANCH start} Determines whether you entered an @ sign in response to the prompt. If so, control passes to the routine named *start* (when you use this routine, substitute an appropriate range name in the {BRANCH} command). If you did not enter an @ sign at the prompt, control of the macro passes to the next cell (B3).

{MENU}Ctemp~ ~ Copies the entry from *temp* to the current cell.

{DOWN}{BRANCH \m} Moves the cell pointer down and transfers control back to the cell named *\m*, restarting the routine.

The dynamic macro presented earlier presents a problem in choosing a flag. Because the {GETNUMBER} command stores all nonnumeric entries as ERR, the macro can't detect a specific character as the interrupt flag. Instead, the macro can watch for an entry that results in ERR. When a user makes a nonnumeric entry, the macro branches appropriately. Such a macro appears next. Cells B1, B2, and B7 in this figure are named *\i, next,* and *brk* respectively. Also, *next* contains the following formula:

+ "{GETNUMBER Enter a value ,"&@CELLPOINTER("address")&"}"

```
         A          B          C          D          E          F
1  \i        {RECALC next}
2  next      {GETNUMBER Enter a value ,$B$14}
3            {IF @ISERR(@CELLPOINTER("contents"))}{BRANCH brk}
4            {DOWN}
5            {BRANCH \i}
6
7  brk       {MENU}E~{BRANCH start}
```

Here's how the macro works:

{**RECALC next**}   Updates the formula in *next* based on the position of the cell pointer.

{**GETNUMBER Enter a value ,B14**}   Displays the prompt *Enter a value* and directs data entry to the current cell. If the user makes a nonnumeric entry, *Symphony* stores the entry as ERR.

{**IF @ISERR(@CELLPOINTER("contents"))**}{**BRANCH start**}   Determines whether the content of the current cell is ERR. If so, the macro branches to the cell named *brk*; otherwise, the macro continues processing with the next cell (B4). It moves the cell pointer down and restarts, updating the dynamic macro command, accepting input, and so on. The commands in the cell named *brk* are as follows:

{**MENU**}**E~**{**BRANCH start**}   Erases the current cell and transfers control to the routine named *start*. Erasing the cell removes the ERR from the current cell, cleaning up the worksheet before the macro continues.

DECEMBER 1986

3

Entering Data in Large Ranges

More information about macros
that help you put data into your worksheet.

BY DANIEL GASTEIGER

In the previous chapter we began with the premise that *1-2-3* or *Symphony*'s worksheet becomes useful only when it contains data. We designed several data-entry macro routines that help you put data directly into the worksheet. The techniques we presented facilitated data entry in worksheet columns. This chapter will explore macro routines that speed up data entry into multiple-column-and-row ranges.

QUICK AND DIRTY

Many macros can help you enter ranges of data. Most involve a set of commands that accepts data for a particular cell, moves the cell pointer to the right, accepts data, moves right, and so on, until you've entered an entire row's worth of information. The macro then moves the cell pointer to the leftmost column of the data-entry range and down one row so you can begin the process again. The following is such a macro:

	A	B	C	D	E
1	\m	{?}~{RIGHT}			
2		{?}~{RIGHT}{?}~{RIGHT}{?}~{RIGHT}			
3		{?}~{DOWN}{LEFT 4}			
4		{BRANCH \m}			

Enter the macro as shown and assign the label in cell A1 as the name for cell B1:

cell pointer to the top-left corner of the range that will receive data (cell B7 in this example) and start the macro by holding down the MACRO key and pressing M. Though the screen remains static, you know a macro is running because the *Macro* indicator appears in the bottom border of the screen. Here's how the macro works:

{?}~{RIGHT} Causes the macro to pause until you press Return, then presses Return RightArrow. When the macro pauses at a {?} command, you can press any keys. Generally, you would type an entry and press Return. The entry can consist of a label, a value, or even a formula. When you press Return, *Symphony* processes the command following the {?} command. In this case, the tilde (~) enters whatever you've typed into the current cell. The {RIGHT} command moves the cell pointer to the adjacent column.

{?}~{RIGHT}{?}~{RIGHT}{?}~{RIGHT} Accepts input into the current cell, moves the pointer, accepts input, moves the pointer, and accepts input. Notice that the macro will work as described even if you omit the tildes following each {?} command. Including the tildes makes the macro more versatile. While the macro pauses, you can access menu commands that end with a single press of the Return key.

For example, you can select MENU Width Set, widen the current column, and press Return. The cell pointer still moves to the right, leaving the current cell blank. Use the Arrow keys to move the pointer back and type the missing entry, then use them to enter the data and return the cell pointer to the proper cell.

{?}~{DOWN}{LEFT 4} Accepts input into the current cell, then moves the cell pointer down and back to the first column of the data-entry range.

{BRANCH \m} Transfers control of the macro to the cell named \m, restarting the data-entry routine. The macro pauses to accept input for each of five cells in a row, moves the cell pointer to the first column of data in the next row, and repeats itself until you stop it by pressing the Break key (on most computers, hold down the Control key and press Break). When you stop a macro this way, you create an error condition in *Symphony*. Simply press the Escape or Return key to clear the error.

This macro is perfect for many data-entry tasks, but it has some limitations. As explained, the {?} command causes a macro to pause. During the pause, a user can press any keys, access menus, and move around on the worksheet, or, as you would hope, enter data. But if your users are inexperienced or ill-behaved, they could destroy data or become confused.

The process of moving the cell pointer from cell to cell is slow and becomes tedious when your routine must accept many columns' worth of data. In fact, with such a simple data-entry routine, it's easy to become disoriented on the worksheet as you enter more and more rows of data. Ideally your data-entry routines should tell you what information to enter each time the macro pauses.

PROMPTED DATA ENTRY

In the last chapter we adapted the {GETLABEL} and {GETNUMBER} commands to accept entries into the current cell. Each of these commands displays a prompt in the control panel, then stores your entry in a specified cell. There is no built-in mechanism to have the {GETLABEL} and {GETNUMBER} commands accept data directly into the current cell, so we devised some techniques to get around this shortcoming. We've used a combination of those techniques to create a data-entry macro that doesn't move the cell pointer to and fro on the worksheet.

The macro relies on dynamic macro code to create a prompt appropriate to the column in which you're entering data. The macro also relies on an intermediate cell to receive data you enter before storing the data in the desired range. We'll see how all this works when we describe the macro's step-by-step operations.

```
        A         B         C         D       E
1   \n        {FOR col,0,4,1,inprout}
2             {LET row,row+1}{BRANCH \n}
3
4   inprout   {RECALC next}
5   next      {GETLABEL Enter Name ,temp}
6             {PUT inprange,col,row,temp}
7
8   temp
9   row                   1
10  col
11
12  Name      Employee #  Extension Room
```

To try out this macro, enter the labels as shown but leave cell B5 blank for the moment. Assign range names by selecting MENU Range Name Labels Right, indicating range A1..A10, and pressing Return. Then assign the name *inprange* to range A12..D8000. Note that each cell in the first row of *inprange* contains a label designating the type of data you'll enter for each column. Now enter the following formula in the cell named *next* (B5).

$$+ \text{``\{GETLABEL Enter''\&@INDEX(inprange,col,0)\&`` ,temp\}''}$$

Finish by entering the number 1 into the cell named *row* (B9). The macro is ready to run. To use the macro, hold down the MACRO key and press N. The location of the cell pointer when you start the macro is not important. Here's what happens:

{FOR col,0,4,1,inprout} Starts a FOR loop. The {FOR} command performs a subroutine a predetermined number of times in a process called looping. The arguments of the {FOR} command are instructions describing the behavior of the loop. The first argument, in this case *col*, is the name of the cell that counts how many times the loop processes the counter. When the loop begins, *Symphony* places the value of the second argument, 0, into the counter cell *col*. Then, if the value of the counter cell isn't equal to or greater than the value of the third argument, 4, *Symphony* processes the subroutine named *inprout*. When the subroutine finishes processing, *Symphony* increases the value of the counter by the value of the {FOR} command's fourth argument, compares the result with the command's third argument, and repeats the subroutine. When the value of the counter exceeds or is equal to the value of the {FOR} command's third argument, *Symphony* stops processing the loop and macro control passes to the command following the {FOR} command.

The following are the commands in the subroutine named *inprout:*

{RECALC next}   Recalculates the cell named *next*. This updates the formula in *next* based on the current value of *col*.

{GETLABEL Enter Name ,temp}   Although this appears as a label, it is actually the result of the formula you created earlier, + "{GETLABEL Enter" &@INDEX(inprange,col,0)&" ,temp}".

This formula uses the @INDEX function to create a prompt for a {GETLABEL} command. The @INDEX function returns a value or label found at a specified column and row offset from the top-left corner of a range. In this case, the @INDEX function returns the label located *col* columns to the right and 0 rows from the top of the range named *inprange*. On the first pass of the {FOR} loop, the @INDEX function produces the label *Name*, on the second pass the function produces the label *Employee*, and so on. *Symphony* concatenates the indexed labels with the literal strings "{GETLABEL Enter " and " ,temp}", producing a recognizable {GETLABEL} command.

The command displays an appropriate prompt in the control panel and pauses for you to enter data. *Symphony* stores your entry as a label in the cell named *temp*.

{PUT inprange,col,row,temp}   Copies your entry to the appropriate location in the data-entry range. The {PUT} command places a value into the cell located a specified number of columns and rows from the top-left corner of a range. In this case, the command copies *temp* to the cell that is *col* columns to the right and *row* rows down from the top-left corner of the range named *inprange*. The value of *col* is determined by the state of the {FOR} loop in progress. That value can be either 0, 1, 2, or 3. The value of *row* is determined by how many times the {FOR} command has restarted. Every four times *Symphony* processes the subroutine, control of the macro shifts to the {LET} command in cell B2.

{LET row,row + 1}{BRANCH \n}   Adds 1 to the value in *row* and restarts the macro. As stated above, *row* is a counter that keeps track of which row in the input range should receive the current data entries.

IN CASE YOU'RE CONFUSED

Let's summarize the macro's process. The macro uses a {FOR} loop to keep track of which column should receive the data you enter. The {FOR} loop processes four times, and the macro accepts data into one row across four different columns. When the loop finishes processing, the macro increases a counter that keeps track of which row is to receive data. The macro then restarts and runs the {FOR} loop to accept data into the four columns of this new row.

The worksheet doesn't appear to change as long as the macro is running. You'll see changes in the control panel, but the data you enter will not appear on the worksheet until you stop the macro by pressing the Break key.

As suggested previously, if you're using this routine in a macro for other people, you may want to make it possible for users to stop the data-entry routine without stopping the macro. One way to do this involves two changes to the macro: insert a row below the string formula in the subroutine (in this case, below row 5) and enter the following:

{IF temp = "@"}{FORBREAK}

Then insert a row below the {FOR} command in cell B1 and enter:

{IF temp = "@"}{BRANCH other}

These mean, "If the entry in *temp* is an "at" sign (@), stop the {FOR} loop and transfer macro control to the cell named *other*." Users will be able to exit from the data entry routine by entering a single at sign in response to any prompt.

Finally, if other people will be using the macro, consider preparing a message screen that displays while they are entering data. The message might read, *Data Entry in progress*, or *Hang in there*, or whatever, but it should reassure users that their data is going somewhere, even though the screen appears static.

JANUARY 1987

4

Building Formulas

A collection of observations about when and how to use macros when creating formulas.

BY DANIEL GASTEIGER

Macros that build formulas are common. They vary in complexity from simple, three-keystroke macros to intricate, multiline macros. Some are clever solutions to difficult problems (such as creating formulas that contain mixed absolute and relative range references); others are simply time wasters. In fact, the type of formula-building macro you create should depend on the type of formula your macro will be creating.

From the macro writer's perspective, formulas fall into four categories:

1. short, simple formulas requiring so few keystrokes that the macro may not be worth the effort
2. longer formulas whose relative and absolute references are always to ranges of unchanging sizes
3. formulas that refer only to named ranges
4. formulas whose relative and absolute references are to ranges that can vary in size with time

The first category includes formulas that give rise to such macros as @TODAY~(@NOW~ in *1-2-3* Release 2/2.01), @SIN({LEFT})~, +{LEFT}/2~ and so on. The longer formulas from the second category suggest macros such as those that appear on the next page.

To create these macros, enter them as shown (remember to start each cell entry with a label prefix). Then assign the labels in column A as names to the adjacent cells of column B; point to cell A1, press slash, select Range Name Labels Right, and press

139

	A	B	C	D	E
1	\f	+{RIGHT}~({LEFT}{LEFT}{LEFT}*			
2		{LEFT}{LEFT}+.05*{LEFT})~			
3					
4	\s	@SUM({UP}{UP}.{UP}{UP}{UP}{UP},			
5		{DOWN}{DOWN})*.05~			

End DownArrow Return. To run the macros, place the cell pointer in cell D12 and, while holding down the MACRO key, press the letter of the macro's name. (If your computer lacks a MACRO key, consult your *1-2-3* documentation for information on invoking macros.)

These odd-looking macros create formulas by moving the cell pointer. If the macros look confusing, try manually entering the keystrokes to see how the formulas are built.

Exactly what the macros do isn't important to this discussion. It is important to note that each macro creates a formula using an unchanging set of pointer movements. In other words, each formula that either macro creates has relative references identical to every other formula that that macro creates.

With formulas of this type, it's more efficient to create the formula once manually, then copy it to the desired cells. To speed the copying process, write a simple one-line macro:

	C	D	E
7	\t	/Cformula~	
8			
9	formula	0	

In this example, cells D7 and D9 are named \t and *formula*, respectively. Cell D9 contains the formula + E9–(A9 ∗ B9 + 0.05 ∗ C9). It evaluates to 0 because there are no values in the cells it references (in Release 2, the formula evaluates to ERR since there is a label in cell C9). When the macro copies this formula to cell D12 (point to D12 and press MACRO-T), the formula's references adjust accordingly. The copy matches the formula created by the macro named \f in the previous illustration. This macro replicates the formula almost twice as quickly as does the original macro.

The third category of formulas for which you might write macros is that of formulas that always refer to the same ranges — usually named ranges. People often use relative references to create formulas, then later want to create copies of the formulas, referring to exactly the same cells.

The easiest way to accomplish this is to turn the formula into a label by inserting a label prefix, copy the label to the desired cells, then edit out the label prefixes. If you need to use the formula often, turn it into a macro by copying a label version of it into its own cell, adding a tilde, and assigning a macro name. The following macro enters a formula into the current cell. The formula it creates originally existed in cell D3. We created the macro by pointing to the original formula, pressing EDIT Home ' Return, and copying the resulting label to \v (cell B11). Then we pointed to B11 and pressed EDIT ~ Return. Whenever you run the macro, it produces an identical copy of the formula:

	A	B	C	D
11	\v	@VLOOKUP(D1,F7..I12,D2)+D5~		

The fourth category of formulas, which contain absolute and relative references to ranges that can vary in size, can sometimes give rise to tricky macros. These formulas might refer to ranges that vary depending on the amount of data entered during a day, or they might require some combination of mixed and absolute range references specific to each range or column of data to which they refer.

Let's say that you've finished entering a column of data and want to sum all the values in the column. You might use the following macro:

	A	B	C	D
13	\a	@SUM({UP}.{END}{UP})~		

The macro assumes that the data you wish to sum begins in the cell directly above the current cell. It also assumes that the data falls in contiguous cells. If any cells in the range you wish to sum lack data, the macro fails to sum the column.

When dealing with columns, the macro should indicate the entire column of data from the cell pointer to the last column entry whether or not there are gaps in the data. The following macro does just that by summing everything below the cell pointer in the current column (as long as there is data below the cell pointer):

	A	B	C	D	E
15	\d	/WIC~{RIGHT}@SUM({DOWN}.{LEFT}{END}			
16		{DOWN}{RIGHT}{END}{UP})~{LEFT}			
17		/WDC~			

You can write a similar macro to sum all the entries in a row, but you may find that the technique has limited use. As your worksheets increase in size, macros that insert and delete rows and columns can become excruciatingly slow. You might save time by writing formulas manually. Also, because the macro inserts and deletes columns or rows, use it cautiously. A carelessly inserted row or column might upset the flow of control of the macro.

In a previous chapter, we presented a macro that creates a formula having both relative and absolute cell references. The formula calculates student rankings based on comparisons of student grades. Because the formula relied on a mixed relative and absolute address to calculate the ranks, there were no simple keystroke sequences to create the formula at any worksheet location (one day you might want the formula starting in cell C3, another day in cell F9). The following is the macro we presented, accompanied by a list of students and the grades by which they should be ranked:

```
        A           B           C           D           E
19  \r          1{DOWN}{LEFT}/RNCgrade2~~
20              {GOTO}bottom~+grade2~
21              {EDIT}{HOME}{DEL}'~
22              {GOTO}grade2~{RIGHT}
23              @IF(grade2={UP}{LEFT},{UP},
24              @COUNT({UP}{LEFT}{ABS}~.
25  bottom
26              ))~
27              /C~.{LEFT}{END}{DOWN}{RIGHT}~
28
29
30              Student     Grade       Rank
31              Jones           100
32              Smith            98
33              Brown            97
34              White            97
35              Evans            86
36              Fox              84
37              Healy            84
```

To use the macro, enter it as shown and assign the labels in column A as names to the adjacent cells of column B. Sort the database using *Grade* as the primary sort key, then place the cell pointer in cell D31 and start the macro by holding down the MACRO key and pressing R.

The formula the macro creates contains an @COUNT function that keeps track of how many students are in the table up to the current row. It does this by using a range reference that is absolute at one end and relative at the other. When you run the macro in this example, the @COUNT function in the formula in cell D32 reads @COUNT(C31..C32). In cell D33 this function reads @COUNT(C31..C33), in cell D34 it reads @COUNT(C31..C34), and so on. Here's how the macro works:

1{DOWN}{LEFT}/RNCgrade2 ~ ~   Enters 1 into the current cell, then assigns the name *grade2* to the second cell of the *Grade* column.

{GOTO}bottom~ + grade2~   Enters the formula *+ grade2* into the cell named *bottom*.

{EDIT}{HOME}{DEL}'~   Converts the formula in *bottom* into a label that represents the cell address of *grade2*.

{GOTO}grade2~{RIGHT}   Moves the cell pointer to the second cell of the *Rank* column. This is the cell that receives the first copy of the formula.

@IF(grade2 = {UP}{LEFT},{UP},   Begins typing the formula in the control panel. Note that the illustration shows the screen as it should look when you create the macro. When you enter the macro, begin this statement and the next by typing a label prefix (apostrophe).

@COUNT({UP}{LEFT}{ABS}~.   Continues typing the formula, creating the absolute reference needed in the @COUNT function. The macro presses Return before it finishes typing the formula. This places *1-2-3* in Edit mode, producing a beep on most computers (ignore the beep). The macro then types a period, which indicates that this will be a range reference as opposed to a single-cell reference. By now the next cell contains a label version of the relative address needed in the formula. *1-2-3* appends that address to the formula in the control panel.

))~   Finishes typing the formula and enters it into the cell.

/C~.{LEFT}{END}{DOWN}{RIGHT}~   Copies the finished formula throughout the column.

A WORD ABOUT MOVING RANGE NAMES

In the past I've argued that macros that move range names around should delete a range name before reassigning the name to another cell or range. When you assign a name to a cell referenced in a formula, the formula becomes "attached" to the range name. When you then use the Range Name Create command to reassign the name, *1-2-3* reassigns the attached formulaic references to match the range name reference. This can destroy a worksheet's integrity.

There's another good reason for deleting a range name before reassigning it: When you reassign a range name using the Range Name Create command, *1-2-3* assumes that you have indeed reassigned formulaic references. If your worksheet is in automatic recalculation mode, *1-2-3* recalculates each time you reassign a name using Range Name Create. When you assign a range name for the first time, however, *1-2-3* doesn't recalculate. In short, a macro that deletes a range name before reassigning the name can run considerably faster than a macro that reassigns names using the Range Name Create command.

5

@INDEX and the {PUT} Command

We explore some of the powerful macro tools
in *1-2-3* Releases 2, 2.01, and *Symphony*.

BY DANIEL GASTEIGER

Many of the letters we receive concern the topic of converting columns of data from one form to another. This might mean increasing every value in a column by 5%, dividing every value by 100, or truncating every label to three characters. For every letter we receive asking for a macro that does some type of conversion, we receive a letter describing such a macro. Ironically, you can do almost all of these conversions quite rapidly without using a macro.

There are times when a macro approach to converting data is appropriate, such as when increasing every value in a column by 5%. This column is within a table composed of 20 columns by 800 rows, and the worksheet is precariously close to filling your computer's memory. Under these circumstances, converting the single column of data is best left to a macro. Let's look first at the nonmacro approach to data conversion and then use the @INDEX and {PUT} commands to build a data-conversion macro.

MANUAL DATA CONVERSION

The data we use for this example is arbitrary. Since purely arbitrary data is boring, let's create a scenario. Bill recently quit his job selling hotdogs, burgers, and drinks at hockey games and started managing a small retail booth for his sister. The booth is in the lobby of the skating rink, and Bill sells several types of hockey-related souvenirs. The following is a portion of the worksheet that Bill uses to keep track of inventory for his sister's business (there are several more columns and rows of data, but we'll assume that the illustration shows the entire model):

	A	B	C	D	E
11	Item	Code #	Wholesale	Retail	Quantity
12	T-shirt	C00033	$3.55	$10.95	189
13	S-shirt	C00048	$5.35	$19.95	76
14	Banner	D10023	$0.30	$2.00	251
15	Pennant	D10089	$0.15	$1.50	341
16	S-Shaker	D10102	$0.25	$2.00	147
17	Pencil	I80003	$0.01	$0.25	1564
18	Mug	I80008	$1.50	$5.95	328

Shortly after taking over the booth, Bill realizes that his sister's prices are significantly lower than the prices of her competitors. He decides to increase the retail price of every item by 5%. These are the steps he follows to update his worksheet:

Place the cell pointer anywhere in column E — cell E12 is a good choice. Press slash, select Worksheet Insert Column, and press Return. With the cell pointer in cell E12, enter the formula +D12*1.05. Then copy the formula to range E12..E18: Select /Copy and press Return, period, LeftArrow, End, DownArrow, RightArrow, Return. The formulas you've just created in column E represent retail prices 5% greater than the values in column D. Use the Range Value command to copy the new values back into column D: Select /Range Value, indicate range E12..E18, press Return, indicate cell D12, and press Return. Finally, delete column E: With the cell pointer in column E, select /Worksheet Delete Column, and press Return.

Inserting columns in very large worksheets is time-consuming. You can generally leave out that step if there is an available blank column in which to create the conversion formulas. Simply enter the first formula, copy it down the blank column, use the Range Value command to copy the resulting values back to the column you're converting, and finally erase the conversion formulas from the worksheet.

INDEXING DATA

As stated earlier, the task of converting columnar data in a complicated worksheet is best left to a macro. But before we present such a macro, let's explore some of the tools we'll be using.

The @INDEX function is the backbone of the data-conversion process. Understanding this function is important to understanding the macro that uses it (there are plenty of macros that convert data without using the @INDEX function, but we won't discuss them here).

The @INDEX function returns a value found at a specified column and row offset from the top-left corner of a table. To better understand what this means, start with a worksheet that looks like the one containing Bill's data (shown earlier), and enter the labels shown in the figure below:

	A	B	C	D	
1	col				
2	row				
3					
4	curval				

Assign the labels as range names to the adjacent cells of column B: Select /Range Name Labels Right, indicate range A1..A4, and press Return. Assign the name *table* to range A11..E18: Select /Range Name Create, enter *table*, indicate range A11..E18, and press Return. Finally, enter the formula @INDEX(table,col, row) into the cell named *curval* (cell B4). The word *Item* should appear in the cell.

Item appears because the @INDEX function returns the value that is *col* (zero) columns to the right and *row* (zero) rows down from the top-left corner of the range named *table*. Now move the cell pointer to *col* (cell B1) and enter the value 1. The @INDEX formula in cell B4 returns *Code #* — the value that is one column to the right and zero rows down from the top-left corner of the range named *table*. We're interested in the *Retail* column of the table, so enter the value 3 into *col*. The word *Retail* appears in the cell named *curval*.

To look at values in the *Retail* column other than the column header, simply enter a numeric offset value into the cell named *row* (cell B2). Now *row* is blank and therefore equals zero. Point to *row* and enter the value 1; the formula in *curval* evaluates to 10.95 — the entry that is three columns to the right and one row down from the top-left corner of *table*. Enter a 2 into *row*, and the @INDEX function yields the value 19.95.

THE CALCULATION

We've found a way to extract values from the table, but our goal is to replace existing values in the table with new values. Right now the @INDEX function in *curval* refers to a cell within the column we're trying to convert. We can use the resulting value in a calculation that produces the desired replacement value.

For example, the value of *curval* is 19.95 — the second numeric value in the column to be converted. To increase that value by 5%, simply multiply by 1.05. Do this by entering the formula +B4*1.05 into cell B5. Then, so that you can identify this value easily, label the cell by entering *convert* into cell A5 and assigning *convert* as the range name for cell B5. Cell B5 will always calculate a value that is 5% greater than the value of *curval* (if *curval* has a label value, cell B5 will show either ERR or 0, depending on which release of *1-2-3* you're using).

See how this works by changing the offset value in *row*: Move the cell pointer to *row* and enter 1. *Convert* evaluates to 11.4975. Change *row* to equal 3; *convert* becomes 2.10 — 5% greater than the value that is three columns to the right and three rows down from the top-left corner of *table*.

THE REPLACEMENT

The @INDEX function gets a value from a table, and a simple formula calculates a conversion value based on the indexed value. For this to be useful, we need a way to place the conversion value into the table in place of the indexed value. The {PUT} command is ideal for the task.

The {PUT} command behaves like the @INDEX function in reverse. The @INDEX function, as we mentioned, retrieves a value from a specified column and row offset within a table; the {PUT} command places a value at a specified column and row offset in a table.

The command takes the form {PUT *table,col,row, value*}, where *table* identifies the table in which a value will be placed, *col* identifies the column offset, *row* identifies the row offset, and *value* identifies the value to be placed in the table. To see how this works, enter labels as shown in the following illustration:

	A	B	C	D	E
9	\p	{PUT table,col,row,"TEST"}~			

Name this one-line macro \p: Select /Range Name Labels Right, indicate cell A9, and press Return. Make sure that *col* and *row* each contain the value 3, then hold down the MACRO key (Alt on most keyboards) and press P. The word *TEST* should appear in cell D14 — three columns to the right and three rows down from the top-left corner of *table*. Change the value of *row* to 1 and run the macro again; *TEST* appears in cell D12. Repair the changes to your table by entering the value 10.95 into cell D12 and the value 2 into cell D14.

FINALLY, THE MACRO

After the preceding discussion, putting these pieces together into a macro that increases every value in a column by 5% is anticlimactic. In fact, the only piece missing is a {FOR} command. A {FOR} command controls what is called a FOR loop, a series of commands that repeats a prespecified number of times. The command takes the following format:

{FOR *counter,start,stop,step,routine*}

When a FOR loop begins, *1-2-3* places the *start* value into *counter*, then compares the value of *counter* with the value of *stop*. If *counter* is equal to or greater than *stop* (unless *step* is a negative number), the loop stops and control passes to the command immediately following the {FOR} command. If *counter* is less than *stop*, *1-2-3* processes the commands beginning in the cell named *routine*. When *routine* finishes processing, *1-2-3* adds *step* to *counter*, compares the new value with the *stop* value, and so on. Put this to use by entering labels as shown in the following illustration. Note that the label in *p* (cell B9) has been edited. We've removed the ending tilde, inserted the command {RECALC block}, and changed *TEST* to *convert*:

	A	B	C	D	E	F
7	\c	{FOR row,1,@ROWS(table)-1,1,\p}~				
8						
9	\p	{RECALC block}{PUT table,col,row,convert}				
10						

Assign *c* as the range name for cell B7: Select /Range Name Labels Right, indicate cell A7, and press Return. Then assign the name *block* to range B1..B5: Select /Range Name Create, enter *block*, indicate range B1..B5, and press Return.

Your macro is ready to convert data. Be sure that the value of *col* is 3, then hold down the MACRO key and press C. In moments the updated values appear in column D.

IS IT VERSATILE?

You can use this macro to manipulate almost any columnar worksheet data. Its greatest weakness is in getting it to erase all cells that evaluate to zero. Adapting it to that task makes it pretty clunky, but the menu option in Release 2/2.01 that lets you suppress display of zero-valued cells eliminates the need for such a macro.

Bill also didn't like the coding system his sister had been using, so he decided to reduce the number of characters in each product's code number. He eliminated the middle two characters from each code and still had a unique identification number for each product. He used the data-conversion macro to update the worksheet appropriately.

To see how this works, enter the value 1 into the cell named *col* (B1), and replace the formula in *convert* to read as follows:

@LEFT(B4,2)&@RIGHT(B4,2)

With *col* equal to 1, the @INDEX function in *curval* and the {PUT} command in the macro will refer to the second column of *table* when you run the macro. The macro will use the new formula in *convert* to alter each code number as described.

6

Fast Data Tables

Write a macro that outraces the Data Table command.

BY DANIEL GASTEIGER

I'm a strong advocate of nonmacro solutions to worksheet problems. If you don't need a macro to do the job, don't use a macro. But rules are fun when they have exceptions, and the "avoid macros" rule has some exceptions. In this chapter we'll write a macro that can outperform *1-2-3*'s Data Table command under certain circumstances.

/DATA TABLE 1-WAY

The Data Table command provides an easy way to reuse a collection of interrelated formulas. For example, the following worksheet contains information on a hypothetical collection of stock certificates. The certificates belong to a struggling investor named Albert who buys Gadmonics stock twice a year if the value drops below $15 a share. Albert has bought stock on several occasions, so he's made entries for each lot of stock. He plans to sell when his profit on the sale will cover the purchase of the quarter horse he's always wanted:

	F	G	H	I	J	K	L
1	Gadmonics:		$21.00				
2							
3	Purdate	Price	Shares	Expend	Current	Profit	Percent
4	Jun-84	$14.4	30	$432.0	$630.0	$198.0	45.83%
5	Oct-84	$14.8	29	$429.2	$609.0	$179.8	41.89%
6	Oct-85	$14.2	32	$454.4	$672.0	$217.6	47.89%
7						========	
8						$595.4	

149

Cell H1 in the figure contains the current price of Gadmonics stock. Columns F, G, and H contain the purchase date, the purchase price, and the number of shares purchased, respectively. Column I calculates Albert's expenditure for the original stock purchase (*Price* times *Shares*), and column J calculates the current value of each lot of stock (*Shares* times the current price — cell H1). Column K calculates the profit Albert would realize if he sold at the current price (*Current* minus *Expend*), and column L calculates the percentage increase or decrease in value of each lot from the day that Albert bought (*Profit* divided by *Expend*). Cell K8 sums the values in column K, calculating Albert's total profit if he should sell at the stock's current value.

To determine the lowest acceptable price at which to sell his stock, Albert can substitute different values into cell H1 until he produces an appealing value in cell K8. However, this might require several guesses before zeroing in on the desired value — particularly if dealing with a larger and more intricate model. Albert can easily reduce his effort by using the Data Table command. To try this, prepare your worksheet as follows:

Create the described worksheet, then move the cell pointer to cell F9. Use the Data Fill command to enter a sequence of values down column F running from 20 to 30 in increments of .2: select /Data Fill, indicate F9..F59 and press Return, enter 20, enter .2, and enter 30. Enter the formula + K8 into cell G8. You're ready to use the Data Table command.

With the cell pointer in cell F8, select /Data Table 1. *1-2-3* prompts for the Table range; indicate F8..G58 and press Return. *1-2-3* prompts for the input cell; indicate cell H1 and press Return. *1-2-3* fills in the table with newly calculated values.

The Data Table command substitutes each value from the leftmost column of the Table range, one by one into the input cell. For each substitution, *1-2-3* recalculates the entire worksheet, including the formula at the top of the second column (and subsequent columns) of the table, based on the substituted value. The result of the calculation for each substituted value appears in the table to the right of the originally substituted value.

After generating the table, Albert can scan the resulting values until he finds a profit value corresponding to the purchase price of the horse he wishes to buy. Directly to the left of that value, he'll find the corresponding value that Gadmonics stock must realize before he can afford to buy the horse.

DATABASES AND TABLES

Perhaps the most powerful use of data tables arises in work with *1-2-3* databases. When working with a database containing financial information — such as a check register dealing with several different accounts — you might want to sum or average values associated with each subcategory of records in the database. For example, the following database contains check entries from three different accounts:

	A	B	C	D	E	F
10			Account			
11						$3,040.00
12	Num	Date	Account	Withdraw	Deposit	Total
13	151	05-Mar	1003	$534.56		$2,505.44
14	152	07-Mar	1003	$728.32		$1,777.12
15		07-Mar	1008		$8,192.00	$9,969.12
16	153	09-Mar	1005	$1,098.50		$8,870.62
17	154	09-Mar	1008	$432.00		$8,438.62
18	155	12-Mar	1005	$976.13		$7,462.49

To follow this example, create the database by entering the information as shown, using the formula +F11–D13+E13 in cell F13 and the formula +F13–D14+E14 in cell F14. Then copy cell F14 to range F14..F18. Assign *crit* as the name for range C10..C11, and assign *dbase* as the name for range A12..F18. These named ranges will serve as Criterion and Database ranges. Adjust the column widths to accommodate the data when you format cells to display as shown in the figure.

At first glance, if you want to sum all the withdrawals made from each account, you might establish three different Criterion ranges (one for each account) and enter three separate @DSUM formulas. (The @DSUM formula is similar to the @SUM formula, but it sums only those items that fit the criteria you specify in the formula.) This is a simple solution for only three accounts, but if you're dealing with dozens of accounts, creating all the needed Criterion ranges becomes tedious. The alternative is to create a data table whose input cell is embedded in a database Criterion range.

To see how this works, create a data table following these instructions: Move the cell pointer to cell H13, and enter the label *Account*. Select /Data Query Input, and enter *dbase*. Select Criterion and enter *crit*, then select Output and press Return. Finally, select Unique. *1-2-3* creates a list of account numbers starting in cell H14. Select Quit to return to Ready mode.

Move the cell pointer to cell I13 and enter the formula @DSUM(dbase,3,crit). The formula evaluates to 3769.51, which is the sum of all the withdrawals shown in the database. To calculate the sum of withdrawals from account number 1005, enter that account number into cell C11, the second cell of the Criterion range. The @DSUM formula in cell I13 recalculates to 2074.63.

You're ready to use the Data Table command to fill in the second column of the table you've created starting in cell H13. The content of the Criterion range is not important, since *1-2-3* ignores that value while it generates the table values. Select /Data Table 1, then indicate H13..I16 as the Table range and cell C11 as the input cell. *1-2-3* fills in the table, placing the sums of withdrawals for each account number below the formula in column I. Your data table should look like the illustration on the next page.

	H	I	J
13	Account	3769.51	
14	1003	1262.88	
15	1008	432	
16	1005	2074.63	

MATTERS OF SPEED

It took *1-2-3* less than a second to calculate the data table you just created. However, when you generate data tables in very large worksheets, you might have to wait several minutes for *1-2-3* to finish the calculations. Even with recalculation set to manual, *1-2-3* recalculates the entire worksheet when it generates a data table. In very large worksheets you can often save time by creating a macro that generates the data table.

The following illustration shows a macro that generates a data table identical to the one we created in the last example:

	A	B	C	D	E
1	\t	/C~test~			
2		/XI@COUNT(test)=0~/XQ			
3		{RIGHT}			
4		@DSUM(dbase,3,crit){CALC}~			
5		{DOWN}{LEFT}/XG\t~			

To use the macro, enter it as shown and assign the name \t to cell B1 and the name *test* to range C11..D11. When you use this type of macro in a large worksheet, set recalculation to manual before you run the macro (/Worksheet Global Recalculation Manual). Place the cell pointer in cell H14, and start the macro by holding down the MACRO key and pressing T. (If your computer lacks a MACRO key, consult your *1-2-3* documentation for information on invoking macros.) Here's what happens:

/C~test~   Copies the contents of the current cell to the range named *test*. This places a copy of the first account number from the table into the Criterion range.

/XI@COUNT(test) = $\emptyset$~/XQ   Determines whether or not @COUNT(test) evaluates to $\emptyset$. If @COUNT(test) evaluates to $\emptyset$, the macro stops. @COUNT(test) will evaluate to $\emptyset$ if the cell pointer lies in a blank cell (hence at the end of the table); it evaluates to 2 if the cell pointer lies in a cell containing data.

{RIGHT}   Moves the cell pointer one cell to the right, to the second column of the table.

@DSUM(dbase,3,crit){CALC}~   Enters the current value of the formula @DSUM(dbase,3,crit) into the current cell. Note that although this entry seems tobegin with an at sign (@), it is a label. When you create the macro, start this entry with a label prefix character (').

{DOWN}{LEFT}/XG\t~   Moves the cell pointer down and left to the next account number in the table, then restarts the macro. The macro continues copying account numbers into the Criterion range, entering the sums of withdrawals for each account number into the table and so on until *1-2-3* tries to process a blank cell. The macro stops when it reaches a blank cell, and *1-2-3* returns to Ready mode.

CLOSING THOUGHTS

You can modify this macro to accommodate larger data tables by adding one {RIGHT} command and a new formula for each added column. For example, the following macro generates two columns of values, one reflecting the sums of the withdrawals for each account number, the other reflecting the average withdrawal for each account.

	A	B	C	D	E
1	\t	/C~test~			
2		/XI@COUNT(test)=0~/XQ			
3		{RIGHT}			
4		@DSUM(dbase,3,crit){CALC}~			
5		{RIGHT}@DAVG(dbase,3,crit){CALC}~			
6		{DOWN}{LEFT}{LEFT}/XG\t~			

Finally, use this macro technique judiciously. As stated, for small worksheets the Data Table command will outperform the macro. On enormous worksheets a macro can reduce the time it takes to generate a table by more than 50% (for some tables your savings can push 90%). As your worksheets grow larger and you find yourself waiting too long for *1-2-3* to recalculate, try writing a macro.

NOTES FOR RELEASE 2/2.01 USERS

The techniques described in the main article apply equally well to *1-2-3* Release 2/2.01. But Release 2/2.01 users should take advantage of the advanced macro commands. I created the first macro shown above in Release 2 and used it to generate a table in a loaded worksheet. The macro finished its task in about 14 seconds (run time will vary depending on your setup), better than half the time it took with the Data Table command. I then created the macro in the following illustration and used it to generate the same table in the same worksheet. The macro completed the table in just 6 seconds.

The macro is designed to work with the check register database described previously. Once you've entered the model, created the table as described, and

	A	B	C	D	E	F
1	\t	{FOR count,1,@ROWS(table)-1,1,data}~				
2						
3	count					
4						
5	data	{LET test,@INDEX(table,0,count)}				
6		{PUT table,1,count,@DSUM(dbase,3,crit)}				

entered the macro as shown, assign range names as follows: \t, B1; *count*, B3; *data*, B5; *table*, H13..I16.

The macro assumes that you've already assigned the following range names: *crit*, C10..C11; *dbase*, A12..F18; *test*, C11..D11.

You can reassign *test* to cell C11, although the macro will work without the change. To use it, hold down the MACRO key and press T. Here's what happens:

{FOR count,1,@ROWS(table)–1,1,data}~ Starts a FOR loop. A FOR loop is a set of commands that *1-2-3* processes a predetermined number of times. For this particular {FOR} command, *1-2-3* uses the cell named *count* (the first argument of the command) to keep track of how many times the loop processes. The {FOR} command puts the value 1 (the command's second argument) into *count* and compares *count* with the command's third argument: @ROWS(table)–1. If *count* is less than @ROWS(table)–1, *1-2-3* processes the commands starting in the cell named *data* (the command's fifth argument). When it finishes processing the commands in *data*, *1-2-3* increases the value of *count* by 1 (the command's fourth argument), compares *count* with @ROWS(table)–1, processes the commands starting in the cell named *data*, and repeats the cycle until the counter equals the value of @ROWS(table)–1.

The following are the steps that *1-2-3* processes for each iteration of the FOR loop:

{LET test,@INDEX(table,0,count)} Assigns the value of @INDEX (table, 0, count) to the cell named *test*. @INDEX(table,0,count) evaluates to one of the account numbers in the table. *1-2-3* interprets this formula to mean "Return the value found in *table* at the coordinates 0,*count*." The first coordinate, 0, is the column coordinate and refers to the first column of the table. The second coordinate, *count*, is the row coordinate. The row coordinate changes each time *1-2-3* processes the loop, so on the first pass the formula evaluates to 1003, on the second pass it equals 1008, and so on.

{PUT table,1,count,@DSUM(dbase,3,crit)} Places the value of the formula @DSUM(dbase,3,crit) into the table at the coordinates 1,*count*. These coordinates refer to the same row as those of the last step, but they refer to the second column of the table rather than the first.

7

Fast Two-Way Data Tables

This macro can significantly outperform the built-in Data Table 2 command.

BY DANIEL GASTEIGER

In the previous chapter, we presented a macro that calculates one-way data tables. The macro can, under certain circumstances, outperform *1-2-3*'s built-in Data Table 1 command. That column prompted several readers to write and ask for a macro that calculates two-way data tables.

With a little effort you can create a macro-driven, two-way data table, and yes, the macro is fast. The macro is so fast that it can make *1-2-3*'s Data Table 2 command look like a computer error.

Let's first create a standard two-way data table, explore some of the tools our macro will use, and finally, put the pieces together and create a macro that generates a two-way data table.

CONSIDER A LOAN

The following illustration shows a worksheet you might use to generate a table of mortgage payments:

	A	B	C	D	E	F
18		0.90	0.0925	0.095	0.0975	0.1
19	$90,000					
20	$100,000					
21	$110,000					
22	$120,000					
23	$130,000					

Row 18 contains numbers that represent annual interest rates, and column A contains various principal amounts. We'll generate a table that shows what your monthly payments will be if you obtain a 30-year mortgage for any of the principal amounts at any of the interest rates.

To generate the data table, enter the values as shown and assign the name *morttab* to range A18..F23: Press slash, select Range Name Create, enter *morttab*, indicate range A18..F23, and press Return. Enter labels in column A as shown below:

	A	B	C
4	princ		
5	intr		

Then assign the labels as names for the adjacent cells of column B: Press slash, select Range Name Labels Right, indicate range A4..A5, and press Return. The range names you've created are not needed to generate a data table, but they make the task easier and will come in handy later on when we create the macro.

Enter the following formula into cell A18:

$$@PMT(princ,intr/12,360)$$

You're ready to generate the data table: Press slash and select Data Table 2. Enter *morttab* in response to the prompt for the Table range. Indicate *princ* as the first input cell and press Return, then indicate *intr* as the second input cell and press Return. *1-2-3* fills in the table.

The values that *1-2-3* generates are the monthly payments you would make on a 30-year mortgage, given a principal amount from column A paired with a particular interest rate from row 18.

BUT IT WAS FAST

Because *1-2-3* generates the data table rapidly, you might wonder how a macro could be any faster. In fact, for a table in such a small worksheet model, a macro wouldn't be faster. However, to appreciate how slowly the Data Table command can operate, simply enter several hundred formulas into the current worksheet, erase range B18..F23 (press slash, select Range Erase, indicate B18..F23, and press Return), and regenerate the table (press the TABLE key). The bigger your worksheet model, the longer *1-2-3* takes to calculate a data table.

In one test model, *1-2-3* calculated a two-way data table in slightly more than 12 minutes. In the same worksheet, the macro we'll create calculated the same table in 11 seconds. Your results will vary, depending on your computer system and the nature of the formulas in your worksheet model.

Let's look at a few of the tools you'll use to create a two-way data-table macro. But first, erase the formula in cell A18 so that it doesn't clutter the display while we work.

THE VARIABLES

The two-way data-table macro must have a mechanism by which it selects the values to use in calculations. For each of the cells in range B19..F23, the macro must calculate the formula @PMT(princ,intr/12,360), where *princ* represents a principal amount from column A, *intr* represents an interest rate from row 18, and 360 is the total number of payments in a 30-year mortgage. We'll use the @INDEX function to select the values as needed.

The @INDEX function returns values located at specified column and row offsets from the top-left corner of a range. For example, in this worksheet the formula @INDEX(morttab,2,0) would return .0925-the value that is 2 columns to the right and 0 rows down from the top-left corner of *morttab*. The formula @INDEX(morttab,0,3) would return 110,000 — the value that is 0 columns to the right and 3 rows down from the top-left corner of *morttab*.

We'll control where our @INDEX functions look for data by entering column and row offset values into cells referenced by the functions. To see how this works, enter labels as shown in the illustration at the top of the next column and assign the labels as names for the adjacent cells of column B: Press slash, select Range Name Labels Right, indicate range A1..A2, and press Return:

	A	B	C
1	col		
2	row		

Now enter the formula @INDEX(morttab,0,row) into the cell named *princ* and the formula @INDEX (morttab,col,0) into the cell named *intr*. Because its column offset value is 0, the @INDEX function in *princ* can find values only in the first column of *morttab*. Likewise, because its row offset value is 0, the formula in *intr* can find values only in the first row of *morttab*. Right now both functions refer to the top-left corner cell of the table (*col* and *row* are blank and therefore equal zero).

Enter 1 into *col*; *intr* updates and becomes 0.09. Enter 2 into *row*, and *princ* becomes 100,000. Given a formula that relies on the values in *princ* and *intr*, we would then have all the formulas necessary to calculate a two-way data table. Create that formula by first entering the label *payment* into cell A7 and naming cell B7 *payment*. Then enter @PMT(princ, intr/12,360) into *payment*. This formula should evaluate to 804.6226.

Move the cell pointer to *row* (cell B2) and enter 1; *payment* becomes 724.1603. Move to *col* (cell B1) and enter 2; *payment* becomes 740.4078. Enter 3 and *payment* becomes 756.7687. Enter 4, then enter 5, each time observing the change in the value of *payment*. Once you've entered 5, you will have seen every value that *1-2-3* will calculate for the first row of the data table. To calculate each of the values in the second row of the table, enter 2 into *row* and enter first 1, then 2, then 3, and so on into *col*. Now that we have a mechanism to calculate every value for the table, we need to control the process that automatically places each calculated value into the appropriate table cell.

PUTTING

While the @INDEX function provides a way to get information out of a table, the macro {PUT} command lets you place information into a table. The {PUT} command is similar to the @INDEX function in that its behavior is determined by arguments identifying a table and by column and row offsets. The {PUT} command also requires an argument that specifies what *1-2-3* should place in the identified table.

For example, if a macro processed the command {PUT morttab,2,3,88888}, *1-2-3* would place the value 88888 into the cell that is 2 columns to the right and 3 rows down from the top-left corner of *morttab*.

Our macro will use the command {PUT morttab,col,row,payment} to place calculated values into the table.

This leads us to our final requirement: a mechanism that keeps track of which cells are being filled.

LOOPS

Our two-way data-table macro uses the {FOR} command to control the table-creation process. The {FOR} command causes a macro to loop (repeat a set of commands) a prespecified number of times. *1-2-3* uses a counter cell on the worksheet to keep track of how many times the macro loops. Each time the loop processes, the counter increases in value by a set interval (a FOR loop counter can also decrease in value, depending on the parameters you supply when you write the command).

The {FOR} command takes the following form:

{FOR *counter,start,stop,step,routine*}

When a macro processes this command, *1-2-3* places the value of *start* into the cell named *counter* and compares *counter* with *stop*. If *counter* is greater than *stop*, the macro continues processing with the command immediately following the {FOR} command. Otherwise, the macro processes the commands found in the cell named *routine*. When *routine* finishes processing, *1-2-3* adds the value of *step* to *counter*, then compares *counter* and *stop*, and if *counter* doesn't exceed *stop*, the macro again processes *routine*.

You can create formulas that rely on the counter cells of {FOR} commands. This provides a simple way to generate several different results from the same formula or set of formulas. For example, if your {FOR} command uses a cell named *counter* as the counter cell, the formula *+counter* will have a different value with each loop of the macro.

The macro in the following illustration exploits the {FOR} command to generate a two-way data table:

	A	B	C	D	E	F
9	\m	{FOR row,1,@ROWS(morttab)-1,1,across}~				
10						
11	across	{FOR col,1,@COLS(morttab)-1,1,fillit}				
12						
13	fillit	{RECALC block}				
14		{PUT morttab,col,row,payment}				

To create the macro, continue with the worksheet you've been using to follow this discussion and enter labels as shown. Then assign the labels of column A as range names for the adjacent cells of column B: Press slash, select Range Name Labels Right, indicate range A9..A13, and press Return. Finally, assign the name *block* to range B1..B7. To run the macro, hold down the MACRO key (Alt on most computers) and press M. Here's what happens:

{FOR row,1,@ROWS(morttab)–1,1,across} ~ Starts a FOR loop that uses the cell named *row* as a counter and processes one fewer times than there are rows in the table. Because the loop starts counting at 1, *row* receives the value 1 on the first pass of the loop. This means that the @INDEX function in *princ* returns the first principal amount from column A of the table. On the second pass of the loop, *princ* returns the second principal amount from the table, and so on. For each pass of the loop, *1-2-3* processes commands starting with the cell named *across*.

{FOR col,1,@COLS(morttab)–1,1,fillit} Starts a second FOR loop that processes the routine named *fillit*. This second loop uses *col* as a counter and processes one fewer times than there are columns in the table. The loop starts counting at 1, causing the @INDEX function in *intr* to return the value .09. With each pass of the loop, *intr* changes to represent a different interest rate from the table. Here are the steps of the routine named *fillit*:

{RECALC block} Updates the formulas in the range named *block*. For this application, all the formulas involved in calculating the table recalculate with one {RECALC} command. It is possible, however, to create models in which a single recalculation won't do. If your model uses several interrelated formulas, include them in the range described by this {RECALC} command. Also, use a repeat count ({RECALC block,3}, for example) to ensure that your table calculates properly.

   {PUT morttab,col,row,payment}   Places the current value of *payment* into the table. *1-2-3* places the value at the column and row offset described by the loop counters *col* and *row*. Hence for each pass of the second loop, the payment value ends up in a different column of a particular row.

HOW IT WORKS

These FOR loops can be confusing, so let's summarize the process. The macro contains two FOR loops that run concurrently. For each iteration of the first loop, there are five iterations of the second loop. And for each iteration of the first loop, the second loop restarts. This arrangement of loops is called nesting.

   The first loop increases a row counter; the second loop increases a column counter. These two counters let @INDEX functions find data in the table's borders. An @PMT function uses the indexed values to calculate monthly mortgage payments on each combination of principal and interest. Finally, a {PUT} command places the calculated payments into the table.

   You can modify the model to handle almost any table by first creating the table and then reassigning the name *morttab* to encompass the new data. Don't delete the original range name *morttab* before you reassign it or you may have to rewrite your formulas for the macro to work properly. Also, the model isn't limited to calculating loan payments. Whatever formula you use in *payment* should in some way rely on the cells named *princ* and *intr*, but these cells can be linked through a variety of calculations.

   Play around with this model, then create some of your own. Put your own formulas into the worksheet, and compare the macro's speed against that of the Data Table 2 command. In the next chapter we'll take a look at a macro-driven three-way data table.

MAY 1987

8

Three-Way Data Tables

Generate tables of data that rely on three variables.

BY DANIEL GASTEIGER

We've seen how convenient one- and two-way data tables can be in using a single set of formulas to calculate several values. A one-way data table calculates a set of values from formulas that rely on a single variable; a two-way data table uses two variables in its calculations.

In the previous chapter, we used the @INDEX function and the {PUT} and {FOR} commands to build a macro that calculates two-way data tables. We designed that macro to save time with data-table calculations. This time we'll use the same tools to create a macro that generates three-way data tables.

A 3-D WORKSHEET?

A two-way data table consists of a row of values adjoining a column of values, two Input cells, and a formula that relies on the values of the Input cells. On the next page is a small *1-2-3* two-way data table we'll use to generate values that represent payments on an automobile loan.

To prepare this table, enter the labels shown in cells A19, A20, and A21. Assign range names by pressing slash, selecting Range Name Labels Right, indicating range A19..A21, and pressing Return. Enter the values shown in row 23, then enter the percentages shown in column B. To enter 2.0%, for example, point to cell B24 and enter *2%*. Format range B24..B29 for percent with one decimal place: Select /Range Format Percent, enter 1, indicate B24..B29, and press Return. Enter the formula @PMT(princ,int/12,years*12) into cell B23. Assign a currency format with no

	A	B	C	D	E	F	G
19	int						
20	years						
21	princ	5000					
22							
23		ERR	1	2	3	4	5
24		2.0%					
25		4.0%					
26		6.0%					
27		8.0%					
28		10.0%					
29		12.0%					

decimal places to range C24..G29: Select /Range Format Currency, enter 0, indicate C24..G29, and press Return. Finally, enter the value 5000 into cell B21.

The formula in cell B23 calculates the monthly payment on a $5,000 loan. The loan's payback period resides in the cell named *years*; the interest rate appears in *int*. Select /Data Table 2, indicate B23..G29 as the Table range, and press Return. Then indicate *int* (B19) as the first Input cell, press Return, indicate *years* (B20) as the second Input cell, and press Return once more. *1-2-3* fills the table with values.

To make the calculations, *1-2-3* substitutes a percent from column B in Input cell 1 (*int*), substitutes a value from row 23 in Input cell 2 (*years*), and places the resulting value of the table's formula into the appropriate cell in the table.

You might look at such a table to get an idea of the price range you can afford when shopping for a car. The lowest monthly payment shown in the calculated table appears in cell G24. This is the amount you would pay each month if you borrowed $5,000 at 2% interest with a five-year payback period. You're more likely to find higher interest rates on five-year loans, so look down the column at the payments associated with 8%, 10%, and 12% interest rates.

This table provides some figures that can help you zero in on an appropriate car loan. Naturally, you want the shortest-term, lowest-interest loan you can afford, but you rarely know how much you'll need to borrow before you've talked turkey with a salesperson. You may be surprised by the value of your trade-in, or you may find that the options you want add another $1,000 to the purchase price. In any case, this table would be more useful if you could vary the principal amount in the calculations just as you vary the term and interest rate. One way to do this is to add a third dimension to your data table.

3-D IN TWO DIMENSIONS

If you think of row 23 of your two-way table as the X axis and column B as the Y axis, you need to add a Z axis to create a three-way table. The Z axis would contain different loan principals for buying a car.

Imagine a three-way data table as being a pile of two-way data tables that extends into the depths of your computer's monitor. You can see only the topmost two-way table as you look at the screen, and you can identify that table by the value stored in the top-left corner ($5,000). If you could rotate the display, your three-way table might look like the following:

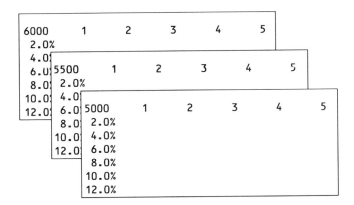

When *1-2-3* fills in this table, each layer will contain values that result from the combination of three values: the principal amount from the top-left corner, the interest rates from the left column, and the terms from the top row.

1-2-3 Releases 1A, 2, and 2.01 are two-dimensional spreadsheets. We'll display a three-dimensional table by peeling apart the table's layers and putting each one on the worksheet.

Start with the worksheet described earlier and replace the contents of cell B23 with the value 3500. Then erase range C24..G29: Select /Range Erase, indicate C24..G29, and press Return.

For this example, we're going to generate a six-layer table that calculates payments for six different loans. Start by copying the entire Table range as follows: Select /Copy, indicate B23..G61 as the range to copy from, and press Return. Then indicate cell B31 as the range to copy to and press Return. Enter the values 4000, 4500, 5000, 5500, and 6000 into cells B31, B39, B47, B55, and B63, respectively. As you do this, notice that each cell into which you make an entry falls in the top-left corner of a layer of the three-dimensional table.

Erase the entries in range A19..B21 and delete all assigned range names: Select /Range Erase, indicate A19..B21, and press Return; then Select /Range Name Reset. You're ready to create a macro and calculate the data table.

A 3-D MACRO

To create the macro that generates a three-way data table, enter labels as shown in column A and in cells B12, B14 and B19 of the following illustration. Note that cells B1 through B10 contain formulas, as do cells B15, B17, and B20. Leave these cells blank for now and we'll enter the formulas after assigning some necessary range names.

	A	B	C	D	E	F
1	numlays	6			layer35	
2	layer				layer40	
3	curlay	layer35			layer45	
4	col				layer50	
5	row				layer55	
6	layval	3500			layer60	
7	rowval	3500				
8	colval	3500				
9						
10	result	1020833.				
11						
12	\t	{FOR layer,0,numlays-1,1,\m}~				
13						
14	\m	{RECALC block}{RECALC program}				
15		{FOR row,1,@ROWS(layer35)-1,1,across}				
16						
17	across	{FOR col,1,@COLS(layer35)-1,1,fillit}				
18						
19	fillit	{RECALC block}				
20		{PUT layer35,col,row,result}				

The macro requires that each layer of the data table have a unique name. The specific range names aren't important, so we'll use a simple naming scheme for this discussion. Select /Range Name Create, enter *layer35*, indicate range B23..G29, and press Return. This assigns *layer35* as the name for the first layer of the three-way table. Name the remaining layers as follows:

B31..G37   *layer40*
B39..G45   *layer45*
B47..G53   *layer50*
B55..G61   *layer55*
B63..G69   *layer60*

List these names in column E, starting in cell E1 as shown in the figure, then assign the name *names* to range E1..E6. Assign the labels of column A as range names for the adjacent cells of column B: Select /Range Name Labels Right, indicate range

A1..A19, and press Return. Then assign the name *block* to range B1..B10 and the name *program* to range B15..B20. Finally, enter formulas in the cells indicated by the following table:

numlays (B1)	@COUNT(names)
curlay (B3)	@INDEX(names,Ø,layer)
layval (B6)	@INDEX(@@(curlay),Ø,Ø)
rowval (B7)	@INDEX(@@(curlay),Ø,row)
colval (B8)	@INDEX(@@(curlay),col,Ø)
result (B10)	@PMT(layval,rowval/12,colval 12)
B15	+ "{FOR row,1,@ROWS("&curlay&")–1,1,across}"
B17	+ "{FOR col,1,@COLS("&curlay&")–1,1,fillit}"
B20	+ "{PUT "&curlay&",col,row, result}"

You're ready to generate a three-way data table. But before you do, save the worksheet so that you'll have a clean copy to work with should you wish to adapt the macro to another set of calculations.

To run the macro, hold down the MACRO key (Alt on most computers) and press T. The only change to your worksheet is the appearance of the CMD indicator in the bottom border of your display. *1-2-3* appears dormant for about a minute, then the screen flickers, and your data table is calculated. Press the PageDown key to peruse the monthly payments for loans at varying interest rates, periods, and principal amounts.

THE GENERAL IDEA

Adequately explaining how this macro works would wear off the tips of my fingers. Instead, we'll look at some of the macro's key pieces and leave you to explore how they fit together.

To understand this macro fully, start by rereading the previous chapter. There we created a macro that efficiently calculates two-way data tables. We've reused that macro, with a few modifications, in this column.

Once you've entered the labels, range names, and formulas of the three-way data-table macro, range A15..B20 of the worksheet appears identical to the previous chapter's macro. The purpose of these lines of macro instructions is to fill a single layer of the three-way data table — essentially to calculate a two-way data table. The remaining additions and changes to the previous chapter's model let *1-2-3* reuse the two-way table macro as often as needed to fill each layer in your three-way table.

Look once again at your worksheet and notice the difference between cells A15 through B20 of this macro and the two-way data-table macro described in the previous chapter. Here cells B15, B17, and B20 contain string formulas that resemble macro commands. When you start the macro, these formulas look like commands that refer to the first layer named in *names* (range E1..E6). As shown in the illustration, before you run the macro, these commands refer to the table layer named *layer35*.

Once *1-2-3* calculates every value for the layer named *layer35*, the macro increases the value of a counter cell (*layer*) upon which these formulas rely. The formulas update and refer to a new layer — the second one listed in *names*. *1-2-3* calculates every value for the second layer of the table, increases the value of the counter cell again, and so on, repeating the process for each layer of the three-way data table. When the macro stops, several cells will return ERR. This is because the counters exceed the number of columns and rows in the table's ranges. It has no bearing on the macro's function or on the table's accuracy.

A second key to understanding this macro is to understand the mechanism that provides access to data from each of the different layers of the table. Whenever the macro increases the value of the counter named *layer*, the formulas in *layval*, *rowval*, and *colval* adjust and refer to a different layer of the table. To see this in action, retrieve the original model (shown in figure 3) and move the cell pointer to *layer* (cell B2). Enter the value 1 and notice the changes to your worksheet. *Curlay* now reads *layer40*, and *layval*, *rowval*, and *colval* each read 4000. (Also, the macro commands in cells B15, B17, and B20 now refer to the layer named *layer40*). Enter 2 into *layer*, and the formulas update once more.

Layval, *rowval*, and *colval* rely on the arcane @@ function to return values from whatever table layer is described in *curlay*. Each of the formulas in these cells contains the function @@(curlay), which means "return the value found in the cell or range named in *curlay*."

SOME FINAL THOUGHTS

This macro generates a three-way table whose values rely on only one formula — the formula in the cell named *result*. But you can adapt the macro to handle almost any set of calculations. To do this, establish a chain of formulas that rely on the cells named *layval*, *rowval*, and *colval*. The formula in *result* must always be the end product of this chain. When you create your own model for the three-way table to use in its calculations, reassign the range name *block* to encompass every formula on which *result* relies.

Try to arrange the formulas in *block* so that they update properly with one rowwise recalculation of *block*. The macro updates the formulas in *block* once per table value, but it does not use a natural order of recalculation. If your model is too complex to update with just one rowwise recalculation, add a repeat count to the {RECALC} command in *fillit*.

If you wish to add another layer to your table, simply enter the layer's name at the end of the list in column E and expand the range named *names* to include the addition. The values in the borders of a layer need not match the values in the borders of any other layer; likewise, a layer's dimensions need not match the dimensions of other layers. One layer might have 6 rows and 6 columns, while another might have 60 rows and 60 columns.

This is a rather intricate collection of techniques for what appears to be a simple problem. If a three-way data table is basically a pile of two-way data tables, why not write a macro that repeats the Data Table 2 command once per layer?

The answer is performance. The Data Table commands are slow. In a large worksheet, a macro can leave the Data Table commands in the dust. Even in a small worksheet like this one, the described three-way data-table macro will outperform a macro that repeats the Data Table 2 command six times.

JUNE 1987

9

Data Table Revisited

The data-table macros drew plenty of reader feedback; we address the issues.

BY DANIEL GASTEIGER

When we presented a macro that could, under certain circumstances, calculate a one-way data table faster than the Data Table 1 command, readers asked for a two-way data-table macro. When we explored such a macro, we received a second wave of letters.

Several readers reported the time savings they realized by using the macro. Others reported on time trials in which the macro took longer to calculate a table than did the Data Table 2 command. Still other readers described nonmacro techniques that calculate data tables more quickly than either the macro or the Data Table 2 command. But most overwhelming were reader's requests for help adapting the macro to applications other than calculating mortgage payments. Let's reexamine the two-way Data-table macro and explore the issues our readers have raised.

THE PROBLEM

Two-way data tables provide a means by which you can easily reuse a single set of calculations. These calculations must rely in some way on values in two cells on the worksheet. Our example substituted interest and principal amounts into the @PMT function. The table calculated monthly mortgage payments based on each pairing of an interest rate and a principal amount.

The illustration shows the worksheet we created. It contains an uncalculated two-way data table starting in cell A18. It also contains a macro to calculate values for that table:

```
        A            B         C        D       E        F
1  col
2  row
3
4  princ              0
5  intr               0
6
7  payment            0
8
9  \m           {FOR row,1,@ROWS(morttab)-1,1,across}~
10
11 across       {FOR col,1,@COLS(morttab)-1,1,fillit}
12
13 fillit    {RECALC block}
14           {PUT morttab,col,row,payment}
15
16
17
18          0      0.09    0.0925    0.095   0.0975        0.1
19   $90,000
20  $100,000
21  $110,000
22  $120,000
23  $130,000
```

To create the model, start in a blank worksheet and enter the labels and numbers as shown. The cells that display 0 contain formulas, so leave them blank for now. Assign the labels in column A as range names for the adjacent cells of column B: Press slash, select Range Name Labels Right, and indicate range A1..A13. Then use the Range Name Create command to assign the name *block* to range B1..B7 and the name *morttab* to range A18..F23. Assign a currency format to cell A18 and to range A19..F23: Press slash, select Range Format Currency, enter 0, and indicate the range. Enter the following formulas in the indicated cells:

Cell	Formula
B4	@INDEX(morttab,0,row)
B5	@INDEX(morttab,col,0)
B7	@PMT(princ,intr/12,360)
A18	@PMT(princ,intr/12,360)

Disregard the *Circ* indicator that *1-2-3* displays when you enter the last formula. The circular reference doesn't invalidate the model.

To calculate the table the old-fashioned way, select /Data Table 2. Enter *morttab* in response to the prompt for the Table range. Indicate *princ* as the first input cell and indicate *intr* as the second input cell.

The values that *1-2-3* generates are the monthly payments you would make on a 30-year mortgage, given a principal amount from column A paired with a particular interest rate from row 18. Disregard the ERRs that appear in cells B4, B5, B7, and A18. These ERRs don't affect the model.

To have the macro generate the table, first erase the values that the Data Table 2 command generated: Select /Range Erase and indicate range B19..F23. Then hold down the MACRO key (Alt on most computers) and press M. The macro takes about as long to generate the table as the Data Table 2 command does. When it has finished, cells B4, B5, and B7 will display ERR. Once again, you can disregard these alerts.

TIME TRIALS

In previous chapters we claimed that the macro can generate the data table faster than the Data Table command can. Yet in this example, the macro and the Data Table command are almost evenly matched. And as stated earlier, several readers who ran time trials with the macro and the Data Table command reported that the macro was slower.

In response to these time trials, we admonish you to use whatever works best in your particular situation. In general, the larger the worksheet relative to the size of the table generated, the more efficient the macro.

For example, if you create a 6-row-by-6-column table in a blank worksheet, the Data Table 2 command and the macro might each take three seconds to calculate the table. However, as you increase the contents of the worksheet without changing the table's size, the Data Table 2 command will take longer and longer to calculate the table. The macro will continue to generate the table in three seconds.

A NONMACRO ALTERNATIVE

If you made it past the speed issue, you might have realized that there is yet a faster way to generate this table. Several readers wrote to describe a formula that uses mixed absolute and relative cell references.

To see how this works, erase the macro-generated table values: Select /Range Erase and indicate range B19..F23. Enter the following formula into cell B19:

$$@PMT(\$A19,B\$18/12,360)$$

Copy the formula throughout the Table range: Select /Copy and indicate cell B19 as the From range and B19..F23 as the To range. Now you can change any value in either border of the table and *1-2-3* will instantly update the corresponding calculations.

This approach is a fine alternative for the table we're discussing. In fact, you can calculate many of your tables by designing a single, mixed-reference formula and copying it throughout the Table range. But there are limitations to this approach.

A table calculated by a formula copied throughout the Table range uses more memory than a macro-generated table. You might not have enough memory for so many formulas, especially in large worksheets where the macro is most efficient. This approach also limits you to creating tables that rely on only one cell's worth of calculations. Suppose the table values you wish to calculate rely on a set of linked formulas? Or suppose the table's calculations involved some database operations? Under these circumstances, you must resort to the Data Table command or a macro.

Many readers have asked how to adapt the macro for these situations. How can they make the two-way data-table macro work with a database and Criterion range? Let's look at one approach.

REDESIGN

Leave everything in your worksheet intact except for the table beginning in row 18. Erase the entire table by selecting /Range Erase and indicating range A18..F23. Then reformat the range: Select /Range Format Reset and indicate range A18..F23. Enter the database as shown in the following illustration:

	A	B	C	D
20	Item	Code	Dept	Cost
21	Pencils	4	100	6.54
22	L pads	4	150	10.92
23	Lunch	8	100	89.72
24	Wine	8	100	32.5
25	Bl pens	4	150	7.54
26	Monitor	6	100	385.37

Name the database *dbase*: Select /Range Name Create, enter *dbase*, and indicate range A20..D26. This database represents a list of a small company's expenditures. Expenditures are coded: 4 indicates office supplies, 6 indicates office equipment, and 8 indicates entertainment expenses. The company is broken up into departments, each with its own account. We'll use a table to calculate each department's total expenditure by type.

Copy the *Code* and *Dept* field headers up two rows: Select /Copy, indicate B20..C20 as the From range, then indicate cell B18 as the To range. These copies will become part of a Criterion range: Select /Range Name Create, enter *crit*, and indicate range B18..C19. Assign the name *var1* to cell B19 and the name *var2* to cell C19.

Enter a new table as shown below:

	A	B	C	D
29		100	150	
30	4			
31	6			
32	8			

Reassign the name *morttab* to encompass the new table: Select /Range Name Create, enter *morttab*, and indicate range A29..C32. Do not delete the range name before you reassign it or you'll have to reenter some of the formulas that refer to the range.

Modify the macro routine named *fillit* as follows:

	A	B	C	D	E
13	fillit	{RECALC block}			
14		{LET var1,princ}{LET var2,intr}			
15		{RECALC block}			
16		{PUT morttab,col,row,payment}			

Finally, enter the following formula into the cell named *payment*:

@DSUM(dbase,3,crit)

Were we to build this model from scratch, we'd assign range names more appropriate to the task at hand. But because we're adapting an older macro, we've reduced our effort and preserved the existing range names. The macro is ready to fly. To try it out, hold down the MACRO key and press M. Once the macro has finished, cells B4 and B5 will contain ERRs; however, your table will contain the sums of each department's expenditures. The ERRs will not affect future runs of the macro. Here's how it works:

{FOR row,1,@ROWS(morttab)–1,1,across} ~   Starts a FOR loop that runs the routine named *across* once for each row in the range named *morttab*.

{FOR col,1,@COLS(morttab)–1,1,fillit}   Starts a FOR loop that runs the routine named *fillit* once for each column in *morttab*.

{RECALC block}   Recalculates the range named *block* and updates the formulas based on the new values of *col* and *row* (refer to the previous chapter for a more in-depth explanation of these procedures). This step assures that the @INDEX functions in *princ* and *intr* extract the appropriate values from the table's borders.

{LET var1,princ}{LET var2,intr}   Assigns the current values of *princ* and *intr* to the cells named *var1* and *var2*, respectively. These cells are within the Criterion range used by the @DSUM function in the cell named *payment*. It seems that we could have omitted this step and placed the @INDEX functions directly into the Criterion range. However, *1-2-3* is likely to misinterpret an @INDEX function that appears in a database Criterion range.

{**RECALC block**} Updates the formulas once more. This recalculation updates the value of *payment* based on the new contents of the Criterion range.

{**PUT morttab,col,row,payment**} Places the current value of *payment* into the appropriate cell of the table.

When you run this macro on such a small database in such a small worksheet, you'll wait longer for results than you would if you used the Data Table 2 command. But as stated earlier, as you increase the size of the worksheet — particularly the number of formulas in the worksheet — this macro will begin to outperform the Data Table command. In very large worksheets there will be no contest.

As you move forward from this example, you'll probably encounter some new problems. Hack around for a while until you find a technique that works. A little patience and trial and error are all you need to produce variations on this model that will work for you.

OCTOBER 1987

10

Concatenation and Mailing Labels

Use macros to chain together strings and create attractive
mailing labels from addresses stored in a database.

BY DANIEL GASTEIGER

Adding numbers together is child's play for *1-2-3*. Adding labels together is another matter. Generally, *1-2-3* Release 1A does not recognize labels and gives them the value of zero in formulas. At first glance it appears that in *1-2-3* it's not possible to do arithmetic with labels (adding them, comparing them, and breaking them into pieces). But looks are deceiving. (Release 2/2.01 users see note at end of this article.)

In other chapters, we've explored techniques to compare labels and used them in macros that look up labels in tables. This time we'll explore *concatenation* — the process of chaining together labels from two (or more) different cells to create single-cell entries. Along the way we'll develop a macro that extracts mailing addresses from a database and prints them on continuous feed, adhesive paper labels.

WHAT IS A DATABASE?

A *1-2-3* database is a collection of information on the worksheet. Each set of related information is called a record. For example, in a database of addresses, all the information about one person is considered a record. A record occupies a single row of the database, and you can have as many records as there are rows on the worksheet minus one.

Each record is divided into distinct categories called fields. An address database might have one field for first name, a second for last name, a third for street address, and so on. Each field of a *1-2-3* database is in its own column headed by the name of the field. The following illustration shows a simple address database containing four records:

	A	B	C	D	E	F
17	First	Last	Street	City	St	Zip
18	Mary	Crumps	1310 Lychee Ave	Meadville	NY	14835
19	Allison	Jakes	88 Welshire St	Enfield	MA	02133
20	Scott	Monk	303 Parkway Blvd	Colonie	MA	02167
21	Barbara	Walley	#1B Clara Donlon	Elks	NY	14848

When you store information in database format, you can use Data Query commands to find and extract selected information and to delete specified records with little effort. If you store several hundred names and addresses, the Data Query commands make it easy to look up any address without paging through the entire database. This makes a database far more useful than a simple list of information.

An address database is even more useful when you can use its data to print mailing labels. The addresses in a database are not in a convenient format for printing on paper labels, but a macro can print each record in the standard address format automatically.

A SIMPLE APPROACH

You've probably received mail that was addressed by a computer. Such letters often have unattractive address labels with large gaps between the first and last names and unusual spacing between the city, state, and zip code. This is because your name and address don't fit perfectly into the spaces the programmers allowed in creating a mailing-label generator. The following short macro illustrates this point by printing address labels using the database shown earlier:

	A	B	C	D
1	\l	/PPOOUQAQ		
2	loop	/PPR{BS}.{RIGHT}~G		
3		R{BS}{RIGHT}{RIGHT}~G		
4		R{BS}{RIGHT}{RIGHT}		
5		{RIGHT}.{RIGHT}{RIGHT}~		
6		GLLLLLLQ		
7		{DOWN}/RNChere~{RIGHT}~		
8		/XI@COUNT(here)=0~/RNdhere~/XQ		
9		/RNDhere~/XGloop~		

To use the macro, enter it as shown. Then assign the range names \l and *loop* by placing the cell pointer in A1 and selecting /Range Name Labels Right, then pressing Down Return. For now use regular 8-1/2-by-11-inch paper, but when you print mailing labels, you'll need the adhesive, one-across 1 7/16-inch labels. This macro assumes you're using continuous-feed labels. If your printer lacks a form-feeding device, you'll have to nurse it through the printing process to keep the paper from shifting.

My Epson FX-80 printer has trouble feeding labels because its sprocket wheels don't move close enough together to engage both sets of perforations on the labels. If you have the same problem, try rolling tractor-fed 8 1/2-by-11-inch paper into the printer, then roll the labels in front of the paper. If you're printing many labels, you'll have lots of blank paper to refold later on, but the paper labels will probably feed more successfully.

Place the cell pointer in the first cell of the first record of the database — in this case, cell A18 — then start the macro by holding down the MACRO key and pressing L (if your computer lacks a MACRO key, consult your *1-2-3* documentation for instructions on starting macros). Here's what happens:

/PPOOUQAQ   Presses slash and selects Print Printer Options Other Unformatted Quit Align Quit. This tells *1-2-3* to print without margins and page breaks and resets alignment so that the position of the printhead is treated as the top of the page. When you are using mailing labels, you should align the printhead about two lines below the top of the first label before you start the macro.

/PPR{BS}.{RIGHT}~G   Presses slash and selects Print Printer Range, cancels the last print range with the {BS} command (Backspace), and sets a new range, two cells across. It then prints the range — the first and last names of the current record of the database.

R{BS}{RIGHT}{RIGHT}~G   Selects Range and resets the print range two cells to the right. Then prints the new print range, the *Street* field of the database.

R{BS}{RIGHT}{RIGHT}   Selects Range and starts to reset the print range again.

{RIGHT}.{RIGHT}{RIGHT}~   Finishes setting the new print range to include the *City, St*, and *Zip* fields of the current record.

GLLLLLLQ   Prints the print range and advances the paper six lines, then returns to READY mode. This finishes printing the first mailing label and positions the paper to print the next.

{DOWN}/RNChere~{RIGHT}~   Moves the cell pointer down and assigns the range name *here* to the first two cells of the current row.

/XI@COUNT(here) = 0~/RNDhere~/XQ   Deletes the range name *here* and stops the macro if there are no entries in the range named *here*. This step stops the macro when all the addresses have been printed. Until then, *here* contains the first and last names of the current record, so @COUNT(here) equals two. When *here* is created on the row after the last record of the database, @COUNT(here) equals zero, so the macro stops. It deletes the range name *here* before it stops so that you don't get unexpected results the next time you use the macro.

/RNDhere~/XGloop~ Deletes the range name *here* and sends the macro to process keystrokes in the cell named *loop*. This step processes if the preceding step does not stop the macro. *Loop* is the second cell of the macro. It prints the first line of the new address indicated by the cell pointer. The macro prints each address, followed by six blank lines, until it has printed everything in the database.

The success of this macro hinges on your having set the worksheet column widths so that each entry is entirely visible. If column widths are too narrow, parts of entries will be hidden behind other entries, and some of the fields will be merged on the printed mailing labels.

Unfortunately, when the columns are wide enough to hold the longest entries, you'll have wide gaps between short entries. In the database shown above, Allison Jakes's name is spaced properly, but Mary Crumps's is not. The labels printed by this macro will look computer generated.

HOW DOES 1-2-3 CONCATENATE?

There are at least three ways to concatenate labels in *1-2-3*, each of which gives you complete control over the spacing between words in your printed mailing labels. We'll use the simplest to build a mailing-label generator.

The following macro concatenates labels from two adjacent cells into a cell named *name*:

	A	B	C	D
1	\c	/C~first~{RIGHT}		
2		/C~last~		
3		{GOTO}name~		
4	first			
5	last	~		
6		~		
7				
8	name			

Enter the macro as shown and assign the labels in column A as range names for the adjacent cells in column B using the Range Name Labels Right command. Enter your first name in cell A12 and your last name in cell B12. Put the cell pointer in cell A12 (the one containing your first name) and start the macro by holding down the MACRO key and pressing C. Here's what happens:

/C~first~{RIGHT} Copies from the current cell to the cell named *first*, then moves the cell pointer one cell to the right.

/C~last~ Copies from this new cell to the cell named *last*. Both *first* and *last* are within the body of the macro.

{**GOTO**}**name~** Sends the cell pointer to the cell named *name* (B8 in the example). By this point the next two cells of the macro contain your first and last names, respectively. These are typed back-to-back in the control panel.

~ Enters your first and last names into the current cell. If your name is Mary Crumps, *name* receives the label *MaryCrumps*.

Normally, you want a single space between the first and last names in a mailing label. Likewise, in an address label there should be a comma and a space after the name of the city, and three spaces between the state name and the zip code. Your macro can insert these spaces as it concatenates the labels. To have the macro in the example insert a space between your first and last names, move the cell pointer to the cell named *last* and insert a row (press /Worksheet Insert Row Return). Now type a single space and enter it into the cell between those named *first* and *last*.

THE MAILING-LABEL GENERATOR

The following macro produces mailing labels by concatenating database entries into a single-cell print range:

	A	B	C	D
1	\l	/RNDhere~/PPOOUQRlabel~AQ		
2	loop	/RNChere~~/C~first~{RIGHT}		
3	here	/C~last~{RIGHT}		
4		/C~street~{RIGHT}		
5		/C~city~{RIGHT}		
6		/C~st~{RIGHT}		
7		/C~zip~{GOTO}label~		
8	first			
9				
10	last			
11		{DOWN}{DOWN}		
12	city			
13		,		
14	st			
15				
16	zip			
17		~/PPGQ{GOTO}here~		
18		/RNDhere~{DOWN}/XGloop~		

This uses the same database presented earlier, but I've moved it down to row 20 of the worksheet to make room for the macro. When you enter the macro in column B, enter a single space in cell B9, a comma followed by a single space in cell B13, and three spaces in cell B15. Then enter the associated labels in column A. Assign range names by placing the cell pointer in cell A1 and pressing slash, then select Range

Name Labels Right and indicate the range A1..A16, finishing with Return.

Before running the macro, move to cell F2, enter the label *street*, and use the Range Name Labels Right command to assign this as the name for cell G2. Move to cell G1 and set the width of column G to 40 using the Worksheet Column Set-Width command. Then assign the name *label* to G1..G9. Finally, move the cell pointer to the first field of the first record of the database, and start the macro by pressing MACRO-L.

This macro builds the mailing address in the range named *label,* then prints that range. Since *label* is nine cells deep, your printer spaces down to the first line of the next paper label after it prints the current address. The macro then moves to the next database record and loops back to build a new mailing label. The macro stops when there is no entry in the first column of the database. Here's how it works:

/RNDhere~/PPOOUQRlabel~AQ   Deletes the range name *here*, then sets the print format to unformatted, assigns *label* as the print range, and establishes the current position of the printhead as the line where the first address should begin. When you assigned range names for this macro, you assigned *here* as the name for cell B3. The macro deletes that name in the first step, so the next step can reassign it. The macro doesn't delete the range name *here* when it stops, so this step is necessary if you intend to use the macro more than once. (See "Moving Range Names" for further rationale on this step.)

/RNChere~ ~/C~first~{RIGHT}   Assigns the name *here* to the current cell, copies the contents of that cell to the cell named *first*, then moves the cell pointer to the right.

/C~last~{RIGHT}   Copies the contents of the current cell to the cell named *last*, then moves the cell pointer to the right. Both *first* and *last* are within the body of the macro and will be concatenated into the range named *label* in a later step.

/C~street~{RIGHT}   Copies the contents of the current cell to the cell named *street* and moves the cell pointer to the right — *street* is within the range named *label*.

/C~city~{RIGHT}   Copies the current cell to *city*, and moves the cell pointer right.

/C~st~{RIGHT}   Copies the current cell to *st* and moves right.

/C~zip~{GOTO}label~   Copies the current cell to *zip* and sends the cell pointer to the first cell of the range named *label*. By now the next cell of the macro (*first*) contains the first name of the first address in the database. The macro types it in the control panel. The cell between *first* and *last* contains a single space, which the macro types after the first name in the control panel. Then it types the last name contained in the next cell.

{DOWN}{DOWN}   Moves the cell pointer down twice, entering the concatenated first and last names into the first cell of *label*. By now the next five cells of the macro contain the city, a comma and space, the state, three spaces, and the zip code, respectively. The macro concatenates these into the control panel.

~/PPGQ{GOTO}here~   Enters the concatenated city, state, and zip code into the third cell of *label*, prints *label*, and sends the cell pointer to the range named *here* — the first cell of the record in the database that the macro just printed as an address label.

/RNDhere~{DOWN}/XGloop~   Deletes the range name *here*, moves the cell pointer down, and transfers control of the macro to the cell named *loop*. The macro assigns *here* as the name for the first cell of this next record in the database, moves across the record copying the entries into the appropriate cells on the worksheet, prints the range named *label*, and so on, until it reaches the end of the database. At that point it copies blank cells into the macro and stops when it tries to process the cell named *first*.

FINAL CONSIDERATIONS

This macro fails if your database contains either blank cells or numeric entries. Just as the macro stops when it finds the end of the database, so will it stop if it copies a blank cell into any of the cells named *first*, *last*, *city*, *st*, or *zip*.

If you wish to leave a field in a record blank, enter a label-prefix character in the cell and your macro won't fail. Likewise, when you enter a number into your database, precede it with a label prefix or the macro won't be able to process it. *1-2-3* helps you remember to do this because it rejects number/label combinations, such as *615 East State St,* that aren't preceded with a label prefix. Likewise, when you enter a zip code that begins with zero, if you omit the label prefix, *1-2-3* removes the leading zero. Any zip code not entered as a label will stop the macro before it reaches the end of the database.

MOVING RANGE NAMES

Have you ever written a macro that moves a range name around the worksheet? A moving range name typically keeps track of a point to which you'd like the cell pointer to return after a macro routine finishes running. Sometimes you use a moving range name to test values in a column or row until your macro finds a particular value. In any case, moving range names can be dangerous.

When you assign a range name to a cell referenced by formulas in other cells, those formulas become "attached" to the range name. If you use the Range Name Create command to move the range name, the formulas adjust so that they also refer to the new cell. This is devastating if you move a range name down a column whose entries are used in rowwise sums. When the range name reaches the bottom of the column, all the sums refer to one cell.

To avoid problems with moving range names, delete range names before reassigning them. When moving the range name *here*, instead of using the command sequence /RNChere~ {BS}~, use the command sequence /RNDhere~/RNChere~ ~.

NOTES FOR RELEASE 2/2.01 USERS

Concatenation in *1-2-3* Release 2/2.01 is as easy as numeric addition. To concatenate labels, you use the ampersand (&) as the operator in a formula. For example, cell A3 in the following worksheet contains the formula +A1&B1:

	A	B	C
1	Jean	Chung	
2			
3	JeanChung		

To concatenate specific characters into a label, enclose the characters in quotation marks. The value of the formula in A3 becomes *Jean Chung* if you rewrite the formula to read +A1&" "&B1.

Release 2/2.01's ability to use formulas to concatenate labels reduces the effort of writing a mailing-label generator. The following macro produces mailing labels from the database presented at the beginning of this column.

	A	B	C	D
1	\l	/PPOOUQRlabel~AQ		
2	loop	{IF @CELLPOINTER("type")="b"}{QUIT}		
3		/C{RIGHT 5}~first~		
4		{RECALC label}		
5		/PPGQ{DOWN}		
6		{BRANCH loop}		

Enter the macro above the database as shown, and assign range names as indicated by the labels in column A. Then copy the database field headers into the third row above the top of the database; go to cell A17, press slash, select Copy, indicate cells A17..F17, press Return, move the cell pointer up three rows (to cell A14), and finish with Return. Assign these labels as range names to the cells directly below them; press slash and select Range Name Labels Down, then press End Right Return.

Go to G1 and set the column width to 40, then enter the following formula into the cell:

@S(first)&" "&@S(last)

Press the DownArrow key and then enter the following formula into cell G2:

@S(street)

Press DownArrow once more, and enter the following formula into cell G3:

@S(city)&", "&@S(st)&" "&@S(zip)

Use the @S function as shown to prevent blank cells from causing the formulas to equal ERR.

Now assign the range name *label* to cells G1..G9. Align the printhead of your printer with the line of the first label on which you want the address to begin. Move the cell pointer to the first field of the first record of the database and start the macro. Here's what happens:

/PPOOUQRlabel ~ AQ   Sets print options to unformatted (no margins or page breaks) and assigns *label* as the print range. *Label* is a nine-cell range containing the string formulas that will calculate each mailing address.

{IF @CELLPOINTER("type") = "b"}{QUIT}   Stops the macro if the current cell is blank. This happens when the macro finishes printing every record in the database (assuming each record includes an entry in the first field).

/C{RIGHT 5} ~ first~   Copies the current database record to the range starting with the cell named *first*. This puts each field entry into a named cell used by the formulas in the cell named *label*.

{RECALC label}   Recalculates the new values of the formulas in *label* based on the current database entry.

/PPGQ{DOWN}   Prints *label* and moves the cell pointer down to the next database record.

{BRANCH loop}   Sends control of the macro to the cell named *loop*. *Loop* determines whether or not the current cell is blank, stopping the macro if it is and passing control to the next cell if it isn't. The macro continues processing until it encounters a blank cell in the first column of the database (normally the end of the database).

FEBRUARY 1986

4

FOR SYMPHONY,
BUT NOT EXCLUSIVELY

This section is dedicated to the approximately 25% of *LOTUS* readers who use *Symphony* in addition to or instead of *1-2-3*. However, it also contains a couple of articles that are relevant to *1-2-3* as well. The section starts with some utilities that ease your way through *Symphony*'s SHEET, DOC, FORM, and COMM operating environments. The Learn mode, an automated method of creating macros, is presented, along with the details of using the Macro Library Manager — Hyperspace.

The chapter on hard-disk utilities doesn't assume a high level of knowledge about DOS, directories, and the mechanical workings of your fixed disk. Try this chapter, and if you run into unknown terms, check your DOS manual for a quick refresher.

The two chapters on multiple files contain ideas that users of both *1-2-3* and *Symphony* will find helpful. If you need to print several worksheets, combine information from different files, or split a large application into smaller parts, these articles help you understand and automate that process.

1

Utilities

These short, simple macros can speed up your everyday tasks.

BY DANIEL GASTEIGER

Despite the enormous power of the *Symphony* Command Language, one of the greatest uses for macros is in creating simple utilities. Utility macros perform tasks you repeat often while creating or working in your worksheet models. Utilities are generally short, simple macros that may be useful in many different models. In this chapter we present some utilities that even first-time *Symphony* users can put to work.

WORKSHEET UTILITIES

Some worksheet-related tasks are common to almost every model. For example, you probably often adjust the widths of individual columns. The following macro eliminates some of the keystrokes required to adjust column widths.

	A	B	C	D
1	\w	{MENU}WS		
2				

The macro itself is in cell B1. It is nothing more than a label representing the keystrokes you want *Symphony* to perform. The label in cell A1 represents the macro's name. When you enter this label, remember to type a label-prefix character (an apostrophe) before the backslash; otherwise, *Symphony* will repeat the letter *W* across the width of the cell. To assign \w as the macro's name, start with the cell pointer in cell A1. Press the MENU key, select Range Name Labels Right, and press Return. Use these commands to name all the macros in this column.

To run the macro, place the cell pointer in any cell of a column whose width you want to adjust; then hold down the MACRO key and press W. (*Symphony's* documentation identifies the MACRO key for your brand of computer.) The macro presses the MENU key and selects Width Set. You can either use the Arrow keys to adjust the width or type a number. In either case, finish the Width Set command by pressing Return.

Symphony Release 1.1/1.2 users can also use a variation of this macro. The following macro hides the current column:

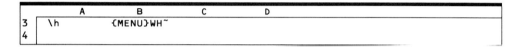

	A	B	C	D
3	\h	{MENU}WH~		
4				

Once you've entered and named this macro, you can hide any column with just two keystrokes; first point to the column, then hold down the MACRO key and press H. The macro simply presses MENU, selects Width Hide, and finishes with Return.

DATE UTILITIES

Sometimes you wish to keep track of your worksheet usage. For example, if you update a particular file once a week, it's useful to mark the file with the current date so that you don't accidentally enter the same data twice in a week.

The @NOW function reads your computer's built-in clock and generates a serial number that represents the current date and time. You can enter @NOW into a cell and set the method of recalculation to manual so that when you recalculate and save the worksheet, you preserve the serial number that represents the moment of recalculation.

You'll have more freedom if you use a macro that stores only the value of the @NOW function in the worksheet without the underlying @NOW formula. This way you can leave the recalculation method set to automatic. Whenever you update the file, you can run the macro before saving:

	A	B	C	D
5	\n	{LET date,@NOW}~		
6				
7	date			

This macro uses two named cells: \n is the name of the cell containing the macro's initial code, and *date* is the name of the cell that will hold the date serial number after you run the macro. You can assign both range names at once using the Range Name Labels Right command. To display the serial number as a recognizable date, give the cell named *date* a date format: point to *date*, press MENU, select Format Date 4, and press Return.

The macro doesn't need a tilde to work; the tilde simply forces *Symphony* to display the results of the macro. (*Symphony* doesn't update a worksheet after it processes a {LET} command until you try to do something else with the worksheet.) In other words, *date* will contain the current date when the macro is finished, but without a tilde, the date won't be displayed.

One tedious task associated with worksheet models is entering dates using the @DATE function. A simple macro to speed up the process follows:

	A	B	C	D
9	\d	@DATE({?})~		

The macro simply types *@DATE(* in the control panel and pauses. You type the year, a comma, the month, a comma, the day, and then press Return. The macro finishes the function by typing a closing parenthesis and pressing Return.

You may be used to the mixed-up format of *Symphony*'s @DATE function and still forget that you have to type the year first, then the month and day. The following macro lets you enter dates in a more familiar way:

	A	B	C	D
1	\d	@DATE({?},{?}){EDIT}		
2		{HOME}{RIGHT 6}{?}),~		
3		{MENU}FD4~		

When you use it, start by placing the pointer in the cell that will receive the date. Here's how it works:

@DATE({?},{?}){EDIT} Types *@DATE(* in the control panel and pauses. You type the desired month and press Return. The macro types a comma and pauses again. You type the desired day and press Return. The macro types a closing parenthesis and presses the EDIT key.

{HOME}{RIGHT 6}{?},~ Sends the cursor to the beginning of the entry in the control panel, then moves the cursor six characters to the right and pauses. This positions the cursor to place the year in the correct location in the @DATE function. You type the desired year and press Return. The macro types a comma and enters the finished function into the current cell.

{**MENU**}**FD4~**   Gives the current cell *Symphony*'s full international date format.

You can adapt this macro to speed up columnar data entry. Simply add the following line of commands as the last step:

{DOWN}{BRANCH \d}

This moves the cell pointer down and restarts the macro each time you press Return. When you've finished entering dates, stop the macro by pressing the Break key (Control-Break on IBM computers.) Clear the resulting error indicator by pressing Escape.

You may feel that pressing Return after typing the month and again after typing the day is not a natural way to enter dates. The following macro, suggested by Joe Yu of Lotus Development Corp., lets you enter dates in the familiar month/day/year format (for example, 3/15/86).

	A	B	C	D	E
1	\d	{GETLABEL "Enter date ",date}			
2		@DATEVALUE(date){CALC}~			
3		{MENU}FD4~			
4					
5	date	7/4/85			

Enter it as shown and assign the labels in column A as names for the adjacent cells of column B: select MENU Range Name Labels Right, indicate A1..A5, and press Return.

To use the macro, point to a blank cell, hold down the MACRO key, and press D. *Symphony* prompts for the date. Type the date as you are accustomed to seeing dates, 3/6/85, for example. *Symphony* enters the serial number for that date into the current cell.

You can modify this macro to enter dates in consecutive cells of the current column by entering the steps {DOWN}{BRANCH \d} into cell B4. Hold down the Control key and press Break to stop the macro when you've finished entering dates.

OTHER WORKSHEET UTILITIES

Worksheet utility macros abound. You can automate any routine task. For example, the macro on the next page converts all formulas in the current column — from the cell pointer down to the last column entry — into their current values. To run the macro, position the pointer in the first cell in the column you want to modify, then hold down the MACRO key and press V.

	A	B	C	D
21	\v	{MENU}RV{END}{PGDN}{END}{UP}~~		

The following simple macro erases the contents of the current cell, reducing your effort by one third. Just position the pointer in the cell you want to erase and invoke the macro.

	A	B	C	D
23	\e	{MENU}E~		

FORM WINDOW UTILITIES

Utilities aren't limited to use in the worksheet. You create macros on the worksheet, but you can use them in any window, with one caveat: A macro designed for use in one window may not work in another window. For example, if your macro presses the MENU key, it will work differently in each window type because each window type has its own menu. Let's look at a few FORM window utilities.

Once you've accumulated many entries in a database created using the FORM window's Generate command, you may want to locate a particular entry in a hurry. You generally know some, but not all, information about the record.

For example, an address database may include people's first and last names; the names of their companies; and their street addresses, cities, states, zip codes, and phone numbers. You could use this database when making sales calls. If you're contacting Biobonding Amalgamated, for example, your database could supply the name and phone number of your sales contact within that company.

To learn this information without a macro, you would begin in a FORM window. Press the MENU key and select Criteria Edit. Use an Arrowkey to move the cursor to the *Company Name* field, then type the first three or so letters of the name of the company you're seeking — in this case, *Bio* — following by an asterisk, and press Return. Press the Insert key, Escape, and select Use from the menu that appears. If any of your database records contain company names beginning with *Bio, Symphony* will display one, noting in the control panel how many matches it has found. You can page through the matching records until you find the one you want. To return to viewing the entire database, press MENU and select Criteria Ignore.

The following macros can speed up this process. To create them, begin with a worksheet containing a database, switch to a SHEET window (press the TYPE key and select SHEET), and find an empty space on the worksheet above and to the right of the database Definition range:

	A	B	C	D
25	\c	{MENU}CE{?}~{INSERT}		
26		{ESCAPE}U		
27				
28	\i	{MENU}CE{DELETE}Y		
29		{ESCAPE}I		

Once you've created the macros, switch back to a FORM window before using them. The first macro assigns a criterion to match. Start it by pressing MACRO-C. Here's what happens:

{MENU}CE{?}~{INSERT} Presses MENU and selects Criteria Edit, then pauses. You can move the cursor and type a single entry in the form that *Symphony* presents. When you press Return, the macro presses Return to finish your entry, and then presses the INSERT key.

{ESCAPE}U Presses Escape and selects Use from the menu that appears. This is so quick that you probably won't see it happen. *Symphony* presents the matching records. If there are no matches, *Symphony* beeps and ERROR flashes in the environment indicator in the top-right corner of the screen; clear the error by pressing Escape.

When you've finished viewing the matching records, run the second macro by pressing MACRO-I. Here's what happens:

{MENU}CE{DELETE}Y Presses MENU, selects Criteria Edit, presses the Delete key, and selects Y from the resulting menu. This deletes the criterion record.

{ESCAPE}I Presses Escape and selects Ignore from the resulting menu. This returns you to the standard FORM window, letting you view all the database records.

When you add new records to a database, *Symphony* places them after the existing records. If you prefer to keep your database alphabetized, set sort keys in your Database settings sheet and run the following macro when you finish entering data in the FORM window:

	A	B	C	D
31	\s	{MENU}RA		

If you prefer to change on a daily basis the field on which *Symphony* keys the sort order, you can use the following macro in the FORM window:

	A	B	C	D
33	\k	{MENU}SS1{?}~~Q		

This macro presses MENU and selects Settings Sort-Keys 1st-Key, then pauses while you indicate the column on which *Symphony* should base the sort order. You may have to press Escape once at this point to unanchor the cell pointer. When you press Return to signal that you've finished, the macro continues processing. It presses Return twice: once to enter the choice you've made, and again to indicate an ascending or descending sort order (*Symphony* uses ascending unless you indicate otherwise). Then the macro selects Quit to return to the FORM window.

THE COMM WINDOW

COMM window menus offer easy ways to telephone and log onto other computers, so utilities that perform these functions are not particularly useful. However, if you ever try to phone a popular bulletin board service that's busy all the time, you may want to use this macro:

	A	B	C	D	E
35	\p	{ONERROR again}			
36		{M}PC~			
37		{BEEP 1}{BEEP 2}			
38		{BEEP 3}{BEEP 4}			
39					
40	again	{WAIT @NOW+@TIME(0,5,0)}			
41		{BRANCH \p}			

Once you've prepared the Communications settings sheet, complete with the type of phone you're using and the phone number you wish to call, use this macro to make your connection. You must be in a COMM window when you run the macro. Here's how it works:

{ONERROR again} Begins error trapping. If an error occurs while the macro is running, *Symphony* will immediately start processing keystrokes in the cell named *again*.

{MENU}PC~ Presses MENU, selects Phone Call, and presses Return. *Symphony* dials the number you stored in the settings sheet and tries to connect with the computer at that number. If the bulletin board you're calling is in use (you receive a busy signal), an error results. The macro processes the routine named *again*. If

Symphony completes the connection, your computer produces four beeps of differing tones, alerting you that the macro succeeded. You can turn down the volume of your modem and do other work while your macro tries to make a connection.

{WAIT @NOW + @TIME($0,5,0$)}   Causes your macro to pause for five minutes. *Symphony* processes this code if an error has occurred. You can change the duration of the pause by replacing the 5 in the minutes position with another number. If you want less than a minute's pause between attempted phone calls, change the 5 to 0 and replace the rightmost 0 in the expression with the number of seconds of the desired pause.

{BRANCH \p}   Restarts the macro. *Symphony* once again tries to connect. The loop continues until the bulletin board is available.

MAY 1986

2

Word-Processing Macros Help Organize Files

Simplify your word-processing chores with macros
that print documents, set up DOC windows,
and create quick memo headers.

BY DANIEL GASTEIGER

I use *Symphony* for all my word processing, and I've found an effective way to save time and organize my files. Rather than save each document in a different file, I keep all related documents in one file. Memos are in a file called MEMO.WRK, letters are in LETTERS.WRK, and articles in ARTICLES.WRK. This arrangement has several advantages over the traditional one-document-per-file approach:

- I can easily refer to an old document while working on a new one.
- I can name a window for each document, giving myself a 13-character reminder instead of the 8 characters allowed on file names.
- If I forget the name of a document I'm trying to find, I can page through all my documents quickly by pressing the WINDOW key instead of retrieving each file.
- Most important, I can expedite my work by using a single collection of macros.

The collection of macros I use depends on the type of document a worksheet contains. Some macros are useful in almost any word-processing file. One macro sets up the word-processing area. When I start a new document, the macro opens a DOC window restricted to the first available empty column of the worksheet. With the worksheet column width set at 72, I can create one document per worksheet column until I run out of memory.

I have two printing macros. The first prints one copy of whatever is in the current window. The other asks how many copies of the document to print, then prints the required number.

Several of my word-processing macros consist of print attribute characters. They allow me to create underlined, italic, and boldface text. Finally, there is a macro in my MEMO file that creates standard memo headings.

SETTING UP THE WORKSHEET

To create this system, start in a blank SHEET window and set the default column width to 72 by pressing MENU and selecting Settings Width 72, then pressing Return and selecting Quit. Next use the MENU Width Set command to set the width of column A to 5 and the width of column B to 50. Column A will hold the macro names; column B will hold the macros themselves. Columns C through IV will hold documents as you create them.

Enter the following macro in columns A and B of the worksheet, starting in cell A1:

```
        A                    B
1   \n           {WINDOWSOFF}
2                {SERVICES}WC{?}~
3                D~RR{BS}{HOME}
4                {RIGHT col}
5                {TAB}{END}{DOWN}~Q
6                {HOME}
7                {LET col,col+1}
8                {WINDOWSON}
9
10  col                              2
```

This macro creates windows to hold new documents. Notice the range name *col* and the macro name *\n* in column A. Assign both names by putting the cell pointer in cell A1, pressing MENU, selecting Range Name Labels Right, then pressing End, PageDown, and Return. Before you run this macro for the first time, enter 2 in the cell named *col* (in this case, cell B10). Then you are ready to go. You can be in any window working on any document when you press MACRO-N, and the macro will prompt you for a window name and create a new window for you. Here's what happens step-by-step:

{WINDOWSOFF} Tells *Symphony* to stop "showing the action" of the windows. The screen remains static until the macro finds a {WINDOWSON} statement, even though the macro is making changes on the worksheet. This keeps the screen from flickering and speeds up the macro.

{SERVICES}WC{?}~ Presses the SERVICES key and selects Window Create. The {?} command halts the macro until you enter a window name that should describe the document you will place in the window. For instance, the name of the window holding this article is SYM WORD PROC. Type the name and press Return. Note that the {?} command "absorbs" the Return you press after typing the window name. Without the tilde (~), *Symphony* won't accept the name for the new window. Also be aware that *Symphony* lets you press any valid keys (such as Escape) while it pauses at a {?} command. If you back out of the menu by pressing the Escape key or decide not to create a window, don't press Return because doing so will "crash" the macro. Instead, hold down the Control key and press Break to stop the Macro, then clear the flashing ERROR indicator by pressing Escape.

D~RR{BS}{HOME} Tells *Symphony* to create a DOC window the same size as the current window. It then starts to set the Window Restrict range. When the macro selects RR (Restrict Range) from the menu, *Symphony* offers to assign the same Restrict range as that of the window in which you started the macro. {BS} (pressing the Backspace key) cancels that choice, and {HOME} sends the cell pointer to cell A1.

{RIGHT col} Moves the cell pointer to the right the number of times indicated in the cell named *col*. On the first run, *col* holds the number 2. Hence, the cell pointer moves to cell C1.

{TAB}{END}{DOWN}~Q Anchors the cell pointer, highlights the entire column as the Restrict range, and presses Return. It then quits the Window settings sheet.

{HOME} Sends the cursor to the home position in the new DOC window.

{LET col, col + 1} Increases the value of *col* by 1. The next time you run the macro, the {RIGHT col} command will move the cell pointer one more column to the right; the new column will be used as the Restrict range for the next window.

{WINDOWSON} Tells *Symphony* to start showing the action. The screen redraws, leaving you ready to start typing.

PRINTING FANCY TEXT

Because I often emphasize words and phrases in my memos and articles, I use the macros shown on the next page to save a few keystrokes.

The \b, \i, and \u macros each generate a marker that tells *Symphony* to print

	A	B
12	\b	▲ B
13		
14	\i	▲ I
15		
16	\u	▲ U
17		
18	\e	▼

whatever follows in bold, italic, or underlined text, respectively. Each consists of a begin-attribute character (▲), followed by the letter code of the desired attribute. The macro named \e types an end-attribute character (▼), which tells *Symphony* to stop using the current print attribute.

Normally you create a begin-attribute character by pressing the COMPOSE key and then pressing BA, or by holding down the Control key and pressing B. Macros can't push the COMPOSE or Control keys, so you have to include the attribute characters within the body of the macro. To write each of the begin-attribute macros, put the cell pointer on the appropriate cell, hold down the Control key and press B, then type the letter that corresponds to the attribute you wish the macro to produce, and press Return. To write the \e macro, go to the appropriate cell, press Control-E, and finish with Return. I use only bold, italic, and underlined attributes, although many others are available (see table). One other note: Not all printers or printer drivers can produce every print attribute. Experiment to determine which type styles your printer can produce.

Once you have entered these macros, you are ready to go. Whenever you are typing a document and want to emphasize some text, hold down the MACRO key and press the letter corresponding to the attribute type you want—for example, press MACRO-U to produce underlined text. Type the words you want emphasized, then press MACRO-E to indicate where you want the emphasis to end.

THE PRINT MACROS

I have two macros to handle printing. The one I use most often prints the current document:

	A	B
20	\p	{SERVICES}PAGPQ
21		

PRINT ATTRIBUTE TABLE

Code	Print Attribute
B	bold
I	italic
U	underlined
+	superscript
–	subscript
X	struck through
0	bold italic
1	bold underlined
2	bold italic underlined
3	italic underlined
4	bold superscript
5	italic superscript
6	bold subscript
7	italic subscript
8	bold italic subscript
9	bold italic superscript
S	applies attribute to everything, including spaces
Q	cancels attribute S

(S and Q are unaffected by begin- and end-attribute characters.)

When I press MACRO-P, the macro presses SERVICES and selects Print Align Go Page-Advance Quit. *Symphony* prints the current document as long as I am viewing it through a DOC window and have no print source defined on the Print settings sheet.

The following macro asks how many copies I want of the current document and then prints that many:

```
        A                          B
22 \c        {GETNUMBER "How many copies?",count}
23           {SERVICES}PA
24           {FOR inc,1,count,1,loop}
25           Q
26
27 loop      GPA{RETURN}
28 inc
29 count
```

The labels \c, *loop, inc,* and *count* are the names of cells to their right. Name them all at once by going to the cell containing \c, pressing MENU and selecting Range Name Labels Right, then pressing End, DownArrow, End, DownArrow, and Return. Align the paper in your printer. Then, from within any document window, press MACRO-C. This is what happens:

{GETNUMBER "How many copies?",count}   The prompt *How many copies?* appears in the control panel and the macro pauses until you press Return. *Symphony* stores your entry in the cell named *count.* If you enter a label instead of a number, you will discover a problem with *Symphony.* Instead of beeping and letting you fix the entry, *Symphony* stores the value ERR in *count.* This puts the macro in a permanent loop, and *Symphony* won't stop printing copies until you press Control-Break several times quickly. To clear the flashing ERROR indicator, press Escape. To compensate for this problem, add the following line right after the {GETNUMBER} command:

$$\{IF \ @ISERR(count)\}\{BEEP\}\{BRANCH \backslash c\}$$

{SERVICES}PA   Presses SERVICES and selects Print Align. This tells *Symphony* that the printhead of the printer is at the top of the page.

{FOR inc,1,count,1,loop}   Starts a loop. The macro performs the commands found in the cell named *loop* the number of times indicated in the cell named *count* before proceeding to the next step. The instructions in *loop* are GPA{RETURN} or Go Page-Advance Align {RETURN}. Go causes a copy of the document to print, Page-Advance causes paper to eject to the top of a new page, Align resets the page counter, and {RETURN} marks the end of the loop — the macro continues processing the {FOR} statement.

Q   Selects Quit from the print menu and returns *Symphony* to Ready mode.

QUICK MEMO HEADERS

I wrote the following macro for a friend, and now I use it regularly:

	A	B
31	\m	M E M O~~~
32		{?}~~~
33		TO: {?}~
34		FROM: {?}~
35		SUBJECT: ▲ B{?}▼~~
36		

After running the \n macro described earlier, you will be faced with a blank DOC window with the cursor in the top-left corner. Run the \m macro, and here's what happens:

M E M O~ ~ ~   Types M E M O and presses three Returns.

{?}~ ~ ~   Waits for you to type the date and press Return, then presses Return three times.

TO: **{?}**~   Types TO: and waits for you to type the name of the addressee, then presses Return.

FROM: **{?}**~   Types FROM: and waits for you to type your name.

SUBJECT:▲**B{?}**▼~ ~   Types SUBJECT: and the begin-attribute character, followed by a B (for boldface), or you may want to use U (for underline) if your printer cannot print boldface text. It pauses for you to enter the subject of the memo, then it types the end-attribute character and presses Return twice. You are now free to type the body of your memo.

Try putting together a worksheet using these macros and save it. Call it up when you want to do word processing, and save it under a different name. When your working file takes up too much memory, retrieve the blank version, use it, then save with a different file name. You will be surprised at how many documents you can create in one file.

JUNE 1985

3

Learn Mode

We take a quick look at Learn mode.

BY DANIEL GASTEIGER

Imagine you're involved in a project that requires you to repeat the same set of keystrokes until you're overcome with boredom. For example, your worksheet contains 100 columns of data in contiguous rows. You want to assign currency and percent formats to alternate columns: currency to the first column, percent to the next, then currency, and so on.

You can format each column individually, or you can write a macro to do it for you. If you decide to write a macro, you can write the macro from scratch, or you can have *Symphony*'s Learn mode create most of the macro for you.

Symphony's Learn mode is like a keystroke tape recorder. As you work with *Symphony*, Learn mode records onto the worksheet every keystroke you make. Once you assign a range name to the range containing the recording (or to the first cell of that range), you can make *Symphony* "play back" the recorded keystrokes.

USING LEARN MODE

To continue our example, fill a 20-row by 16- column range with arbitrary data; to do this, press MENU, select Range Fill, indicate range A2..P21, and press Return four times. Now select an empty area of the worksheet to use as the recording area or Learn range. This area should be many tens of rows deep. For maximum flexibility, use an entire column containing no entries. Select SERVICES Settings Learn Range, indicate the column that will serve as the recording area (for this example, indicate range R1..R8192), press Return, and select Quit Quit.

You're ready to record. Move the cell pointer to the top of the first column you want to format (A2) and press the LEARN key. *Symphony* lights the Learn indicator at the bottom of your screen. Do exactly what you would do to format the first two columns of data, indicating ranges only by pointing. Then leave yourself ready to format the third column. Here is the procedure:

Select MENU Format Currency 0, press Return, and press End DownArrow Return. Press RightArrow MENU, select Format % 0, press Return, and press End DownArrow Return. Finally, press RightArrow. Now press the LEARN key to turn off Learn mode. *Symphony* has recorded your keystrokes beginning in cell R1.

Assign the name \f (or any other single letter) to cell R1: select MENU Range Name Create, enter \f, and enter *r1*. You've created a macro. If you've followed these instructions exactly, your cell pointer is now on cell C2. Hold down the MACRO key and press F. *Symphony* assigns a currency format with no decimal places to column C and a percent format with no decimal places to column D, finally leaving the cell pointer at the top of column E. Run the macro several times to format the remaining columns of data.

The macro that *Symphony* creates in Learn mode is a collection of labels on the worksheet, just like any macro you create. You can edit the macro as you would any of your own.

LEARN MODE PITFALLS

Learn mode can save time as you create simple macros because it stores keystrokes exactly as you make them. For the most part, you needn't debug Learn mode macros because they repeat whatever process you've already performed manually. There are, however, some pitfalls.

Macros that involve pointing don't always do what you have in mind. Let's say you use a Learn mode macro to create formulas in column D of the worksheet. As you create the formulas for the first time, you move the cell pointer to columns A, B, and C several times. When you replay the recorded keystrokes, *Symphony* tries to move the cell pointer to the left as many columns as you did originally. You will have problems if you then run the Learn mode macro starting with the cell pointer in column A, B, or C. The pointer will hit the worksheet's left border when enough {LEFT} commands are processed.

A second Learn mode pitfall is that it encourages users to create useless macros. Avoiding this pitfall requires only a little common sense: Why write a macro that creates a model when you have to build the model to create the macro? If your Learn mode macro re-creates a worksheet that you use often, do away with the macro. Simply save a copy of the model that the macro creates. Retrieving a finished model is quicker than retrieving and running a macro that builds the model.

These pitfalls are minor compared to the benefit you get from Learn mode. Creating simple macros is a breeze when you let *Symphony* do most of the work for you. However, I'm not a fan of Learn mode because I'm a sloppy typist. Learn mode records every keystroke you make. If you're as sloppy as I am, your Learn mode macros will be rife with {BACKSPACE} and {ESCAPE} commands (Learn mode doesn't use the abbreviations {BS} and {ESC}). You might take as long editing out the superfluous commands as you would writing the macros in the first place.

OCTOBER 1986

4

Jump into Hyperspace: The Symphony Macro Library Manager

This *Symphony* Add-In lets you create off-the-sheet macros that retrieve files, erase worksheets, and pass data from one worksheet to another.

BY DANIEL GASTEIGER

Symphony Release 1.1/1.2's Macro Library Manager adds an exciting dimension to macro writing. With the Macro Library Manager, nicknamed Hyperspace at Lotus, you can create macros to be used on any worksheet, at any time, without copying them from one worksheet to another. A macro in Hyperspace can perform almost any task you can perform via the keyboard, including starting new worksheets from scratch and retrieving files from disk. Here, we look at Hyperspace with some considerations for both the beginning and the advanced user.

AN OVERVIEW

The Macro Library Manager is an Add-In application that comes with *Symphony* Release 1.1/1.2. You can use Hyperspace by putting the Help and Tutorial Disk in drive A on a two-disk system or by copying it into the directory containing your *Symphony* program files on a hard-disk system—the latter happens automatically when you follow the install instructions in the *Symphony* documentation. Once in *Symphony*, you press SERVICES and select Application Attach, point to MACROMGR.APP, and press Return. You can then either invoke Hyperspace from the Applications menu or select Macros from the SERVICES menu to gain access to the Macro Library Manager's commands.

Three of the commands are particularly significant. One menu choice, Save, allows you to indicate any range on the worksheet to send to Hyperspace. The range is saved on disk as a file with an MLB extension. Also, a copy of the range is placed in RAM, independent of the worksheet (into the proverbial hyperspace). Finally, all the data (numbers, labels, formulas, and range names) contained in the range vanish from the worksheet.

Another command, Edit, brings a copy of a library into the worksheet from Hyperspace. If you have sent a range into Hyperspace with the SERVICES Macros Save command (or with SERVICES Macros Load, which we'll get to in a minute), you can get a copy of it back by using the SERVICES Macros Edit command. This allows you to make changes to the library. The changes must once again be saved via SERVICES Macros Save.

SERVICES Macros Load copies a macro library from disk directly to Hyperspace. You use Macros Load at the beginning of a session to gain access to a library that you created and saved during a previous session.

HOW DOES A LIBRARY WORK?

Having a macro library in Hyperspace is like having two worksheets in memory at once. The Symphony worksheet remains 8,192 rows by 256 columns, while you can create macro libraries consisting of any range of rows or columns containing up to 16,376 cells.

Here are some rules for using Hyperspace:

- All formulas can refer only to the library or worksheet in which they are contained. Formulas on a *Symphony* worksheet cannot refer to data in a Hyperspace library, nor can formulas in Hyperspace refer to data on a *Symphony* worksheet.
- You can pass data between libraries and the worksheet by using macro command keywords such as {LET} and {PUT}.
- A Hyperspace library has no cell coordinates. Because of this, any data in Hyperspace that you wish a macro to be able to use must be contained in named ranges.
- While processing, a macro looks for range names used in bracketed command statements, first on the worksheet, then in libraries in Hyperspace. If a range name isn't on the worksheet, the macro looks for it in the library that was loaded into Hyperspace earliest in your current work session. If the range name isn't in that library, the macro looks for it in the second earliest loaded library, and so on until the named range is found. If the macro fails to find the named range on

either the worksheet or any of the libraries in memory, it stops and displays an *Invalid range...* error message. This search order allows you to use the same range name in every library you create, as well as on the current worksheet. When the macro processes, it uses only the first occurrence of a range name that it finds along the described path. For example, if you have one library in Hyperspace and a range name occurs both on the worksheet and in the library, the macro uses the range on the worksheet.

▪ You can have up to ten macro libraries in Hyperspace at a time.

SOME EXAMPLES

1. Formulas can refer to only the worksheet or library in which they are contained. Therefore, if you placed the range A1..B3 of the following worksheet into Hyperspace, the formula it contains would be meaningless (it would evaluate to zero).

	A	B	C	D
1	@SUM(C1..D3)		1	2
2			2	2
3			3	1

For the formula to evaluate properly, the entire range A1..D3 must be contained in the same library.

2. Any data in Hyperspace that you wish a macro to be able to use must be contained in named ranges. In the following worksheet, cell B1 is named \m and cell B4 is named *number*. If you place the range A1...B4 into Hyperspace and run the macro (by pressing MACRO-M), the macro places a zero in cell A1 and an eight in cell A2. Remember that once you place A1..B4 in Hyperspace using the SERVICES Macros Save command, that portion of the worksheet will be blank:

	A	B
1	\m	{LET a1,a4}
2		{LET a2,number}
3		
4	number	8

Here's how it works:

{LET a1,a4}   Puts the value found in cell A4 into cell A1. Since a Hyperspace library has no cell coordinates, *Symphony* finds A1 and A4 on the worksheet when it evaluates this expression.

{LET a2,number} Puts the value found in the cell named *number* into cell A2. Since *number* is a named range in Hyperspace, *Symphony* can find it in the library and place the value it contains in cell A2.

3. You can pass data between libraries and the worksheet by using macro command keywords such as {LET} and {PUT}. In this example, cell B1 is named \m, and cell B4 is named *number*. If you send the range A1..B4 into Hyperspace and run the macro by pressing MACRO-M, cell A1 on the worksheet receives the value eight, but cell A2 receives a meaningless formula. When the macro finishes, *Symphony* is in edit mode because it can't find the range named *number* anywhere on the worksheet.

	A	B
1	\m	{LET a1,number}
2		{GOTO}a2~+number~
3		
4	number	8

DO I WANT TO USE HYPERSPACE?

Everyone who uses utility macros can benefit from Hyperspace. Utilities are short macros that help speed things up as you design worksheet models. Many people create their own collection of utilities. Rather than create a dummy worksheet from which to start all other worksheets, you can place all your utilities into macro libraries. When you start *Symphony*, simply load the libraries into Hyperspace, and all your utilities are available from any worksheet. You don't have to worry about where to start building an application, because its location won't interfere with the macros in Hyperspace.

If you design macro-driven worksheet applications for other people, Hyperspace can make your job easier. You can lock libraries as you create them so that only people knowing the password can view them using the SERVICES Macros Edit command. This lets you protect both your macros and your sensitive data from unauthorized alterations, with one special consideration: Data within named ranges in a macro library can be obliterated by carelessly written (or carefully written, depending on the intent of the user) macros. Here's how this works:

You create a macro library containing both a table named *table* and a macro that uses the table in @VLOOKUP and @INDEX functions to place values on the worksheet. Let's say an unwary user in your department creates a Hyperspace macro library that also contains a table named *table* and a macro that puts data into the table using {GETNUMBER} and {PUT} statements. When the user loads your library into Hyperspace, followed by his library, then runs his macro, the {PUT} statements in his macro alter the table in the library you created. If his macro deals with large amounts of data, he may spend hours updating the wrong table before discovering the error. Fortunately, with the library locked, there's no way for your coworker to save the changes he has made to your table, and he can retrieve the original data using SERVICES Macros Load.

Similarly, anything within a named range in Hyperspace should be considered accessible information to anyone with a little macro savvy. Your coworker, learning that the Hyperspace library you have supplied contains a table named *table*, can write a macro using {LET} statements and the @INDEX function to examine the data in the table.

To help users avoid problems with conflicting range names in Hyperspace libraries, the Macro Library Manager includes the Macros Name-List command. This works like the Menu Range Name Table command in the *Symphony* SHEET window, but it produces only a list of the range names in a particular library (remember that libraries contain no cell coordinates). When you create a new macro library, you can begin by loading other libraries you'll be using with the new one and creating a name list for each library. Then you'll know which names to avoid using in the new library.

GETTING HYPERSPACE TO TAKE CONTROL

When you write an application for other people to use, you'll probably want a macro to start running automatically when the worksheet is loaded. To do this, press SERVICES and select Settings Auto-Execute Set, then either point to the first cell of the desired macro or type the name of the macro and press Return. Save the worksheet; the next time you retrieve it, the macro will begin running as soon as it is loaded.

Making a macro in a Hyperspace library start automatically requires more elaborate preparation. First attach Hyperspace to *Symphony*. If you are using a hard disk, you copied Hyperspace onto it when you installed *Symphony*. To make Hyperspace available on a two-disk system, insert the Help and Tutorial Disk in drive A. In either case, press SERVICES and select Application Attach. Then point to MACROMGR.APP and press Return.

Now create the following macro:

	A	B	C	D
1	{SERVICES}MLstartup~Y{ESCAPE}			
2	{BRANCH applic}			

Here, *startup* is the name of the library that contains the macro, and *applic* is the name of the macro in the library. Press SERVICES, select Settings Auto-Execute Set, point to cell A1, and press Return. Finally, save the worksheet. Whenever you have attached the Macro Library Manager and you retrieve this worksheet, here's what happens:

{**SERVICES**}**MLstartup~Y**{**ESCAPE**}   Presses SERVICES and selects Macros Load, then enters *startup* as the name of the library to load from disk into Hyperspace. If a copy of *startup* already exists in Hyperspace, it is replaced by the copy on disk.

{**BRANCH applic**}   Sends the macro looking for keystrokes to the cell named *applic*. Since *applic* is not on the worksheet, *Symphony* looks for it in Hyperspace and, finding it there, continues processing that macro. A good first command to use in *applic* is {SERVICES}NY, which erases the current worksheet, leaving the macro to run unfettered.

JULY 1985

5

Hard-Disk Utilities

Use macros to manage the directories on your hard disk.

BY DANIEL GASTEIGER

Having a hard-disk system is like building a small library onto your personal study. You have ample space to store information, a convenient cataloging mechanism, and room, should the need arise, for other users to store and browse through information.

But as you add more files and directories to your hard disk, finding specific information becomes more difficult. When the subdirectories of your subdirectories have subdirectories, you can get lost looking around for files. And even when you keep your directory structure simple, you can end up with more directory names than you really need. You compound problems when several users share a single hard-disk system.

In this article, we'll discuss some macros that you can use to navigate the directories on your hard disk.

THE IDEAL DISK MANAGER

Many users store worksheet files in several subdirectories of their hard disks. Some people put their correspondence in one directory, their reports in another, special projects in a third, personal files in a fourth, and so on. Other users share a hard disk within their work groups, and each group member has a separate directory in which to store worksheets.

If, for whatever reason, your hard disk contains more than one data directory, you probably don't start every worksheet session intending to work from the same directory. It would be useful if a directory manager could take control automatically when you start *Symphony* and give you a chance to select the desired directory.

Ideally, a directory manager should be available to provide easy access to any directory — without complicating *Symphony*'s simple procedure for changing directories. This manager should know what directories exist on the disk and should be easy to update when you create new directories or delete old ones. We'll try to satisfy these requirements as we design macros that manage hard-disk directories.

A SIMPLE MANAGER

To begin, let's create a short macro. In an empty worksheet, enter labels as shown in the illustration at the bottom of the page.

We've set the column widths in our illustration to reveal the contents of each cell in the macro. You needn't adjust your column widths at all. Simply enter the labels shown and remember to start with an apostrophe label prefix when you make an entry that begins with a backslash. Also, replace the path names used in rows 3 and 6 of the illustration with path names appropriate for your hard disk. For example, if your hard disk has a directory named JEAN, replace the word REPORTS in cells D3 and D6 with JEAN.

Finally, assign range names to cells B1 and B3: Press MENU, select Range Name Labels Right, indicate A1..A3, and press Return. Your macro is ready to run. Hold down the MACRO key and press D. *Symphony* displays a menu of available directory path names. Point to the name of the directory you wish to use and press Return; *Symphony* makes the selected directory current. Because several items in the menu begin with a backslash character, you should make selections only by pointing and pressing Return. If you type a backslash while *Symphony* displays the menu, you select the leftmost menu choice that begins with a backslash (which happens to be \ in this example).

	A	B	C	D	E
1	\d	{MENUBRANCH dirm}			
2					
3	dirm	\	\sym	\reports	\sym\graph
4		Use root directory	Change directory	Change directory	Change directory
5		{S}FD{ESC}	{S}FD{ESC}	{S}FD{ESC}	{S}FD{ESC}
6		\~	\sym~	\reports~	\sym\graph~

WHAT'S GOING ON?

The macro we've created generates a user-defined menu based on information stored in the worksheet. The macro's first command, {MENUBRANCH dirm}, means "use the instructions that begin in the cell named *dirm* to create a menu in the control panel."

The menu instructions consist of two rows of labels. The first row (B3..E3) represents the short prompts of the menu — the individual menu selections. The second row of instructions (B4..E4) represents the menu's long prompts. These are the extra bits of information about a selection that appear when you point to the selection's short prompt on the actual menu.

When the macro displays the menu in the control panel, you can make a selection by highlighting the desired choice and pressing Return. When you make a selection, the macro continues processing commands that appear in the cell directly beneath the selection's long prompt in the menu instructions. For example, when you select \REPORTS from the menu in this example, the macro continues processing commands in cell D5.

The commands in cell D5 are {S}FD{ESC}. These mean "press SERVICES, select File Directory, and press Escape." At this point *Symphony* is ready to receive the path name of the directory you wish to make current. The macro processes the keystrokes in cell D6 and enters REPORTS as the new path name. *Symphony* processes a similar set of commands for whichever menu selection you make.

This macro has three limitations. The first is the minor annoyance that you are the disk manager's manager. When you add or delete a directory from the hard disk, you also must update the macro to account for the change. Life would be easier if the macro could update itself when you change the directory structure of your hard disk.

The macro's second limitation is in its use of the {MENUBRANCH} command. A user-defined menu can contain no more than eight selections. With nine directories or more, this macro becomes obsolete.

The third limitation is its worksheet dependency. In its present form, this macro works only within the current worksheet. When you retrieve a different file or start a new file, you'll no longer be able to change directories with just a few keystrokes. We can overcome this limitation by putting the directory macro into Hyperspace.

MAKING THE JUMP

Hyperspace is better known as the *Symphony* Macro Library Manager — an add-in utility that lets you store macros in your computer's RAM but not on the worksheet. The macros remain in memory even when you retrieve a worksheet or erase the current worksheet.

Assuming you use Release 1.1 or 1.2 of *Symphony*, you copied the Hyperspace program file onto your hard disk along with the rest of the program's files. To use Hyperspace, first attach it to *Symphony*: Press SERVICES, select Application Attach, point to the item MACROMGR.APP, press Return, and select Quit. This adds the selection Macros to the SERVICES menu.

Now put your directory-menu macro into a Hyperspace library: Press SERVICES, select Macros Save, enter a file name — say, DIRECT — indicate range A1..E6, press Return, and select No. The macro disappears from the worksheet.

Symphony saves a copy of the macro on disk and writes a copy in RAM. To run the macro, simply hold down the MACRO key and press D, just as you did when the macro resided on the worksheet. You can run the macro from within any worksheet as long as the worksheet does not contain a range named \d.

THE NINTH DIRECTORY

Going beyond the eight-item limit of *Symphony*'s user-defined menus is not easy to do with a Hyperspace macro. Let's start with a macro on the worksheet, then adapt it for use in Hyperspace.

Start with a blank worksheet and enter labels as shown in the following illustration, substituting your own list of directory path names for the list that begins in cell B8:

```
        A          B          C          D          E          F
1   \c            {END}{PGDN}{GOTO}paths~{?}
2                 {LET newdir,@CELLPOINTER("contents")}
3                 {SERVICES}FD{ESC}{newdir}~
4
5   newdir
6
7
8   paths         \
9                 \Thelma
10                \Wesley         Point to your
11                \Butch          directory's name
12                \Agnes          and press Return.
13                \Wilma
14                \Gordy
15                \Symphony
16                \Symphony\graphs
```

Assign the labels in column A as range names for the adjacent cells of column B: Press MENU, select Range Name Labels Right, indicate range A1..A8, and press Return. When you start the macro by pressing MACRO-C, here's what happens:

{END}{PGDN}{GOTO}paths~{?} Presses the End key followed by the PageDown key, then presses GOTO, enters *paths* as the target address, and pauses. These commands send the cell pointer to the bottom of the worksheet and then back to the first cell in the list of path names. Sending the cell pointer off-screen ensures that the display will show both the top of the path-name list and the message entered in column D when the macro pauses. While the macro pauses, you can use the Arrow keys to move the cell pointer around on the worksheet.

   {LET newdir,@CELLPOINTER("contents")}   Places a copy of the contents of the current cell into the cell named *newdir*.

   {SERVICES}FD{ESC}{newdir}~   Presses SERVICES, selects File Directory, presses Escape, calls *newdir* as a subroutine, and presses Return. When your macro calls the subroutine named *newdir, Symphony* is ready to accept a path-name specification. Because the previous macro step copied your selected path name into *newdir*, calling *newdir* as a subroutine types your selected path name into the control panel. The tilde finishes the entry.

   A macro of this type can handle as many directories as you can create on your hard disk, but the macro is worksheet-dependent. You can't pop the macro into Hyperspace and expect it to perform as intended because you can't point to cell entries that are stored in Hyperspace. If you're willing to trade a full-screen display of available path names for a line-by-line display, you can write a similar macro that works in Hyperspace and so is available for use with every worksheet.

A HYPERSPACE UTILITY

If you wish to save the work you've done so far, do so, then erase everything from the worksheet but the list of path names. Delete all the range names (MENU Range Name Reset Yes), and move the list of path names to cell A1: Press MENU, select Move, indicate the range holding the list (B8..B16 in our model), and press Return Home Return.

   Enter labels as shown in the following illustration, omitting, for now, the contents of cell E12:

   Assign the labels in column D as range names for the adjacent cells of column E: Press MENU, select Range Name Labels Right, indicate D1..D16, and press Return. Assign the name *paths* to the range that contains the list of your disk's path names: Press MENU, select Range Name Create, enter *paths*, indicate the range (A1..A9 in our model), and press Return. Assign the name *block* to range E11..E12. Finally, enter the formula @INDEX(paths,0,row) into the cell named *form* (E12).

   Put the macro, including the list of path names, into Hyperspace: Press SERVICES, select Macros Save, and enter a file name — DIRS. Then indicate range A1..E17 (if your list of path names is longer than ours, make sure that the range you specify encompasses the entire list), press Return, and select No. Once again, the macro disappears from the worksheet. To run the macro, press MACRO-M.

   When you start the macro, the first path name in the list appears in the control panel. When you press the DownArrow or UpArrow key, *Symphony* displays a

```
          D          E         F         G         H
 1  \m            {form}
 2                {GET stroke}
 3                {IF stroke="~"}{BRANCH select}
 4                {IF stroke="{ESCAPE}"}{ESC}{QUIT}
 5                {IF stroke="{DOWN}"}{LET row,row-1}
 6                {IF stroke="{UP}"}{LET row,row+1}
 7                {IF row=-1}{LET row,@ROWS(paths)-1}
 8                {IF row=@ROWS(paths)}{LET row,0}
 9                {ESC}{RECALC block}{BRANCH \m}
10
11  row
12  form          \
13
14  stroke
15
16  select        {ESC}
17                {SERVICES}FD{ESC}{form}~
```

different path name in the control panel. To make a directory current, press UpArrow or DownArrow until the path name is visible, then press Return. If you decide not to change directories, simply press Escape. Here's how the macro works:

{form} Calls the subroutine named *form*. *Form* contains a formula that returns a path name from the list of path names. At this point, *form* returns the first name in the list. *Symphony* types that name in the control panel.

{GET stroke} Causes the macro to pause until you press a key, then stores a label representation of the keystroke in the cell named *stroke*.

{IF stroke = "~"}{BRANCH select} Determines whether the content of *stroke* is a tilde. If *stroke* contains a tilde, the macro continues processing commands in the cell named *select*; otherwise, control of the macro passes to the next cell.

{IF stroke = "{ESCAPE}"}{ESC}{QUIT} Presses Escape and stops the macro if you've pressed the Escape key.

{IF stroke = "{DOWN}"}{LET row,row–1} Decreases the value of the cell named *row* if you've pressed the DownArrow key.

{IF stroke = "{UP}"}{LET row,row + 1} Increases the value of the cell named *row* if you've pressed the UpArrow key.

{IF row = –1}{LET row,@ROWS(paths)–1} Prevents the value of *row* from dropping below 0. *Row* is a counter used in the @INDEX formula to keep track of which path name from the list is displayed in the control panel. When *row* equals 0, *Symphony* displays the first path name. When *row* equals 3, *Symphony* displays the fourth path name, and so on. If the value of *row* dropped below 0, the @INDEX formula would return ERR.

{IF row = @ROWS(paths)}{LET row,0} Prevents the value of *row* from exceeding the number of entries in *paths*.

{ESC}{RECALC block}{BRANCH \m} Presses Escape to clear the control panel, updates the range named *block* so that *form* returns a new path name (assuming you've pressed UpArrow or DownArrow), and restarts the macro. The macro types the new label from *form* into the control panel, pauses to intercept your keystroke, and so on until you press Return or Escape.

As stated earlier, if you press Return while the macro is running, control of the macro transfers to the cell named *select*.

{ESC} Presses Escape to clear the path name displayed in the control panel.

{SERVICES}FD{ESC}{form}~ Presses SERVICES, selects File Directory, presses Escape to clear the existing directory specification, calls the subroutine *form*, and presses Return to enter the selected path name in response to *Symphony*'s prompt.

JUNE 1987

6

Multiple Files

Printing several worksheets and combining data from different sources are easy with macros.

BY DANIEL GASTEIGER

If you use *Symphony* regularly, you probably have more than one worksheet file. Most likely you have many files containing different financial models, reports, databases, and other applications. Often the data in one file is similar to the data in another file. Other times a single file gets so large that it becomes unmanageable, and you divide it into smaller files. In either case you may want to manipulate information from several different files.

With a little planning you can write macros that automatically print reports from several files or that combine data from different files to generate cumulative totals. In this chapter we'll look at ways to print the contents of several different files.

PRINTING FROM SEVERAL WORKSHEETS

Have you ever written several letters, each in its own worksheet, and finally gotten around to printing them out? It's pretty frustrating to retrieve a file, print it, retrieve another file, print it, and so on. Before you face this situation again, consider the following. (Users of *Symphony* Release 1.1/1.2 and higher should also refer to the "Macros in Hyperspace" note at the end of the article.)

A few factors contribute to the success of a macro that works with data from different worksheets. The data contained in each file should be similar and should be arranged in a standard format. These restrictions ensure that a macro can find needed data in each accessed file.

The names you assign to the files your macro will use can play a part in how you design your macro. If, for example, you intend to print sequentially 20 memos from 20 different files, you could assign file names such as MEMO1, MEMO2, MEMO3, and so on. Your macro could then use a counting mechanism such as a {FOR} command to keep track of which files to print. Alternatively, when you're working with sales data divided by state into separate files, the file names might be quite dissimilar. Your macro will have to rely on a different file-management scheme.

Let's say you've written 20 memos in 20 different files. Each memo is in a DOC window starting in cell A1 of the worksheet. You've assigned sequentially numbered names to the files as you saved them so that each is named with three letters — standing for July — followed by a number: JUL1, JUL2, JUL3, and so on. To print the files automatically, create a worksheet as follows.

In a blank worksheet create a DOC window restricted to the first eight columns. To do this, press SERVICES and select Window Create. Then enter a name for the new window — call this one MEMOS. Select DOC and press Return to accept the current window size as the size for the new window, then select Restrict Range, indicate range A1..H8192, and press Return. Finally, select Quit; *Symphony* presents you with a blank DOC window.

Press the WINDOW key to make the original SHEET window current and enter the following macro as shown in columns J and K, omitting for now the entry in cell K10:

```
       J            K         L        M        N        O
 1  flnm
 2  cnt
 3
 4  \p           {ONERROR stop}{BLANK cnt}
 5               {SERVICES}WUmemos~{HOME}
 6               {GETLABEL "Enter common characters: ",flnm}
 7  loop         {ERASE}{END}{HOME}
 8               {LET cnt,cnt+1}
 9               {RECALC next}
10  next            ERR
11               {SERVICES}PAGPQ
12               {BRANCH loop}
13
14  stop         {BEEP 1}{BEEP 2}{BEEP 3}
```

Assign the labels in column J as range names for the cells to their right; to do this, press MENU, select Range Name Labels Right, indicate range J1..J14, and press Return. Now enter the following formula in the cell named *next* (K10):

+ ''{SERVICES}FCCEIF''&flnm&@STRING(cnt,∅)&''~ ''

The cell displays ERR when you enter the formula but will change while the macro runs to equal the command sequences {SERVICES}FCCEIFjul1~ {SERVICES}FCCEIFjul2~, and so on. To run the macro, hold down the MACRO key and press P. The MACRO key is identified in the *Symphony* documentation. Here's how the macro works:

{ONERROR stop}{BLANK cnt}   Begins error trapping and erases the cell named *cnt*. Should an error occur while the macro is running, control will pass directly to the cell named *stop*. *Stop* contains the commands {BEEP 1}{BEEP 2} {BEEP 3}, which simply produce three different tones, telling you that the macro has finished running. The {ONERROR} command anticipates that the macro will eventually generate a file name that doesn't exist on disk. When *Symphony* tries to combine a nonexistent file, an error occurs.

{SERVICES}WUmemos~{HOME}   Presses SERVICES and selects Window Use, indicating MEMOS as the name of the window to use, then sends the cursor to the top-left corner of the DOC window.

{GETLABEL ''Enter common characters: '', flnm}   Displays the prompt *Enter common characters:* in the control panel and places your entry as a label in the cell named *flnm*. The prompt reminds you to indicate the characters common to each file name your macro will process. Since you named each of your files JUL followed by a number, you enter *jul* in response to this prompt.

{ERASE}{END}{HOME}~   Erases the current contents of the DOC window. This clears column A to receive the data that the macro will combine from other files.

{LET cnt,cnt + 1}   Increases the value of *cnt* by one. By this point during the macro's first pass (the macro loops through this step once for each file it prints) — the cell named *flnm* contains the characters JUL, and the cell named *cnt* contains the number one.

{RECALC next}   Recalculates the formula in the cell named *next*. On the first pass of the macro, the formula equals {SERVICES}FCCEIFjul1~. *Symphony* processes the commands in *next* (cell K10), combining JUL1 into column A of the worksheet.

{SERVICES}PAGPQ   Presses SERVICES and selects Print Align Go Page-Advance Quit. *Symphony* prints everything in the current window.

{BRANCH loop}   Transfers control of the macro to the cell named *loop* (cell K7). The macro erases the contents of the current window, increases the value of *cnt*, combines the next file in the sequence, prints the file, and so on until it has processed every file in the sequence. When there is a gap in the sequence or the last file has been processed, an error occurs and the macro processes the commands in the cell named *stop*.

PRINTING EVERYTHING

Let's suppose you have a floppy disk (or a directory) that holds several memos in dissimilarly named files. Each file has the same format: a memo entered through a DOC window into column A of the worksheet. But the file names bear no resemblance to each other. You want to print every file on the disk (or in the directory).

Start by setting up windows as described in the preceding section, but instead of entering the first macro described, use the following one (omitting for now the ERR shown in cell K8):

```
        J           K       L       M
1  cnt
2
3  \p          {BLANK table}{BLANK cnt}
4              {SERVICES}WUmemos~{HOME}
5              {SERVICES}FT~Wtable~
6  loop        {ERASE}{END}{HOME}~
7              {RECALC next}
8  next            ERR
9              {SERVICES}PAGPQ
10             {LET cnt,cnt+1}
11             {BRANCH loop}
12
13 table
```

Use the MENU Range Name Labels Right command to name cells K1, K3, K6, and K8 as *cnt*, *\p*, *loop*, and *next*, respectively. Assign the range name *table* to range K13..M8192. Enter the following formula into the cell named *next* (cell K8):

$$+\text{``\{SERVICES\}FCCEIF''}\&@INDEX(table,0,cnt)\&\text{``}\sim\text{''}$$

The formula equals ERR when you first enter it in the worksheet. By the time control of the macro passes to this cell, the formula will refer to the first entry of a file table that the macro creates in the range named *table*. Assuming that NAME is the name of the first entry, this formula will equal {SERVICES}FCCEIFNAME.WRK~ ({SERVICES}FCCEIFNAME.WR1~ in *Symphony* Release 1.1/1.2) on the macro's first pass. The macro loops, increasing the value of a counter (*cnt*) each time. Since the @INDEX function in this formula uses *cnt* as one of its arguments, this formula refers to a different name in the file table with each pass through the loop.

Finally, be sure that *Symphony* is using the proper directory or floppy disk by pressing SERVICES and selecting File Directory. If the desired drive or directory shows in the control panel, press Return; otherwise, reassign the default directory by pressing Escape and entering the full path name of the directory you want the macro to use. When you're ready to print, hold down the MACRO key and press P. Here's what happens:

{BLANK table}{BLANK cnt}   Erases the contents of the range named *table* and of the cell named *cnt*.

{SERVICES}WUmemos~{HOME}   Makes the MEMOS window current and moves the cursor to the top-left corner of the window.

{SERVICES}FT~Wtable~   Presses SERVICES, selects File Table, presses Return to cause *Symphony* to create a table of files contained in the default directory, selects Worksheet, indicates *table* as the range in which to create the table, and presses Return. *Symphony* creates a list in the range named *table* of the worksheet files contained in the current directory.

{ERASE}{END}{HOME}~   Erases the contents of the current window (MEMOS).

{RECALC next}   Recalculates the formula in the cell named *next*, the next cell in the macro. When the macro processes *next*, it combines the file currently indexed in *table* by the value in the cell named *cnt*. If *cnt* indexes a blank cell, the macro stops.

{SERVICES}PAGPQ   Prints the current contents of the MEMOS window.

{LET cnt,cnt + 1}   Increases the value of *cnt* by one.

{BRANCH loop}   Transfers control of the macro to the cell named *loop*. The macro erases the MEMOS window, updates the formula in *next* based on the new value of *cnt*, combines the next file in the list, prints the file, and so on until the macro has printed every file specified in the table.

QUICK AND DIRTY

If you find either of these techniques useful, save the macros you've created under a memorable file name. Then whenever you face a large printing task, you can retrieve the macro and let it rip. If you're not organized enough to reuse a macro, try using this quick-and-dirty approach to printing several different files.

Begin as described up to the first illustration in the section headed "Printing from Several Worksheets." Instead of writing the macro shown, manually issue the SERVICES File Table command, creating a file table starting in cell J1. Erase the data that appears in columns K and L after you issue the File Table command, leaving only the file names in column J. Remove the names of any files you don't want to print by deleting the rows of the worksheet containing those file names (MENU Delete Rows). Enter the following formula into cell K1 and copy it down the column as far as entries extend in column J:

$$+ \text{``}\{S\}FCCEIF\text{''}\&j1\&\text{``}\sim\{S\}PAGPQ\{M\}E\{END\}\{HOME\}\sim\text{''}$$

Assign the name *go* to cell K1. You've just created a macro. Press the WINDOW key to return to the window named MEMOS. Then press Home and start the macro.

The success of each of the macros we've discussed relies on having your documents reside in column A of your worksheets. If data in any of the files to be printed lies to the right of column A, the macros may not succeed in printing all the data. In the next chapter we'll look at some macros that help you work with different file formats.

MACROS IN HYPERSPACE

These macros will work as well from within the Macro Library Manager (Hyperspace) as they do from a standard *Symphony* worksheet, but using Hyperspace gives you a little more flexibility. A macro stored in Hyperspace can retrieve each file without destroying the macro. You needn't worry about using a standard layout for each file you intend to print. Merely assign a print range and other settings in each file. These settings will remain intact when the macro retrieves the file. This means that with the right macro design, you needn't design a worksheet in which to combine the files you want to print. If you're using Hyperspace, rewrite as follows the first macro described in the text:

	A	B	C	D	E	F
1	flnm					
2	cnt					
3						
4	\p	{BLANK cnt}{HOME}				
5		{GETLABEL "Enter common characters: ",flnm}				
6	loop	{LET cnt,cnt+1}				
7		{RECALC next}				
8	next	ERR				
9		{SERVICES}PAGPQ				
10		{BRANCH loop}				

The cell named *next* shows the value ERR in the illustration. Replace this with the following formula:

$$+ \text{``\{SERVICES\}FR''\&flnm\&@STRING(cnt,0)\&``~''}$$

With this macro in Hyperspace, you can hold down the MACRO key and press P, enter a few characters in response to the prompt, and *Symphony* will retrieve and print a series of sequentially numbered files. Note that this macro lacks an {ONERROR} statement. This is because of an apparent bug in Hyperspace. Though an {ONERROR} command in Hyperspace seems to prevent an error condition from arising, it fails to transfer control of the macro to the cell named in the statement.

When you've entered the macro and assigned its range names, put it in Hyperspace by first attaching the *Symphony* Macro Library Manager. If you're using a two-floppy-disk system, put the Help disk in drive A. On any system, press SERVICES, select Application Attach, point to MACROMGR.APP, and press Return. Then select Quit, press SERVICES, and select Macros. Select Save, assign a name to the library (name it PRINT), and press Return. Indicate range A1..B10, press Return, and select No. The macro is ready to run. Hold down the MACRO key and press P, answer the prompt, and *Symphony* will print your worksheets automatically.

Special thanks to Burch Downman of Houston, Tex., who supplied the quick-and-dirty solution presented in this chapter.

JULY 1986

7

More Multiple Files

This collection of observations and techniques
will help you build multifile applications and models
that otherwise wouldn't fit in your computer's RAM.

BY DANIEL GASTEIGER

Y ou don't need to be a computer whiz to end up feeling cramped by your
computer's on-board memory. If you're starting with the minimum amount of
RAM required to run *Symphony*, even rather small worksheet models will produce a
MEM indicator to signal that you've run out of memory. Stuffing your computer with
640 kilobytes of RAM will give you more room to stretch out, but eventually even this
can prove too limiting. When your worksheets begin to overload your computer's
memory, it's time to subdivide.

Many of the problems you solve with a worksheet involve subsets of data and
their associated calculations all tied together with summary calculations that render
the information you want. You can extract subsets of a worksheet into their own files
and work individually with each set of calculations. Then, when you've produced the
desired calculations from each worksheet subset, you can combine the results into a
single file that summarizes the calculations from the other files. The process is
cumbersome at best, but with a little effort, you can streamline it with macros.

In a previous chapter we explored some techniques that let you sequentially print
documents from several different files. In this chapter we'll discuss other ways to use
data from several different worksheets, and we'll apply the techniques to some
common worksheet-related problems.

222

A FILE-COMBINE ACCUMULATOR

On page 248, we present a worksheet that was designed for Bill, a hawker at hockey games. We'll use the same scenario to describe a simple technique that involves working with two different files.

After each game, Bill wants to see only his accumulated profits broken down by item so that he can decide which items need better promotion. (Should he be yelling "Dogs," "Burgers," or "Drinks"?)

During the game, Bill jots down the number of burgers, hotdogs, and drinks he sells. After a game he plugs the numbers into the *Today's Sales* column on his worksheet. Cell D5 in the *Today's Profit* column contains the formula +C5*B5*.35, which calculates 35 percent of the cash value of the hotdogs he sold that day. This is his profit on hotdog sales. By copying this formula to cells D6 and D7, Bill can also calculate his profits on burger and drink sales. Cell D9 contains the formula @SUM(D5..D7), which calculates Bill's total profit for the game. Bill copies this formula to cell E9 to calculate the season's accumulated profit. His worksheet appears below.

Bill has already entered one game's worth of sales in the *Today's Sales* column. Now he must decide what to put in the *Total Profit* column. He could set the recalculation method to manual, enter the formula +D5+E5 into cell E5, and then copy the formula to cells E6 and E7. However, these circular references would add *Today's Profit* to *Total Profit* every time the worksheet recalculated. Unfortunately, this model is just the corner of a worksheet containing several other models that Bill calculates more often than once per game. Bill's life would be easier if he could let *Symphony* recalculate automatically.

```
        A          B        C        D        E
 1                     Monthly Sales
 2
 3                    Today's  Today's  Total
 4               Price  Sales    Profit   Profit
 5  Hotdogs      $1.00     53   $18.55
 6  Burgers      $1.40     27   $13.23
 7  Drinks       $0.75     48   $12.60
 8            ===================================
 9                    Totals   $44.38   $0.00
```

After the first game, Bill can use the MENU Range Values command to copy the current values of the *Today's Profit* column into the *Total Profit* column. For each successive game, Bill will need a method to add the new *Today's Profit* values to the existing *Total Profit* values.

Bill can do this manually by using the File Xtract command. He points to the first cell of the *Today's Profit* column and presses SERVICES. He selects File Xtract

Values, enters a temporary file name (TEMP, for this discussion), indicates the day's earnings (D5..D7) as the range to extract, and presses Return. *Symphony* creates a disk file that contains the current values of the day's profits starting in cell A1.

Now Bill points to the first cell of the *Total Profit* column (cell E5), and combines the file he just created. He presses SERVICES and selects File Combine Add Entire-File Ignore Values, indicates TEMP.WRK (or TEMP.WR1 for Release 1.1/1.2 users), and presses Return. *Symphony* adds the extracted values to the existing values in the *Total Profit* column. Finally, Bill erases the temporary file (because he's a neat son of a gun). The following is a macro that performs these steps automatically:

	A	B	C	D
13	\a	{SERVICES}FXVtemp~{DOWN 2}~		
14		{RIGHT}		
15		{SERVICES}FCAEIVtemp~		
16		{SERVICES}FEWtemp~Y		

To use the macro, enter it as shown and assign \a as the name for cell B13; point to cell A13, press MENU, select Range Name Labels Right, and press Return. Point to the first cell of the *Today's Profit* column (cell D5) and start the macro by holding down the MACRO key and pressing A. With this macro in his worksheet, Bill can enter his sales volumes for the day in the *Today's Sales* column and easily update the accumulated *Total Profit* column.

MODULAR MODELS

When you divide large models up into smaller units or modules, you can manage the modules using file-extract and file-combine techniques similar to the one that Bill's macro uses. The primary consideration in setting up such models is to structure each module similarly so that you can easily adapt data combined from one module to data combined from another module.

Generally, there are three approaches to automating multiple file applications. One is to put the macro that controls the different files into its own master worksheet. The macro combines data from each of the modules into the master worksheet and performs summary calculations in that worksheet. The second approach is to put a controlling macro into each module. The controlling macros each perform their necessary maintenance tasks, then retrieve the next module in a predetermined sequence. Each module's macro is set to start running automatically when *Symphony* retrieves the module, so control of the macro passes from one module to the next until results are consolidated. The third approach is to create a macro in Hyperspace (the *Symphony* Release 1.1/1.2 Macro Library Manager) that manages the worksheet modules and produces a summary statement. Let's look at a simple example that uses both of the first two approaches listed.

BILL'S BOSS

Bill is a member of a three-person sales force. Each of the salespeople reports directly to Hannah, the head hawker. To increase sales, Hannah has created a worksheet similar to Bill's for each of the salespeople. She has instructed each of her salespeople to keep track of the numbers of hotdogs, hamburgers, and drinks they sell during a game. They each submit these numbers to her, and she updates their files, prints reports for each salesperson, and ultimately produces a summary worksheet of the business's entire sales to date.

It's unlikely that all of this data would fill the memory of even the leanest computer, but you can apply the techniques the model uses to modularize any *Symphony* application. Also, the application we'll design for Hannah is not the most efficient we could create, but it is adequate for the job she has to do. It demonstrates macros that pass control from one worksheet to the next and macros in a master worksheet that combine data from several independent worksheet modules.

THE MODULES

The modules that contain each salesperson's data look almost identical to Bill's worksheet (shown earlier). Hannah has entered a salesperson's name into the title of each worksheet so that she can easily identify the data with which she's working. The module she designed for Bill's data is shown below.

```
       A         B        C        D        E
1                Bill's Monthly Sales
2
3                        Today's  Today's  Total
4                Price    Sales    Take     Take
5  Hotdogs       $1.00             $0.00
6  Burgers       $1.40             $0.00
7  Drinks        $0.75             $0.00
8                ===================================
9                        Totals   $0.00    $0.00
```

Note that Hannah isn't interested in Bill's profits so much as she's interested in her take from Bill's sales. Her worksheet reflects that interest by using the following formula in cell D5:

$$+C5*B5*0.65$$

This calculates 65 percent of the total that Bill should have collected from his concession's sales during the game — the amount Hannah collects from Bill as her cut to cover expenses and her own profits. The module that Hannah creates for Bill's sales also contains the following macro:

	A	B	C	D	E
13	\i	{BLANK daysales}{DRAW}			
14		{GOTO}daysales~			
15		{?}{DOWN}{?}{DOWN}			
16		{?}~{SERVICES}FXVtemp~daytake~			
17		{GOTO}tottake~			
18		{SERVICES}FCAEIVtemp~			
19		{SERVICES}FS~Y			
20		{SERVICES}PAGPQ			
21		{SERVICES}FEWtemp~Y			
22		{SERVICES}FRanna~			

To use the macro, enter it as shown and use the MENU Range Name Create command to assign the following range names:

daysales	C5..C7
daytake	D5..D7
tottake	E5..E7

Then assign a print range that encompasses Bill's sales data; press SERVICES, select Print Settings Source Range, indicate A1..E9, press Return, and select Quit Quit. Finally, save the file under the name BILL; select SERVICES File Save, type *bill*, and press Return. (If you're using floppy disks, use only one disk throughout this entire discussion. If you're using a hard disk, use only one directory.)

Before this macro will function properly, you'll have to create all of its associated modules. Start by creating a file named ANNA. Anna is one of Bill's coworkers. This second file will contain Anna's accumulated sales data. Create the file by modifying the copy of Bill's file currently in memory.

Edit the title across the top of the worksheet to read *Anna's Monthly Sales*. Modify the last line of the macro (cell B22) to read {SERVICES}FRjean~ . Then set the macro to run automatically when *Symphony* retrieves the file: press SERVICES, select Settings Auto-Execute Set, enter \i, and select Quit. Now save the file under the name ANNA: press SERVICES, select File Save, press Escape, and enter *anna*.

The macro in the file named ANNA finishes by retrieving a file named JEAN. Jean is the third person on Hannah's sales team. Create a worksheet module for Jean as you did for Anna by changing the title in row 1 of the worksheet and by modifying the last line of macro code to read {SERVICES}FRmaster~. Since you've already set the macro named *i* to run automatically, simply save your work under the file name JEAN.

The macro in JEAN finishes by retrieving a file named MASTER. MASTER will hold the accumulated daily totals as well as the accumulated monthly totals for the concessions' sales. Create MASTER as you did the other files by modifying the original file still in memory. Edit the title to read *Accumulated Sales Totals*, then replace the existing macro with the one in the following illustration:

```
      A         B          C         D
13  \i        {BLANK daysales}{DRAW}
14            {GOTO}daysales~
15            {comb}bill~
16            {comb}anna~
17            {comb}jean~
18            {SERVICES}FXVtemp~daytake~
19            {GOTO}tottake~
20            {SERVICES}FCAEIVtemp~
21            {SERVICES}FS~Y
22            {SERVICES}PAGPQ
23            {SERVICES}FEWtemp~Y
24
25  comb      {SERVICES}FCANdaysales~IV
```

To create this macro, erase the existing macro: point to cell B13, select MENU Erase, and press End DownArrow Return. Then enter the new macro, including the labels in cells A25 and B25. Name cell B25 *comb*, then save the file under the name MASTER. Your multiple-worksheet application is ready for a test run.

To try out the model, retrieve the disk copy of the file named BILL, then start the macro it contains by holding down the MACRO key and pressing I. Here's what happens:

{BLANK daysales}{DRAW}   Erases the *daysales* range and redraws the screen to display the change.

{GOTO}daysales~   Sends the cell pointer to the first cell of the range named *daysales*.

{?}{DOWN}{?}{DOWN}   Causes the macro to pause until you press Return, then moves the cell pointer down, pauses again until you press Return, and moves the cell pointer down. At each pause you enter the number of hotdogs or burgers that Bill sold at the game that day.

{?}~{SERVICES}FXVtemp~daytake~   Causes the macro to pause until you press Return (so you can enter the number of drinks that Bill sold), then extracts the range named *daytake* into a file named TEMP. *Daytake* contains the formulas that calculate Hannah's income for the day.

{GOTO}tottake~   Sends the cell pointer to the first cell of the range named *tottake*.

{SERVICES}FCAEIVtemp~   Adds the values from the file named TEMP to the values in the current column. This updates the running totals of the month's earnings.

{SERVICES}FS~Y   Saves the newly updated file under its original file name, BILL.

{SERVICES}PAGPQ   Prints the sales figures.

{SERVICES}FEWtemp~Y   Erases the temporary file named TEMP that the macro created earlier.

{SERVICES}FRanna   Retrieves the file named ANNA. Since ANNA contains an autoexecute macro nearly identical to this macro, the process starts again. *Symphony* accepts data for Anna's sales, updates the *Total Take* figures, saves the file, prints a report, and retrieves the file named JEAN.

The process repeats for the file named JEAN, but the macro in JEAN retrieves MASTER, which contains a different autoexecute macro. MASTER's macro works as follows:

{BLANK daysales}{DRAW}   Erases the range named *daysales* and redraws the screen.

{GOTO}daysales~   Sends the cell pointer to the first cell of the range named *daysales*.

{comb}bill~   Calls the subroutine named *comb*. *Comb* starts to issue a command sequence that combines information from a disk file into the current worksheet. The subroutine presses SERVICES and selects File Combine Add Named-Range, enters *daysales* as the name of the range to combine from the disk file, and selects Ignore Values. Then the subroutine ends and control of the macro returns to the commands *bill~*, which indicate BILL as the disk file from which to combine data.

{comb}anna~   Repeats the commands of the last step, but combines data from the file named ANNA. Because the subroutine uses the File Combine Add option, *Symphony* adds the values from ANNA to the values previously combined from BILL.

{comb}jean~   Repeats the previous step, but combines data from the file named JEAN. The balance of the macro extracts the values from the *Today's Take* column and combines them into the *Total Take* column, just as each of the individual modules did to calculate their own running totals. Then the macro prints a report of the day's earnings and the earnings to date.

IS IT TIME TO SUBDIVIDE?

As expressed earlier, all the data in this model could easily fit into one worksheet. Splitting things up into separate modules was more trouble than it was worth. Still, these techniques are useful in many situations. As you build models that push the limit of your computer's memory, consider using macros to manage multiple-file applications. Note that as related worksheet modules grow, they may no longer fit together on a single floppy disk. Your macros may need to include commands that prompt you to change disks from time to time — particularly if your sales force is much larger than Hannah's.

AUGUST 1986

8

Mailing Labels

Symphony macros that create mailing labels.

BY DANIEL GASTEIGER

In a previous *1-2-3* Macros column, we presented several macros that print mailing labels from a *1-2-3* database. Many readers have since asked if the same techniques work in *Symphony*. They do, but there are easier and more efficient ways to print mailing labels using *Symphony*.

In *1-2-3* you must manually create each database structure (Database, Criterion, Sort, and Extract ranges), as well as any desired data-entry and print routines, on the worksheet. You would need several macros to match the built-in database capabilities of *Symphony*'s FORM window.

Let's examine a *Symphony* macro that prints mailing labels from a database in a SHEET window. Then, to emphasize the maxim that nonmacro alternatives are often better, we'll use *Symphony*'s automatic report generator to print labels more quickly. If you already have a database of names and addresses that uses a FORM window, you'll probably prefer the report-generator method described later in this article.

A SIMPLE DATABASE

A *Symphony* database is a collection of information stored as records on the worksheet. Each record occupies its own row and contains information about a unique item or individual. For example, each record of an address database might contain a person's first and last names, title, company name, street address, city, state, and zip code.

	A	B	C	D	E	F	G	H
19	First	Last	Title	Company	Street	City	State	Zip
20	Edgar	Kilter	Systems Analyst	Oh!Data	883 Pine St	Colter Gap	WY	33477
21	Kathleen	Menace		BC Pets, Inc	Felmore Blvd	Altoona	MT	73832
22	Wynne	Lai	Software Consultant		63 Woodcliff Ave	Walleysville	MA	02217
23	Constance	Cranch			304 Kendall Pl	Toohey	IA	42647
24	Carlton	Singh	Vice President	Golden Galoshes	572 The Parkway	Los Trellos	CA	92142

FIGURE 1

A record is divided into discrete pieces of information called fields, which occupy adjacent columns of the worksheet. You identify the fields by placing labels called field names at the top of each database column. The column containing first names might be headed with the label *First,* the column containing last names with the label *Last,* and so on. Figure 1 shows the field names and the first five records of an address database.

Notice that all the data entries are labels, including zip codes, and that some records lack information, as is the case with most databases. The database does not contain, for example, a title for Kathleen Menace. Whenever there is no appropriate information for a particular field, the corresponding cell is blank. We'll have to consider these details as we build a mailing-label generator.

ADDRESS-LABEL FORMULAS

Database information is stored in rows, while address labels are arranged in blocks. The fastest way to transform a data record into a mailing label is through string formulas. It's not a simple task.

We'll create the shortest possible macro to print addresses on tractor-fed, adhesive, 1 7/16-inch labels. The macro relies entirely on two sets of formulas for its speed and simplicity. One set uses the @INDEX function to reference each row of the database. The other set builds the mailing-label addresses based on the values of the first set. Theoretically, you could combine the formulas into a single set that both indexes the database and builds the mailing labels, but the resulting formulas would be unwieldy.

Copy the field names to the first row of the worksheet. To do this, press MENU, select Copy, indicate range A19..H19, press Return, indicate cell A1, and press Return. Enter the label *vert* in column A two rows above the database (cell A17), and use the Range Name Labels Right command to assign this as the name for the adjacent cell in column B. Assign *dbase* as the name for range A19..H24 (press MENU, select Range Name Create, type *dbase*, press Return, indicate range A19..H24, and press

	J	K	L	M	N	O	P	Q	R	S	T	U
1	@S(!first)&@IF(@ISSTRING(first)+@ISSTRING(last)=2," ","")&@S(!last)											
2	@CHOOSE(@ISSTRING(title)+@ISSTRING(company),@S(!street),@S(!title)&@S(!company),@S(!title))											
3	@CHOOSE(@ISSTRING(title)+@ISSTRING(company),@S(!city)&", "&@S(!state)&" "&@S(!zip),@S(!street),@S(!company))											
4	@CHOOSE(@ISSTRING(title)+@ISSTRING(company),"",@S(!city)&", "&@S(!state)&" "&@S(zip),@S(!street))											
5	@CHOOSE(@ISSTRING(title)+@ISSTRING(company),"","",@S(!city)&", "&@S(!state)&" "&@S(!zip))											

FIGURE 2

Return), and assign the labels in the first row of the worksheet as names for the cells directly below them (go to cell A1, press MENU, select Range Name Labels Down, and press End RightArrow Return).

Enter the following in the cell named *first* (A2):

$$@INDEX(\$dbase,@COUNT(\$A\$1..A1)-1,\$vert)$$

Copy it across the row through the cell named *zip* (H2) by putting the cell pointer in *first* (A2) and pressing MENU; then select Copy and press Return Tab UpArrow End RightArrow DownArrow Return. Row 2 of the worksheet will appear to contain copies of the database field names.

The @INDEX function looks for a value contained in a range. You describe the position of the desired value by supplying both column and row offsets from the top-left corner of the range. In this case the indexed range is *dbase* and the column offset is @COUNT(A1..A1)-1, which, when you copy the formula, equals 0 in *first*, 1 in *last*, 2 in *title*, and so on. The row offset is the value of the cell named *vert*, which is currently 0.

To see how these formulas will work when you create the mailing-label macro, enter a 1 in the cell named *vert* (B17). The @INDEX formulas now refer to the first data record and the worksheet updates accordingly. Enter a 2 in *vert*, and the @INDEX formulas reference the second data record. We'll design a macro that increases the value of *vert*, prints a range containing formulas that refer to the @INDEX formulas, increases the value of *vert* again, and so on until it has printed once for each record in the database.

STRING FORMULAS

The second set of formulas is rather tricky. As mentioned earlier, these formulas need to account for the fact that some records in the database lack information in one or more fields. The set of formulas in figure 2 accounts for the possibilities that your records contain a person's title but not a company name, a person's company name but not a title, both a title and a company name, or neither a title nor a company name. The formulas also work if a record contains a person's first and last names, a first or a last name only, or neither a first nor a last name. In any case, these formulas always expect to find entries in the street, city, and state fields, although zip codes aren't necessary (you can argue with the post office).

Because these formulas are so long, I recommend that you enter them first as labels (start each one by typing an apostrophe). Start in cell J1, putting one formula in each of the cells in range J1..J5. Then copy the block of labels from J1..J5 to range A4..A8. Finally, remove the label prefix from each copy in column A (point to each cell and press EDIT Home Delete Return). If *Symphony* doesn't accept the resulting formula because of a typing error, press Escape and return to the original label version in column J. Edit that label to match the corresponding formula in figure 2, recopy it to column A, and again remove the label prefix. Repeat this procedure for each formula until both the label versions in column J and the nonlabel versions in column A are accurate. When you've finished, cells A4 through A8 should contain Kathleen Menace's complete address.

The technique I've described for creating long formulas has two advantages over entering the formulas directly into column A. First, if you wish to modify a standard formula, you must deal with cell and range addresses rather than the names assigned to those addresses. This is because *Symphony* doesn't display range names in Edit mode. With label versions of the working formulas, you can copy the labels, make changes to the copies, and copy the new labels into position before removing the label prefixes. This preserves both the original formulas and the new versions as labels in case you wish to edit them further.

Second, when you create label versions of complex formulas that use range names, you can reuse the formulas from one application to another simply by combining them into a new worksheet and removing the label prefixes. As long as the appropriate range names exist in the new worksheet, you can place the labels anywhere and expect them to work as intended. I've shared these and similar formulas with several people at the Lotus offices by extracting the label versions into their own files and handing them around on floppy disks.

Once you've created the formulas, point to the cell named *vert* (B17) and enter the number 1. The formulas update instantly to display Edgar Kilter's address. Enter a 2 and the formulas display Kathleen Menace's address, adjusted to account for the empty title field. Enter a 3 into *vert* and the formulas display Wynne Lai's address, adjusted for lack of a company name. When you enter a 4, you see the three lines of Constance Cranch's address; when you enter a 5, you see all five lines of Carlton Singh's address. If you're using *Symphony* 1.1/1.2 and you enter a 6 into *vert,* all your formulas display ERR (in earlier releases of *Symphony,* the address formulas will be blank). This is because a vertical offset of six falls outside the range named *dbase*; the range named in the @INDEX formulas. When you work with a larger database, be sure *dbase* encompasses the entire range.

This stepping process is similar to the process our macro will perform when it uses the formulas to print mailing labels. I'll let you figure out just how the mailing-label formulas work.

THE MACRO

After all this work, the actual mailing-label macro is anticlimactic. It occupies only two cells:

	A	B	C
13	\m	{FOR vert,1,@ROWS(dbase)-1,1,print}	
14			
15	print	{SERVICES}PGQ	
16			
17	vert	0	

Enter it as shown (the illustration also shows *vert,* which you named earlier) and assign the labels in column A as range names for the adjacent cells of column B (use the Range Name Labels Right command). Press SERVICES, select Print Settings Source Range, indicate A3..D11, and press Return. Select Margins No-Margins, which disables pagination, and return to the worksheet by selecting Quit Quit.

Here's one more thought before you start printing: Sprocket wheels on some printers can't engage both sets of perforations on narrow paper stock. I recommend loading standard 8-1/2-by-11-inch continuous-feed paper before loading the labels. Load the continuous-feed labels in front of the paper, engaging the perforations on the left side of the paper backing. You'll have piles of paper to refold when you finish printing, but your labels will probably feed more smoothly. Align the printhead of your printer just below the top edge of the first adhesive label.

Start the macro by holding down the MACRO key and pressing M. Here's what happens:

{FOR vert,1,@ROWS(dbase)−1,1,print} Starts a FOR loop. This {FOR} command instructs *Symphony* to process the macro routine named *print* once for each row of the database, except the row containing the field names. It keeps track of its progress by first setting the value of *vert* to 1 and comparing it to the Stop value: @ROWS(dbase)–1. If *vert* is the greater value, the FOR loop stops; otherwise, it processes the routine named *print* and increases the value of *vert* by one. It continues increasing *vert*, comparing the result against the value of @ROWS(dbase)–1. It processes the *print* routine as long as the value of *vert* is less than the Stop value.

{SERVICES}PGQ   Prints the current contents of the Print range that you set before you ran the macro. This routine processes once for each pass of the loop, and since the formulas in the Print range rely indirectly on the increasing value of *vert*, this command sequence prints a different address on each pass. *Symphony* spaces the printed labels properly because you have disabled pagination and indicated a nine-line Print range, which corresponds exactly to the spacing between the adhesive-backed labels.

A FORM WINDOW DATABASE

When you create a database using the FORM window's Generate command, *Symphony* establishes several interrelated worksheet structures: the Database, Criterion, Output, Entry, Definition, and Report ranges. *Symphony* also assigns the database field names as range names for the cells directly below them in the database. You can create formulas that refer to these range names (the first database entry) and assign these formulas as a Report range. Then when you print using the database as the source, *Symphony* prints one copy of the Report range for each record, adjusting the formulas accordingly. The outcome is identical to that of the macro, except that the report generator is faster. With the report generator you have the added advantage of being able to indicate to *Symphony* precisely which records to print as labels simply by entering instructions in a criterion record. The *Symphony* documentation contains instructions on using criterion matching.

We'll create a database in a FORM window and use the formulas in figure 2 to print mailing labels using *Symphony*'s built-in report generator. If you've already entered the formulas as described, extract the label versions to their own file so that you'll be able to use them later; assuming the labels are in cells J1..J5, press SERVICES, select File Xtract Formulas, enter a file name (such as FORMULAS), and indicate range J1..J5. You may also wish to save the work you've done so far, though you won't be needing it for the remainder of this discussion. Clear the worksheet by pressing SERVICES and selecting New Yes.

Enter labels as shown in the illustration on the next page.

	A	B	C
1	First:L:20		
2	Last:L:20		
3	Title:L:45		
4	Company:L:45		
5	Street:L:45		
6	City:L:20		
7	State:L:5		
8	Zip:L:9		

The words in these labels will become the field names of a new database. The colon-letter and colon-number combinations following the words describe the type of entries the fields will contain; for example, :L indicates a label field, and :25 indicates that the field should accept up to 25 characters per entry.

Turn the current window into a FORM window by pressing the TYPE key and selecting FORM. The window appears blank, and the message *(No Definition range defined)* appears in the control panel. Ignore the message and press MENU, then select Generate Label, and press Return twice. You are asked to specify the range of field names. Indicate range A1..A8 and press Return. A data-entry form appears on your screen.

Enter the records shown in figure 1. To enter data in a FORM window, type the appropriate information for the current field (look for the cursor) and press Return. The cursor moves to the next field so that you can make the next entry. If you lack information for a particular field, leave the line blank by pressing Return. When you've entered all the information for a form (be sure to press Return even after the last field entry), place the record into the database by pressing the Insert key. A new blank form appears on your screen and *Symphony* displays in the control panel the messages *Inserting Record 2* and *New Record*. Enter the remaining records from figure 1.

You can move among records you've already entered by pressing the PageUp and PageDown keys. Also, the Home key takes you directly to the first database record, and the End key takes you to the last. You can begin entering a new record by pressing first the End key and then PageDown. You can change a field entry in any record by pointing to it and simply retyping it or by pressing the EDIT key and using the Arrow, Delete, and Backspace keys. When you've finished editing, press Return.

MACRO-FREE ADDRESS LABELS

Symphony stores the information you enter into data-entry forms in rows of the worksheet. Rather than explain how the information is laid out, I'll present the steps necessary to print mailing labels from that information. We'll do most of our work in a SHEET window.

Press the SWITCH key. The window changes back to a SHEET window. Notice that the contents of the worksheet have changed dramatically. Move the cell pointer to cell G1 and combine the file that you created earlier named LABELS (press SERVICES, select File Combine Copy Entire-file Ignore Formulas, point to the LABELS file name, and press Return). If you didn't create a labels file as described in the text, enter the formulas shown in figure 2 following the instructions in the section called "String Formulas."

Copy the label versions of the formulas to cell C2 and edit out the label prefixes. The formulas will refer to the first record in the database. Switch back to the FORM window (press the SWITCH key) and press MENU. Select Settings Cancel Report, then select Report Main. Indicate range C1..D9, press Return, and select Quit Quit. Be sure your printer is ready to go, then press SERVICES. Select Print Settings Source Database and press Return. Select Margins No-Margins Quit, and finally select Go. *Symphony* prints the mailing labels automatically without a macro!

THOUGHTS IN CLOSING

You can use *Symphony*'s built-in report generator to print any material that contains information stored in a database. *Symphony* prints one copy of the Report range for each database record (when you use criterion matching, *Symphony* prints only records that meet the criteria). Relative cell and range references in formulas in the Report range adjust downward one row with each copy of the range that *Symphony* prints. If those formulas begin by referring to the first row of the database, they will refer to a different record on each pass.

Refer to the *Symphony* documentation for more details on working with databases and the report generator. Overall, using the report generator is far easier than designing macros to perform the same task, and the report generator invariably prints more quickly than does a macro. Again I encourage you to seek a nonmacro approach before wrestling with the *Symphony* Command Language.

Special thanks to Andrew Feinstein of White Plains, N.Y., whose entry in the February 1986 contest helped shape this chapter.

JUNE 1986

SECTION

5

MORE POWER FOR
1-2-3 RELEASE 1A

Release 1A was the *1-2-3* standard for almost two years. During that time it also became the standard spreadsheet in most businesses. Even after Release 2 became available in the fall of 1985, many people continued to feel that their needs were still satisfied by the older version. A majority of you are using the newer releases but our research indicates that over 25% of *LOTUS* readers still use 1A at least some of the time.

In fact, there are ways to get Release 1A to provide many of the advanced capabilities of the later releases. These macro-based tricks were the pride of early *1-2-3* experts. You can't duplicate all the advanced capabilities, and you've got to do some fancy footwork to accomplish those you can duplicate. But if you absolutely refuse to upgrade, this section contains some techniques to push *1-2-3* Release 1A far beyond its creators' vision. You will learn how to use the Data Fill command to approximate the {FOR} macro command keyword, how to use Range Justify for word processing, and how to use the @D functions to approximate label arithmetic.

In truth, if any of these capabilities are particularly important to you, it would be worth upgrading to a more advanced version of *1-2-3*, which will make these tasks simple instead of heroic. Still these articles contain many useful tricks and techniques that all *1-2-3* users will find helpful.

1

Some Short, Powerful Macros Speed Everyday Tasks

These routines automatically set column widths,
turn formulas into labels and back, date-stamp worksheets,
and more.

BY DANIEL GASTEIGER

When you're building a model, there are many operations you do repeatedly — recalculate, change column widths, save the file. You can use macros for each of these and build a collection of macros that you can incorporate into every worksheet. Here are some of the most useful ones.

This is a familiar experience. You select manual recalculation (/Worksheet Global Recalculation Manual) so that you don't have to wait through lengthy recalculations every time you make a cell entry. You spend three hours building an enormous model. Finally, with the last formula in place, you press the CALC key and lean back to watch the spreadsheet magic. The WAIT indicator flashes for a minute before you turn to other work while *1-2-3* recalculates, but you find yourself glancing at the screen every 20 seconds to see whether the recalculation is finished.

With a simple macro, the program will beep when it finishes calculating. Here is a routine that will produce a beep:

	A	B	C	D
1	\b	{HOME}{UP}{UP}{UP}		
2				

Go to cell A1, type '\b, and press Return. In cell B1 enter {HOME}{UP} {UP}{UP}. Finally, assign \b as the range name for cell B1 by putting the cell pointer on cell A1, issuing the command /Range Name Labels Right, and pressing Return. You must name all *1-2-3* macros with a backslash (\) and letter combination. To start a macro, hold down the MACRO key and press the letter of the macro's name. If your computer lacks a MACRO key, consult the macro section of the *1-2-3* manual.

If you combine this macro with the {CALC} command, *1-2-3* signals when it finishes recalculating the worksheet:

	A	B	C	D
1	\c	{CALC}{HOME}{UP}{UP}{UP}		
2				

After you enter the macro as shown and assign the name \c , you can recalculate the worksheet by holding down the MACRO key and pressing C. When recalculation finishes, the cell pointer jumps to A1 and throws itself against the edge of the worksheet three times, causing *1-2-3* to beep. Unfortunately, if you start the macro while you are working in cell H357, it is a long trip back.

Here is a better approach:

	A	B	C	D
1	\c	{CALC}/BBB{ESC}		
2				

This causes the worksheet to recalculate; after this, the macro tries to select B from the main menu three times. Since there is no such menu item, *1-2-3* beeps and {ESC} returns *1-2-3* to Ready mode.

You can replace the {CALC} command with the {TABLE} command to recalculate large tables, or you can place the routine /BBB{ESC} alone anywhere within a larger macro to have *1-2-3* signal when it finishes a subroutine or discovers that you have entered an illegal value.

SMALL MACROS FOR BIG JOBS

The "beep" macro is a utility — a small routine that helps you to perform large tasks efficiently. You can make any series of keystrokes you often use into a utility.

When you are creating a model, you probably change column widths frequently. The following macro helps speed things up:

	A	B	C	D
3	\w	/WCS		
4				

When you press MACRO-W, the macro selects /Worksheet Column-Width Set. Adjust the width of the current column by typing a value between zero and 73 or by pressing the LeftArrow and RightArrow keys and then pressing Return.

FORMULAS TO LABELS AND LABELS TO FORMULAS

Even the best typists make mistakes. Sometimes you finish typing a long formula, press Return, and find yourself in edit mode because you have mistyped a cell address, range name, or @function. If you do not know what you have done wrong or you need to fix something elsewhere on the worksheet before the formula will work, press Home and type and apostrophe, then press Return. Your formula will appear as a label in the cell and you will not lose what you have typed. Now you can make corrections in other cells, then return to this cell and remove the label prefix (by pressing EDIT Home Delete Return).

With the following macros on your worksheet, if you find yourself in Edit mode, you can turn your formula into a label by pressing MACRO-O, and turn it back to a formula by pressing MACRO-F.

	A	B	C	D
5	\o	{HOME}'~		
6				
7	\f	{EDIT}{EDIT}{DEL}~		
8				

You may write a formula and later realize that you need an exact copy of it somewhere else on the worksheet. Unfortunately, if you use *1-2-3*'s Copy command, the relative addresses in the formula adjust, and the copied formula will refer to cells different from the original ones. One solution to the problem is to make all the cell and range references of the original formula absolute before making copies. You can then copy the formula anywhere, and it will evaluate just as the original did. Another solution is to turn the formula into a label (by pressing EDIT Home, typing an apostrophe, and pressing Return), copy the formula to the target cell, and remove the label prefix (by using the \f macro shown above). The utility to speed this up is:

	A	B	C	D
9	\l	{EDIT}{HOME}'~		
10				

To use it, put the cell pointer on the formula you wish to copy and press MACRO-L. Copy the resulting label wherever you wish. Then with the cell pointer highlighting the original formula, press MACRO-F. Finally, go to the copy of the formula (remember, this is still a label) and press MACRO-F once more.

DATE-STAMPING YOUR WORKSHEET

Sometimes you would like your worksheet to display the date on which it was modified. It's also useful to tag historical information, such as a day's stock prices, with the day's date.

The @TODAY function alone cannot do either of these things. @TODAY relies upon the date you enter in DOS when you start your computer or the date set automatically by your built-in clock. If DOS has been given the correct date and time, entering @TODAY into a cell and giving it a date format causes today's date to be displayed. But if you save the worksheet and retrieve it tomorrow, tomorrow's date will be displayed instead.

To date-stamp a worksheet, put the cell pointer on an empty cell and type *@TODAY*. Then, before pressing Return, press the CALC key. The current value of @TODAY will appear in the control panel. Enter it into the cell by pressing Return.

The value of @TODAY is a serial number that you can format in *1-2-3* to display as a date. Leave the cell pointer on the cell containing the serial number and press the slash key. Then select Range Format Date 1 and press Return.

If you are working in cell D1, your worksheet probably looks like this:

	D	E	F	G
1	********			
2				

This is because column D is not wide enough to display the entire date. Use the \w macro that was described earlier to increase the width of that column until the date appears.

The following macro performs these steps for you:

	A	B	C	D
11	\n	@TODAY		
12		{CALC}~		
13		/RFD1~		
14		/WCS10~		

Since the macro sets the width of the current column to 10, don't use it in columns whose widths you have already changed. If you plan to always date-stamp in the same cell, rewrite the macro as follows:

	A	B	C	D
16	\t	@TODAY		
17		{CALC}~		

The first time you use the macro, manually set the column width to 10 and give the cell the proper date format. To run the macro, put the cell pointer on that cell and press MACRO-T. The new date that appears in the cell will not change when you retrieve the worksheet on another day.

Another version of the date-stamp macro performs a different part of the task for you. Start by naming the cell you wish to date-stamp. Do this by putting the cell pointer on that cell and pressing the slash key. Then select Range Name Create, type *date*, and finish by pressing Return twice. Use the \w macro to set the column width to 10. Press slash, select Range Format Date 1, and then press Return to give the cell a date format.

Now write the following macro:

	A	B	C	D
19	\d	/DFdate~@TODAY~~~		
20				

When you run this macro, *1-2-3* enters the serial number for today's date into the cell named *date* and leaves you wherever you are on the worksheet. You need not point at the date-stamp target cell before running the macro. The macro selects Data Fill from the main menu and indicates *date* as the range to fill. It assigns the current value of @TODAY rather than the formula as the Start value, and it accepts the defaults for the Step and Stop values. Since *date* is a single cell range, the Data Fill command does not use Step and Stop values.

SAVE A WORKSHEET WITH TWO KEYSTROKES

When you are creating a large model, you probably save your worksheet about every 15 minutes so that you will have a backup copy if your computer accidentally shuts down. Instead of pressing all the keys needed to save a file, you can write a macro to do the job for you. The following macro saves a file named PROJECT:

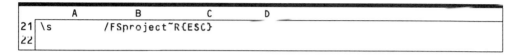

```
         A            B          C          D
21  \s          /FSproject~R{ESC}
22
```

This is a dangerous macro. If you have already saved a worksheet called PROJECT on the data disk you are using and you run this macro from within a different worksheet, the original PROJECT worksheet will be erased. Before you write and use this type of macro, be sure you have chosen a unique file name for the current worksheet.

This macro will work whether or not you already have a copy of the file named PROJECT on the disk. When you press MACRO-S, the macro selects /File Save and enters the file name (in this case PROJECT). If a file with that name exists, the macro selects Replace from the menu, replaces the old copy with a new copy, and presses the Escape key. If a file with that name does not exist on the disk, your macro creates a new file. It then types R in the control panel and presses the Escape key to clear the R.

PUTTING THEM ALL TOGETHER

Utilities are truly useful when you can use them in any worksheet. You can do this by creating a library of macros on a blank worksheet and by always building new worksheets from that worksheet. Start by entering the macros in columns A and B of a worksheet so that they appear like the illustration on the next page

You may not necessarily want to include all of these macros, and you may have a few of your own that you wish to include. Once you enter them as shown, put the cell pointer in cell A1 and select /Range Name Labels Right. You will be prompted to indicate a range containing the labels. Press the PageDown key and then Return. By doing this, you name all the macros in one step.

	A	B	C	D
1	\c	{CALC}/BBB{ESC}		
2				
3	\w	/WCS		
4				
5	\o	{HOME}'~		
6				
7	\f	{EDIT}{HOME}{DEL}~		
8				
9	\l	{EDIT}{HOME}'~		
10				
11	\n	@TODAY		
12		{CALC}~		
13		/RFD1~		
14		/WCS10~		
15				
16	\t	@TODAY		
17		{CALC}~		
18				
19	\d	/DFdate~@TODAY~~~		
20				
21	\s	/FSproject~R{ESC}		
22				

Go to cell D1 and press MACRO-N, then name the cell *date*. Place the cell pointer on the macro named \s and save the file as LIBRARY. From now on, when you start to create a new worksheet, retrieve LIBRARY. When it is loaded into memory, the cell pointer will still be on the macro named \s. This will remind you to change the file name in the macro so that when you use the macro to save, you will not erase a file you created earlier.

Now you are ready to go. Build your worksheet as always, but take advantage of the collection of macro utilities to make the job easier. You can move the entire macro library to an out-of-the-way location before you start. To do so, press Home, then select /Move and highlight the macros and their names. Press Return, then move the pointer to the cell that will receive the top-left corner of the library and press Return. If you do this, remember where you move your library. Inserting or deleting a row in the wrong place can destroy macros. When you use the \s macro to save your work, the original copy of LIBRARY remains on disk, and you will save your current work under the name that you placed into the macro when you first retrieved the worksheet.

JUNE 1985

2

Macro Skill with Data Fill

These macros can help you accumulate running totals and print multiple copies.

BY DANIEL GASTEIGER

Macros save keystrokes, decrease the amount of time you spend thinking about what you are doing, and perform repetitive tasks so that you don't have to. Let's look at a macro that asks how many copies of a document you wish to print and then prints the requested number. On the way, we'll look at the Data Fill command and a few ways you can use it to shorten your macro routines.

/DATA FILL

The Data Fill command puts a sequence of numbers into a range on the worksheet. It works this way: Press slash and select Data Fill. Highlight a range, for instance A8..A20, and press Return. Enter a Start value — the number that *1-2-3* will put in the first cell of the range to fill. Enter a step value — the amount by which *1-2-3* will change the previously used value for each cell that it fills. If the Step value is positive, *1-2-3* increases the value from cell to cell; if it is negative, *1-2-3* decreases the value. Finally, enter a Stop value — the highest or lowest number that *1-2-3* should use for the data fill. *1-2-3* fills the range cell by cell. It puts the Start value in the first cell, adds the Step value to it, and puts the result in the next cell, again adds the Step value for the third cell, and so on, until either the range is filled or the value to be entered into the range exceeds the Stop value.

   The Data Fill command accepts numbers, cell references, range names, formulas, and @functions for the Start, Step, and Stop values. But rather than putting actual cell references or formulas into the range being filled, *1-2-3* enters only the current values of the referenced cells or formulas. One example of this looks like this:

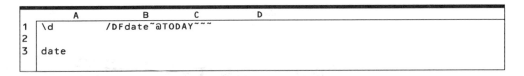

	A	B	C	D
1	\d	/DFdate~@TODAY~~~		
2				
3	date			

Date is a single cell range. You can name it at the same time you name the macro by going to cell A1 and pressing slash (/). Then select Range Name Labels Right and press End DownArrow Return. Start the macro by holding down the MACRO key and pressing D.

The Data Fill command ignores the Step and Stop values you give it when it fills a single cell; therefore, the only value it uses when you run this macro is the Start value. In this case the Start value is @TODAY, and as mentioned earlier, the /Data Fill command assigns the current value of @TODAY, rather than the formula itself, to the cell named *date*.

AN ACCUMULATOR

You can take advantage of the Data Fill command to generate values wherever it is inappropriate to write formulas. For example, the following worksheet is designed for Bill, a hawker at hockey games. After each game, Bill wants to see only his accumulated profits broken down by item so that he can decide which items need better promotion. (Should he be yelling ''Dogs,'' ''Burgers,'' or ''Drinks''?)

During the game Bill records on a notepad the number of burgers, hotdogs, and drinks he sells. After a game he plugs the numbers into the Today's Sales column on his worksheet. Cell D5 in the Today's Profit column contains the formula +C5*B5*.35, which calculates 35 percent of the cash value of the hotdogs he sold that day. This is his profit on hotdog sales. By copying this formula to cells D6 and D7, Bill can calculate his profits on burger and drink sales. Cell D9 contains the formula @SUM(D5..D7), which calculates Bill's total profit for the game. The same formula is copied to cell E9; this calculates the season's accumulated profit.

Bill has already entered one game's worth of sales in the Today's Sales column. Now he must decide what to put in the Total Profit column. He could select /Worksheet Global Recalculation Manual, then enter the formula +D5+E5 into cell E5, and copy it to cells E6 and E7. However these circular references would add Today's Profit to Total Profit every time Bill pressed the CALC key. (See ''The CIRC Indicator''.) Unfortunately, this model is just the corner of a worksheet containing

	A	B	C	D	E
1			Monthly	Sales	
2					
3			Today's	Today's	Total
4		Price	Sales	Profit	Profit
5	Hotdogs	$1.00	53	$18.55	
6	Burgers	$1.40	27	$13.23	
7	Drinks	$0.75	48	$12.60	
8		======	========	========	=======
9			Totals	$44.38	$0.00

several other models that Bill calculates more often than once per game. The following macro, devised to fill the Total Profit column with the season's accumulated profits, uses the Data Fill command:

	A	B	C	D
12	\a	/DFtothot~tothot+dayhot~~~		
13		/DFtotburg~totburg+dayburg~~~		
14		/DFtotdrink~totdrink+daydrink~~~		

Assign the following range names by selecting /Range Name Create:

dayhot   D5   *tothot*   E5
dayburg D6   *totburg* E6
daydrink D7   *totdrink* E7

After Bill has changed the values in the Today's Sales column, he presses MACRO-A. Here's what happens:

/DFtothot~tothot + dayhot~ ~ ~   Places the value, not the formula, of *tothot + dayhot* in the cell named *tothot*. On the first run *tothot + dayhot* equals $18.50 ($0 + $18.50). On the next run, this value will equal $18.50 plus whatever the profits are for the next game.

/DFtotburg~totburg + dayburg~ ~ ~ Places the value of *totburg + dayburg* in the cell named *totburg*.

/DFtotdrink~totdrink + daydrink~ ~ ~   Places the value of *totdrink + daydrink* in the cell named *totdrink*.

Since the Data Fill command enters values instead of formulas, you need not set Worksheet Recalculation to Manual to maintain the correct season totals in the Total Profit column.

PRINTING MULTIPLE COPIES

A permanent loop macro repeats its steps continuously until you stop it with the Break key. Here is a looping macro that uses the Data Fill command to keep track of the number of times it has repeated its task. It allows you to specify how many copies of a print range you want to print. It then prints that number:

	A	B	C	D
1	\p	/PPR{?}~Q		
2		/XNHow many copies? ~copies~		
3		/REcounter~		
4	loop	/PPAGPQ		
5		/DFcounter~counter+1~~~		
6		/XI(counter>=copies)~/XQ		
7		/XGloop~		
8				
9	copies			
10	counter			

I often write macros in the top-left corner of my worksheets and place data and reports either below or to the right of the macros. If this arrangement later becomes a problem, I use the Move command to move the macros out of the way. You can put this macro anywhere as long as all of its pieces are in place. Once you enter it on the worksheet, go to the cell containing the label \p, and select /Range Name Labels Right. Then press End DownArrow End DownArrow DownArrow Return. This names the cells to the right of the labels with range names *\p, loop, copies,* and *counter.*

Finally, to run the macro, press MACRO-P. Check the *1-2-3* manual for instructions on invoking macros.) Here's what happens:

/PPR{?}~Q   Presses slash and selects Print Printer Range. The macro pauses here and allows you to highlight the range to print. If you have previously highlighted a range, you can press Return to reselect that range or you can cancel the range by pressing the Backspace key, and then assign a new range. When you press Return, *1-2-3* accepts the range to print and then exits from the Print menu.

/XNHow many copies? ~copies~   Displays the prompt *How many copies?* and places the number you type in the cell named *copies* when you press Return. The /XN command allows you to enter only a number. If you accidentally enter a label while the prompt is displayed, *1-2-3* beeps and displays the error message *Illegal number input.* Simply press Return and reenter the number.

/REcounter~   Erases the cell named counter. This guarantees that the macro will loop the correct number of times.

/PPAGPQ Presses the slash key, then selects Print Printer Align Go Page-Advance Quit. This prints one copy of the Print range, ejects the paper to the top of the next page, and exits from the Print menu.

/DFcounter~counter + 1 ~ ~ ~   Increases the value of the cell named *counter* by 1.

/XI(counter > = copies)~/XQ   If the value of *counter* is greater than or equal to the value of the cell named *copies*, the macro stops. Let's say you have entered 3 in response to the prompt *How many copies?* When the macro has printed one copy of the Print range, *counter* will equal 1. The macro will continue processing in the cell following the /XI statement.

/XGloop~   Continues processing keystrokes in the cell named *loop*.

The macro goes to the cell named *loop*, prints another copy of the Print range, then increases the value of the cell named *counter* by 1 and compares *counter* with *copies*. Again, if you have entered 3 to the prompt *How many copies?*, the macro processes the next cell's instructions that send it back to loop for a third printing, *counter* increases by 1 (it equals 3), and the macro once more compares *counter* with *copies*. Now *counter* and *copies* agree (they both equal 3), so the macro processes the /XQ command and quits.

These are just a few uses of the Data Fill command. Experiment with it, and you will find many other ways that Data Fill can help you write short, fast macros.

THE CIRC INDICATOR

A formula that refers to itself is a circular reference. When this kind of formula exists, *1-2-3* reacts by illuminating the CIRC indicator along the bottom border of your screen. Most circular references change in value each time the worksheet recalculates. For instance, the value of the formula on the following worksheet will increase by 5 for each recalculation:

	A	B	C	D
1	+A1+B1	5		
2				

It means "add the value of cell B1 to the value of cell A1." When you first enter the formula, cell A1 evaluates to 5. When you press the CALC key or enter something elsewhere on the worksheet, the formula evaluates to 10. Remember, changing a value on the worksheet causes the entire worksheet to recalculate. After the next recalculation, the formula equals 15, and so on.

You can control circular references by issuing the Worksheet Global Recalculation Manual command. This disables automatic recalculation. Cells containing circular references will then change in value only when you press the CALC key. In general, it is best to avoid creating circular references in the first place.

_____

JULY 1985

3

Using Range Justify

Concatenating and parsing labels is not
1-2-3 Release 1A's forté, but macros using the Range Justify
command do both of these tasks and more.

BY DANIEL GASTEIGER

At first glance, labels in Release 1A of *1-2-3* don't appear to be dynamic. There are no string operators that add together (concatenate) or break apart (parse) labels, and labels in formulas equal zero.

In previous articles we've looked at techniques that determine whether labels are equal, look up and edit labels in tables or databases, and concatenate labels into mailing addresses. In this chapter we'll explore the Range Justify command and use it in macros to concatenate and parse labels.

CHAINING TOGETHER

We previously showed a macro that combines names from two adjacent cells into a cell named *name*. The following is a variation of that macro; it combines names from adjacent columns into the column to their right:

	A	B	C	D
1	\m	/C~first~{RIGHT}		
2		/C~last~{RIGHT}		
3	first			
4	last			
5		{DOWN}{LEFT}{LEFT}		
6		/XG\m~		

To run the macro, enter it as shown and assign the labels in column A as range names to the corresponding cells of column B; go to cell A1 and press slash, select Range Name Labels Right, and press End DownArrow DownArrow Return. Enter a list of first names in column A, with matching last names in column B, starting in cell A8:

	A	B	C	D
8	Willy	Hackman		
9	Beth	Riceburned		
10	Tex	Malone		

Place the cell pointer in A8, highlighting the initial first name, then start the macro by holding down the MACRO key and pressing M. (Consult your *1-2-3* documentation for information on invoking macros). Here's what happens:

/C~first~{RIGHT}   Copies the contents of the current cell to the cell named *first* within the macro, then moves the cell pointer one cell to the right.

/C~last~{RIGHT}   Copies from the current cell to the cell named *last* and moves the cell pointer to the right. By now the next cell of the macro contains a first name, and the one after it contains a last name. The macro types these back-to-back in the control panel.

{DOWN}{LEFT}{LEFT}   Moves the cell pointer down, entering the concatenated first and last names into the cell, then moves the cell pointer two cells to the left, over the next first name in your list.

/XG\m~   Sends the macro looking for keystrokes to the cell named \m. The macro restarts, concatenating the next name, moving down, and so on. It stops when it has concatenated all the names because it copies blank cells into *first* and *last*, leaving nothing for the macro to process.

You can easily modify your macro to add a space between the first and last names by inserting a row above the cell named *last* (B4) and entering a single space into the new, empty cell B4.

This is a self-modifying macro, so called because it rewrites itself while it runs, producing different results based on the modifications. In this case, the macro rewrites instructions in the cells named *first* and *last*, modifying the words that the fourth macro step enters into the worksheet. The technique is useful as long as you are certain that there will be no blanks within the list of labels you wish to combine. If your list lacks just one name, the macro fails before it concatenates the last entry, producing unpredictable and probably undesirable results.

WHAT IS RANGE JUSTIFY?

Almost everything about *1-2-3* is geared toward manipulating numeric data, but Range Justify is different. It lets you drastically alter the appearance of non-numeric data. The Range Justify command arranges labels to fit within the width you specify. For example, starting with a blank worksheet, enter the label *Now is the time for all good men...* into cell A1.

With the cell pointer in A1, press /Range Justify; indicate A1..C1 and press Return. The words that extend past the indicated right margin (cell C1) move down and become long labels in column A. When you indicate more than one row to the Range Justify command, *1-2-3* tries to fit all the text within the range you specified. If there is not enough room, you receive the error message *Justify range is full*. Whatever didn't fit within the range is included in the bottom-left cell of the range. It's important to understand that the justified labels remain in one column; they do not occupy cells to the right. The justification range serves only as a guideline for the width into which the labels should fit.

You can justify a column of contiguous labels simply by indicating a one-row justification range. *1-2-3* rearranges everything below the specified row down to the first nonlabel cell.

The Range Justify command lets you restructure text to fit whatever format your models require and can even give you a rudimentary word-processing capability. To do all this, it splits long labels apart (or pieces them together if need be) at blank spaces, effectively parsing (or concatenating) the labels.

CHAINING TOGETHER REVISITED

To concatenate a pair of labels using the Range Justify command, the labels must reside in vertically adjacent cells. To see how this works, start with a blank worksheet, then enter your first name in A1 and your last name in A2. Now point to cell A1 and press /Range Justify RightArrow RightArrow Return. Assuming there are fewer than 27 characters in your name, it appears as a single label in cell A1. *1-2-3* automatically places a space after the last character of the upper cell before it attaches the contents from the lower cell. Here's the macro we discussed earlier rewritten with the Range Justify command:

```
        A         B         C         D         E
1  \m          /RNCtest~{RIGHT}
2              /XI@COUNT(test)=0~/RNDtest~/XQ
3              /C~d1~{RIGHT}
4              /C~d2~{RIGHT}
5              /RJd1~/Cd1~~
6              /RNDtest~
7              {DOWN}{LEFT}{LEFT}
8              /XG\m~
```

To use the macro, enter it as shown and assign *m* as the range name for cell B1. Then set the width of column D to 35 by pointing to cell D1 and pressing /Worksheet Column-Width Set 35 Return. Finally, enter a list of first and last names in columns A and B starting in cell A10, as you did for the first example:

	A	B	C
10	Willy	Hackman	
11	Beth	Riceburned	
12	Tex	Malone	

Point to the initial first name of your list (cell A10) and start the macro. Here's what happens:

/RNCtest~{RIGHT}~   Assigns *test* as the name for the current cell and the cell to its right.

/XI@COUNT(test) = 0 ~/RNDtest~/XQ   Deletes the range name *test* and stops the macro if @COUNT(test) equals zero. The @COUNT function determines how many cells in a specified range contain data. @COUNT of a single cell equals one whether or not it contains data, while @COUNT of a larger range equals the number of cells in the range that contain labels, numbers, or formulas. When the macro assigns *test* to the first row below your list of names, @COUNT(test) equals zero, so the macro stops.

/C~d1~{RIGHT}   Copies from the current cell to cell D1, then moves the cell pointer to the right. This macro violates the convention of using range names in macros because the Range Justify command moves and destroys range names assigned to the column being justified. Reassigning those names each time they are destroyed creates more work for you and slows down your macro.

/C~d2~{RIGHT}   Copies from the current cell to cell D2, then moves the cell pointer to the right.

/RJd1~/Cd1~ ~   Justifies cell D1, pulling the contents of D2 up to fill out the width of the cell, then copies the resulting label to the current cell. If the combined first and last names contain more than 35 characters, *1-2-3* leaves them in separate cells and copies only the first name into position alongside your list. Therefore, you must adjust the width of column D to allow for the longest labels you'll be concatenating.

/RNDtest~   Deletes the range name *test* so that the macro can reassign it to the next row of your list.

{DOWN}{LEFT}{LEFT}   Moves the cell pointer down and to the left, to the first name of the next person on your list.

/XG\m~   Restarts the macro. As implied earlier, the macro continues looping until it encounters the blank cells at the end of the list.

This technique is ideal for combining names, addresses, and sentences made up of collections of words in different cells. *1-2-3* adds spaces where appropriate when combining labels with the Range Justify command. If you don't want the spaces added, use the technique presented in the first macro and create self-modifying code.

A RANGE JUSTIFY PARSER

1-2-3 can't always fit the specified labels within the width you indicate. You can use this to advantage when you want to separate pieces of labels into several cells. To see how this works, start once again with a blank worksheet. Set the width of column A to 1, and enter your first and last names into cell A1. Now issue the Range Justify command: select /Range Justify, then press Return. Your first name remains in cell A1, and your last name moves to cell A2.

You can use this technique to solve the problem of manipulating data imported from other computers. Generally, when you retrieve data from other computers via modem, your communications program creates a file of long labels. You bring such files into your worksheet using the File Import command.

Let's say you've imported a file containing a column of dates into your worksheet starting in row 14. The first few rows of data look like this:

	A	B	C	D
14	03/15/85			
15	03/29/85			
16	04/01/85			
17	04/06/85			

You'd like to use these dates in some calculations using *1-2-3*'s date serial numbers, but besides being labels instead of numbers, the dates are not in the proper format for use with the @DATE function. The following macro replaces each date label with its corresponding serial number:

	A	B	C	D	E	F
1	\d	/RNChere~{RIGHT}~				
2		/XI@COUNT(here)=0~/RNDhere~/XQ				
3		{GOTO}d1~/Chere~~{EDIT}				
4		{LEFT}{LEFT}{BS} {LEFT}				
5		{LEFT}{LEFT}{BS} ~/RJ~				
6		{EDIT}{HOME}{DEL}{DOWN}				
7		{EDIT}{HOME}{DEL}{DOWN}				
8		{EDIT}{HOME}{DEL}~				
9		{GOTO}here~				
10		@DATE(d3,d1,d2){CALC}~				
11		/REd1..d3~/RNDhere~{DOWN}				
12		/XG\d~				

Before you run the macro, set the width of column D to 1; go to any cell in column D and press /Worksheet Column-Width Set, type *1*, and press Return. Point to the first date you wish to convert (cell A14 in this case) and start the macro. Here's what happens:

/RNChere~{RIGHT}~   Assigns the range name *here* to the range including the current cell and the cell to its right.

/XI@COUNT(here)=0~/RNDhere~/XQ   Deletes the name *here* and stops the macro if @COUNT of *here* equals zero. This stops the macro when it has processed the last date label in the column.

{GOTO}d1~/Chere~~{EDIT}   Sends the cell pointer to D1 and copies the contents of the range named *here* to D1, then presses EDIT. Since *here* is a two-cell range, this step copies both the date label and a blank cell to cells D1 and E1. Whatever it copies to E1 is not important since the remainder of the macro ignores that cell. This step leaves *1-2-3* in Edit mode, ready to alter the contents of cell D1.

{LEFT}{LEFT}{BS} {LEFT}   Moves the cursor two characters to the left, presses Backspace to erase the rightmost slash in the label, types a space to replace the slash, and moves the cursor left once more.

{LEFT}{LEFT}{BS} ~/RJ~   Moves the cursor to the left two more spaces, erases the second slash in the label, replacing it with a space, and issues the Range Justify command. Because the width of the column is set to 1, each portion of the address ends up in a separate cell in the column.

{EDIT}{HOME}{DEL}{DOWN}   Presses EDIT, Home, Delete, and Down. This removes the label prefix from the cell, leaving a numeric value rather than a label. The cell pointer ends up in cell D2.

{EDIT}{HOME}{DEL}{DOWN}   Removes the label prefix from this cell, using the same keystrokes as the last step. The cell pointer ends up in cell D3.

{EDIT}{HOME}{DEL}~   Once again removes the label prefix, turning this last of the three cells containing pieces of the copy of the original label date into a numeric entry.

{GOTO}here~   Sends the cell pointer back to the cell named *here*. This is the cell containing the original date label that the macro just finished parsing.

@DATE(d3,d1,d2){CALC}~   Types the @DATE formula into the control panel, using references to the three cells containing the parsed values, then presses the CALC key, which turns the formula into a value and enters the value into the current cell.

/REd1..d3~/RNDhere~{DOWN}   Erases the parsed values from D1..D3, deletes the name *here* so that the macro can reuse it later, then moves the cell pointer to the next date label in the list.

/XG\d~   Restarts the macro, making it repeat the steps described above for the next date label.

This parsing technique has applications beyond converting data imported from other computers. You could use it to salvage other worksheet data that would be more useful if restructured. Or you can create routines that extract individual words or characters from within long labels, based on their positions within the labels. Taking the idea to extremes, you can use all of the label-arithmetic techniques we've explored to date in this column to create a search-and-replace macro that replaces every occurrence of a word within a block of text with some other word.

NOTES FOR RELEASE 2/2.01 USERS

Though you can use the techniques described in this column in *1-2-3* Release 2/2.01, there are simpler ways to accomplish the same tasks. In Release 2/2.01, labels have string values. This means you can do arithmetic with them similar to the arithmetic you do with numbers.

To concatenate labels, use the ampersand (&) operator. For example, cell A1 of the following worksheet contains the formula +A3&B3:

	A	B	C	D
1	JeanChung			
2				
3	Jean	Chung		

Because it is a formula, +A3&B3 changes appropriately when you change the contents of either cells A3 or B3. You have no need to write a macro to concatenate the labels. See Section 3, Chapter 10 for a Release 2 macro that uses this type of concatenation to print mailing labels.

Parsing in Release 2/2.01 is almost as easy as concatenation. Before you write formulas to parse data, review the section about the Data Parse command in the *1-2-3* manual. This command parses date labels as we did in the previous example. Here's how it works with that same data starting in cell A14:

Move the cell pointer to the first line of data you wish to parse. Press slash and select Data Parse Format-Line Create; *1-2-3* inserts a row and places a label that contains parsing instructions in the new blank cell. Select Input-Column and indicate the entire column of labels, including the format line, then press Return. Select Output-Range, indicate the cell directly under the format line (in this case, cell A15), and press Return. Finally, select Go. *1-2-3* replaces the date labels with date serial numbers.

To extract a particular word from a sentence, consider using the @LEFT, @RIGHT, @MID, and other string-handling @functions. These are tricky if you want to extract a word from within a long label — the last word in each of several labels of different lengths, for example. If you place the label in a cell with a width of 1 and issue the Range Justify command, pressing End DownArrow puts you at the label's last word. You might need several cells of string formulas to do this without the Range Justify command.

MARCH 1986

4

Label Arithmetic

Using 1-2-3 Release 1A @D functions and self-modifying macros, you can perform label arithmetic you may not have believed possible.

BY DANIEL GASTEIGER

1 -2-3 Release 1A is definitely a tool for number crunchers, but it can manipulate text as well as numbers. In this chapter we look at some techniques for comparing labels (strings) in *1-2-3*.

WHY COMPARE STRINGS?

By comparing numbers, you can determine whether income exceeds expenses, how much money you will have left after acquiring a new company, and what the year's profit margin will be. By comparing labels, you can find entries in a database, sort databases, and determine whether an item occurs in a list.

1-2-3 uses Data Query commands to perform these label-comparison tasks for you. When you put a word in a Criterion range, you can use the Data Query Find command to view every data record that meets the criterion. With the Data Query Extract command, you can copy records that meet the criterion into an Output range. Using the Data Sort command, you can quickly arrange data in alphabetical order.

@D functions increase *1-2-3*'s string handling power. By defining a Database range, an offset, and a Criterion range, you can determine how many times a label appears in a list (@DCOUNT), the first occurrence of a label in a list (@DMIN), and the last occurrence of a label in a list (@DMAX).

ARE THE LABELS EQUAL?

I'm often asked how to compare two labels on a *1-2-3* worksheet. Because the value of cells containing labels equals zero in formulas and functions, there seems to be no way to determine whether one label is identical to another. But it can be done. First, examine the following worksheet:

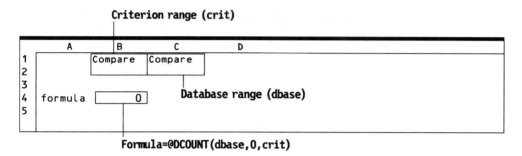

The range C1..C2 in this example is named *dbase*, and B1..B2 is named *crit*. The label *Compare* in cell C1 is the field name for a Database range, and the label *Compare* in cell B1 is the field name for a matching Criterion range. The cell named *formula* (B4) contains the formula @DCOUNT(dbase,0,crit). The @DCOUNT function calculates the number of data records that match a value contained in a Criterion range. In this case, *dbase* is the database, although it contains only one field, and *crit* is the Criterion range. When you put a label in the empty cell of each range (cells B2 and C2), *formula* generates a one if the labels are identical or a zero if they are not.

LABELS IN LISTS

Let's say your macro asks a user to enter a name, then compares the name against a list to determine whether it is already on the list. If you expand the range named *dbase* downward, your macro can handle a list containing up to 2,047 records. The macro on the following page checks the word you type against the list. If the word is already on the list, the macro displays the message *That animal is already on the list* in the control panel. If the word is not already on the list, the macro adds the word to the list and expands *dbase* downward to include the new record.

Then assign the range names \m, *msg,* and *hld* by going to cell A1, pressing the slash key, selecting Range Name Labels Right, and then pressing End DownArrow End DownArrow Return. Also assign the range name *crit* to the range B13..B14 and

```
        A           B           C           D           E
1  \m           /XLEnter animal type ~hld~
2               /XI@DCOUNT(dbase,0,crit)<>0~/XMmsg~
3               {GOTO}dbase~
4               {END}{DOWN}{DOWN}
5               /Chld~
6               /RNCdbase~{DOWN}~
7               /XG\m~
8
9  msg          That animal is already on the list
10              (press Return to continue)
11              /XG\m~
12
13              Compare     Compare
14 hld                      dog
15                          wombat
16                          jerboa
17                          hyrax
```

dbase to the range C13..C17. Finally, start the macro by holding down the MACRO key and pressing M. (Consult the macros section of your *1-2-3* manual for instructions on invoking macros.)

Here's what happens:

/XLEnter animal type ~hld~   Displays the prompt *Enter animal type* in the control panel, treats what you type as a label, and places it in the cell named *hld*. Notice that *hld* is the lower cell of the Criterion range (cell B14). Whatever you enter becomes the new criterion for @D formulas.

/XI@DCOUNT(dbase,0,crit)<>0~/XMmsg~   Transfers the flow of the macro to the menu instructions named *msg* if the label stored in the Criterion range (*crit*) matches an entry in the Database range (*dbase*). If there is no match, the macro continues in the next cell. Notice that when there is a match, this step uses the /XM command to produce a user-defined menu. The menu consists of a single choice that reads *That animal is already on the list* and its associated long prompt (*press Return to continue*). When the user presses Return, the macro processes the command /XG\m~, which sends it looking for keystrokes to the cell named \m, the first cell of the macro. The process then starts again.

{GOTO}dbase~   Sends the cell pointer to the top of the range named *dbase* (cell C13 in this example).

{END}{DOWN}{DOWN}   Sends the cell pointer to the cell below the last entry in the range named *dbase*. This works only if there is already at least one entry in *dbase*. When you adapt this macro for your own applications, be sure to create *dbase* as a two-cell range and place an entry in the empty cell before you run the macro.

/Chld~ ~   Copies the label from the cell named *bld* to the current cell.

/RNCdbase~{DOWN}~   Extends the range named *dbase* downward one row to include the new entry. The new entry becomes another item in the list against which your macro compares future entries; you cannot make the same entry twice.

/XG\m~   Sends the cell pointer looking for keystrokes to the cell named \m, the first cell of the macro. The macro displays the *Enter animal type* prompt, compares the entry against the expanded list, and accepts it if it is not already on the list or rejects it if it is already present.

NOT A PERFECT SOLUTION

The @DCOUNT function has some quirks. If you leave the lower cell of the range named *crit* blank, everything except empty cells in the database is considered a match to the criterion. As you can see from the first illustration, *formula* generates a zero, although both the Criterion and Database cells are blank and therefore equal. When you enter any record into the database, *formula* generates a one until you enter a nonmatching criterion into the Criterion cell.

A second quirk of the @DCOUNT function is its ability to use wild-card characters in making comparisons. A question mark included in a label in the Criterion range matches any character in the same position in a data record. The criterion *wr?te* matches the records *write* and *wrote*. An asterisk at the end of a label in a criterion matches all characters from that point onward in a data record. The criterion *wr** matches the records *wrote, writing,* and *writhing*. Because of these quirks, *1-2-3* cannot handle all of your label comparisons, but it is adequate for most applications.

MORE MAGIC

The @DCOUNT function lets you write macros that manipulate labels by comparing one against another or one against a list. Your applications may be as simple as the data-entry routine we discussed here, or they may be complex applications driven by menus that allow English language responses. In the next chapter we'll explore the @DMIN and @DMAX functions by using them to find and edit records in databases.

OCTOBER 1985

5

Label Lookup in 1-2-3

This unorthodox use of @D functions in *1-2-3* Release 1A lets you look up labels in tables and edit records in a database.

BY DANIEL GASTEIGER

In the previous chapter, we used the @D functions of *1-2-3*, Release 1A, to compare labels. Using the @DCOUNT function, we determined whether two labels were identical or whether a label we entered already existed in a list on our worksheet. In this chapter we'll see how to use the @DMIN and @DMAX functions to locate labels in tables and to edit database entries, tasks that are absent from *1-2-3*'s fundamental capabilities.

WORKING WITH DATABASES

A *1-2-3* database is a collection of information stored as records in individual rows of the worksheet. A record is made up of fields that contain specific information about the item it describes. For example, as a manager of a zoo or animal-breeding farm, you might create a database containing one record for each animal, each record containing separate fields for the animal's name, type, location, and date of birth. A part of such a database looks like this:

	A	B	C	D
12	Name	Type	Location	DOB
13	Carlton	wombat	Pen #6	Aug-84
14	Portnoy	jerboa	Terrarium #2	Feb-85
15	Hiram	hyrax	Terrarium #2D	Jan-85
16	Fred	ocelot	Veterinarian	Nov-78
17	Paco	paca	Cage #8	Oct-84

Let's say you want to use this database to determine the whereabouts of particular animals in the collection. Because of the database's size, you can use the Data Query Extract command to make the task easier. To do this, follow our example by entering the data as shown (use the @DATE function to enter dates in the *DOB* column and format the column using the Range Format command, selecting Date 3 as the format). Then select /Range Name Create, type *dbase*, press Return, and indicate the range A12..D17, finishing with Return. (Range names used in this article are arbitrary. Feel free to substitute whatever names you please.)

Next establish a Criterion range on the worksheet. The Criterion range needed to locate individual animals by name consists of two cells. One contains the field heading *Name*, which coincides with the field heading of the *Name* column in the database. The second, directly below the first, will receive the name of the animal you wish to find using the Data Query Extract command. Name this two-cell Criterion range *crit* (B9..B10).

Establish an Output range on the worksheet. For this example, the Output range is two cells deep. The upper cell contains the field heading *Location*, matching the field header of the *Location* column in the database. The lower cell is blank. When you perform the extract, it will receive the *Location* entry from the record in the database that matches the criterion. Name this range *Output* (D9..D10).

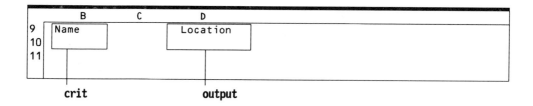

To perform an extract, you must first set Input, Criterion, and Output ranges using the /Data Query menu. Press slash and select Data Query Input; type *dbase* and press Return. Select Criterion and enter *crit*, then select Output and enter *output*. Finally, select Quit; *1-2-3* returns to Ready mode.

With these settings established, enter an animal's name into the Criterion range (go to cell B10 and enter *Fred*, for example), and select /Data Query Extract. Fred's whereabouts — Veterinarian — appear in the Output range. Select Quit to leave the menu.

After doing one extract, you can do another simply by entering a new animal's name in the Criterion range and pressing the QUERY key. The QUERY key repeats the last query operation you selected from the menus; it is one of *1-2-3*'s great timesavers once you master its use.

LIMITATIONS AND ALTERNATIVES

If several of your animals are named Fred and each has its own entry in the database, this model generates the error message *Too many records for Output range* when you issue the /Data Query Extract command. When you clear the message by pressing Escape, the location of the first Fred in your database appears in the Output range.

To accommodate several animals of the same name, modify your Criterion range to allow a selection criterion for animal type. To do this, enter the word *Type* into cell C9. Press slash and select Range Name Create, enter *crit* (or select it by pointing), then press RightArrow and Return. Now, to find out where Fred the ocelot is, enter *Fred* into the *Name* column of the Criterion range (cell B10) and *ocelot* into the *Type* column (cell C10). The /Data Query Extract command should no longer produce an error message.

The Data Query Extract command is a powerful tool for looking up labels. Unfortunately, it does not allow you to make changes to database entries that it finds. You need a way to move the cell pointer to Fred's entry in the database so that you can update his record when he returns from the veterinarian. *1-2-3*'s /Data Query Find command lets you view Fred's entry in the database, but you can't edit the entry while viewing, and the cell pointer returns to its starting point when you end the Query Find command.

DO IT WITH A MACRO

The "Query Find and Edit" macro relies on a few unusual macro techniques. First, it requires an extra column in your database to hold a serial number for each entry. Second, it uses the @DMIN function to build a target cell address for a {GOTO} command, violating our convention of using only range names within macros. This makes the technique rigid, but it should prove useful for most database applications.

Enter the label *Serial* in cell E12 of the worksheet. This is the heading for a new column of the database. Move the cell pointer down to E13 and press slash (/). Then select Data Fill, indicate cells E13..E17, and press Return. Enter 1 as the Start number, 1 as the Step number, and accept the default (2047) as the Stop number; *1-2-3* fills the range with numbers from 1 to 5. Select /Range Name Create to extend the range *dbase* one column to the right.

Whenever you add or delete records from your database, refill the *Serial* column through the last database entry. Exclude the *Serial* column from the Data range if you sort the database. This preserves its order so that your macro will continue to work.

To make this discussion easier to follow, assume that no animals in your database have the same name. Also eliminate the Output range from your worksheet. Use the Range Erase command to erase cells C9..D10. Then use the Range Name Delete command to delete the range name *output*, and use Range Name Create to shrink the range *crit* to B9..B10. Now enter the label *holder* into cell A10 and assign it as the name for cell B10 using the /Range Name Labels Right command. Your worksheet should look like this:

	A	B	C	D	E
9		Name			
10	holder				
11					
12	Name	Type	Location	DOB	Serial
13	Carlton	wombat	Pen #6	Aug-84	1
14	Portnoy	jerboa	Terrarium #2	Feb-85	2
15	Hiram	hyrax	Terrarium #2D	Jan-85	3
16	Fred	ocelot	Veterinarian	Nov-78	4
17	Paco	paca	Cage #8	Oct-84	5

The following is a "Query Find and Edit" macro for a *1-2-3* database:

	A	B	C	D	E
1	\m	/LXEnter animal's name: ~holder~			
2		/XI@ISERR(@DMIN(dbase,4,crit))~/XG\m~			
3		{GOTO}rownum~			
4		@DMIN(dbase,4,crit)+12{CALC}{HOME}'~			
5		{GOTO}A			
6	rownum				
7		~{RIGHT}{RIGHT}			

Enter it on the worksheet as shown, and assign the labels \m and *rownum* as range names for the cells to their right; go to cell A1 and press slash, then select Range Name Labels RightArrow and press End DownArrow Return. To start the macro, hold down the MACRO key and press M (if your computer lacks a MACRO key, consult your *1-2-3* manual for instructions on starting macros). Here's what happens:

/XLEnter animal's name: ~holder~   Displays the prompt *Enter animal's name* in the control panel, then enters what you type as a label into the cell named *holder*. Since *holder* is within the Criterion range, the name you enter becomes the criterion for *1-2-3*'s database operations.

/XI@ISERR(@DMIN(dbase,4,crit))~/XG\m~   Restarts the macro if the name you entered is not in the database. This step helps keep the macro from crashing if you make a typing error.

{GOTO}rownum~ Sends the cell pointer to the cell named *rownum. Rownum* is a cell within the body of the macro (B6 in the illustration). It is empty on the macro's first run and filled with data by the next macro step.

@DMIN(dbase,4,crit) + 12{CALC}{HOME}'~   Evaluates the formula @DMIN(dbase,4,crit) + 12 and enters the result as a label into *rownum*. The @DMIN part of the formula equals the value found in the fifth column of the database (the *Serial* field) in the record that matches the criterion. If you entered *Fred* in response to the prompt, @DMIN(dbase,4,crit) equals 4 (Fred's is the fourth record in the database). Using @DMAX gives the same result as long as there is only one Fred in the database. The database starts in row 12 of the worksheet, so adding 12 to 4 gives the row number of Fred's record. Your database can start on any row as long as you replace 12 with the appropriate row number.

{GOTO}A   Starts a {GOTO} command. A is the first column of the database. The following cell (*rownum*) by now contains a label version of the proper row number that completes the target address of the {GOTO} command.

~{RIGHT}{RIGHT}   Finishes the {GOTO} command, sending the cell pointer to the first field of the appropriate record in the database, then moves the pointer two cells to the right, landing on the location of whatever animal you named in response to the prompt. You can change the entry, browse the record and those around it, and restart the macro to locate a different record.

VARIATIONS ON A THEME

Your macro need not send you into the database to update records. With a few changes, your macro can ask the animal's location and record it directly into the database. Here's how it looks:

	A	B	C	D	E
1	\m	/XLEnter animal's name: ~holder~			
2		/XI@ISERR(@DMIN(dbase,4,crit))~/XG\m~			
3		{GOTO}rownum~			
4		@DMIN(dbase,4,crit)+12{CALC}{HOME}'~			
5		/XLEnter animal's location: ~C			
6	rownum				
7		~			

And here's how it works. Cells B1 through B4 are unchanged from the original macro. They prompt for the animal's name, check to be sure the name is in the database, and enter the row number of the animal's record as a label into the cell named *rownum*. Cell B5 is different.

/XLEnter animal's location: ~C   Starts a /XL command by displaying the prompt *Enter animal's location* in the control panel. Whatever you type is entered as a label into the cell specified after the tilde (~). This is a cell whose address begins with the C on this line and finishes with the row number contained on the next line; the /XL command itself ends with the tilde on the last line of the macro. C is the *Location* column of the database, hence your response to the prompt is entered directly into the appropriate row and field of the database.

You have access through this macro to any field of the database by changing the column letter in the second /XL command. And you are not limited to viewing and replacing entries. Your macro can copy entries from within a database (replicating the Data Query Extract command discussed earlier) or even edit existing entries to mark accounts paid, for example.

1-2-3 Release 1A users have been frustrated with *1-2-3*'s apparent inability to let them edit found entries in a database. The techniques outlined above should satisfy most users and open the door to powerful database applications.

NOVEMBER 1985

SECTION
6

FOR ADVANCED USERS:
Helping Yourself, Helping Others

L ike any other kind of programming, writing macros can be challenging as well as productive. The goal is to create a semi- or fully-automated worksheet that limits the possibility of error while operating at maximum speed and efficiency.

Advanced macro writers often create models for use by other people; a challenging task. Among the design and technical issues discussed in these articles are how to write structured code, how to display help messages, how to capture and evaluate user keystrokes before they are entered into the worksheet, and how to distribute revised versions of an already distributed model. This technique alone can save you hundreds of hours of administrative time, winning the respect of both users and your own boss.

To finish off the section, we've included three chapters on very advanced techniques using the new macro I/O commands to directly read and write ASCII files, gain greater control over your printed output, and create graphic display enhancements on your monitor.

While a couple of articles in this section were written with *Symphony* in mind, they are all of use to *1-2-3* users except "More Messages," which discusses methods of using *Symphony*'s windowing capabilities to give users information.

1

Questions to Ask Before You Write Code

Address these concerns with your client before you begin any development effort.

BY DANIEL GASTEIGER

You might not have asked for the job. You might not even know you have the job. But if you're creating worksheets that other people use, then like it or not, you're a developer. And if you're writing templates to other users' specifications, you're in about as deep as you can get.

If you are writing templates to other people's specifications, then you've probably also rewritten templates, and rewritten them, and rewritten them. A template built to a user's specifications is rarely the template that the user wants. But if you make the right moves before you start developing a template, you can reduce the amount of time you'll spend rewriting it. Here are a few thoughts on how to play the game.

WHAT DO THEY WANT?

Key to any development effort is determining exactly what your client wants. Get your clients to describe their needs in terms of the information they need to process and the output they wish to produce.

Clients have a penchant for describing their needs in terms of the techniques a model will use. Generally, this type of information is useless. A client might ask for a database that uses lookup tables and some kind of string formulas to print a monthly report. Through questioning you might find that your client has names and addresses of 500 people who should receive a monthly report of the contents of a particular database. The template that does this is significantly different from one that generates a monthly report based on a database that contains information about 500 people. In either case, you might use string formulas and lookup tables. On the other hand, until you're actually designing the model, its elements are not relevant.

Strive with your client to define all the tasks that people will perform with the model. From what source will the data originate? Will users enter data? In what form will the data be? What needs to happen to the data? Will it be sorted? Will it be graphed? What kinds of reports will be needed? What should be the format of the reports? How much data are you discussing? Keep your first discussions about a project in these terms, and try to be exhaustive. Until these questions are answered, you don't know for sure if you've got a job to do.

DO THEY REALLY WANT IT?

An exhaustive list of tasks that the client wants a template to perform should contain items that fulfill the client's wildest hopes. Ask the client to guess what the template's most unlikely application might be. Some of the items suggested might happen by accident anyway, and these extra items provide a good starting point to pare down the model's complexity.

And paring is what you should do. Your client will be most satisfied with a model that is simple and easy to use. If their list of features includes the kitchen sink, help them realize that they don't need a sink to change a light bulb. Your client might describe a complete text and data-management tool that lets them enter, edit, select, erase, and sort information with ease. They may not know that they're describing *Symphony*'s FORM window, which makes your job easier if they're also using *Symphony*.

Whatever the case, make sure that your clients need the features they describe. While you're at it, establish why the client wants a particular feature. Knowing a feature's use can help you design it to fit well with the rest of the model. Features that will be used once a year shouldn't be as prominent in the model as features that are used daily. Also, frequently used features should be the most elegant and streamlined so that the client doesn't think your model is a clunker.

SHOULD THEY REALLY WANT IT?

People tend toward inertia, particularly with regard to using computers. Most end users want to use what they're already using. If a new product or tool requires significant training (or sounds as though it might), then forget it. In fact, you probably know a few people in your organization who still haven't gotten around to trying out their computers.

This inertia problem can lead clients to ask for products that don't make much sense. For example, many businesses accumulate piles of information each day and need a tool that lets them store and analyze that information. *1-2-3* and *Symphony* might be ideal for performing analysis, but there is a logical upper limit to the amount of information the software can handle. If your clients are dealing with several hundred data records a day, you might help them (and yourself) most by convincing them to use a package other than *1-2-3* or *Symphony*. Failing this, look forward to creating a template that shuffles data from one file to another and takes hours to complete tasks that other commercially available software could do in minutes.

The point is, it makes sense to do some things with *1-2-3* and *Symphony*, but not all things. If your clients see these products as the only acceptable tools, and you see a considerably superior alternative, try to sell the alternative. If alternate products don't offer significantly more efficiency or ease of use (even if they are better suited to the task), accept the clients' inertia and stick with what they know.

WHO'S GOING TO USE IT?

Determine who the end users of your model will be. If you can presuppose a high level of experience with *1-2-3* or *Symphony*, your model can be less rigid and leave room for interpretation (but don't go overboard in this direction). If your end users are just learning the software, your model should assume that they'll have difficulty and should guide them carefully.

Advanced users will be frustrated by an over-prompted, confining template, while beginners are likely to get nowhere with a very sketchy model. Documentation can help the beginners along, and you should determine early what form the documentation should take. Will the users expect on-line help? Will one-line prompts and menus offer enough guidance? Should off-line documentation reiterate the *1-2-3* or *Symphony* manuals, or can you assume that users will know the fundamentals?

You should also determine what kind of training you or someone else will be expected to provide with the template. If end users are simply going to receive a copy of the model and be on their own, the documentation will probably be quite involved. However, if each user will receive some training with the model, your documentation might simply help the trainer to train.

Of course, you can knock a model together in a few days' time, and it's nice to be able to promise that, but be cautious about making this offer. Have you allowed time for testing your model? For demonstrating it and making refinements based on your client's reactions? For writing supporting documentation? Does the client anticipate a need to learn how to use the model, or should the model be idiotproof? Make sure your client allows you enough time to do a thorough job. Better to estimate three extra weeks into the task and never use them than to miss a projected delivery date.

WHO'S GOING TO SUPPORT IT?

Here's my favorite question: Once the template is in use, who fixes damaged copies? Who makes changes when changes are needed? Who fixes the model when an end user finds a flaw? If you're the one, establish limits before you build the model. Your job should be to build the template to specifications. If you're being paid for that effort, establish right away that future modifications mean more work and more pay.

Ongoing maintenance can also be costly. If the model works when it leaves your hands but comes back broken, do you expect to make the repairs? Do your models suffer design flaws that lead them to breakdown, or are the flaws in your user base? If you identify problems in the user community, you might decide to build macro-driven templates that lock the user out of the worksheet. If your models are self-destructing, it's time for you to take a refresher course.

Of course, a responsible developer will guarantee a model. If someone discovers bugs after you distribute the template, it's in your best interest to make repairs quickly and to help people out of any jams you might have caused them.

Explore all of these issues before you begin creating a template for someone else's use. But don't stop here. For big projects, work out a plan and review it with your client before you begin development. In many cases, you can create a prototype of the product and demonstrate it before you finalize the design.

Some developers advocate mapping out the worksheet, writing documentation, and flowcharting the whole mess before writing a line of code. But a worksheet is malleable enough that in many cases you can build and rebuild a model more quickly than you can map the whole thing out in advance. Once you've dealt with the fundamental issues, you'll have to decide which development strategy works best for you.

OCTOBER 1987

2

Basic Spreadsheet Layout

Some basics about designing templates for use by other people.

BY DONALD E. KLAMON

There is no best way to structure a worksheet, but there are many bad ways. This article will help you identify and avoid layout problems before they occur. The problems we'll discuss are caused by that necessary evil of all worksheet templates: the user. There is no way to construct a truly indestructible template, but you can minimize the chances of a user damaging your models.

We'll focus on applications that reside entirely on the worksheet, and we'll assume that you're working either with *1-2-3* Release 2 or higher or with *Symphony*. *Symphony* users should also refer to the *"Symphony* Models" section. These observations should help avert disaster while you're creating a model and later when it's pressed into service.

FREEDOM

The first issue to consider in designing a worksheet is that of control versus versatility. If your model is macro-driven and provides no escape from macro control, your worksheets can be relatively unstructured with impunity. You must still consider whether the macros will insert and delete rows or columns, whether you've left room for the worksheet to expand as needed, and whether you've left room in which to modify the macros themselves if the need arises.

Whether the model is entirely macro-controlled or not, your worksheet will probably contain several different work areas. These will normally consist of the user's work area, the developer's workspace, and common areas. Let's consider how you might lay out each of these spaces.

USER'S AREA

This is the area of the template that the user sees. It usually consists of one or more ranges whose contents and structures are determined by the nature of the application. Generally, the user's area contains space for data entry, word processing, data analysis, and sometimes even "free play." Few general rules apply to the layout of this area. Your primary concern should be with the location of the user areas in relation to other parts of the model.

Structure the user areas so that the most likely changes you or your users will make in the future will have the least impact. If you're likely to insert rows or columns into a particular table, don't put another table beside it. However, if you're not likely to alter a table, segregate it with other stable worksheet structures. For example, you're not likely to delete one month's worth of data in a series of twelve months' worth. Therefore, it is fairly safe to stack such tables several deep in the worksheet, matching columns by month.

Leave extra room within the user areas. If you're unlikely to add new headings later on, leave some room within the template. Blank rows can improve the model's look, and they provide room for future expansion.

Leave blank rows and columns between user's work areas. Try to give the most volatile sections room to expand and contract. Databases, for example, tend to grow downward and are easiest to manage when they fall below other worksheet structures. Financial records that expand monthly will most likely need space to expand to the right.

Consider that everything to the right of newly inserted columns moves to the right. After several updates of an ever-expanding model, data structures might end up in uncharted territory. Try to place expanding worksheet structures at the frontier.

DEVELOPER'S AREA

When you build a model, you create structures all over the worksheet. None of these structures are immune to change over time, though some are more likely than others to change. Generally, developers create a set of structures that users never see. These might consist of macros, documentation, tables, and variables upon which other structures rely.

When you create a model, keep these "invisible" structures together in their own area. If you're writing macros, set aside a range of 10 columns by several more rows than the macro will require. For the most part, your macros will occupy only one column of the developer's area. However, thorough developers take time to label named cells and include descriptive text about each macro step in the worksheet. Also, macro instructions that generate user-defined menus require as many as nine columns (eight choices and a blank column to the right of the last choice). Ten columns should handle any macro you write.

A macro often relies on one or more cells outside of the macro to keep track of its own processing. These cells might be {FOR} loop counters, formulas that perform intermediate calculations, or logical expressions involved in determining the macro's flow of control. The function of your macros will be easier to deduce if you collect these variables into a compact range. They're easy to find if you put them in a space above or below your macros, but because macros tend to grow downward, put the variables above the macros.

The overwhelming key to preserving the integrity of your macros and their supporting structures is to protect them from row and column insertions and deletions. Inserting rows indiscriminately will bring any macro to its knees. Inserting columns can dismember your macro-driven menus. You can best protect these structures by locating them diagonally above the user's area of the worksheet.

COMMON AREAS

Assuming you've left "free-play" areas in your model, you've probably also included "controlled-play" areas. These are areas with which the user interacts in a fairly predictable manner. For example, this area might include a data-entry form managed by the Range Input command (in *1-2-3*) or *Symphony* Release 1.2 using the INPUT.APP add-in, or perhaps a number of cells involved in necessary but seldom-used calculations.

The volatility of these structures will determine where you place them on the worksheet. Your user's area will most likely expand downward and to the right. The most static, partially controlled areas will be relatively safe if they fall above the user's area and as far to the left as possible to the the left of the user's area and as high on the worksheet as possible. Database Output ranges, however should fall to one side or the other of the user's area, as Output ranges can dramatically alter the contents of a worksheet. The figure on the next page diagrams a worksheet template.

SYMPHONY MODELS

Symphony provides tools that let you segregate worksheet structures and better protect them from damage. With *Symphony* a collage of worksheet elements can appear to users as a well-organized application.

A Restrict range segregates one worksheet structure from all the others. Inserting

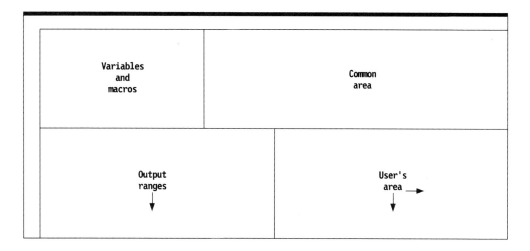

and deleting rows and columns in a restricted window affects only the area of the worksheet within the window's Restrict range. For the most part, you should enclose newly created structures within their own windows or enclose several related structures within one window.

For example, once you generate a database, restrict the window containing it. The Restrict range should encompass the database's related ranges, the database itself (plus room for downward growth — often this extends to the last row of the worksheet), and several columns to the right of the database to allow for expansion.

Once you have enclosed all of the individual elements of your models in windows, you can move easily from element to element simply by pressing the WINDOW key. However, life is never as easy as this sounds.

Don't be seduced by *Symphony*'s windowing capability. It's easy to create more windows than you can easily manage. Also, without some type of plan, you could end up with one worksheet structure stuck plumb in the middle of another's expansion space. Create a layout that accounts for the varying volatility of the worksheet structures the model uses. Don't put databases below databases or DOC windows on top of DOC windows. Leave room for these structures to expand.

Finally, consider the *Symphony* Macro Library Manager (Hyperspace). Hyperspace lets you put macros and their associated ranges and tables into libraries that don't reside on the worksheet. This clears up the worksheet, apparently simplifying its layout. But be warned: Macro applications in Hyperspace require more planning than do worksheet macros.

Macros in Hyperspace may not be able to perform database calculations unless their associated database is also in Hyperspace. In addition, macros in Hyperspace cannot include dynamic code (that is, string formulas that evaluate to macro commands) that refers to the current worksheets. Because of these things, worksheets used with Hyperspace macros may need to include "exchange" areas: space preserved to receive data, formulas, and macro code, which are dropped out of Hyperspace under macro control.

CLOSING THOUGHTS

Placing macros and their associated ranges in the top-left corner of the worksheet provides a hidden benefit. With this arrangement you can conceal the macros behind fixed worksheet titles. Simply adjust the display (by moving the cell pointer) so that your macros are off-screen, and place the cell pointer to the right of the column you wish to use as a border. If your macros are in columns A through J, column K should be the leftmost visible column and the cell pointer should be in column L. Then select /Worksheet Titles Vertical (in *Symphony*, MENU Settings Titles Vertical). Your macros will remain off-screen until someone makes a concerted effort to view them.

Not all worksheet models will require premeditated design, while some will require excruciating attention to detail. However, the rationale behind the described layout follows for every model you build: Figure out where the user is likely to batter your template, and guard against possible damage. While you're working on that, I'll try to figure out how to eliminate the user and make our jobs easier.

FEBRUARY 1987

3

Are Your Models User Friendly?

Some considerations for seeing that your users make the most of your models.

BY DONALD E. KLAMON

One day over lunch, our firm's informal developer's group talked about how we make our models user friendly. We were surprised by the number and variety of ways we came up with. Some techniques came from user requests, but most arose during the testing process when, for example, a user made an assumption the developer never dreamed of. Not all types of user friendliness are appropriate for every model you create, but here are some general concepts and suggestions to get you started.

CAN THIS MODEL BE USED?

The first consideration is whether people can actually use your models. This is not quite as silly as it seems. A developer often has a very powerful machine with lots of memory. A user may have a less powerful machine. When you build a model, take care that its minimum hardware and memory requirements do not exceed the minimum configuration in the user community. Consider the size of the model in another way: If the model takes a long time to load, it may not get used often. I have seen models that took more than five minutes to load into a PC's memory. If your models are very large, consider alternatives, such as splitting your model into two smaller, more manageable models.

Another configuration concern is the software release your users have. In *1-2-3*, for example, you may want to write one model for Release 1A and another for Release 2/2.01. In this case, you should also ensure that the Release 1A version of the model can easily transfer to later releases as people upgrade.

FROM THE USER'S PERSPECTIVE

Systems analysts and designers rarely think the same way users think. Therefore, it is helpful to involve one or more users in the development of a model. If you can get a cross section of users to act as guinea pigs, you can anticipate problems and generally make models acceptable at all levels of expertise.

The overall design, within and between models, should reflect the way people do business. For example, the rows and columns for data input should be in the same order as the user's input document. At the least, the worksheet should be set up in a way that is logically consistent with the data to be entered. Where possible, make your model's structure and performance as similar as you can to that of the other models extant in your user community. Also consider the primary tasks: If the main concern is to transfer data to a mainframe, you should make this portion of the model and the process as easy as possible. If most of your users have floppy-disk systems, you may want to keep the models small enough so that users aren't constantly changing disks. If the user requires several print options, it might be worthwhile to build a custom print menu into the model to make the process easier.

CUSTOMIZED MENUS AND MACROS

Menus and macros, in combination, are the mechanics that make the most visible addition to models. Customized menus can have a structure similar to *1-2-3* and *Symphony* command menus. That is, you can have multiple main menus and specialized submenus. Be sure to include in each submenu an option that returns the user to the previous menu or to Ready mode. People will occasionally make inappropriate or incorrect menu choices, and there should be an easy path back.

If many people will use your models, consider building in help screens by storing explanatory labels somewhere on the worksheet. If someone selects the Help option from the custom menu, a macro can copy the labels to a portion of the current screen or move the cell pointer to the labels' location. Of course, you must provide a way to get back to the previous location.

Make sure to design your models so that, after people get into the menu, there will not be major problems if they just press Return. *1-2-3* and *Symphony* use this philosophy. For example, the default (first) option after selecting Quit from the main menu is No, so users can't make a catastrophic mistake by pressing Return to accept the default option.

EFFECTIVE DOCUMENTATION

Users have widely divergent perspectives on documentation. To some, it is the first step in learning the models; to others, it is a last resort to be used only in case of crisis. You can make the documentation a user-friendly element of the package, if it is well done.

Try to write the documentation in nontechnical language and define new terminology, and try to make it understandable to all users. This means writing to the lowest common denominator without insulting the advanced user (a neat trick at best). The documentation should cover not only how to use the model in the normal course of events but also what to do when things go wrong. Explain what each model does. Explain the calculations; otherwise, someone will think they're wrong and "fix" them. Also mention any default values and explain why you used them.

In most user communities, there are some advanced users who will dissect your model to learn what they can. Why not help them? You can do this in a separate section of the documentation. Begin with the architecture of the model and list the macros and menus, giving their locations and some information about their functions. Often a developer will build some "back doors" into a model. These are hidden macros that get you to the macro area, the menu area, or somewhere else on the worksheet. You use these during the development process to avoid wasting time removing titles and protection and moving around the model. If you leave them in the model, mention these back doors for the convenience of your advanced users and so that they know to include back doors in their own models.

By giving this help to advanced users, you make their examination of your model more efficient, and you make your model an educational tool as well as a production template.

AN AUDIT TRAIL FOR USERS

Rarely are models used only once. Usually they are used several times in a trial-and-error process to zero in on the final numbers. Because of this, users often end up with many printouts reflecting various stages of the process. You should give users a way to differentiate the printouts. This may be as easy as including an @TODAY or @NOW function to print the current date. Your model should also prompt users to input information on the project, cost center, division, iteration, or whatever is necessary to uniquely identify the printout.

To avoid confusion and help identify a printout, you might have a macro print other information, such as default values, percentage assumptions, or user-selected calculation options. If the model is designed to consolidate other models, the printout might list the files that have been consolidated.

SHORTCUTS

While models should be user friendly, you can take this idea a bit too far. You want to make sure that a model isn't so friendly that no one wants to use it. For example, many data-entry macros annoy users by forcing them to suffer long pauses after each entry they make. Try to make your models efficient as well as friendly.

Make sure to design your models so that users enter data only once. If the model requires users to enter identical data in several worksheets, you can devise a macro to perform a file-combine operation to bring data from one model into another. This makes it easier for the user and minimizes the opportunity for error.

If your models have custom menus, make sure that the first character of each option is different. This way, the knowledgeable user can select an option by pressing the option's first character rather than highlighting the option and pressing Return.

VEHICLES FOR CHANGE

There is no doubt that some of your models will change over time, whether they need only minor alterations or complete replacement. If people don't have the correct model, their work can be counterproductive. In addition, the best way to make a model more useful is to listen for feedback. Therefore, you need to devise ways to both deal with changes to the model and communicate with the user community.

For starters, you might put into the documentation a form that people can send back to you containing information necessary to contact them for subsequent changes. Reciprocally, make sure that users have a vehicle for requesting changes. It's best to coordinate this within user areas, but each user should know how to contact you if something is wrong or inefficient. When I wrote my first models, I was also the user, but other users made valuable suggestions. No developer can think of everything—tap the collective experience of your users to make your models better.

Keep copies of all versions of each model, what changes were made when, and the effect of these changes. You might also give each version a new release number and effective date. This greatly simplifies conversations about the current model or the latest changes.

At a minimum, keep in touch with someone in each area who can coordinate the distribution of changes and updates. If there are many models in use in your organization, you could publish a regular newsletter with the latest version of each model and instructions for getting updates.

MODELING

Many production templates are used as production vehicles only. Somehow, we lose track of the idea that we can and should use them as models to play what-if games, which help determine strategies and plans. You can encourage users to take advantage of this modeling capability in several ways.

Don't make the user change all of the data to do some modeling. For calculated amounts like subtotals or totals, leave one cell at the left of each row for a percentage. The result of each formula in a row would be multiplied by that percentage. To see the effect of cutting 25%, for example, just change the percent cell in that row from the default of 100% to 75% and recalculate. This feature should be accompanied by a menu option or macro that resets all percent cells to 100%.

If your model has a file-saving routine, give the user an option to save under a new file name rather than replace the original template with a modified copy having the same name.

MODEL ABUSE

It doesn't matter how completely a model addresses the needs of its users; there will always be people who want to make their own "improvements." I have found that even threats don't deter these helpers. The only successful approach is to work with them, explain what you have done, and tell them some of the risks they run by making changes.

Explain the model's formulas in the documentation. If one user changes a formula, at least other users can determine what is wrong and change it back. Let users know what changes have been made with each update and why. Also, make it clear in your documentation that an update may not work if the user changes the model. You may not be able to alter habits, but at least you can make people aware of the potential price.

USE YOUR USERS

As soon as you put titles on rows and columns, your model is user friendly; it's just a matter of degree from that point on.

The single key to making a model user friendly is to get to know the users. Your job is to make their tasks easier and more productive. Take their complaints as suggestions — whenever a model does something the user doesn't want or doesn't do something the user does want, it shows you a way to make the model better. The improvement may be only a note in the documentation, but even that can increase the friendliness of the model by saving people time and frustration. The greater the cross section of people involved in the development and testing, the more likely your model will be accepted, used, and productive.

And finally, don't ignore small segments of your user community, such as the helpful fixers and the advanced users. By addressing them, you can often enlist their assistance instead of working at cross-purposes. If you listen carefully to your users, you wind up looking like the expert.

OCTOBER 1987

4

Writing Structured Macros

Breaking complex macros into reusable subroutines lets you mix and match command sequences and spot errors quickly.

BY TIMOTHY BERRY

Do your *1-2-3* macros resemble spaghetti? Do you use stream-of-consciousness to write serpentine lines of macro instructions? Is it easier to rewrite than to modify your macros? If so, the techniques of structured programming can help you unscramble and organize your macros. Even if you write solid, well-designed, functional macros, giving them structure makes it easier to modify and document them.

Structured programming is nothing more than bringing common sense to the process of writing computer instructions. It entails organizing instructions and procedures into modules that you can use as the building blocks of a larger macro. You can write and test as well as expand and modify each module separately. Most of the problems that macros are designed to solve contain logically definable parts, such as input and output routines, menu presentations, and calculations. Structured programming lets you build these parts separately and combine them to form a sophisticated macro. An advantage of structured programming is that you can draft others to write and test macro segments for you. Doing so reduces the time usually spent debugging large macros. When properly organized and administered, this team approach to macro writing is quite satisfying.

	A	B	C	D	E	F
1	/XNInput starting value~~					
2	{RIGHT}					
3	/XNInput final value~~					
4	{RIGHT}					
5	/XNInput number of periods~~					
6	{RIGHT}					
7	(({LEFT}{LEFT}{LEFT}{LEFT}{LEFT}^(1/({LEFT}-1)))-1~					
8						
9						
10						
11						
12						
13						
14						
15						
16						
17						
18						

FIGURE 1A

FIGURES 1A & 1B. The essence of a structured approach to macro programming is illustrated by this typical financial calculation. Here compound average growth rate is determined by a macro. The unstructured macro in 1A provides few clues as to what's going on. Its straight-line nature makes it difficult to follow the logic. The structured version of the same macro in 1B clearly delineates macro segments by grouping them according to function and assigning descriptive range names to each group. The segment named \m controls the macro's overall flow of logic by calling subroutines as needed. Each subroutine ends with an instruction that returns control to the main macro segment. Subroutines are identified with range names rather than cell locations to provide them with mobility, self-documentation, and a measure of protection.

PROVIDING STRUCTURE

You can force almost any computer programming language to exhibit structure. Even BASIC, notorious for its lack of structure and long lines of winding logic linked by confusing Goto and If-Then statements, can be conquered. In some BASIC programs, only the author has a clear idea of what is going on at any given point in the code. On the other hand, PASCAL programmers praise PASCAL for its structure, which makes the writing of clear, logically organized programs almost second nature. In reality, BASIC programs may or may not be structured and PASCAL programs may or may not be confusing. This is also true of macros. The structure emerges as you write a macro; it is not inherent in the language.

Figures 1A and 1B shows two macros that calculate compound average growth rates. This common financial calculation can be broken into the following components: the input of variables—starting and ending values and a number of periods; the calculation of intermediate values; and the output of results. A *1-2-3* macro written to solve this problem can be divided into similar parts or subroutines.

```
        H        I       J        K        L
1  \m        /XCinput1st~{RIGHT}
2            /XCinputlast~{RIGHT}
3            /XCinputpeds~{RIGHT}
4            /XCcagrcalc~
5
6  input1st  /XNInput starting value~~
7            /RNCfirst~
8            /XR
9
10 inputlast /XNInput final value~~
11           /RNClast~~
12           /XR
13
14 inputpeds /XNInput number of periods~~
15           /RNCperiods~~
16           /XR
17
18 cagrcalc  ((last/first)^(1/(periods-1)))-1~
```

FIGURE 1B

An unstructured *1-2-3* macro that calculates compound average growth rates appears in figure 1A. Only after completing a detailed reading of each statement in the macro will you understand what is going on. A structured version of the same program appears in figure 1B. Here the macro appears as individual modules, and each module is a subroutine. Each subroutine is placed in a named range, and subroutines are used as needed. The macro named *\m* oversees the entire operation, using subroutines named *input1st, inputlast, inputpeds,* and *cagrcalc* during execution. This macro depends on several key elements for its structure. The most important is the subroutine call.

In a subroutine call, groups of macro instructions are summoned for use by the main or control segment of a macro. These groups of instructions are identified by specific range names such as *input1st* and *inputlast*. Once subroutines are executed, they return control to the main macro with a /XR command. If you want a choice of functions within a macro, you can include a subroutine that provides branching to various macro segments. Such a subroutine presents a choice of menu options. Once you make a choice, the branching subroutine directs program flow accordingly.

The structured macro in figure 1B illustrates how range names combined with subroutines break simple programs into logically definable blocks. Each of the subroutines included in the macro is identified by a range name created by using the Range Name Labels Right command. The macro segment named *\m* calls other subroutines by range name with the following command: /XCrange name. When a subroutine is complete, it returns to the macro named *\m* by executing the /XR command. For example, when you run the macro named *\m*, it calls the *input1st* subroutine, which prompts you for the first value (/XN*input starting value* ~ ~). Once you supply this value, the subroutine assigns the range name *first* to the cell holding the value so that it can be used in a later calculation. Then the /XR command ends the subroutine and *m* macro resumes control. The main program segment then calls the *inputlast* subroutine with the /XC*inputlast* instruction. This subroutine calling procedure is repeated as each instruction in the main body of *m* is executed.

Although *1-2-3* macros can identify and call subroutines by cell locations (for example, /XCM204), there are good reasons for using range names rather than cell addresses as subroutines names. First, you can keep track of range names. Second, when you treat subroutines as named ranges, you can easily change their worksheet location. Third, named ranges are not affected by the insertion or deletion of rows and columns. You can move named ranges to out-of-the-way worksheet locations, and *1-2-3* can still find them when necessary. If you give subroutines exact cell locations, *1-2-3* may be able to call them only once during the course of executing a macro.

EXPANDING STRUCTURED MACROS

It's clear that writing structured macros requires a little more effort than writing unstructured ones. Is it worth the trouble? In most cases, yes. Even when you are writing simple, one-line macros, doing so in a structured manner will allow you to expand on a solid, reusable base of macro routines. Eventually, you can create a library of routines to mix and match as your spreadsheet calculations require. For example, look at figure 2.

Here a few additional subroutines give our initial structured macro some extra power. These subroutines enable the macro to check the *periods* value you specify before running the macro. The *periods* value is the time over which the growth rate is calculated. After accepting input for the first value, the macro calls the *subright* subroutine, which moves the cell pointer to the right (*periods-1*). This produces a block of cells equal to the number of periods. Once this block has been generated, the macro accepts the last value and proceeds with computation.

As computation proceeds, the expanded macro jumps back to the cells between *first* and *last* and fills in intermediate values. The output is:

	A	B	C	D	E	F	G
1	100.0	131.6	173.2	228.0	300.0	31.6%	
2							

Because the original version of this macro was well structured, these changes are relatively easy to make. With slight modifications to the main body of the original

	A	B	C	D	E	F
1	\m	/XCinputpeds~				
2		/XCinput1st~				
3		/XCsubright~				
4		/XCinputlast~{RIGHT}				
5		/XCcagrcalc~				
6		/XCsubform~				
7		/XCsubcopy~				
8		/XCinit~				
9						
10	cagrcalc	((last/first)^(1/(periods-1)))-1~{EDIT}{CALC}~				
11		/RFP~~/RNCrate~~				
12		/XR				
13						
14	inputpeds	/XI(periods>1#AND#periods<25)~/XR				
15		/XNEnter number of periods (2-24): ~periods~				
16		/XGinputpeds~				
17						
18	init	/RNDfirst~				
19		/RNDlast~				
20		/RNDrate~				
21		/XR				
22						
23	subright	{RIGHT}/XIperiods=2~/XR				
24		{RIGHT}/XIperiods=3~/XR				
25		{RIGHT}/XIperiods=4~/XR				
26		{RIGHT}/XIperiods=5~/XR				
27		{RIGHT}/XIperiods=6~/XR				
28		{RIGHT}/XIperiods=7~/XR				
29		{RIGHT}/XIperiods=8~/XR				
30		{RIGHT}/XIperiods=9~/XR				
31		{RIGHT}/XIperiods=10~/XR				
32		{RIGHT}/XIperiods=11~/XR				
33		{RIGHT}/XIperiods=12~/XR				
34		{RIGHT}/XIperiods=13~/XR				
35		{RIGHT}/XIperiods=14~/XR				
36		{RIGHT}/XIperiods=15~/XR				
37		{RIGHT}/XIperiods=16~/XR				
38		{RIGHT}/XIperiods=17~/XR				
39		{RIGHT}/XIperiods=18~/XR				
40		{RIGHT}/XIperiods=19~/XR				
41		{RIGHT}/XIperiods=20~/XR				
42		{RIGHT}/XIperiods=21~/XR				
43		{RIGHT}/XIperiods=22~/XR				
44		{RIGHT}/XIperiods=23~/XR				
45		{RIGHT}/XIperiods=24~/XR				
46						
47	subform	{GOTO}first~				
48		{RIGHT}				
49		+{LEFT}*(1+$rate)~/RF,1~~				
50		/XR				
51						
52	subcopy	/C~.{END}{RIGHT}{LEFT}~				
53		/XR				
54						
55	periods	6				

FIGURE 2. The original growth rate macro can be expanded by additional subroutines. Adding the *init, subright, subform,* and *subcopy* routines allows it to display the intermediate values calculated in the course of determining final values. The *subright* routine produces a block of cells equal to the number of periods. By jumping back to the cells between *first* and *last* in the *init* subroutine as the macro executes, intermediate values are recorded and displayed. Besides adding subroutines, slight modifications of the *main* and *inputpeds* are also required.

	A	B	C	D	E	F
58	\n	/XMstartup~				
59						
60	startup	Ends	GRate			
61		Define thDefine starting point and growth rate
62		/XG\m~	/XGgrate~			
63						
64	grate	/XCinputpeds~				
65		/XCinput1st~				
66		/XCsubright~				
67		/RNClast~~{RIGHT}				
68		/XCinputrate~				
69		/XCsubform~				
70		/XCsubcopy~				
71		/XCinit~				
72						
73	inputrate	/XNInput growth rate (decimal) ~~			
74		/RNCrate~~/RFP~~				
75		/XR				

FIGURE 3. **Menu-driven macro program branching is achieved by adding these additional subroutines to the existing macro. Here you will be prompted to choose between two methods of building a projection row. When you start the macro by pressing MACRO-N, you are offered two options: Ends and GRate. Selecting Ends causes control to shift to the original macro routine (\m), while selecting GRate (growth rate) shifts control to the instructions in the routine named *grate*. The *inputrate* subroutine is added to accept the initial growth rate figure.**

macro and the subroutine named *inputpeds*, the added subroutines, *init, subright, subform,* and *subcopy* do the trick.

STRUCTURING WITH MENUS

Having built the macro shown in figure 2, there is a quick and almost easy progression to the macro shown in figure 3. This program lets you choose between two ways of building a projection row. The first option defines starting and ending points, calculates a growth rate, then fills in the intermediate values. The second option prompts for a starting point and for a growth or interest rate, then projects from the starting point to the end of the period using that rate. The second row-building option of figure 3 specifying a growth rate is built almost entirely from subroutines written and tested for the macro in figure 2. Only the *inputrate* subroutine had to be added.

These two program options are linked by a menu that presents a choice of program functions. The /XM command in figure 3 provides a menu with the two choices Ends and GRate. If you choose Ends, the macro processes the instruction /XG\m contained in cell B62. This transfers control to the original macro named \m (shown in figure 2). If GRate (growth rate) is chosen, the macro executes the commands in the routine named *grate* in figure 3. Again, additional program features are added to existing macros as subroutines rather than writing entire macros from scratch.

It may take an extra measure of discipline to think of macros as confederations of independent subroutines. And it may seem farfetched to view your fellow spreadsheet creators as members of a corporate macro-writing team. Nevertheless, both concepts are valid. As the tasks you commission your macros to perform become more complex, the advantages of a structured approach to macro programming become increasingly evident.

AUGUST 1985

5

Messages

With these techniques your macros can request information from users or guide them through your applications.

BY DANIEL GASTEIGER

Software applications often "converse" with the people who use them. *Symphony*, for example, presents menus when you press the appropriate keys and responds with prompts that lead you through the process you select. When you ask *Symphony* to do something it can't do, it displays an error message to help you better understand the problem. Finally, when you can't remember the procedure required to produce a desired result, you can press the HELP key for guidance.

When you design applications for others, or even for yourself, your macros can supply the same types of assistance. In this first article of two on presenting guidance within your applications, we'll look at some of the macro commands and other techniques to help your macros converse with their users.

SOME COMMON COMMUNICATIONS

The most *Symphony*-like dialogue you can create with a macro is produced by a user-defined menu. The {MENUBRANCH} and {MENUCALL} commands follow instructions stored on the worksheet to generate moving pointer menus in the control panel. These custom menus can contain up to eight choices.

To create menu instructions, place labels representing the menu choices in adjacent cells of one row and labels representing their corresponding explanations, called long prompts, in the following row. Then place commands appropriate to each menu choice in the cells below the long prompts of the menu instructions. For clarity, name the cell representing the first menu choice with a range name that indicates the purpose of the menu. For example, a menu that gives the option of erasing a data-entry range might be named *wipeout*. The following macro illustrates a simple, two-choice menu that confirms whether or not the user wants to erase the contents of a data-entry range named *input*:

	A	B	C	D
1	\e	{MENUBRANCH wipeout}		
2				
3	wipeout	No	Yes	
4		Don't erase	Erase input range	
5			{BLANK input}	
6			{CALC}	

To try the macro, enter it as shown and assign the range names \e and *wipeout* by pointing to cell A1 and issuing the command sequence Range Name Labels Right End Down Return. Assign the name *input* to range B8..B12 and put some arbitrary data into these cells. Finally, start the macro by holding down the MACRO key and pressing E.

Symphony displays the custom menu. Select No or Yes as you would from any *Symphony* menu. When you select No, the macro stops processing because no commands follow the long prompt for No in the menu instructions. When you select Yes, the macro's {BLANK input} command erases the range named *input*, and its {CALC} command updates the worksheet to illuminate the result of the erasure.

OTHER USES FOR MENUS

If you replace the {MENUBRANCH} command in the example with a {MENUCALL} command, there is no apparent difference in the function of the macro. There is, however, a difference in the way the commands operate. The command {MENUBRANCH wipeout} presents a menu based on the instructions that start in the cell named *wipeout* and sends the macro down whatever path the user chooses. The command {MENUCALL wipeout} presents the same menu, but once the macro has processed all the commands associated with the user's choice, the macro processes the commands immediately following the {MENUCALL} command.

The round-trip nature of the {MENUCALL} command lets you use it to create one- or two-line messages in the control panel. You might use such a message to remind users of tasks they must perform before *Symphony* starts a procedure. For example, your macro could instruct the user to align the paper in the printer before it starts printing or to place a particular disk in the data drive before it saves a file.

The following macro saves the current file, asks you to put a new disk into the data drive, then saves the file a second time, creating a backup:

	A	B	C	D	E
1	\s	{SERVICES}FS{ESC}filename~Y{ESC}			
2		{MENUCALL newdisk}			
3		{SERVICES}FS~Y{ESC}			
4					
5					
6	newdisk	Press Return to proceed			
7		Place backup disk in data drive			
8					

An alternate macro for hard-disk users follows:

	A	B	C	D	E
1	\s	{SERVICES}FS{ESC}filename~Y{ESC}			
2		{MENUCALL newdisk}			
3		{SERVICES}FS{ESC}A:\filename~Y{ESC}			
4					
5					
6	newdisk	Press Return to proceed			
7		Place backup disk in drive A			
8					

Here's how these macros work:

{SERVICES}FS{ESC}filename~Y{ESC}   Names the worksheet FILENAME and saves it. If a file named FILENAME already exists, the Y in this command causes *Symphony* to save over it, replacing the original file; the {ESC} command does nothing. If FILENAME doesn't exist, *Symphony* saves, then types the Y in the control panel, immediately erasing it with the {ESC} command.

{MENUCALL newdisk}   Displays a menu in the control panel based on the instructions beginning in the cell named *newdisk*. Because this menu has only one choice, pressing the pointer-movement keys has no effect on it. The menu instructs users to place a backup disk in the data drive and press Return to continue, though it will also continue if they press the Escape key or type the first letter of the menu choice (P, in this example). In any case, because no commands follow the long prompt of the menu instructions, the macro finishes processing the {MENUCALL} command and proceeds to the next step.

{SERVICES}FS~Y{ESC}   Saves the file under the file name it used in the first step of the macro. The hard-disk macro uses the commands:

{SERVICE}FS{ESC}A:\filename~Y{ESC}

This saves a second copy of the file on the A drive rather than in the current directory of the hard disk. When you create this macro, you must also substitute your own file name for the name *filename* in this command.

QUICK INSTRUCTIONS

The {MENUBRANCH} and {MENUCALL} commands let your macros converse with users in a familiar way. The {GETLABEL} and {GETNUMBER} commands also present messages in the control panel, though they work a little differently. The {GETLABEL} and {GETNUMBER} commands prompt users for information to store on the worksheet. For example, when a macro processes the following command, it displays the prompt *Enter applicant's phone* in the control panel and stores whatever you type as a label in the cell named *phone:*

{GETLABEL Enter applicant's phone,phone}

The {GETNUMBER} command accepts only numbers or formulas and stores the numeric value of whatever entry you make in response to its prompt.

You can use either command to display messages in the control panel. Simply assign a range name to a cell that will receive your response to the message. Use this range name in every {GETLABEL} or {GETNUMBER} command when using these functions solely to give directions. For example, the three steps shown below are taken from a longer macro. They simply recalculate the worksheet, remind the user to align the printer paper to the top of the page, and print a copy of the current document:

	B	C	D	E	F
25	{CALC}				
26	{GETLABEL Align paper and press Return,trash}				
27	{S}PAGPQ				

Users can type anything in response to the prompt, but the macro won't proceed until they press Return. If they have typed anything, *Symphony* stores it as a label in the cell named *trash*; otherwise, *Symphony* stores a label-prefix character in that cell. If you use a {GETNUMBER} command instead of {GETLABEL}, *Symphony* stores the value ERR in the cell named *trash*.

PROLONGED PROMPTS

The techniques covered so far present messages that stay on-screen only until someone acts on them. But you might want to present instructions to which the user can refer throughout a work session. *Symphony* gives you several easy ways to do this. One way is to type the desired messages directly into the window where people do their work. For example, the following simple model contains instructions for keeping track of transactions in a checking account (it already contains one entry):

```
        A      B         C           D        E         F
 1  Enter your starting balance in cell F10.  Then enter the
 2  check numbers, the dates and descriptions of each
 3  transaction, and the amounts--either withdrawal or
 4  deposit--in the appropriate columns, one transaction per
 5  row.  If the balance does not appear when you enter the
 6  amount of the transaction, copy the formula in column F
 7  farther down the worksheet.
 8
 9  Check Date    Description    Withdrawal Deposit   Balance
10  ---------------enter starting balance here----->>  858.58
11    105 Mar-85 Electric            15.32            843.26
```

The formula in cell F11 is:

$$@IF(@COUNT(D11..E11) = 0, ``'', F10-D11 + E11)$$

It equals nothing (a label prefix) if there are no entries in the *Withdrawal* or *Deposit* columns of the current row; otherwise, it equals the amount of the previous cell, minus the value of the *Withdrawal* column, plus the value of the *Deposit* column. Although it doesn't show, I've copied it through cell F100, which allows for several weeks of postings before I need to copy it farther down the column. I'll leave it to you to figure out other details of the model.

The instructions for this model are visible only when you're working in the top-left corner of the worksheet. Ideally, you want instructions to show at all times. You can freeze these instructions on-screen with the MENU Settings Titles command.

Once you've created the worksheet, move the cell pointer to the row below the last line of information you wish to retain on-screen. In this example, you wish to keep the column headers on-screen even when your data scrolls up out of view. Put the cell pointer in row 10, and issue the commands MENU Settings Titles Horizontal Quit. Now the instructions and column headers remain visible as long as you work in columns A through F of the worksheet.

This technique becomes more useful as you add macros to help users with the model. With the macros off-screen to one side of the workspace, you can "lock in" a list of their names and reminders of their functions on-screen.

Unfortunately, the MENU Settings Titles command applies only to a SHEET window. Creating on-screen messages for other window types requires more effort.

Putting messages in a FORM window is perhaps the easiest. You need only include the message in the window's Entry range for *Symphony* to display it. To see how this works, create a small database.

Start with a blank worksheet (SERVICES New Yes). Enter the labels *Name* in cell A1 and *Phone* in cell A2. Press TYPE and select FORM, then press MENU and select Generate Label; type 15 and press Return twice. Finally, indicate cells A1..A2 and press Return. A data-entry form appears on your monitor.

To use the form, type a name and press Return. The flashing cursor moves to the next line. Type a phone number and press Return. Enter the data on this form into the underlying worksheet by pressing the Insert key. *Symphony* presents a new blank form. Continue filling in the blanks and using the Insert key to enter forms into the worksheet. Within a form, move from blank to blank by pressing the UpArrow and DownArrow keys. Use the PageUp and PageDown keys to move among forms you've already entered. The Home key takes you directly to the first entry you made, while End takes you to the last entry. Pressing PageDown while viewing the last entry produces a new blank form. Consult your *Symphony* documentation for more information on working in a FORM window.

To put messages in a FORM window, you must return to a SHEET window. To do this press the SWITCH key. The top-left corner of your worksheet appears below:

	A	B	C
1	Name		
2	Phone		
3			
4	Name _____		
5	Phone_____		
6			
7	Name	Value	Type
8	Name		L:15
9	Phone		L:15
10			
11	Name	Phone	
12		0	0

Move to cell A6 and insert as many rows as you'll need for your instructions. For this example, insert six rows (press MENU and select Insert Rows, press the DownArrow key 5 times, and press Return). Now position your message in the blank cells below the labels in cells A4 and A5. For example, move to cell A7 and enter *Press End PageDown to begin new entry*. Finally, reassign the range name of the database Entry range to include the new cells.

The database Entry range consists of the cells containing the fill-in-the-blanks form that *Symphony* displays when you use a FORM window. *Symphony* names this range when you use the Generate command to create a form. To reassign the range name, press MENU and select Range Name Create; then point to the range name that consists of the database name connected by an underline to the letters EN. In most cases this will be MAIN__EN. Press Return and use the DownArrow key to extend the range to include the message, finishing with Return. Finally, use the SWITCH key to change back to a FORM window. The message remains on-screen as long as you use the form.

FEBRUARY 1986

6

More Messages

In this chapter we explore more techniques
you can use to present messages to people
who use your macro applications.

BY DANIEL GASTEIGER

When you write *Symphony* macros for others, your macros must tell their users which keys to press and what information to supply, or the macros must verify that they are carrying out a procedure. In the last chapter we looked at some macro commands you can use to provide one- or two-line messages. We also looked at techniques to produce messages on the screen in both SHEET and FORM windows. In this chapter we'll show how to put messages to users on your screen in any window and how you can use these techniques to create error messages and help screens.

MESSAGE WINDOWS

Sometimes you want a message to remain visible as long as a user works on a particular task. Your macros can use *Symphony*'s windowing capability to do this. If an application requires work in many different windows, you can put instructions in their own windows to simplify procedures even more.

Let's say you've created a database application that lets users enter data in a FORM window. You've preset the settings sheet to sort the database in a particular order, and you want to leave a message on the screen telling users how to sort the database when they've finished the data entry. This is just part of a larger application that uses several other windows to monitor the model's usage and generate reports, but for this discussion, we'll deal only with activity within the FORM window.

As we saw in the last chapter, some messages can reside within their associated windows. To place a message in a FORM window, include it in the database's Entry range. Alternatively, messages can reside in their own windows, sharing the screen with the windows in which the users work. Before we describe these message windows and the macros that control them, let's review some basics about *Symphony* windows.

THE WINDOWED WORKSHEET

If you were to create a worksheet on paper to match the size of *Symphony*'s worksheet, the paper would measure about 150 feet high by 16 feet wide. Since you couldn't view the entire worksheet on even the largest monitor, *Symphony* provides windows through which to view smaller, more manageable sections of the worksheet.

Although the windows stay pretty much in the same place on-screen, you can think of them as being movable. When you move the pointer to a cell outside the visable area of a window, you can drag the window along, uncovering a new section of the worksheet.

Symphony keeps track of the windows you create by "stacking" them. When you create a window, *Symphony* puts it on top of the stack, pushing the other windows down. If you press the WINDOW key, *Symphony* pulls the bottommost active window from the stack and places it on top. A window is inactive if you've hidden it either with the SERVICES Window Hide or the SERVICES Window Isolate commands. The SERVICES Window Use command brings any window in the stack to the top.

You can assign a Restrict range to any *Symphony* window to define the worksheet area that you can view through the window. The window in which you start a work session is initially unrestricted, giving you access to the entire worksheet, but you can restrict the window's accessible area to as little as a single cell.

Your view of the worksheet isn't the only thing affected by the window's Restrict range. Some commands that profoundly change the worksheet are also restricted. For example, inserting and deleting rows and columns does not affect the worksheet outside the current window's Restrict range, although you can indicate any cell on the worksheet as the source or target cells in move and copy operations.

Take care to use Restrict ranges when you build multiwindow applications; if you don't, you might unintentionally alter or destroy data. One approach is to build applications from left to right and from top to bottom, putting pieces that will take up the greatest number of rows as far to the left as possible. Your databases will then start in column A, with macros, reports, and Extract ranges trailing off toward the two-lettered columns.

I like to put macros into a nine- or ten-column section of the worksheet and access them through a window called MACROS. I reserve a block of cells near the top right of this section for counters, holders, and other cells whose contents change often while the macros run. When I need to create message windows, I put the text they will contain above the macros and create separate windows to view them.

PUTTING IT ALL TOGETHER

Following this suggested format, the simple database model described earlier might occupy the worksheet as shown:

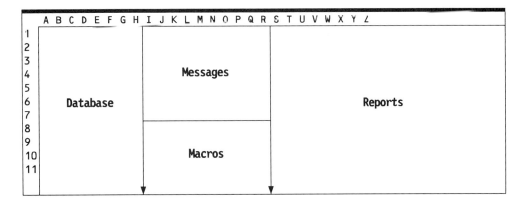

It's beyond the scope of this article to describe all the steps required to create the model. We'll present the general idea and leave you to fill in the rest, or you can use this as a starting point to create other applications using message windows.

Start with a blank worksheet and create a database containing six fields, one each for first name, last name, street address, city, state, and zip code. You can create it using the MENU Generate command in a FORM window. For this discussion, we'll assume your database form resides in a window named MAIN. Once you've generated the database, set MAIN's Restrict range to access only the width of the database and its associated Definition range.

Also, extend the Restrict range to the bottom of the worksheet so that the database has plenty of room to grow. To do this, press SERVICES and select Window Settings Restrict Range. *Symphony* highlights the entire screen, displaying the current Restrict range. Press Backspace to cancel that range, indicate the range A1..H8192, press Return, then select Quit Quit.

Create the window that will contain your macros by pressing SERVICES and selecting Window Create. Type MACROS as the window name and press Return. Press Return to select SHEET as the window type; press Return once more to accept the current window size as the size for the new window. Finally, select Restrict Range, press Backspace and indicate J1..R8192, then press Return and select Quit Quit.

Enter the label *Press MACRO-S to sort the database* into cell J1, then create a window to contain it as follows: Press SERVICES and select Window Create. Type MESSAGE as the window name and press Return. Press Return to select SHEET, then press the Tab key or the Period key twice to move the blinking cursor marking the free corner of the highlight to the top-left corner. Shrink the window by repeatedly pressing the DownArrow key until it includes only three rows, then press Return. Select Borders Line Quit. The new message window overlays the macros window across the bottom of the screen.

If you change to a different window (either MAIN or MACROS), the message window is buried. Resize MAIN so that both it and the message window can be on the screen at once. To do this, press the WINDOW key to bring MAIN to the top. Then press SERVICES, select Window Layout, press the UpArrow key four times, press Return, and select Quit.

The following macro steps put both windows on the screen, leaving MAIN active:

	J	K	L	M
10		{SERVICES}WUmessage~		
11		{SERVICES}WI		
12		{SERVICES}WUmain~		

You can run these steps from within any window to gain access to your database. Here's how they work:

{SERVICES}WUmessage~ Makes the message window active.

{SERVICES}WI Isolates the message window, hiding all others.

{SERVICES}WUmain~ Makes the FORM window active, leaving the message window visible. MAIN and MESSAGE are the only active windows (the only ones you can access with the WINDOW key).

You can use this macro sequence pretty much whenever you wish to clear the screen and display specific windows. Start by displaying the window that will be on the screen but not in use, isolate that window, then display the window in which your users will work. When you build large models, substitute {S} for {SERVICES} to save time and effort.

If you want several one-line messages to appear in several different windows (or in several different circumstances), you can put all the messages in one window and use a simple subroutine to control which message gets displayed. To do this, expand MESSAGE's Restrict Range to get a few more worksheet rows (J1..R7, for example). Then enter a different message into each row of the window (if you're trying these techniques as you read along, enter several nonsense messages). The message-controlling subroutine looks like the example that follows:

```
        J          K          L          M
18│ mess    {DEFINE row:value}
19│         {SERVICES}WUmessage~
20│         {SERVICES}WI
21│         {HOME}{DOWN row-1}
22│
23│ row
```

As noted in the worksheet, cells K18 and K23 are named *mess* and *row*, respectively. Once you've created this subroutine, your macro can call up a message with the command {mess n}, where *n* is the number corresponding to the row in which the message resides. To see how this works, enter the subroutine in your MACROS window as shown, then enter the following macro:

```
        J          K          L          M
14│ \t      {mess 3}
15│         {S}WUmain~
```

Assign the labels contained in column J as range names for the adjacent cells of column K; point to cell J14 and issue the command sequence MENU Range Name Labels Right, then press End DownArrow End DownArrow Return. Start the macro by holding down the MACRO key and pressing T. Here's what happens:

{**mess 3**}   Calls the subroutine named *mess* (from the previous figure), passing along the value, or argument, 3. *Symphony* flags this command as the point in the macro to return to after it finishes processing the subroutine as follows:

{**DEFINE row:value**}   Places the value of the argument into the cell named *row*.

{**SERVICES**}**WUmessage~**   Makes the window named MESSAGE current.

{**SERVICES**}**WI**   Isolates MESSAGE, hiding all other windows.

{**HOME**}{**DOWN row–1**}   Sends the cell pointer to the top of the message window, then moves it down to the message indicated in the cell named *row*. In this example, the subroutine call passes the value 3 to the cell named *row*; the cell pointer moves down two rows (3 minus 1) to the third message. At this point, the macro returns to the step immediately after the subroutine call (cell K15).

{**S**}**WUmain~**   Brings the window named MAIN out of hiding, leaving the message on the screen.

Whenever you want your macro to change windows and update the associated message, simply use a subroutine call with an argument that matches the number of the appropriate message.

PROVIDING HELP

There are enough ways to create help screens in *Symphony* to take up several macro columns. All that distinguishes a help screen from any other message is the space it requires to convey information. A help screen is typically just that: a screenful of helpful information.

To create useful help screens, you must anticipate your users' needs. If they're working in a database, they may want direction on editing records, moving between records, searching for specific information, and so on. Your screens should provide enough help to get users through a session without bogging them (or your model) down with superfluous details.

Put your help screens off to one side (perhaps below your macros or in the columns adjacent to them). You can place each help screen within its own restricted window or place all of them in a single window with a large Restrict range. In either case, be cautious if you later restructure your worksheet—globally inserting and deleting columns and rows can move worksheet information out from under a window's Restrict range.

Creating help windows is the same as creating other windows, so I'll let you figure out that process. Getting users to make the most of help windows is a little trickier. Taking the model from our earlier example, you could create a macro that displays a single help screen while waiting for the user to press Return. Let's assume the help screen is in a window named HELP1, sized to fit on the screen without obscuring the message window.

Before you create the macro, include the message *Press Return to resume work in the database* within your message window and remember its row number (row 2 for this example—the original message, *Press MACRO-S to sort the database,* is in row 1). Then enter the steps as shown here:

	J	K	L	M
36	\7	{mess 2}		
37		{S}WUhelp1~		
38	back	{GET test}		
39		{IF test<>"~"}{BRANCH back}		
40		{mess 1}		
41		{S}WUmain~		

This macro relies on the subroutine presented earlier, but it won't work properly until you've created a window named HELP1 and a cell named *test*. The macro's name (\7) gives you a simple way to start it. Simply press the USER key twice. Here's what happens:

{mess 2} Calls the subroutine named *mess* and passes the parameter 2. The subroutine displays the message window, isolates it, and moves the window's second message into view.

{S}WUhelp1~ Makes the window named HELP1 visible.

{GET test} Pauses until the user presses a key, then stores the keystroke in the cell named *test*.

{IF test<>"~"}{BRANCH back} Sends the macro to process keystrokes in the previous cell if *test* doesn't contain a tilde (~). This step, coupled with the one before it, creates a simple loop that locks the worksheet until the user presses Return—a necessity disclosed in the message window.

{mess 1} Calls the subroutine to display the first message and isolate the message window.

{S}WUmain~ Brings the database window (MAIN) to the top of the window stack.

This macro won't help your users if they don't know how to use it, so be sure to add a message somewhere on screen (perhaps within the FORM window as described in the last chapter) instructing them to *Press the USER key twice for help*.

CAPTURING KEYSTROKES

In Chapter 8 of this section, we create a macro that intercepts keystrokes, accepting those necessary to accomplish most tasks while rejecting those that might give users too much control over *Symphony*. Help screens are a natural for keystroke-capturing macros.

A macro can't actually "press" the HELP key, but the {GET} command recognizes when that key has been pressed. The following is a bare-bones, keystroke-capturing macro that gives users help when they press the HELP key:

```
      J        K        L        M
44 catch   {GET tst}
45         {IF @VLOOKUP(tst,rjct,0)+1}{BRANCH catch}
46         {IF tst="{HELP}"}{\7}{BRANCH catch}
47 tst     {HELP}
48         {BRANCH catch}
49
50         {
51         {MENU}
52         {SERVICES}
53         {WINDOW}
54         {TYPE}
55         {SWITCH}
```

As usual, columns J's labels indicate the range names for column K's adjacent cells. Also, assign the range name *rjct* to the range K50..K55, which contains a list of the keystrokes that *Symphony* won't allow while the macro is running. Here's how the macro works:

{GET tst}   Pauses until the user presses a key, then stores a label representation of the keystroke in the cell named *tst*.

{IF @VLOOKUP(tst,rjct,∅) + 1}{BRANCH catch}   Restarts the macro if, in the last step, the user pressed one of the keys listed in the range named *rjct*.

{IF tst = "{HELP}"}{\7}{BRANCH catch}   Calls the subroutine named \7 if the user pressed the HELP key, then restarts the macro. This macro, discussed earlier, displays a help screen until the user presses Return. If the user hasn't pressed the HELP key, the macro processes the next step. This cell contains the user's keystroke.

{BRANCH catch}   Restarts the macro. This all happens so quickly that users don't know they are under macro control.

ERROR MESSAGES

No matter what the application, users often try to do things they just shouldn't do, such as entering the wrong type of data (numbers instead of labels or vice versa), pressing the wrong keys, or looking at areas of the worksheet that should remain hidden. If you anticipate these eventualities, you can prepare your macros to deal with them.

For example, you can rewrite the keystroke-capturing routine from the last section to tell users when they've pressed a disabled key. Simply add the following subroutine to the worksheet, and insert a subroutine call into the macro's second line. If the subroutine is named *bad*, the second macro step becomes:

{IF @VLOOKUP(tst,rjct,∅) ı 1}{bad}{BRANCH catch}

Here's the subroutine named *bad*:

	J	K	L	M
57	bad	{mess 3}		
58	prev	{GET tst}		
59		{IF tst<>"~"}{BRANCH prev}		
60		{mess 1}		
61		{S}WUmain~		

It uses the original message-window subroutine to display message 3, which you should place in the message window as *Illegal keystroke, press Return to continue*. Here's how it works:

{mess 3}   Displays the third message in the message window.

{GET tst}   Pauses until the user presses a key, then stores the keystroke in *tst*.

{IF tst<>"~"}{BRANCH prev}   Branches back to the previous step if the user hasn't pressed Return. If the user has pressed Return, the macro continues in the next cell.

{mess 1}   Displays the first message in the message window.

{S}WUmain~   Returns control to window MAIN.

HELP!

If you've been building these examples as you followed the text, by now you have a long column of disjointed routines and subroutines in column J of your worksheet. Although many of the routines work together, they are not necessarily bound to each other. As you create your own applications, take the pieces you need from these examples and work them into your code. But don't stop there—this column barely touches on the myriad techniques for producing help screens and error messages.

MARCH 1986

7

Dynamic Macro Code

Writing string formulas that evaluate to macro commands lets you squeeze even more power out of the macro Command Language.

BY DANIEL GASTEIGER

Before *Symphony,* manipulating strings on a worksheet was cumbersome. Now you can do arithmetic with strings as easily as you do with numbers. This feature is especially useful if you write macros because you can write macro commands that change based on changes in data on the worksheet.

Macros are simply lists of labels on the worksheet. *Symphony* interprets these lists as sequences of commands as though you were typing them at the keyboard. It makes no difference to *Symphony* whether a macro command is a label preceded by a label prefix or one that results from a string calculation. As long as a string formula displays as a valid command by the time it is processed in a macro, the macro interprets it as the command it resembles.

A SIMPLE EXAMPLE

Let's examine cell B1 of the following macro:

	A	B	C	D
1	\f	SELL~		
2				
3	val	30		
4				

Assign the range name \f to cell B1 by putting the cell pointer on cell A1 and issuing the command sequence MENU Range Name Labels Right Return. When you run the macro (hold down the MACRO key and press F — consult your documentation for information about the MACRO key), it enters the word *SELL* into the current cell. In fact, cell B1 contains the following formula:

$$@IF(val<30,\text{``HOLD''},\text{``SELL''})\&\text{``}{\sim}\text{''}$$

This formula equals HOLD~ if the value of the cell named *val* is less than 30 and SELL~ if *val* equals or is greater than 30.

The following variation on this idea enters the word *HOLD* or *SELL* to the right of the current cell, moves down, repeats the process, and so on until you stop the macro by pressing the Break key:

```
         A        B         C          D
1   \g        {RECALC formula}
2             {RIGHT}
3   formula        ERR
4             {DOWN}{LEFT}
5             {BRANCH \g}
6
```

The formula in the cell named *formula* is:

$$@IF(@CELLPOINTER(\text{``contents''})<30,\text{``HOLD''},\text{``SELL''})$$

To run this macro, enter some values into column E as follows:

```
         E        F         G          H
1       30
2       31
3       27
4       31
5       29
6       28
7       31
```

Place the cell pointer on cell E1 and start the macro. Here's what happens:

{RECALC formula} Recalculates the formula in the cell named *formula*. This ensures that it has the proper value when it is processed.

{RIGHT} Moves the cell pointer to the right.

ERR Though this reads ERR in the illustration, by the time it is processed, it equals HOLD or SELL, depending on the value in the cell to the left. It types *HOLD* or *SELL* in the control panel.

{DOWN}{LEFT}   Moves the pointer down and left, entering whatever the last step has typed into the cell.

{BRANCH \g}   Restarts the macro. The {RECALC} command updates the formula based on the value of the current cell, the pointer moves right, and the appropriate word is typed into column F. This loop continues until you stop the macro with the Break key.

A NONMACRO ALTERNATIVE

The preceding example is not an exceptional application of dynamic macro code. Here's how you can do the job more efficiently. Move the cell pointer to cell F1 and enter:

$$@IF(E1<30,``HOLD``,``SELL``)$$

Copy this formula down column F (with the cell pointer in cell F1, press MENU and select Copy, then press Return Left End Down Right Return). Finally, use the Range Values command to turn the formulas into labels (select MENU Range Values and press End Down Return Return). Refer to the section ''Do I Really Need a Macro?'' for more thoughts on efficient problem solving.

One self-modifying macro I recently saw accepted user input, then asked the user to confirm that the input was correct. It appears in the figure below.

	A	B	C	D	E
1	\n	{GETLABEL Enter your name ,name}			
2		{RECALC next}			
3	next	ERR			
4		{IF answer<>"Y"}{BRANCH \n}			
5		{CALC}			
6					
7	name				
8	answer				

Assign range names as follows:

B1 \n
B3 next
B7 name
B8 answer

When you hold the MACRO key and press N, here's what happens:

{GETLABEL Enter your name ,name} Displays the prompt *Enter your name* in the control panel and stores your entry in the cell named *name*.

{RECALC next} Updates the value of the formula in the cell named *next*.

ERR This formula equals ERR in the illustration because it relies on a string in the cell named *name*. *Name* is blank until you run the macro, and therefore equals zero, which cannot be used in a string formula. The formula is as follows:

$$+ \text{``\{GETLABEL Is ''\&name\&`` your name? (Y/N),answer\}''}$$

The {RECALC} command in the previous cell updates this formula with the name you entered in response to the prompt in the first step. When I ran the macro, I entered *Daniel*, so this formula became:

$$\text{\{GETLABEL Is Daniel your name? (Y/N),answer\}}$$

It displayed the prompt *Is Daniel your name? (Y/N)* in the control panel, paused for me to answer, and finally placed my answer in the cell named *answer*.

{IF answer < >"Y"}{BRANCH \n} Branches to \n if you did not type *Y* or *y* in response to the last prompt. (*Symphony* ignores capitalization when it compares letters in conditional statements.)

{CALC} Recalculates the worksheet. This step updates the screen so that you can see the results of the macro when it has finished running. When you use this routine as part of a larger macro, you don't have to recalculate the worksheet at this point.

ENTERING DATA IN THE CURRENT CELL

Sometimes you want your macros to accept data from a user directly into the current cell. Here's a formula that does this:

$$+ \text{``\{GETLABEL Enter a string ,''\&@CELLPOINTER (``address'')\&``\}''}$$

When the cell pointer is in cell B13, this becomes:

$$\text{\{GETLABEL Enter a string ,\$B\$13\}}$$

When the pointer is in F233, it becomes:

$$\text{\{GETLABEL Enter a string ,\$F\$233\}}$$

When you use this formula in a macro, remember to precede it with a {RECALC} command or it may not work as you intend.

COMBINING FORMULAS

The following *1-2-3* worksheet contains a data-entry macro that demonstrates the power of using string formulas as macro commands. Be aware that the cells named *pointer*, *header*, and *formula* (B1, B2, and B5, respectively) contain string formulas rather than labels:

```
        A          B          C        D        E
1  pointer    $A$11
2  header     A10
3
4  \m         {RECALC block}
5  formula    {GETLABEL Enter employee's Name   ,$A$11}
6             {RIGHT}
7             {IF @ISERR(formula)}{DOWN}{END}{LEFT}
8             {BRANCH \m}
9
10 Name       Office     Extension
11
```

The formula in *pointer* is:

@CELLPOINTER("address")

It equals the absolute address of the current cell. The formula in *header* relies on the value of *pointer*. It calculates the address of the cell containing the database field header for the current column. For example, cell A10 contains the field header of column A, so if the cell pointer is in column A, *header* equals A10. Here's the *header* formula in cell B2:

@MID(pointer,1,(@MID(pointer,2,1)< >"$")+1)&"10"

The formula in *formula* looks like this:

+"{GETLABEL Enter employee's "&@@(header) &","&pointer&"}"

It calculates a {GETLABEL} command that includes both the field header of the current column and the current cell address. With the cell pointer in cell A11 of the worksheet, the formula equals:

{GETLABEL Enter employee's Name ,A11}

Name is the database field header for column A. Notice the expression @@(header) in the formula. This @function was not documented in the original

Symphony. It refers to a cell indirectly via another cell. It means "use the value in the cell named in this cell." With the cell pointer in column A, @@(header) equals Name — the value found in the cell named in *header*.

Before you run the macro, assign *block* as the range name for the range B1..B5. Move to cell A11, hold down the MACRO key, and press M. Here's what happens:

{RECALC block} Updates the formulas based on the current position of the cell pointer. When you first start the macro, formulas will have the values shown in the figure.

{GETLABEL Enter employee's Name ,A11} Displays the prompt *Enter employee's Name* in the control panel and places your entry in cell A11 (the current cell).

{RIGHT} Moves the cell pointer to the right.

{IF @ISERR(formula)}{DOWN}{END}{LEFT} Moves the cell pointer down one row and back to column A if *formula* equals ERR. This happens when there is no field name in row 10 of the new column. If there is a field header for this column, the macro skips the movement commands and continues processing in the next cell.

{BRANCH \m} Restarts the macro.

The macro recalculates its formulas based on the location of the cell pointer, creating a prompt appropriate for the current database column and accepting input to the current cell. When there is no field header for a column, the cell pointer moves down and back to column A, allowing you to begin a new entry into your database. As long as you keep field headers in adjacent cells of row 10, you can rearrange, add, and delete fields without rewriting your macro. Your dynamic macro code adjusts automatically.

To make the macro work in *Symphony*, create it as explained, then revise it as follows:

1. Move the range A5..B8 to cell A6; put the cell pointer in cell A5, press MENU, select Move, indicate cells A5..B8, and press Return. Then point to cell A6 and press Return. This opens a blank cell between the first and second macro steps, automatically expanding the range named *block*.

2. Move cell B8 to cell B5; press MENU, select Move, indicate B8, press Return, indicate B5, and press Return.

3. Move cell B9 to cell B8; press MENU, select Move, indicate B9, press Return, indicate B8, and press Return.

4. Edit cell B5 to appear as shown below; point to B5, press the EDIT key, type {BRANCH \m}, and press Return.

{IF @ISERR(formula)}{DOWN}{END}{LEFT}{BRANCH \m}

AVOID CONFUSION

These examples show just a few uses of string formulas within macros. You can use them in file-saving routines, criterion matching macros, and many other applications. But before you write dynamic macro code, explore other possibilities. Macros can be tricky enough without code that changes from one moment to the next. Use dynamic code sparingly and push *Symphony* to its limits.

JANUARY 1986

8

Capturing Keystrokes

Here's a technique that gives *Symphony* users greater freedom within a macro but prevents them from accessing areas of the worksheet you want to keep concealed.

BY DANIEL GASTEIGER

Those who write macros for others sometimes encounter the classic problem of freedom versus control. There may be times when you want users to be able to use some of *Symphony*'s features without interference from the macro. But you don't want them to see sensitive data or possibly destroy macros or data in the worksheet.

Take the case of a macro that manages an address database. It should be able to sort the database, locate records according to selected criteria, and print mailing labels. It should do this in a predictable, crashproof way. It should also let users enter new information into the database and edit existing data without unnecessary restrictions. Essentially, users should be under macro control without knowing it.

It's tempting to write a macro that makes a FORM window current, then stops running so that users can manipulate data with FORM window commands — but it's not a safe practice. Once the macro stops, any *Symphony* command lets users access areas of the worksheet you might want to keep out of their reach. In this chapter we look at a technique that lets others use *Symphony* as it was designed to be used but prevents them from accessing areas of the worksheet you want concealed.

WORKING WITH A DATABASE

One way to turn users loose within *Symphony* but still keep them under control is to create a macro that intercepts their keystrokes and ignores any you don't want them to use. Let's create a simple database to illustrate this technique. (*1-2-3* users will find these techniques useful, although they will need to revise the keystrokes.) The database will store employee names, office numbers, and extensions.

To create the database, start with a blank worksheet (SERVICES New Yes), and enter labels in the worksheet as shown in the figure included at the bottom of this page.

Change to a FORM window by pressing the TYPE key and selecting FORM. The message *No Definition range defined* should appear in the control panel of your display. Press MENU and select Generate Label; enter 15 and press Return to accept the window name as the name for the database. Then indicate cells A1..A4 and finish with Return. A fill-in-the-blanks data-entry form appears in the window.

To use the form, simply type an entry and press Return. *Symphony* moves the cursor to the next blank line (field) on the form, ready to accept the next entry. When you've completed a form (remember to press Return after typing the last entry), press the Insert key. Your work is entered into a row of the underlying worksheet, and you are presented with a blank form for your next record. To follow this example, make several fictitious entries into your database.

Look over entries you've already made by using the movement keys on the numeric keypad. Press Home to view the first entry in your database, End to view the last entry, and PageUp and PageDown to move from one record to the next and back. Move from field to field within a record by pressing the Arrow keys, and change entries you've already made by pressing the EDIT key. This lets you modify database entries just as you do cell entries on the worksheet. To replace an entry in a field, navigate to that field using the Arrow keys, then retype the entry and press Return. To delete an entire record from the database, press the Delete key and answer Yes to the question that appears in the control panel.

	A	B	C	D
1	First			
2	Last			
3	Office			
4	Extension			
5				

These are all the instructions you need in order to enter and edit information in a database using a FORM window. Since working in a FORM window is so easy, almost any macro substitute hinders rather than helps users. The following macro technique lets users work in a FORM window, yet prevents access to other areas of the worksheet.

A MACRO THAT CAPTURES KEYSTROKES

To give a user free run of the FORM window, write a macro that intercepts keystrokes and decides whether or not to process them. The macro should let users use almost every key but reject keystrokes such as SERVICES, WINDOW, and MENU. The following is such a macro:

```
         J        K        L        M        N        O
1   catch    {GET tst}
2            {IF @VLOOKUP(tst,rjct,O)+1}{BRANCH catch}
3   tst
4            {BRANCH catch}
5
6            {
7            {MENU}
8            {SERVICES}
9            {WINDOW}
10           {TYPE}
11           {SWITCH}
12
```

To create the macro, turn the current window back into a SHEET window by pressing the SWITCH key. Move the cell pointer to the right of the database Definition range that *Symphony* created when you issued the Generate command; for this example, move to cell J1. Enter the macro as shown, including the list of characters and macro keywords in cells K6 through K11.

Assign the range names *catch* and *tst* by putting the cell pointer in cell J1, pressing MENU, selecting Range Name Labels Right, and pressing End Down Return. This assigns the labels in the highlighted range as names for the cells to their right. *Tst* is a blank cell within the body of the macro, and it will store each keystroke made while the macro is running; *catch* is the macro's name. Finally, assign the name *rjct* to the range K6..K11. This is the list of keystrokes that your macro will ignore.

Press the SWITCH key to change the window back to a FORM window, then start the macro by pressing the USER key, typing *catch*, and pressing Return. Here's what happens:

{GET tst}   Pauses until the user presses a key, then stores the keystroke in the cell named *tst*.

{IF @VLOOKUP(tst,rjct,∅) + 1}{BRANCH catch}   Restarts the macro if the user's keystroke appears in the list in the range named *rjct*. The @VLOOKUP function tries to find the label stored in the cell named *tst* in the range named *rjct*. If the label is not in the list, @VLOOKUP(tst,rjct,∅) + 1 equals ERR, which *Symphony* interprets as false; the macro proceeds to the next cell. If the label is in the list, the formula equals the position of the label in the list plus 1 (the first position in a list is 1, and adding 1 keeps the formula from equaling 1, which *Symphony* interprets as false); *Symphony* processes the {BRANCH catch} command, restarting the macro.

The next cell of the macro is named *tst*. It contains whatever keystroke the user made. The macro processes that keystroke as it does any macro step, then moves on to the next cell.

{**BRANCH catch**}   Sends the macro looking for keystrokes to the cell named *catch*, which restarts the macro.

This process happens so quickly that except for the *Macro* indicator at the bottom of the screen, users have no clue that a macro is running. They can use any keys except those listed in *rjct*, so work in the FORM window can proceed unhindered. When they press the MENU, SERVICES, WINDOW, TYPE, and SWITCH keys, however, nothing happens.

Notice that the list of excluded keystrokes includes the opening brace ({) used in command-language keywords. If you don't include this character in your list, the macro bombs when the user tries to type a brace.

FURTHER CONSIDERATIONS

To lock users into an application, your macro must start automatically when someone retrieves the worksheet in which it's built. To make this macro start automatically, press SERVICES and select Settings Auto-Execute Set; then type *catch* and press Return.

Also, use the {BREAKOFF} command to prevent users from stopping the macro by pressing the Break key. If this is the first command in the macro, it will protect the worksheet against most users. To edit a worksheet containing an autoexecuting macro that includes the {BREAKOFF} command, press Control-Break while *Symphony* reads the worksheet into memory. Unfortunately, anyone can beat a {BREAKOFF} command this way, but you needn't explain this to the people who will use your application. For now, leave out the {BREAKOFF} command so that you can stop the macro while you're testing it.

BUILDING BIGGER MACROS

As mentioned earlier, you'd probably use the macro presented above as part of a larger macro. In so doing you must give the macro a way both to enter into the routine and to exit from it.

The illustration below shows one simple example of a menu that your macro might present to lead users into the keystroke-capturing routine. It appears on the same worksheet as the first macro, just below the range named *rjct*:

```
           J          K          L          M          N
13  \m          {MENUBRANCH men1}
14              {BRANCH \m}
15
16  men1        Form       Print      Order      Save
17              Use fill-in-the-blanks forms
18              {BRANCH catch}
19
```

To add this routine to your original macro, switch to a SHEET window (if the macro is running, stop it by pressing the Break key, and clear the resulting error by pressing Escape).

I've omitted the long prompts of the menu choices for printing, sorting, and saving the database to show the column containing the menu choice Form. When you create an appropriate menu for your own application, include descriptive long prompts for each menu item.

To follow this example, enter the macro steps as shown and include the following long labels in cells L17, M17, and N17, respectively: *Print a listing of selected records, Sort the listing,* and *Save your work.* Finally, assign the range names \m and *men1* by putting the cell pointer in the cell containing the label \m and issuing the command sequence MENU Range Name Labels Right End Down Return.

Remember to switch back to a FORM window, then hold down the MACRO key and press M. Here's what happens:

{MENUBRANCH men1}   Uses the instructions found starting with the cell named *men1* to create a menu in the control panel. Users can select items as they do with any *Symphony* menu. If they press the Escape key, the macro processes the command immediately following the {MENUBRANCH} command.

{BRANCH \m}   Re-creates the menu if the user presses the Escape key. Users are locked into the menu until they make a selection.

When users select FORM, they are free to use the familiar FORM window commands. This keystroke-capturing routine provides no way back to the menu, but there is an easy way to provide one. Just as you can "turn off" keys with a macro, you can also assign different functions to those keys. The illustration at the top of the next column contains both the menu routine and a revision of the keystroke-capturing routine that returns users to the customized menu when they press the MENU key:

Modify your macro by pointing to any cell in row 2 (cell K2 is a good choice) and pressing MENU Insert Row Return. Then enter {IF tst = "{MENU}"}{BRANCH \m} into cell K2. Now when your macro is capturing keystrokes, it branches back to the {MENUBRANCH} command whenever the user presses the MENU key. If every menu choice ultimately leads back to the customized menu, users are effectively locked into your macro. Be sure your custom menu has a Quit command that saves the file and erases the worksheet.

```
       J         K         L         M         N         O
1   catch   {GET tst}
2           {IF tst="{MENU}"}{BRANCH \m}
3           {IF @VLOOKUP(tst,rjct,0)+1}{BRANCH catch}
4   tst
5           {BRANCH catch}
6
7           {
8           {MENU}
9           {SERVICES}
10          {WINDOW}
11          {TYPE}
12          {SWITCH}
13
14  \m      {MENUBRANCH men1}
15          {BRANCH \m}
16
17  men1    Form      Print     Order     Select
18          Use fill-in-the-blanks forms
19          {BRANCH catch}
20
```

Otherwise, users will have to reboot a new application.

ERROR TRAPPING

Despite your best efforts, you may unwittingly supply doorways into your worksheets. For example, if your macro includes a print routine like the one suggested by the Print option on menu *men1*, users can cause the macro to fail by running that routine while the printer is off-line.

Fortunately, you can guard against this type of problem by using the {ONERROR} command in your macros. This command tells the macro what to do if an error that would normally stop the macro occurs. It takes the form {ONERROR rout,message}, where *rout* is the name of the cell to which the macro branches if an error occurs and *message* is the cell in which *Symphony* stores the error message that it would normally display in the lower-left corner of your screen. This second argument is optional.

{ONERROR} can send the macro back to a menu whenever an error occurs. For this simple macro, use {ONERROR \m}, which simply restarts the macro when it would otherwise crash.

FINISHING THE APPLICATION

Once you are satisfied that your macro works, add the {BREAKOFF} command suggested earlier. Since you know how to beat that command, don't bother saving a backup of your application that lacks this command. If you decide to revise the application, you can retrieve the fully functioning version, erase the {BREAKOFF} command it contains, make and test your revisions, and reenter {BREAKOFF} into the appropriate cell.

If you build your application from the pieces provided here, reassign the autoexecuting macro to bring up your menu rather than the keystroke-capturing routine. Press SERVICES and select Settings Autoexecute Set, then replace the existing range name with the name \m. The following is the final macro without the long prompts and the three subroutines suggested by *men1*'s menu instructions. It is presented this way for greater clarity.

	J	K	L	M	N	O
1	catch	{GET tst}				
2		{IF tst="{MENU}"}{BRANCH \m}				
3		{IF @VLOOKUP(tst,rjct,0)+1}{BRANCH catch}				
4	tst					
5		{BRANCH catch}				
6						
7		{				
8		{SERVICES}				
9		{WINDOW}				
10		{TYPE}				
11		{SWITCH}				
12						
13	\m	{BREAKOFF}				
14		{ONERROR \m}				
15		{MENUBRANCH men1}				
16		{BRANCH \m}				
17						
18	men1	Form	Print	Order	Select	
19		Use fill-in-the-blanks forms				
20		{BRANCH catch}				

Use this as the starting point from which to build your own crashproof macros. The key-catching technique can lock users into any *Symphony* window. When you use this technique, be particularly cautious about giving users access to a SHEET window. There are many ways to alter data on a *Symphony* worksheet without using menu commands.

NOTE

This article discusses techniques that you can use to lock others into your applications, protecting your models from unauthorized tampering. I advocate using {BREAKOFF} as the first command in your macros to prevent people from stopping them by pressing the Break key. I also explain how to override the {BREAKOFF} command by pressing Break while your worksheet loads into memory. However, this works in *Symphony* Releases 1 and 1.01 only.

Don Nadel of Lotus Product Development suggests the following technique that lets *Symphony* Release 1.1/1.2 users regain control of their applications. Start in a blank worksheet and enter the following macro:

	A	B	C	D
1	breakoff {RETURN}			
2				

Assign the label in cell A1 as the range name for cell B1 using the MENU Range Name Labels Right command. Then place the macro into a *Symphony* Macro Library (Hyperspace).

To use Hyperspace on a dual-floppy system, insert the Help and Tutorial Disk in drive A (hard-disk users skip this step) and press SERVICES. Then select Application Attach, point to MACROMGR.APP, press Return, and select Quit.

To place the macro you've just created into Hyperspace, press SERVICES and select Macros Save, enter a name for the library, indicate the range A1..B1, press Return, and select No. This macro in Hyperspace automatically beats the {BREAKOFF} command. When you retrieve a worksheet containing an autoexecute macro that begins with {BREAKOFF}, *Symphony* interprets that command to mean "call the subroutine named *breakoff*" rather than "disable the Break key." Since *breakoff* exists in Hyperspace, *Symphony* branches to it and immediately returns to the macro on the worksheet. You can then stop the macro by pressing the Break key. When you want to test the macro with {BREAKOFF} in effect, remove the macro named *breakoff* from Hyperspace.

DECEMBER 1985

9

Updating Worksheet Models

Use this technique to modify all the worksheet models you've distributed throughout your company.

BY DONALD E. KLAMON

You've developed and distributed your Lotus templates to more than 200 employees, and they've already entered data into their copies of the model. Next thing you know, your boss calls you in and says, "I hope you don't mind, but we're changing the formulas and categories for your models." You might consider 1. killing yourself, 2. killing your boss, or 3. using a self-updating macro.

These are the choices I faced. And although the second option was tempting, I settled on the third.

I work for a financial institution with many offices. I was assigned to produce a package of *1-2-3* templates that could be used for budgeting throughout the institution.

The people who were to use the templates had varying levels of expertise with *1-2-3*. They would be using the templates for budgeting, consolidating data, and preparing data for mainframe use.

Because of the project's scope, I was certain that as soon as I had distributed the model and people had begun to use it, I would have to change it. Someone would decide that one category of expenses really belonged elsewhere on the worksheet. Then someone else would decide that the percentages used to calculate payroll taxes or benefits should be adjusted. As a result, the original specifications for this project would have only a passing resemblance to the final product.

The varied level of PC expertise among the people who would use the program compounded the problem. Only a few of the users knew *1-2-3* well enough to make requested changes. And as different people tinkered with their worksheets, they were likely to come up with incompatible models. All the worksheets had to be alike to ensure proper consolidations. Enter the self-updating model.

SELF-UPDATING MODELS

Each worksheet in the package contains a macro that users can run when they receive an update disk for the model.

The macro (I'll call it the main macro) combines into the worksheet a file from the default data drive. The combined file contains further macro commands that the main macro calls as a subroutine. The subroutine updates the main worksheet and then transfers control back to the main macro. Finally, the main macro erases the area of the worksheet that had contained the combined file and saves the worksheet to ensure that the modifications are preserved. Take the following simple example:

Cell C100 in the original model contained the formula +C95*0.15, which calculates a salary-related benefit. After the model had been distributed, management changed the percentage from 15% to 17%. Fortunately, the original model also contained the macro shown below.

	A	B	C
1	\u	/WGPD	
2		{GOTO}ba1~	
3		/FCCEupdate~	
4		/XCba1~	
5		/REba1..ba1000~	
6		/WGPE/FS~R	

The macro combines a file named UPDATE into the worksheet starting at cell BA1. Then the main macro calls BA1 as a subroutine. For this to work, the file named UPDATE must contain macro commands starting in cell A1. For this example, the commands beginning in cell A1 of UPDATE appear as follows:

	A	B	C
1	{GOTO}c100~		
2	+c95*0.17~		
3	/XR		

Note that the macro in the file named UPDATE neither contains nor refers to range names. This is because *1-2-3* doesn't include range names with the data it combines from other files. When you create a model, you won't know which cells you will need to change later on. Your updating macros will usually refer to cells and ranges by address rather than by range name.

When you create a model, you also won't know how extensive future changes will be. This update macro is quite short, but it might just as well have required tens of lines of code. (This example has a built-in 1,000-line limit for the update macro, but you'll see a bit later how to go beyond that limit.)

At any rate, I circulated copies of the UPDATE file (along with instructions for its use) to everyone who received the original template. It fell to them to copy UPDATE.WKS (I was working with *1-2-3* Release 1A—Release 2/2.01 uses the file-name extension WK1) to their data directories, retrieve their original copies of the model, and update their models by pressing MACRO-U. The *1-2-3* documentation identifies which keys to press to invoke macros. This approach ensured that even novice *1-2-3* users could update their worksheets properly.

MULTIPLE UPDATES

I received three requests for revisions to the model within 45 days of its distribution. These revisions involved basic changes in calculations or functionality. With each new update disk created, there was no guarantee that all users had performed the previous updates.

To account for this, the model included an autoexecuting macro that displayed the same opening screen each time someone retrieved the file. This screen identified the model and displayed the model's release number. The UPDATE files I circulated contained macro instructions that changed this release number. Users could read the opening screen to identify which update they had performed.

The following illustration shows a macro that can update any version of the model regardless of what authorized update had already been done. Note that the release number of the model is in the cell *rev*:

	A	B	C
1	/XIrev>1~/XGba5~	/XIrev>1.1~/XGbb6~	/XIrev>1.2~/XGbc5~
2	{GOTO}c100~	{GOTO}A7~First~	{GOTO}b100~
3	+C95*0.17~	{DOWN}	+b95*.5~
4	{GOTO}rev~1.1~	Enter first name~	{GOTO}rev~1.3~
5	/XCbb1~	{GOTO}rev~1.2~	/XR
6	/REbb1..bb8~	/XCbc1~	
7	/XR	/REbc1..bc5~	
8		/XR	

Those who have not yet updated are working with Release 1 of the model (*rev* = 1). When the first routine, shown in column A of the illustration, takes control of the updating process, it determines that the value of *rev* is not greater than 1. (Remember that when the update file is combined into the original model, the data shown in column A will actually fall in column BA.) The macro then performs the steps shown in column A and completes the first update by changing the value of *rev* to 1.1.

After completing the update, the subroutine calls a second subroutine (shown in column B). This subroutine determines that *rev* is not greater than 1.1, and the macro performs the second revision. It finishes by changing the value of *rev* to 1.2 and calling the subroutine shown in column C.

The subroutine shown in column C also tests the value of *rev* and performs the third and final update. This routine finishes the update by changing *rev* to 1.3. At this point, *1-2-3* is simultaneously processing three subroutines. When the last subroutine is completed, each subroutine in turn relinquishes control to the previous subroutine, erasing completed subroutines as the progression continues. Finally, control passes back to the main macro, which erases the range holding the first update routine.

If you have already updated the model, the macro skips each update routine in turn; the value of *rev* will be greater than 1, so control will transfer to the command that calls the second update routine, and so on.

Therefore, if you try to update a current model, the macro combines the update file, makes several tests, erases the combined macro steps, and returns control to you without changing anything. There's no harm done, and you can be certain you're using the most current revision of the model.

When you get a request to change the model again, you can send out the same update disk with only two changes. You must write the update routine, and you must change the previous update routine to call and then erase the new one.

FINAL CONSIDERATIONS

Don't use the name UPDATE as the file name in each of your updating macros. Give each update file a name tied to the model it updates. This will let you circulate all update files on a single disk—and will prevent anyone from accidentally using an update file intended for one model on a different model.

You can use many different methods to change your original worksheet. Here are four examples:

- The macro sends the cell pointer to a cell and enters the new formula as though someone were sitting at the keyboard typing it.
- The macro copies a label version of the formula to a target location, sends the cell pointer to the target location, and edits out the label-prefix character. (This method is faster than the first for long formulas.)

- The macro sends the cell pointer to a cell and edits the old formula.
- The macro copies or moves a formula from the combined UPDATE file to a target location in the original worksheet.

The last two methods can cause problems and are best avoided. If an unauthorized user has already edited a target formula, having the macro edit the formula could cause unintended results. Combining working formulas into a worksheet requires careful planning and testing to ensure that the macros work as intended.

The original update macro in the main worksheet ends by erasing cells BA1 through BA1000, leaving the worksheet clear of the combined UPDATE file. This apparently limits your first update to 1,000 lines of code, which should be more than enough for any update. *1-2-3* Release 1A users may not have enough RAM to use all 1,000 cells, but you needn't change the macro code—simply write shorter update routines. All later updates can occupy as much of a column as needed. Include the appropriate range references in the Range Erase commands at the end of each subroutine call.

Also, the update macro combines the UPDATE file into the worksheet at cell BA1, which is 52 columns to the right of where the main worksheet starts. This leaves space for worksheet expansion between the end of the model and the update work area. Vary the spacing depending on the size of the models you create.

Finally, be aware that *1-2-3* limits the number of subroutines that can run concurrently. Release 1A can handle only 16 consecutive /XC commands without a /XR command, while the later releases of *1-2-3*, Release 2 and Release 2.01, allow up to 31 consecutive subroutine calls.

Using self-updating macros, you can not only change formulas; you can change macros, add new features to your already-released models, and even build new worksheets. The process is so easy that your users might think nothing of requesting changes whenever they feel the whim. Maybe killing your boss is the best decision after all.

JANUARY 1987

10

File Keywords

Use these command keywords to manipulate files efficiently
and speed up your multiple-file applications.

BY SCOTT TUCKER AND DANIEL GASTEIGER

As you create bigger and bigger applications, you might find that your computer
lacks the RAM you need to put an entire model into a single worksheet. When
you start feeling cramped by your computer's memory, it's time to subdivide — put
portions of a model into separate worksheets, then tie all the pieces together with
macros.

In previous articles we explored several techniques you can use in creating
multiple-file applications. This time we'll examine the command keywords that are
designed to deal with multifile models. Using the keywords described in the next
section, these models let you store and access data in ASCII disk files.

FILE I/O

Manipulating ASCII files with macros is easier than its language is intimidating. Think
of an ASCII file as a greeting card. When you prepare the greeting for mailing, you
first *open* the card, you then *write* a message, and finally you *close* the card. If you
realize you left out some information or said something you wish you hadn't, you can
either throw out the first card and *open* a new one, or *open* the original card to
modify it. Sometimes you're quite happy with what you've written, and you want to
open the card simply to *read* its contents. You might follow along with your finger

as you read, effectively *pointing* to each word as you come to it. And you might sometimes skip over some words, moving your finger to a new position and continuing from there.

This summarizes the processes involved in file I/O. The file I/O command keywords can open a file so that *Symphony* can either write in the file, read from the file, or both read and write (modify) in the file. When your macro opens a file using the write option, *Symphony* creates a new file. If a file with the specified name already exists, *Symphony* erases the file to make way for the new version. Using the read option, your macro can open only a preexisting file. *Symphony* places a pointer at the beginning of the file and the pointer moves forward through the file, keeping track of which characters are read as the macro progresses. *Symphony* cannot write information in a file opened with this option, though your macro can reposition the pointer within the file and continue reading from the new location.

As with the write option, when your macro opens a file using the modify option, *Symphony* places a pointer at the beginning of the file. The macro can read or write in the file starting at the current location of the file pointer. Whatever the macro writes in the file replaces existing information character-for-character. The file pointer moves to the next position in the file whether the macro is reading or writing.

WHICH KEYWORDS?

The *Symphony* Release 1.1/1.2 documentation lists nine command keywords for file I/O (input/output). These commands exist in the original release of *Symphony*, though they aren't mentioned in the documentation. In spite of the omission, all *Symphony* users and users of *1-2-3* Release 2/2.01 can use the file I/O command keywords with impunity. The file I/O keywords, their syntaxes, and their functions appear as follows:

{**OPEN file,mode**}   Opens a disk file named *file* in one of three modes. The modes are "R" for reading, "W" for writing, or "M" (modify) for both reading and writing.

{**READ bytecount,location**}   Copies *bytecount* number of characters from the open disk file to the cell named *location*.

{**READLN location**}   Copies a line of characters from the currently open file to a cell named *location*.

{**WRITE string**}   Copies the characters represented in *string* into the open disk file.

{**WRITELN string**}   Adds a carriage-return line-feed sequence to the characters represented in *string* and copies the resulting string into the open disk file.

{**GETPOS location**}   Stores in *location* a value that represents the position of the byte pointer in the open disk file.

{**SETPOS number**}   Moves the byte pointer in the currently open file to the position represented by *number*.

{**FILESIZE location**}   Stores in *location* a value that represents the number of bytes (characters) in the currently open disk file.

{**CLOSE**}   Closes a disk file opened with the {OPEN} command.

The arguments in these commands consist of literal text (characters enclosed in quotation marks) or of range references. Unlike most macro commands, when a file I/O command succeeds in its task, control of the macro passes to the next cell in the macro. Only if a file I/O command fails does *Symphony* process other commands in the cell containing the command.

SO WHAT?

Suppose your application consists of several sets of data on which you perform several different calculations. Your model might perform some of the calculations so rarely that keeping those calculations in the main worksheet would be inefficient — even though the model would be useless without the calculations. More important, you might wish to run figures unrelated to the main model through the same set of calculations without using the larger model.

Let's say you're writing a comprehensive investment model in *Symphony*. You put the most frequently used portions of the model into a single worksheet, but you put some complex and rarely used calculations into their own worksheets. You want the individual modules to work two ways: You want to be able to use them as stand-alone worksheets complete with macro-driven interface, and you want to automate the modules' calculation powers so that the main model can call them as subroutines. The macro file I/O commands let you easily create such a model.

AN EXAMPLE

The following worksheet calculates the payment per period on a loan for which you know the principal, the interest rate, and the number of payments to be made. This simple calculation hardly deserves its own worksheet, but it serves to illustrate how a module of the type described might work:

```
        A           B           C              D
1           LOAN  ANALYSIS
2     ==================================
3
4     prin                  Principal
5     inter                 Interest Rate/Period
6     num                   Number of Periods
7
8     pay             ERR   Payment/Period
```

To create the worksheet, enter the labels as shown, leaving blank rows 4 through 6 of column B. Assign the labels in column A as range names for the adjacent cells of column B: point to cell A4, press MENU, select Range Name Labels Right, and press End DownArrow End DownArrow Return. Then enter the following formula in the cell named *pay* (B8):

$$@PMT(@VALUE(prin), @VALUE(inter), @VALUE(num))$$

Now create the macro shown in the following figure:

	A	B	C	D
21	file			
22				
23	\m	{OPEN "data.dat","R"}{BRANCH manual}		
24		{READLN prin}		
25		{READLN inter}		
26		{READLN num}		
27		{READLN file}		
28		{CLOSE}		
29		{CALC}		
30		{OPEN "solution.dat","W"}		
31		{WRITELN @STRING(pay,2)}		
32		{CLOSE}		
33		ERR		
34				
35	manual	{MENUBRANCH menu1}{BRANCH manual}		
36				
37	menu1	Input	Save	Quit
38		Enter data	Save the worksheet	Stop the macro
39		{BRANCH inp}	{BRANCH save}	{QUIT}
40				
41	inp	{HOME}		
42		{GETNUMBER "Enter Principal ",prin}		
43		{GETNUMBER "Enter Interest rate ",inter}		
44		{GETNUMBER "Enter Number of payments ",num}		
45		{CALC}		
46				
47	save	{SERVICES}FS~Y		

Use special care in rows 37 through 39, as the entries in these rows fall in four separate columns. Use the Range Name Labels Right command to assign the labels in column A as names for the adjacent cells of column B. Then enter the following formula in cell B33:

$$+``\{SERVICES\}FR"\&file\&``\sim"$$

The formula returns ERR because there is no entry in the cell named *file* (B21).

Finally, set *Symphony* to run the macro automatically when it retrieves the worksheet: press SERVICES, select Settings Auto-Execute Set, enter \m, and select Quit.

Position the pointer in cell A1 and save the file, using the name LOAN for this example, then give the macro a whirl: simply retrieve the file you just saved. When *Symphony* finishes retrieving the worksheet, the macro starts automatically. Here's what happens:

{OPEN "data.dat","R"}{BRANCH manual}   Tries to open the file named DATA.DAT in read mode. If DATA.DAT doesn't exist on the disk, control of the macro transfers to the cell named *manual*. The macro in the master worksheet will create DATA.DAT before it retrieves the loan-calculation module. Since you retrieved the loan-calculation module manually, the file DATA.DAT doesn't exist. Let's examine the macro steps starting in the cell named *manual*.

{MENUBRANCH menu1}{BRANCH manual}   Displays in the control panel the menu whose description begins in the cell named *menu1* (B37). You can select *Input* to enter data, *Save* to save the worksheet as it appears, or *Quit* to stop the macro.

If you select *Input*, the macro prompts you to enter the principal, the interest rate, and the number of payments. *Symphony* recalculates the worksheet, and the payment per period appears in the cell named *pay*. The macro has acted as an independent worksheet.

Let's examine how the macro works when the master worksheet, which you will create later, retrieves the module.

The macro in the master worksheet creates a file named DATA.DAT before it retrieves the loan module. DATA.DAT contains four pieces of information: the principal amount, the interest rate, the number of payments, and the name of the master worksheet — in this case, MASTER. A bit later we'll look at how the master file creates DATA.DAT.

Because DATA.DAT exists, the first step in the macro succeeds in opening the file with the read option, and control of the macro passes to the command in cell B24. Here's what happens:

{READLN prin}   Copies the first line of characters from the open file into the cell named *prin*.

{READLN inter}   Copies the second line of characters from the open file into the cell named *inter*.

{READLN file}   Copies the third line of characters from the open file into cell named *file*.

The following two lines copy the third and fourth lines from the file into the cells named *num* and *file*, respectively.

{CLOSE}   Closes the file.

{CALC}   Recalculates the worksheet.

{**OPEN** "solution.dat","**W**"} Creates a file named SOLUTION.DAT and prepares to write in the file.

{**WRITELN @STRING(pay,2)**} Writes the string equivalent of the value of *pay* in the open file, finishing with a carriage-return line-feed sequence. The file SOLUTION.DAT now contains the result of the loan calculation.

{**CLOSE**} Closes the file named SOLUTION.DAT. By now the next cell in the macro appears as {SERVICES}FRmaster~ because the cell named *file* contains the file name read from DATA.DAT. Its work completed, the macro retrieves MASTER, leaving the file copy of the loan module unchanged. The worksheet has acted as an integral part of a much larger model.

THE MASTER WORKSHEET

The following macro demonstrates some of the pieces you might include in a master worksheet that calls the loan module as a subroutine.

```
         A          B        C        D        E
29│ file      master
30│
31│ princip      10000
32│ interest      0.01
33│ number         48
34│ payment
35│
36│ getpay     {OPEN "solution.dat","R"}{BRANCH nosol}
37│            {READLN payment}
38│            {CLOSE}
39│            {SERVICES}FEOsolution.dat~Y
40│            {CALC}
41│
42│ nosol      {OPEN "data.dat","W"}
43│            {WRITELN @STRING(princip,2)}
44│            {WRITELN @STRING(interest,2)}
45│            {WRITELN @STRING(number,2)}
46│            {WRITELN file}
47│            {CLOSE}
48│            {SERVICES}FS~Y
49│            {SERVICES}FRloan~
```

The labels in column A are names for the adjacent cells of column B. *Princip*, *interest*, and *number* might contain results of the model's calculations, and they might be located anywhere on the worksheet. We've shown them here for convenience. Once you've entered the labels and assigned the range names, assign *getpay* to run automatically when *Symphony* retrieves the worksheet. Save the worksheet under the name MASTER. If you fail to save at this point, your work will be lost when you run the macro.

You can start this macro by pressing the USER key and entering the macro's name, *getpay*. Here's what happens:

{OPEN "solution.dat","R"}{BRANCH nosol}   Tries to open the disk file named SOLUTION.DAT in read mode. If the file doesn't exist, control of the macro passes to the routine named *nosol*; otherwise, the macro continues processing in the next cell. We'll look at the commands in *nosol* in a moment.

{READLN payment}   Copies the contents of the file SOLUTION.DAT to the cell named *payment*. *Payment* now contains the result of the loan calculation that took place in the loan module.

{CLOSE}   Closes the open file.

{SERVICES}FEOsolution.dat~Y   Erases the file named SOLUTION.DAT. This prepares the directory or disk for your next use of the macro.

{CALC}   Recalculates the worksheet and displays the effect of the macro.

When SOLUTION.DAT doesn't exist in the current directory, this happens:

{OPEN "data.dat","W"}   Creates a file named DATA.DAT. If DATA.DAT already exists, this command erases the existing file.

{WRITELN @STRING(princip,2)}   Writes the string equivalent of the value of *princip* in the file named DATA.DAT.

{WRITELN @STRING(interest,2)} As above, but for the contents of *interest*.

{WRITELN @STRING(number,2)} As above, but for the contents of *number*.

{WRITELN file}   Writes the label stored in the cell named *file* (the current file name) in the open file.

{CLOSE}   Closes the DATA.DAT file.

{SERVICES}FS~Y   Saves the current file. This step may be unnecessary, depending on your application. By saving the file, you preserve whatever calculations have taken place to this point. The next command retrieves a different file, effectively erasing the file in memory, so if you need to keep calculations current, this step is important.

{SERVICES}FRloan~   Retrieves the file named LOAN. LOAN is the loan module shown earlier. It will calculate the payment per period based on the information stored in DATA.DAT and store the result in a file named SOLUTION .DAT. The macro in LOAN finishes by retrieving the file that retrieved LOAN in the first place — in this case, MASTER. When this happens, the autoexecute macro in MASTER discovers SOLUTION.DAT and is able to read the payment per period calculation that SOLUTION.DAT holds.

ARE YOU CONFUSED?

The description of the procedure is more confusing than is the procedure itself. The macro in the master worksheet decides what to do based on the presence or absence of a disk file named SOLUTION.DAT. If SOLUTION.DAT exists, the macro reads information from the file. If SOLUTION.DAT doesn't exist, the macro creates an intermediate file, saves the current file, and retrieves the file named LOAN. LOAN creates the file named SOLUTION.DAT and then retrieves the master worksheet, which can now process the contents of the new file.

When you use these techniques in your macros, you can include commands that keep track of what step the macro is processing when it saves itself and retrieves a worksheet module. One way to do this is to have the macro change the autoexecute macro setting. For example, imagine that *getpay* is one of several routines that retrieve other worksheet modules. Each routine can include a command, just before the {SERVICES}FRmodule command, to assign itself as the autoexecute macro. Then when the module retrieves the master worksheet, the macro will continue processing in the routine where it left off.

SEPTEMBER 1986

11

DOS Device File Names

Do something different with the file
I/O macro commands.

BY ROBERT QUINN

As an applications developer, you might feel frustrated by the limitations of *1-2-3* and *Symphony* because it seems the software just can't perform certain tasks. For example, you might want to create multicolored help screens that temporarily pop up over the worksheet. Or perhaps you'd like each page of your report to have three-line headers using several font styles. Maybe an application requires your macro to communicate directly with *Lotus Signal*, a real-time stock quotation system.

Although you haven't found these features described in your software's documentation, they are in the products. You can create them all by using the file input/output (I/O) command keywords. The next two articles explore techniques that enable you to put personal touches into your applications.

THE CONCEPT

The following macro involves an unorthodox use of the file I/O commands:

	A	B	C	D
1	\a	{OPEN "PRN",W}		
2		{WRITELN "This is a sample line."}		
3		{CLOSE}		

Enter the macro shown in the figure into an empty worksheet, then assign the range name \a to the first line of the macro (cell B1). Turn your printer on and run the macro. Your printer prints the sentence *This is a sample line*. Notice the printer's quick response time. Compare that response time with the printer response time of the following two slower macros (for *1-2-3* and *Symphony*, respectively), which assume that a range named *text* contains the sentence *This is a sample line* :

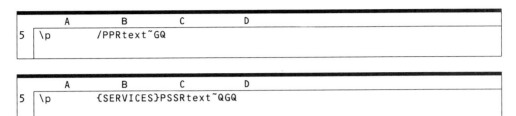

	A	B	C	D
5	\p	/PPRtext~GQ		

	A	B	C	D
5	\p	{SERVICES}PSSRtext~QGQ		

Look at the first macro again. In order to access the printer, that macro uses something called a DOS device file name, which is a file name reserved by DOS for a specific purpose. The device file name PRN, for example, is reserved to redirect normal file output to the default printer of your computer system.

WHAT THE DEVICE FILE NAMES DO

You can use the device file names PRN, LPT1, LPT2, LPT3 (for parallel ports) and AUX, COM1, COM2 (for serial ports) to direct data to printers, modems, and so forth. You can also use the serial port device file names to receive data (the parallel ports are, by definition, for output only).

The device file name CON concerns your console—your computer keyboard and monitor. You've probably used CON when working in DOS, for example, in conjunction with the DOS COPY command to create batch files. DOS interprets the command COPY CON AUTOEXEC.BAT to mean "copy a file named AUTOEXEC.BAT from the console."

Similarly, the command COPY AUTOEXEC.BAT CON copies the contents of the AUTOEXEC.BAT file to the console. The result is the same as the result from issuing the DOS command TYPE AUTOEXEC.BAT.

You can use the CON device file name in a macro to require special types of input from the user. More important, you can use it to send output directly to the screen. When used properly, this device file name lets a macro place any combination of ASCII characters anywhere on the screen in any combination of display attributes (including foreground and background colors, boldface, and so forth).

The NUL device file name, which refers to the null port, might seem odd. Because it represents a nonexistent port, or device, it lets you send data into a void. If you replace references to specific file names with NUL, you can run a macro without modifying an existing file. For example, if your macro uses the command {OPEN "acctsdat",W} to modify an existing file, you can change the command to read

	A	B	C	D
1	¦\027-1			
2	This text is underlined.			
3	¦\027-0			
4	This text isn't underlined.			
5	¦\015			
6	This text is compressed.			
7	¦\018			
8	This text is normal.			

FIGURE 1

This text is underlined.
This text isn't underlined.
This text is compressed.
This text is normal.

FIGURE 1A

{OPEN "NUL",W}. Then you can test the macro without making undesired changes to your disk.

The NUL device file name is not useful for input. Suppose that your *1-2-3* macro uses the commands /FCCEaccts~ (in *Symphony,* {SERVICES}FCCEIFaccts~) to combine a worksheet from disk. If you replace the file name ACCTS with the device file name NUL, the macro fails and produces the error message *Part of file is missing.*

The NUL device file name is particularly useful in debugging macros that use the file I/O keywords (or even the File menu commands).

Your system may recognize device file names other than the ones listed. DOS lets third parties develop custom device file names. For example, *Lotus Signal* uses the custom device file name QUOTES to let *1-2-3* and *Symphony* access real-time stock data.

CUSTOMIZED PRINTING

Let's return to the example that uses the device file name PRN. Besides speed, what does this technique offer that *1-2-3* and *Symphony* Print commands don't? By using the PRN device file name, you can generate printouts that have multiple font styles and print attributes in a single line.

1-2-3 and *Symphony* give you control over your printer by letting you use printer control codes (called setup strings in *1-2-3* and initialization strings in *Symphony*). These codes tell a printer to change the style or nature of the printing characters. We'll use Epson FX-80 printer control codes for this discussion; consult your printer's manual for its list of allowable codes.

In *1-2-3* Releases 2 and 2.01 and in *Symphony*, you can insert printer control codes into any row of a worksheet and thereby change from row to row the style in which your printer prints. For example, when you print the range shown in figure 1, you produce the printout shown in figure 1A.

Every other row of the worksheet in the illustration contains a printer control code. The first control code (in cell A1) consists of the characters \027-1 (you identify the cell contents as a printer control code by starting the entry with two split vertical bars). To the Epson printer, this means "underline everything you type from here onward." The control code in cell A3 (\027-0) means "stop underlining." The code in cell A5 (\015) means "use condensed print," and the code in cell A7 (\018) means "return to normal printing."

Generally, a control code contains a backslash followed by at least three digits. The digits 027 represent ASCII character 27 — the escape character. The digits 015 and 018 represent ASCII characters 15 and 18. If a printer code requires a particular ASCII character (many codes begin with the escape character), you represent the character by entering its ASCII value preceded in your setup string by a backslash.

Using a slightly different notation, you can embed the same printer codes in file I/O macro keywords. This lets you combine several print attributes in a single line of output. The macro in figure 2 illustrates the technique in a *1-2-3* or *Symphony* macro.

This macro opens a file named PRN — essentially opening your printer as an output file. Then the macro sends a line of characters to the printer. The line of characters sent results from a string equation that concatenates several words with several printer-control ASCII characters.

There's a hitch to getting this macro to work properly in *Symphony* and an even bigger hitch for *1-2-3* users. The hitch has to do with the way your software exchanges data with other DOS applications. Lotus products use a character set called LICS, which associates characters with values different from those of ASCII. For example, the English pound character (£) is LICS character number 163, whereas it is ASCII character number 156. To account for these differences, when *1-2-3* and *Symphony* import and export data, they translate the data to ensure its integrity.

Whenever *1-2-3* and *Symphony* import a file or when they export data to a file, they translate LICS to ASCII or ASCII to LICS, based on information stored in the character-translation table. The software also uses this table to translate data exchanged using the file I/O keywords — whether or not you are using DOS device file names.

The default character-translation table in *1-2-3* and *Symphony* translates alpha-numeric characters during output procedures (such as printing). Unfortunately, it doesn't translate the escape character or many other useful characters. When you run the macro shown in figure 2, you won't get the intended results.

```
      A       B        C         D
1 | \f     {OPEN "PRN",W}
2 |        {WRITELN +"Normal, "&@CHAR(15)&"compressed"&@CHAR(18)&", and "&@CHAR(27)&"-1underlined"&@CHAR(27)&"-0}
3 |        {CLOSE}
```

FIGURE 2

TRANSLATIONS

You can customize *Symphony*'s character-translation tables in order to instruct *Symphony* to send the desired printer codes. Start with a blank worksheet and place the pointer in cell A1. Press SERVICES and select Configuration Other File-Translation Generate Current, press Return, and select Quit Quit.

When you return to the worksheet, note that *Symphony* created a table two columns wide and 256 rows long. *Symphony* uses the first column during data output. Each row is assigned the ASCII value that *Symphony* substitutes when outputting the associated LICS character (indicated by the worksheet row number minus 1). *Symphony* uses the second column of the table as the guide for translating incoming data.

For example, move the pointer to cell A164. This row represents the character-translation information for LICS character number 163, the English pound character. The number in cell A164 (156) is the number of the ASCII character that *Symphony* will substitute when outputting LICS character number 163.

Now move the pointer to cell A28. This cell contains the number 32. This means that *Symphony* replaces the LICS character 27 with the ASCII character 32 during file output operations. We want *Symphony* to send ASCII character 27, so we'll replace the number 32 with 27. And because we want to send other ASCII printer codes (for example, ASCII 15 for compressed print), let's change the entire table.

To alter the table, move the pointer to cell A1 and press MENU. Select Range Fill, indicate range A1..A256, and press Return three times. This fills the left column of the table with numbers in sequence from 0 to 255. Using these values, *Symphony* will output whatever numeric code is associated with a particular LICS character. Hence, LICS character 15 is sent as ASCII character 15. Note that because this table is customized for our purposes, you may wish to use *Symphony*'s default character-translation table for other applications. To activate this table, you must first save it and then tie it to *Symphony*.

To save the table, press SERVICES, select Configuration Other File-Translation Generate Save, indicate cell A1, and press Return. Now enter a file name — ASCII, perhaps. *Symphony* saves the table. Tie the table to *Symphony* by selecting Custom from the File-Translation menu and selecting ASCII.CTF. With this new table active,

0	0	64	64	63	199	63	153
32	1	65	65	63	252	63	153
32	2	66	66	63	233	63	153
32	3	67	67	63	226	63	153
32	4	68	68	126	228	142	153
32	5	69	69	63	224	143	153
0	0	70	70	63	229	146	153
32	1	71	71	63	231	128	153
32	2	72	72	63	234	63	153
32	3	73	73	63	235	144	153
32	4	74	74	63	232	63	153
32	5	75	75	63	239	63	153
0	0	76	76	63	238	63	153
13	13	77	77	63	236	63	153
32	14	78	78	63	196	63	153
32	15	79	79	63	197	63	153
32	16	80	80	63	201	63	153
32	17	81	81	63	230	165	153
32	18	82	82	63	198	63	153
32	19	83	83	63	244	63	153
32	20	84	84	126	246	63	153
32	21	85	85	63	242	63	153
32	22	86	86	63	251	153	153
32	23	87	87	63	249	63	153
32	24	88	88	63	253	63	153
32	25	89	89	63	214	63	153
32	26	90	90	32	220	63	153
32	27	91	91	63	162	63	153
32	28	92	92	63	163	154	153
32	29	93	93	63	165	63	153
32	30	94	94	63	166	63	153
32	31	95	95	63	160	225	153
32	32	96	96	159	225	133	153
33	33	97	97	173	237	160	223
34	34	98	98	155	243	131	153
35	35	99	99	156	250	63	173
36	36	100	100	63	241	132	153
37	37	101	101	157	209	134	153
38	38	102	102	158	170	145	181
39	39	103	103	21	186	135	153
40	40	104	104	15	191	138	153
41	41	105	105	63	153	130	153
42	42	106	106	166	153	136	153
43	43	107	107	174	189	137	153
44	44	108	108	63	188	141	153
45	45	109	109	227	161	161	153
46	46	110	110	242	171	140	153
47	47	111	111	246	187	139	153
48	48	112	112	248	153	63	153
49	49	113	113	241	153	164	177
50	50	114	114	253	153	149	174
51	51	115	115	63	153	162	190
52	52	116	116	63	153	147	153
53	53	117	117	230	153	63	153
54	54	118	118	20	153	148	175
55	55	119	119	249	153	63	153
56	56	120	120	63	153	237	176
57	57	121	121	63	153	151	183
58	58	122	122	167	153	163	153
59	59	123	123	175	153	150	153
60	60	124	124	172	153	129	153
61	61	125	125	171	153	152	178
62	62	126	126	243	153	63	153
63	63	127	127	168	153	63	153

FIGURE 3. The default character-translation table used by *1-2-3* and *Symphony* during I/O operations. The numbers on the left of each column represent codes used during output; the numbers on the right, codes for incoming data.

try out the macro shown earlier. When you run the macro (again, assuming you're using an Epson printer), *Symphony* produces the following output:

Normal, compressed, and <u>underlined</u>

For *1-2-3* users, the character-translation table is not easily accessible. No built-in mechanism by which to modify the table exists, but there are some alternatives. Figure 3 illustrates the default character-translation table used by *1-2-3* and *Symphony*. For *1-2-3*, this table resides in the driver set. Using the DOS DEBUG program or a program like *The Norton Utilities*, you can search for this particular sequence of bytes and then modify the sequence to create a custom driver set. Alternatively, you can purchase the *1-2-3* Programmer's Toolbox from Q-Soft Inc. (Midland Park, N.J.), which provides a means to directly customize *1-2-3*'s character-translation table.

CLOSING THOUGHTS

Using the file I/O command keywords to generate printed output gives you greater flexibility than you have with *1-2-3* and *Symphony* Print commands. You can combine different fonts on a single line and even increase the number of lines in your headers and footers, all more quickly than you'd expect from the built-in Print commands.

There is a price, however. Because this technique doesn't use the Print menu, you cannot use your software's printing features (such as margins, pagination, headers, footers, and so forth). You must create these features within your macros.

If your printer is attached to a port other than the default parallel port, simply substitute the port's device file name in your macro's {OPEN} command ({OPEN "COM1",W}, for example).

Finally, watch for other situations in which you might use file I/O keywords to control a process. Many peripherals use the serial and parallel ports on a PC. For example, the *Lotus Signal* receiver attaches to a serial port. And since *Signal* has a programming language of its own, you can use file I/O commands to send special instructions to it and then receive requested data. Other possible applications include capturing data from technical instruments, sending special instructions to plotters, and communicating over local area networks.

In the next chapter, we'll discuss some unusual techniques that use the CON DOS device file name and will give you complete control of your screen. We'll discuss how to use DOS's ANSI.SYS driver to place any combination of ASCII characters (including special graphics characters) anywhere on the screen in any variety of color combinations and screen attributes.

12

Macro Graphics

Use macros to create snazzy graphics anywhere
on your computer's monitor.

BY ROBERT QUINN

et's face it, a worksheet display is dull. Worse is the fact that the look and feel of
your macro-driven template is apparently limited by the environment in which
you develop it. Even a limited ability to control the display graphically could make
the difference between producing just another Lotus template and producing a
template that reflects your or your company's unique style.

In spite of appearances, *1-2-3* and *Symphony* can provide you with powerful
graphics. You access this capability by using the macro file input/output (I/O)
command keywords.

In the previous chapter we saw how to use the macro file I/O commands with the
DOS device file named PRN to control printer output. In this chapter we'll use the
same macro commands and the CON device file name to create snazzy graphic
displays and pop-up messages. Before we proceed, however, let's review some
related topics.

CATCHING UP

The macro file I/O commands let you send data to the DOS logical device file named
PRN, which refers to your printer, more quickly than you can using selections from
1-2-3's or *Symphony*'s Print menus. These commands also let you output printer
control codes (setup or initialization strings) that combine several print attributes in
a single line of text. But there's a trick to using the file I/O keywords to control your
printer.

Whenever *1-2-3* or *Symphony* use the file I/O command keywords to import or export data, the programs convert ASCII codes into LICS codes or vice-versa. The conversion process is mediated by a list of numbers called the character-translation table. The characters that result from this conversion are useless for controlling printers, plotters, and other peripherals. For example, during output *Symphony* and *1-2-3* translate the LICS character 027 (escape) to ASCII character 032 (space), rendering it meaningless as a printer control code. To make your software send the proper printer control codes, you must customize the character-translation table.

To customize *Symphony*'s character-translation table, start with a blank worksheet and press SERVICES. Select Configuration Other File-Translation Generate Current, point to cell A1, press Return, and select Quit Quit. Use the Range Fill command to enter values 0 to 255 in range A1..A256. Then select SERVICES Configuration Other File-Translation Generate Save, point to cell A1, press Return, enter the file name ASCII, select Custom, point to ASCII.CTF, press Return, and select Quit Quit. Finally, erase the current worksheet. The new character-translation table will remain current throughout your current work session or until you elect to use a different table.

There are no commands in *1-2-3* to let you customize its character-translation table. *1-2-3*'s translation table resides in the driver set, so you can customize it with the help of DEBUG or a program like *The Norton Utilities*. Should you wish at any time to use such a program and modify your driver set, in the previous chapter we printed a copy of the table to help you identify the relevant data. For an alternative, Q-Soft Inc. (Midland Park, N.J.) produces the *1-2-3 Programmer's Toolbox*, which provides easy access to the character-translation table.

DISPLAY WRITING

Once you have activated the modified character-translation table, run the following macro several times in an otherwise empty worksheet:

	A	B	C	D
1	\a	{OPEN "CON",W}		
2		{WRITELN "This is a sentence."}		
3		{CLOSE}		

Once per row starting on the left edge of the display, your software writes *This is a sentence*. Each time you run the macro, it generates another copy of the sentence. (If at any point while you're trying these techniques your macros don't behave as described, refer to the notes on "Know Your Users' Systems" at the end of this chapter.) Run the macro repeatedly until a copy of the sentence occupies each row of the worksheet, and notice that the display scrolls when the macro writes on the last line (except, perhaps, the top and bottom borders).

The text that your macro writes on-screen doesn't affect the operation of your software. You can think of the graphic images as being superimposed on the worksheet program. Depending on the brand of your computer and the display driver you've installed, "refreshing" the worksheet, or returning to the original display, is quite easy.

Many users can refresh the display simply by pressing Return or Escape. If that doesn't work, press the DRAW key (*Symphony*) or the CALC key (*1-2-3* and *Symphony*). These approaches should refresh the worksheet for anyone using a toggle-mode driver.

If you're using a shared-mode driver, clearing the custom graphics display might take more effort. In *Symphony*, switching to a GRAPH window and then back to a SHEET window does the most consistently thorough job, though you might be left with extraneous characters in the first row of the display. Again, the behavior of the display depends on your hardware and drivers.

The macro you've just run uses the file I/O command keywords to send data to the DOS device file named CON, which is short for *console*, your computer's keyboard and monitor. The first line of the macro opens CON as a file for output. The macro's second line writes to CON *This is a sentence*, followed by a carriage return and a line-feed. The third macro command closes the device file named CON, ending file I/O operations.

Substitute the {WRITE} command for the {WRITELN} command in this macro. Now when you run the macro, you append another copy of the output sentence to the preceding copy. When you fill a line, output wraps to the next row, and so on, until the entire display begins scrolling upward.

The following macro exploits this scrolling characteristic to erase the screen in an unusual way. To refresh the display after the macro has cleared it, simply press Return:

	A	B	C	D
6	\a	{PANELOFF}{WINDOWSOFF}		
7		{OPEN "CON",W}		
8		{WRITE @REPEAT(@CHAR(10),50)}		
9		{?}		
10		{PANELON}{WINDOWSON}		
11		{CLOSE}		

This macro uses the @REPEAT function and sends 50 copies of the LICS character 10 to the device file named CON. The LICS character (as well as the ASCII character) 10 is the line-feed character, so this macro essentially performs 50 line-feeds, scrolling everything off the display.

By using the {PANELOFF} and {WINDOWSOFF} commands, you prevent your software from updating the display as long as the macro is running. When the macro pauses at the {?} command, your software won't refresh the first and last lines of the display as it might have with the first macro. The {PANELON} and {WINDOWSON} commands at the end of the macro cause the entire screen to redraw, canceling the effects of the I/O commands.

DRAWING PICTURES

So far we've looked only at macros that send text characters to the display. You could almost duplicate these effects with macros that type text in a COMM window. The following macro provides a better sense of the power of the file I/O commands:

	A	B	C	D	E	F
1	\m	{PANELOFF}{WINDOWSOFF}				
2		{LET counter,30}{OPEN "CON",W}				
3		{WRITE @REPEAT(@CHAR(10),50)&@CHAR(13)}				
4	back	{LET counter,counter+1}				
5		{RECALC block}				
6		{IF counter=256}{?}{QUIT}				
7		{WRITE formula}				
8		{BRANCH back}				
9						
10	counter					
11	formula	ERR				

To create the macro, enter it as shown, assign the labels in column A as range names for the adjacent cells of column B, assign the name *block* to the range B10..B11, and enter the following formula into the cell named *formula*:

@STRING(counter,0)&@IF(counter>99, "; ","; ")&@CHAR(counter)&" "

This formula concatenates the string value of *counter* with a semicolon, followed by the LICS character whose code matches the value of *counter*. If you enter the number 234 into *counter*, *formula* appears as in the following illustration:

	A	B	C
10	counter	234	
11	formula	234; e	

The macro first clears the screen, then loops through a series of commands that increases the value of *counter* and sends the value of *formula* to the screen. Because you've customized the character-translation table, the macro's resulting screen display shows ASCII, rather than LICS, characters paired with the characters' values. You can refer to this list when you select characters to generate graphic images.

JUMPING AROUND

So far, we're able to write strings of characters to the display, ultimately filling the screen and causing everything on-screen to scroll upward. But suppose you want to write near the top of the screen and the macro is already writing near the bottom of the screen. Ideally, you should have access to every point on the screen without concern for where your macro has already written.

To accomplish this, you rely on the ANSI.SYS device driver, a utility that comes with every copy of DOS. The ANSI driver interprets escape-character sequences similar to the way a printer interprets setup strings. With the driver active, your macros can send "screen setup strings" and control the positioning, color (or intensity), and behavior of output from {WRITE} and {WRITELN} commands.

To activate the ANSI.SYS driver, you create a file called CONFIG.SYS on your startup disk (or root directory). If your startup disk already contains a CONFIG.SYS file, you should edit that file to contain the command DEVICE = ANSI.SYS. If your startup disk doesn't hold a CONFIG.SYS file, use the COPY CON command, EDLIN, or some other text processor to create the file. The new file's contents should read simply, DEVICE = ANSI.SYS. In any case, once it contains the CONFIG.SYS file, your startup disk must also contain the file named ANSI.SYS, which resides on your original DOS disk. Your DOS manual contains more information about these files and how to create them.

With the CONFIG.SYS file created, restart your computer (hold down the MACRO and Control keys and press Delete). Upon startup DOS reads the CONFIG file and activates the ANSI.SYS driver. You can then provide your macros with the ability to write graphics anywhere on the display.

Load *Symphony* or *1-2-3* again, activate the customized character-translation table, and try out the following macro:

```
        A       B          C         D        E         F
1  \m        {PANELOFF}{WINDOWSOFF}
2           {OPEN "CON",W}
3           {WRITE @CHAR(27)&"[13;19H"}
4           {WRITE @CHAR(27)&"[0;32;44m"}
5           {WRITE " This sentence is in living color!  "}
6           {WRITE @CHAR(27)&"[0m"}
7           {CLOSE}
```

The macro places a green-and-blue message in the center of the display (our apologies to people using monochrome monitors). When you refresh the display and rerun the macro, the message appears in the same position as it did on the first run.

The commands in cells B3 and B4 send control codes to the ANSI.SYS device driver. The command {WRITE @CHAR(27)&"[13;19H"} means "move the cursor to the 13th row and the 19th column of the computer's display." (Note that the ANSI.SYS driver considers a column to be the width of a single character.) The command {WRITE @CHAR(27)&"[0;32;44m"} means "use green as the foreground color and blue as the background color to display the characters that follow." The command in cell B5 of the macro sends the actual text of the message to the screen.

The final {WRITE} command in cell B6 sends a code to reset the display attributes. If the macro did not send a reset code, your display would appear in green and blue when you exited to DOS.

The table lists the ANSI.SYS display control codes. To address the ANSI.SYS device driver, precede each of the listed codes in a {WRITE} command with the escape character (ASCII character 027). For example, to move the cursor home, send the character sequence ESC[H.

Cursor Control Codes

Code	Description
[#;#H	Moves cursor to coordinate defined by #;#, where # represents row
[#;#f	and column, respectively (origin is 1;1)
[H	Moves cursor to the origin
[#H	Moves cursor to row # in current column
[;#H	Moves cursor to column # in current row
[#A	Moves cursor up # rows
[A	Moves cursor up 1 row
[#B	Moves cursor down # rows
[B	Moves cursor down 1 row
[#C	Moves cursor right # columns
[C	Moves cursor right 1 column
[#D	Moves cursor left # rows
[D	Moves cursor left 1 row
[s	Temporarily saves current position of cursor for future recall
[u	Restores cursor to position previously saved by [s

Display Codes

[2J	Erases display using most recent background color and moves cursor to origin (1;1)
[K	Erases from cursor to end of current row
[#;#;#m	Sets character attributes where each # represents a selection from the corresponding column of the following list:

# Attribute	# Foreground	# Background
0 Reset	30 Black	40 Black
1 Intensity	31 Red	41 Red
4 Underscore	32 Green	42 Green
5 Blink	33 Yellow	43 Yellow
7 Reverse	34 Blue	44 Blue
8 Invisible	35 Magenta	45 Magenta
	36 Cyan	46 Cyan
	37 White	47 White

[#h [#1	Sets display mode indicated by #, where # is a number from the following list:

#	Display Mode
0	40 x 25 black-and-white
1	40 x 25 color
2	80 x 25 black-and-white
3	80 x 25 color
4	320 x 200 color (medium-resolution graphics)
5	320 x 200 b&w (medium-resolution graphics)
6	640 x 200 b&w (high-resolution graphics)

Note: There are also escape sequences that redefine keyboard keys. However, because *1-2-3* and *Symphony* control the keyboard directly, the ANSI.SYS keyboard control sequences serve no purpose.

PUTTING IT ALL TOGETHER

The macro at the top of the next page combines several ANSI escape sequences to generate a full-screen graphic.

Decipher the meaning of each of the display control commands used in this macro, then use the ANSI commands in your own macros and create some custom graphics. While you're writing your macros, keep a few things in mind.

Use the {PANELOFF} and {WINDOWSOFF} commands to suppress your software's urge to update the screen and wipe out your custom graphics. Use the {PANELON} and {WINDOWSON} command when you want to refresh the spreadsheet display.

```
         A          B          C        D          E          F
 9  \e        {PANELOFF}{WINDOWSOFF}
10            {OPEN "CON",W}
11            {WRITE @CHAR(27)&"[44m"}
12            {WRITE @CHAR(27)&"[2J"}
13            {WRITE @CHAR(27)&"[13;19H"}
14            {WRITE @CHAR(27)&"[0;31;42m"}
15            {WRITE @CHAR(27)&"[5m"}
16            {WRITE "Another sentence in color."}
17            {WRITE @CHAR(27)&"[0m"}
18            {?}
19            {PANELON}{WINDOWSON}~
20            {CLOSE}
```

Remember to end each sequence of screen control codes with the reset escape sequence. If one macro doesn't send a reset code, then the custom codes will be in effect when the next graphic routine runs. What's more annoying, when you return to DOS, your display will still be using the custom attributes.

This article barely touches on the uses of the DOS device file names and the worksheet techniques associated with their use. With a little effort you can apply these techniques to give your models a unique flavor.

KNOW YOUR USERS' SYSTEMS

It's terribly annoying when you follow all the written instructions to do something and things just don't work. This article might provide one of those annoying experiences. Your success with the described techniques will rely in part on the type of hardware you're using and on the Lotus display driver you've installed for *1-2-3* or *Symphony*.

Generally, monitors have text-display modes and graphics-display modes. While operating in a text-display mode, a monitor can't show graphic images (with the exception of graphic images built from text characters). Conversely, while operating in a graphics-display mode, most monitors will show only images that are created graphically (pixel by pixel).

A text display can update more quickly than a graphic display, so the driver of choice is one that works primarily in text mode and switches to graphics mode only when displaying graphs (a toggle-mode driver). This is most likely what you installed with *1-2-3*. *Symphony* users, however, might have installed drivers that let them view text and graphs simultaneously (shared-mode drivers) and keep the display in graphics mode throughout your work session. A shared-mode driver is likely to cause the described techniques to fail.

We tested several different systems with the techniques described in the article and found many inconsistencies. An IBM with a Color Graphics Adapter worked as described, as did a Compaq Portable and an IBM with a Hercules Monochrome Graphics Card (although the monochrome graphics of the Compaq and Hercules left much to be desired). Each was running with toggle-mode drivers. When we switched to shared-mode drivers, each computer behaved differently. The Compaq still displayed the custom graphics, but refreshing the worksheet display wasn't always easy. And the IBM with a Hercules card simply wouldn't relinquish control of the screen to the *Symphony* macro.

The lesson is clear: Test your macros on the machines that your end users are using. Will the graphics that look great on your EGA monitor look as wonderful on your users' monochrome displays? If you can't ensure consistency from one user's system to the next, you should probably stick with the original worksheet display.

JUNE 1987

SECTION
7

LETTERS TO THE
MACRO EDITOR,
QUESTIONS, AND ADVICE

No book of *LOTUS* reprints would be complete without a letters section. Many of you have told us that the parts of the magazine you like best are the reader contributions in the Good Ideas, Q&A, Macro Letters, reader evaluation, and letters-to-the-editor sections. The reason is that the letter writers are generally addressing the same problems you face. In addition, letters are short, easy to read, bite-size treats that you can scan quickly.

LOTUS has never had to worry about getting enough letters to fill the various letters columns. Quite the opposite. Literally hundreds of letters pour into our offices every month. This is just one manifestation of a uniquely gratifying aspect of *LOTUS*: the intense relationship it has with its readership.

To help you find the information you want, the letters in this section are divided into four very general categories. The first covers such topics as starting, stopping, speeding up, and improving the visual or auditory performance of your macros. The second group covers macro menus, using range names, flow-of-control commands, branching, and subroutines. The third group deals with entering, calculating, erasing, and analyzing data, and throws in some other macro tricks as well. Finally, the fourth group covers ways to find and correct the little mistakes you accidentally built into your macro as well as the macro implications of some bugs that Lotus Development didn't discover until after its products shipped.

GROUP

1

Starting, Stopping, Time and Noise

1. INVOKING MACROS

I have a Hewlett-Packard 110 computer with built-in Lotus software. I cannot, however, locate a MACRO key. Does this mean that my machine cannot perform macro operations?

Lane McDaniel
McDaniel and White
Dallas, Texas

1-2-3 was originally written for the IBM PC and was later rewritten for (ported to) other machines. We don't wish to ignore these machines in our discussions, but even generic discussions might leave out somebody. Here are 1-2-3 ports listed by the keystrokes necessary to start a macro named \m.

While depressing the MACRO key, press M *applies to: Bytec Hyperion, Compaq Portable and Compaq Plus, Data General/One, IBM PCjr and 3270 PC, Tandy Model 1000, Texas Instruments Professional, and Victor 9000.*

While depressing the Control and Shift keys, press M *applies to: DEC Rainbow 100 and 100+, Hewlett-Packard 100 Portable and 150, and Zenith Z-100.*

While depressing the Copy key, press M *applies to: Convergent Technologies NGEN Workstation.*

While depressing the GL key, press M *applies to: Wang Professional.*

And here are some examples of how to stop a macro:

356

COMPUTER	PROCEDURE
DEC Rainbow Tandy 2000	Press Break
IBM PC IBM PC clones Hyperion Data General	Hold down the Control key and press Break
Hewlett-Packard 110 and 150	Hold down the Break and Shift keys and press Stop
Convergent Technologies	Hold down Code and press Cancel
Wang Professional	Hold down Shift and press Cancel
Victor 9000	Press the CLR/Home key
Grid Compass	Hold down the Code and Control keys and press DownArrow

2. UNDOCUMENTED KEYWORDS

I've discovered an undocumented macro keyword. I use {INSERT} in a Release 2 macro to turn on the *Ovr* indicator. This lets your macros overwrite text while *1-2-3* is in Edit mode.

Jack McKinley
Denver Lotus User's Group
Denver, Colo.

There are other undocumented keywords as well. For example, {MENU} acts like the slash key to bring up the menu. You can also shorten the commands {LEFT}, {RIGHT}, {UP}, and {DOWN} to {L},{R},{U}, and {D}, respectively. For example, the command {L 4} is equivalent to the command {LEFT 4}.

3. A MACRO INDEX

I've found that creating a macro index in my worksheet is very helpful. This simple listing saves time, since I no longer have to hunt through my macros to find the one I want. Also, before saving a file I always position the pointer within a cell in the index so that the index displays on the screen when I later retrieve the file.

Richard Tangard
Norwalk, Conn.

4. BREAKING OUT OF A MACRO

I frequently use macros that retrieve files containing an autoexecuting macro. The first line of the autoexecuting macro uses a {BREAKOFF} command to disable the Break key. This prevents other users from stopping the macro and tampering with the worksheet.

Although this is effective, this technique prevents me from retrieving the file to edit the worksheet. To get around this shortcoming, I created a password-protected file called TEST that contains just a number, Ø or 1. To edit the file, I change the contents of TEST from Ø to 1. The second line of my autoexecuting macro contains the File Combine command to combine TEST into the current worksheet. The password must also be included in the macro. In the third line of the macro, an {IF} command tests whether the imported value is Ø or 1. If it is 1, the {QUIT} command stops the macro and lets me edit the worksheet. If the value is Ø, the macro continues.

Jan Novelli
Reseda, Calif.

5. OK, HOLD IT!

I'm having trouble getting the {WAIT} command to work. Whenever I invoke a macro with a statement such as {WAIT @TIME(15,000,000)}, *Symphony* ripples through the {WAIT} statement without pausing. Help!

Richard G. Watkins
Sandy, Utah

The {WAIT} command causes a macro to pause until your computer's internal clock catches up with the time indicated within the {WAIT} command. To get the macro to work properly, use the @NOW and @TIME functions within the {WAIT} command. If you want your macro to pause for 10 seconds, use the statement {WAIT @NOW + @TIME(Ø,Ø,10)}. This means "add 10 seconds to the current time and pause until the computer's clock time equals that sum."

6. THE {BEEP} COMMAND

All releases of *Symphony* accept arguments in the {BEEP} command—a feature undocumented in Release 1. These arguments determine the tone that the {BEEP} command produces. I've written a short macro that recalculates the worksheet and then plays a short tune. Even in the most crowded offices, my users know when their worksheets are finished recalculating.

	A	B	C	D	E
1	\t	{CALC}			
2		{BEEP 2}{WAIT @NOW+@TIME(0,0,.5)}			
3		{BEEP 4}{WAIT @NOW+@TIME(0,0,.5)}			
4		{BEEP 4}{WAIT @NOW+@TIME(0,0,.5)}			
5		{BEEP 1}{WAIT @NOW+@TIME(0,0,.5)}			
6		{BEEP 4}{WAIT @NOW+@TIME(0,0,1)}			
7		{BEEP 2}{WAIT @NOW+@TIME(0,0,.5)}			
8		{BEEP 3}			

Note that the fifth {WAIT} time is longer than the others. Try it and you'll know why.

Brian Underdahl
Graybar Electric Co.
St. Louis, Mo.

Adjust the time indicated in the {WAIT} commands according to the processing speed of your PC. On slower PCs, you might want to eliminate the {WAIT} commands completely. Also note that different computers produce different tones, so this routine might play an unrecognizable tune for many users. Try a similar routine in an {ONERROR} command sequence within a long-running macro. The tune will alert you to problems if you've shifted attention to other matters.

7. MACROS AND RECALCULATION

In a large or complex worksheet, your macro will run faster with the recalculation method set to manual. Then when you want to recalculate the worksheet within a macro, use the {CALC} Command.

David A. Martin
Pennsauken, N.J.

If you use Symphony *or 1-2-3 Release 2 or 2.01, you can reduce recalculation time by using the {RECALC} command. This command instructs 1-2-3 to recalculate a range of cells {RECALC range} rather than the entire worksheet. {RECALC} uses a row-by-row recalculation sequence. If you prefer the recalculation to proceed column-by-column, then use the {RECALCCOL} command.*

Both commands can take up to three arguments in the format {RECALC location,condition,iterations}. The first argument, location, *can be a single cell address, a range of cells, or a range name. The second two arguments are optional. 1-2-3 recalculates and then evaluates the conditional statement of the second argument. If the condition is false, 1-2-3 recalculates* location *again. 1-2-3 continues to recalculate* location *until either the condition is true or the number of recalculations equals the value of* iterations.

Release 1A users can recalculate one cell or a range of cells by copying the cell or range onto itself. Also, editing and reentering a formula recalculates the formula regardless of the recalculation method. Therefore, your macros can use the instructions /Ctest~ test~ or {GOTO}test~{EDIT}~ to recalculate a formula in a cell named test. *The first technique leaves the cell pointer in the current cell, while the second technique moves the cell pointer to the cell named* test.

8. BENCHMARK MACROS

How can I set up a macro so that I can time its execution? This macro will be used for benchmark testing on different PCs.

G.F. Herron
St. Louis, Mo.

A tip submitted by Ed Karl of Wheat Ridge, Colo. can solve your problem. By inserting one line at the beginning and two lines at the end of your macro, you can time the macro's execution. The periods in this figure represent your original macro.

	A	B	C	D
1	\m	{LET start,@NOW}		
2		...		
3		...		
4		{LET stop,@NOW}		
5		{DRAW}		
6				
7	start			
8	stop			
9	time	00:00:00		

Enter the macro as shown, replacing the periods with your original macro. Then use the *Range Name Labels Right* command to assign the labels \m, start, stop, *and* time *as range names for the adjacent cells in column B. In the cell named* time, *enter the formula* +stop–start. *Use the* MENU Format Time 3 *command to assign time formats to* start, stop, *and* time. *Here's how the macro works:*

{**LET start,@NOW**} *Enters the value of @NOW into* start. *Then your macro takes over until* Symphony *processes the following command.*

{**LET stop,@NOW**} *Enters the value of @NOW into* stop.

{**DRAW**} *Redraws the screen so that the formula in* time *will display its new value.*

The formula in time *subtracts* start *from* stop. *The result equals the macro's total processing time.*

9. RUNNING MACROS FROM HYPERSPACE

I store about 20 macros, including one named \c, in the Macro Library. However, I'm unable to invoke \c on one particular worksheet. It works fine on all of my other worksheets. What could be causing this problem?

Alice Moore
Denver, Colo.

Retrieve the problematic worksheet and move the pointer to a blank area. Press MENU and select Range Name Table to see a list of all the range names in the worksheet. If \c is listed, this is the source of the problem. You cannot invoke a macro from the Macro Library if the macro has the same name as a range in your worksheet.

10. FASTER MACROS

Macros within large worksheet models run considerably faster if the Auto-Display setting for each window is set to No. If the MAIN window has this setting, then each window created from the MAIN window will also have the setting.

Brian Underdahl
Graybar Electric Co.
St. Louis, Mo.

Alternatively, you can use the {PANELOFF} and {WINDOWSOFF} macro commands to freeze the screen while a macro is running. These commands tell Symphony *not to redraw the control panel and the window display area. Your macros will run faster, and you'll eliminate the flickering that occurs as the program processes a macro. Use the {PANELON} and {WINDOWSON} commands to restore normal functioning to the display.*

11. REDUCING "FLICKER"

Symphony and *1-2-3* Release 2/2.01 offer two macro commands that significantly decrease run time by stopping the screen from redrawing as *1-2-3* or *Symphony* processes sections of the macro. {WINDOWSOFF} stops *1-2-3* or *Symphony* from redrawing the worksheet until the macro encounters the command {WINDOWSON}. {PANELOFF} stops *1-2-3* or *Symphony* from redrawing the control panel until the macro encounters the {PANELON} command.

A. Larry Aaron
The Rust Engineering Co.
Oak Ridge, Tenn.

Since the screen remains static when you use these two commands, other users may think the macro has crashed. To prevent confusion, insert the macro command {INDICATE Wait} before the {PANELOFF} command. This changes the indicator in the top-right corner of the screen to Wait so the user knows that the macro is still running. Then, before the {PANELON} command, insert another {INDICATE} command to switch to an appropriate indicator, or just use {INDICATE} without an argument to return to normal functioning.

12. WORD BORDERS

Often I need *Symphony* windows with either line borders or no borders (SERVICES Window Settings Borders). However, when a macro operating in such a window uses a command such as {GOTO} or MENU Copy, the window's border returns to standard. Why is this, and is there a way to get around it?

James Tevlin
University of South Alabama
Mobile, Ala.

The SHEET window borders become visible to give you points of reference on the worksheet when you use commands that involve pointing. This is important when you're interacting with Symphony *manually. Macros simply process stored keystrokes as though you were typing them at the keyboard, and* Symphony *reacts as if you are. You must either accept this flickering of the screen while your macros run or disable the screen display altogether. To disable the display, include the {WINDOWSOFF} command in your macro. This freezes the screen image (except for the control panel, which you can turn off separately using the {PANELOFF} command) until* Symphony *processes a {WINDOWSON} command. The macro commands still process, moving the cell pointer about on the worksheet, but the screen remains static.*

GROUP
2

Menus, Range Names, and Subroutines

1. MACRO MENU TIPS

Here are some tips and techniques to enhance your *1-2-3* macro menus:

1. Always have an escape route back to the main user-defined menu. Since M is often used to designate other menu items, we use a backslash (\) as the menu choice that returns users to the main menu.

2. You can use numbers as menu items, as long as you enter them as labels. This is helpful when users must select menu items in a particular sequence.

3. To relate long menu prompts more closely to the corresponding menu items, justify the long prompts so they begin under the menu item. You can do this by adding leading spaces to the long prompts in the menu instructions on the worksheet.

4. Even when the macro displays a user-defined menu, the first line of the control panel displays the contents of the current cell. Since this might be confusing to new users, have your macros position the pointer in a blank cell before calling up the menu.

Daniel Ehrman
Chicago, Ill.

2. MACRO MENUS

I've created a menu using the /XM command. When I run the macro, the error message *Invalid use of Menu command* appears and the macro stops.

Bob Liss
Canton, Ohio

First, make sure you haven't specified more than the limit of eight menu items. Also, make sure the cell to the right of the last menu item is blank. To be on the safe side, use the Range Erase command to clear the cell. Even if the cell looks blank, it might contain a label prefix. If the error condition persists, count the number of all characters in all of the menu items combined. The following table, devised by Lotus Product Support, lists limits for the total number of characters allowed in menus called by the /XM command. These limits exist in each release of 1-2-3.

Number of menu choices	Maximum number of characters
1	77
2	75
3	73
4	71
5	69
6	67
7	65
8	63

To find the maximum number of characters allowed in menus called by {MENUBRANCH} or {MENUCALL}, add two to each total in the preceding table.

3. VARIABLE PROMPTS IN MACRO MENUS

We're all looking for ways to make highly developed spreadsheets more user friendly. Here's one suggestion that does just that.

In a macro menu, the prompt line can be an @IF formula with strings as the second and third arguments. I employ this technique in order to warn users when a menu selection is inoperable because of certain circumstances in the worksheet.

For example, a menu choice might be to extract a database to a separate file. The @IF formula determines whether or not the database is empty. If the database is empty, the prompt *Illegal: empty database* appears below the menu choice. If the database is not empty, the message *Make separate file* appears instead. The formula looks like this:

IF(@ROWS (database)<2,"Illegal:empty database","Make separate file")

Charles Hoke
South Bend, Ind.

Using @IF formulas in the prompt line of a macro menu works only in Symphony *Releases 1.1 and 1.2, as well as in 1-2-3 Release 2/2.01. Using a variable prompt in Release 1 causes an error that stops the macro. The error message that appears is* Illegal MENUBRANCH/MENUCALL menu.

4. NAMING RANGES

Be cautious in choosing the range names you use in your macros. If you try to branch to a cell with a name that looks like a cell address (for example, *q2*), the macro branches to the address rather than to the name. Also, don't assign two or more hyphenated range names each beginning with the same characters, such as *grand-sum* and *grand-total*. If your macro tries to branch to either range, *Symphony* gets confused and branches to the last range rather than the intended range.

James Cienci
Plainville, Conn.

These observations raise some important issues. 1-2-3 *and* Symphony *let you use almost any character in range names. This doesn't mean that you should use every character. Especially avoid using arithmetic, logical, and string operators since these have specific meanings that are confusing both to users and to* 1-2-3 *and* Symphony *when they appear in range names. For example, the range names* grand sum *and* grand-total *probably won't cause any trouble unless there is also a range named* grand *on your worksheet. Then* 1-2-3 *and* Symphony *may try to interpret the name* grand-sum *as the expression* grand *minus* sum. *This could be extremely confusing if you also have a range named* sum *on the worksheet. Many people recommend using underscores to separate parts of range names. This eliminates most problems, but it can cause confusion when you generate a database in a FORM window. If your field names include underscores, the Entry and Definition ranges will be mismatched.*

Even when you use letters alone or combinations of letters and numbers in range names, be cautious. Don't use words that are reserved for the macro processor. For example, if Symphony *encounters the {MENU} command in a macro and you have previously used* menu *as the name of a cell, the program will call the range named* menu *as a subroutine rather than pressing the MENU key.*

5. {KEYNAMES}

In the December 1986 *Symphony* Macro Letters section, you presented a macro that easily deletes range names. The macro uses the formula @CELLPOINTER ("contents")&"~", which resides in a cell named *calc*. You are asking for trouble if you name a range *calc*. In a previous issue of *LOTUS*, there was an article that discussed the importance of using proper range names. I wish I'd read that article before I named a range *calc*, referred to it in a macro, and crashed my program.

You should always avoid using range names that match a function key or a cell address. This might be worth mentioning again.

Gemma Kelly
Mobile Images Canada
Toronto, Ontario

Using calc *as a range name was an oversight on our part. As you point out, this can cause problems with a* Symphony *macro. While running a macro,* Symphony *tries to process a word contained in braces as a subroutine call. If the word doesn't exist as a range name on the worksheet (or in a Macro Library),* Symphony *tries to interpret the word as a special keyname or a command keyword. Finally, if the word is neither an existing range name nor a keyname or command keyword, the macro bombs.*

Because of the progression of this decision-making process, naming a range with a keyname such as menu *is also likely to cause problems. When you later use the keyname {MENU} to mean "Press the MENU key," Symphony misinterprets the command and calls the range named* menu *as a subroutine.*

Thank you for pointing out the oversight.

6. DELETING RANGE NAMES

In a past issue there was a macro tip for deleting range names. The following macro is less complex and doesn't use as much worksheet space.

	A	B
1	\n	{MENU}RND{MENU}

The macro presses MENU and selects Range Name Delete. When *Symphony* prompts for the name to delete, the macro presses the MENU key to list all of the range names on one screen. The macro pauses for you to select a range name to delete. Use the pointer-movement keys to position the pointer over the range name, then press Return.

Greg Baker
Manassas, Va.

7. NESTING LEVELS

I am building a menu-driven application for use by others. The program uses almost 50 {MENUBRANCH} statements. Unfortunately, the macro fails, and *Symphony* displays the error message *Too many nesting levels*. What are nesting levels?

David Dolan-Walace
Neenah, Wisconsin

When you place an operation within another similar operation, you are "nesting" operations. You can nest expressions in a formula by surrounding them with parentheses. Macro commands are nested when one subroutine includes a command to call another subroutine or when a {FOR} loop is still running.

{MENUBRANCH} commands do not call subroutines; therefore, using several of them in a row does not qualify as nesting. However, if you are using {MENUCALL} commands, you may be nesting them by putting several in sequence within your macro. This could cause the error that you describe. Also, be sure that you have not accidentally used a reserved keyword (one of the reserved bracketed macro commands) as a range name on your worksheet. If, for example, you have named a range menu, *give it a different name and delete the range name* menu.

Then when you use {MENU} to mean "press the MENU key," your macro will not attempt to run a subroutine named menu.

8. MULTIPLE BRANCHING

I need to design a macro that will do one of 12 tasks, depending on the current month. One technique is to use {IF} and {BRANCH} statements as follows:

```
        A          B           C        D         E
1  date       24-Jan-86
2
3  \a         {IF @MONTH(date)=1}{BRANCH jan}
4             {IF @MONTH(date)=2}{BRANCH feb}
5             {IF @MONTH(date)=3}{BRANCH mar}
6             {IF @MONTH(date)=4}{BRANCH apr}
7             {IF @MONTH(date)=5}{BRANCH may}
8             {IF @MONTH(date)=6}{BRANCH jun}
9             {IF @MONTH(date)=7}{BRANCH jul}
10            {IF @MONTH(date)=8}{BRANCH aug}
11            {IF @MONTH(date)=9}{BRANCH sep}
12            {IF @MONTH(date)=10}{BRANCH oct}
13            {IF @MONTH(date)=11}{BRANCH nov}
14            {BRANCH dec}
15
```

The cell named *date* (B1) contains the formula @NOW, and each {BRANCH} statement contains the name of a subroutine containing instructions appropriate for the coinciding month (elsewhere on the worksheet). Is there a way to get the same results using the @CHOOSE function?

Thomas Green
Oklahoma Natural Gas
Tulsa, Okla.

The following macro uses the @CHOOSE function as you suggest:

```
        A        B          C
1  date      24-Jan-86
2  month     jan
3
4  \m        {DISPATCH month}
```

Date *(cell B1) contains the formula @NOW, and* month *contains the formula:*

@CHOOSE(@MONTH(date)−1, "jan","feb","mar","apr","may",
"jun","jul","aug","sep","oct","nov","dec")

{DISPATCH month} means "branch to the cell whose name appears in month."

The {DISPATCH} command is documented in the Reference Manual *accompanying Release 1.1 and* Symphony *1.2, as well as the* Symphony Update *booklet included with all copies of* Symphony *Releases 1 and 1.01.*

9. ORDERING /XI COMMANDS

Whenever you write a macro with multiple /XI commands in vertically adjacent cells, your macro will be faster if you put the /XI statements in descending order, from most likely to be true to least likely to be true. For example, the macro shown on the bottom of this page determines the day of the week on which the date in the cell named *date* falls. After the macro enters the day into the cell named *day*, the macro branches to the cell named *next*.

When *1-2-3* evaluates a true condition in the series of /XI statements, the macro processes the keystrokes following the condition. These keystrokes enter the specified day of the week into *day* and then branch to *next*. Say that *date* is most likely to fall on a Monday. Since Monday is the first day tested for in the series of /XI statements, the macro will most often process just the first /XI statement and then branch to *next*. Because the macro branches to *next*, it does not read any more of the /XI statements. If the last /XI statement in the series tested for a Monday, then each time you ran it, the macro would most often read through each /XI statement before finding the condition that was true. This, of course, slows down the macro.

```
      A           B           C          D          E
 1 date
 2 day
 3
 4 \a          {GOTO}day~
 5             /XI@MOD(date,7)=2~Monday~/XGnext~
 6             /XI@MOD(date,7)=3~Tuesday~/XGnext~
 7             /XI@MOD(date,7)=4~Wednesday~/XGnext~
 8             /XI@MOD(date,7)=5~Thursday~/XGnext~
 9             /XI@MOD(date,7)=6~Friday~/XGnext~
10             /XI@MOD(date,7)=0~Saturday~/XGnext~
11             /XI@MOD(date,7)=1~Sunday~
12 next        ...
13
```

Shane Devonshire
Daly City, Calif.

This example isn't particularly useful in Release 2/2.01, though the technique it illustrates applies to all releases of 1-2-3. To display date's *weekday in the cell named* day *(assuming* date *falls after February 1900), enter the following formula into* day:

@Choose(@MOD(date,7),"Saturday","Sunday","Monday","Tuesday",
"Wednesday","Thursday","Friday")

10. ENTERING TILDES

In Release 1A, a macro always recognizes the tilde (~), as the Return key. This prevents you from embedding the tilde within the macro in order to enter it as a character into a cell. However, there is an alternative if you want to use the macro to enter a database criterion such as ~Chicago. Within the macro, just copy the criterion from a designated cell into the Criterion range.

Flo Samuels
San Diego, Calif.

In Releases 2 and 2.01, the keyword { ~ } lets your macro type the tilde character.

11. CREATING FOR-NEXT LOOPS

Can *1-2-3* Release 1A simulate the action of a For-Next loop?

Mike Freeman
Tecmark Computer Services
Vancouver, Washington

For-Next loop is a series of commands that are repeated a finite number of times before the macro either stops or moves on to another series of commands. In 1-2-3 Release 1A *you can control such a loop by arranging the macro commands as follows:*

	A	B	C	D	E	F
1	\m	/REcounter~				
2	loop	macro steps...				
3						
4						
5		/DFcounter~counter+1~~~				
6		/XI(counter>=targ)~/XQ				
7		/XGloop~				
8						
9	targ	3				
10	counter					

Assign the range names \m, loop, targ, *and* counter *using the Range Name Labels Right command. The loop begins in the cell named* loop *and ends with the command /XGloop~. In the cell named* targ, *indicate the number of times the loop should repeat. Each time the macro completes the loop, the value in the cell named* counter *increases. When* targ *and* counter *are equal, the macro stops.*

GROUP
3

Manipulating Data
and Other Tricks

1. DATA ENTRY

Here is a *1-2-3* data-entry macro that lets you make eight entries in each row:

	A	B
1	\e	{?}~{RIGHT}
2		/XI@MOD(@COUNT(entry),8)=0~{LEFT}{END}{LEFT}{DOWN}
3		/XG\e~

Assign the name *entry* to a range eight columns wide, such as A1..H1000. Here's how the macro works:

{?}~{RIGHT} Pauses for user input, then moves the pointer one cell to the right.

/XI@MOD(@COUNT(entry),8) = 0 ~ {LEFT}{END}{LEFT}{DOWN} Determines whether the number of entries in *entry* divided by eight has a remainder. If there is no remainder (that is, there are eight entries in the row), the pointer moves back to the beginning of the row and then down one row—the beginning of the next row.

/XG\e~ Tells the macro to branch back to \e to continue reading keystrokes. This restarts the macro.

For the macro to work properly, you must make an entry into each cell within a row. The entries can be numbers, labels, formulas, or even label prefixes.

Gary Titus
Lansing General Hospital
Lansing, Mich.

To be on the safe side (in case there are entries in the column to the left of entry), replace the {END}{LEFT} command sequence with a series of eight {LEFT} commands. Release 2 and 2.01 users can write more efficient alternatives to this macro.

2. DATA-ENTRY SHORTCUT

Numerical data entry on the IBM numeric keypad is a lot faster when you rename the + key as Return and the * key as Insert. Then you don't have to keep shifting.

	A	B	C	D	E
1	catch	{GFT input}			
2		{IF input="+"}~{BRANCH catch}			
3		{IF input="*"}{INSERT}{BRANCH catch}			
4	input				
5		{BRANCH catch}			

Bernhard Schmidt
San Francisco, Calif.

Be careful of what you try to do while this macro is running. The macro fails if you type certain characters, such as an open brace ({).

3. DATA ENTRY DOWN COLUMN

Here is a looping macro that lets me enter numbers with two decimal places down a column without having to type the decimal point. Since the macro moves the pointer for me, I can press the NumberLock key and use the numeric keypad for data entry rather than for pointer movement.

	A	B
1	\d	{?}~{EDIT}/100
2		{DOWN}{BRANCH \d}

Also, my worksheet contains formulas that subtotal the data I'm entering. To prevent the macro from overwriting the formulas with new data, I protect all the formulas with the Range Protect command. However, an error condition occurs whenever I press Return to move the pointer to the cell below. To prevent the error from stopping the macro, I include an {ONERROR} routine that moves the pointer to the cell below and restarts the macro whenever an error occurs.

To stop a macro with an {ONERROR} routine such as this, press Break (Control-Break on most computers) twice.

Octave Anthaume
Dixifoods Inc.
Lafayette, La.

Since formulas slow down worksheet recalculation, modify your macro so that it enters your data as values rather than as formulas (for example, 23/100). In the following modification, the {CALC} key converts the formula into a value before {DOWN} enters it into the cell.

```
      A       B
1   \e   {IF @CELLPOINTER("type")="b"}{?}/100{CALC}
2        {DOWN}{BRANCH \e}
```

Note the inclusion of an {IF} statement that checks whether the current cell is blank. If the cell is blank, the macro pauses for you to enter a number, then it moves the pointer down to the next row and starts over. If the current cell contains an entry, the macro leaves the contents of the cell intact. Then it moves the pointer down and starts again. With this modified version it's not necessary to protect your formulas, although it's certainly a good practice to do so.

4. ENTERING NUMBERS AS LABELS

I tried to modify the address-writing macro in a Macro Basics column, but when I did, the macro didn't work correctly. When I replaced the P.O. box in the example with a street address that begins with a number, the macro tried to enter the entire address into one cell.

C.K. Wadsworth
Osterville, Mass.

To enter any label that begins with a number, such as a street address, into a cell via a macro, begin that line of macro code with two apostrophes. Also, it's not necessary to use a tilde before {DOWN}, as shown in the Macro Basics column. The keyword {DOWN} will enter the information into the current cell before moving the cell pointer to the row below. An example of the macro you would use is shown in the following figure:

```
      A       B
1   \a   '55 Cambridge Parkway{DOWN}
2        Cambridge, MA 02142~
```

5. FASTER MACROS FOR COPYING

If you have macros performing a lot of copying, and the macros point to the cells that they copy, the macros will be faster if you use @CELLPOINTER("contents") rather than the Copy command or Range Values command. Instead of using a macro statement such as {GOTO}cell1~{M}C~cell2~, use {GOTO}cell1~{LET cell2, @CELLPOINTER("contents")}~. The latter statement runs twice as fast.

Ed Karl
Wheat Ridge, Colo.

6. RANGE PROTECTION IN MACROS

I wrote a macro that copies user-specified ranges in a protected worksheet into an unprotected range. The macro runs successfully once, but on the second try, it ends with an error statement. Can you tell me why?

Walter S. Barnes Jr.
New Orleans Public Service
New Orleans, Louisiana

The Copy command copies both the contents and format of the source range. On the first run of your macro, the unprotected target range receives the protection status of the source range and thus becomes protected. On the second run, the target range is now protected, and the macro fails. To avoid this problem, use the following command sequence immediately ahead of the Copy command:

    {M}RPAname~

Name *is the name of the Copy command's target range.*

7. COPYING RESULTING VALUES

I am having trouble with the Copy command within a macro. I want to copy the value from a specific location in the spreadsheet. This value is the result of an @CHOOSE function. Is there a straightforward way to copy the value of that cell and not the underlying formula? In this macro I need to retain relative references in the formulas.

Tom Lowy
Media, Pa.

If you're using Release 1A, replace the Copy command in your macro with the statement + source{EDIT}{CALC}~. This statement assumes that the pointer is already positioned in the cell to which you want to copy. If the pointer isn't in the target cell, precede this macro statement with a {GOTO} command. Also, you must assign a range name to the cell from which you want to copy. In this example, we used the range name source.

The macro enters the formula + source *into the current cell so that the value that* appears in source *also appears in the current cell. Then the macro presses* {EDIT}{CALC}~, *which removes the underlying formula* + source, *leaving just the remaining value as the cell contents.*

Alternatively, you can use the Data Fill command to copy only the value from one cell to another without moving the cell pointer. In this case, the macro would read /DFtarget~source~ ~ ~. Target represents the cell in which you want the copy to appear, and source *represents the cell holding the* @CHOOSE *formula.*

Release 2/2.01 users can use the Range Value command to copy just the resulting value of a formula or use the command {LET target,source}.

8. USING RANGE VALUE

When using manual recalculation, it's easy to forget to recalculate the worksheet before using the Range Value command. To prevent copying the results of uncalculated formulas, I created a one-line macro — {CALC}/RV{?}~{?}~{CALC}. When you run the macro, it recalculates the worksheet, selects /Range Value, and pauses so that you can indicate the Copy From range and the Copy To range. Finally, it recalculates the worksheet a second time.

Kathleen Laffoday
El Paso, Tex.

9. USING A DOUBLE LOOKUP TABLE

We use the following table to determine the freight rate based on the distances between two zip codes:

	A	B	C	D	E
1		27000	27100	27200	27400
2	27600	125	105	109	80
3	27700	104	84	52	40
4	27800	179	159	163	134
5	27900	325	305	314	285

The distances are located at the intersection of each zip code in the table. Can you suggest a macro that will ask for the origin zip code and the destination zip code, then return the distance at the location of the pointer?

Wayne Riddle
Raleigh, N.C.

We'll assume for this example that the origin zip codes fall in the leftmost column of the table and that the destination codes are in the top row. We'll also assume that the zip codes in your table are labels. Assign the name table *to range A1..E5. Then enter the labels shown in the following figure:*

	A	B	C	D	E	F
8	\f	{GETLABEL "Origin Zip Code? ",origin}				
9		{GETLABEL "Destination Zip Code? ",destin}				
10	\g	@VLOOKUP(origin,table,@HLOOKUP(destin,table,0)){CALC}~				
11						
12	origin					
13	destin					

Use the Range Name Labels Right command to assign the labels in column A as range names for the adjacent cells of column B. Position the pointer in a blank cell and start the macro by holding down the MACRO key and pressing F. The distance between the two zip codes appears in the current cell.

Here's how the macro works:

*{**GETLABEL "Origin Zip Code? ",origin**}Prompts for the origin zip code and enters it in* origin.

*{**GETLABEL "Destination Zip Code? ", destin**} Prompts for the destination zip code and enters it in* destin.

*@**VLOOKUP(origin,table,@HLOOKUP(destin,table,∅)){CALC}~** Enters the value of the double lookup formula into the current cell. The double lookup formula means "Find the value at the intersection of the column containing the destination zip code and the row containing the origin zip code."*

10. CREATING HEADERS WITH THE CURRENT TIME

When we're working on a report, we revise the figures a couple of times each day. It gets confusing when we're not sure if we're looking at the most current report or one that was printed a few hours before. Unfortunately, there is no simple convention that lets you put the current time in the header when you print a report. However, I came across a solution. I use the {CONTENTS} command within a subroutine to write a header with the current time.

Larry D. Wilson
La Crosse, Wis.

The macro at the top of the next page is a slightly modified version of the subroutine.

Enter the labels in columns A and B. Be sure to type a space at the end of the label in cell B5. Assign the range names time1, timesub, *and* time2 *to the adjacent cells in column B with the Range Name Labels Right command. Enter the formula* @NOW *in* time1. *Here's how the macro works:*

*{**RECALC time1**}{**CONTENTS time2,time1,9,120**} Recalculates the formula in* time1. *Then in the cell named* time2, *the macro creates a label that looks like the value in* time1 *with a time format.*

*{**S**}**PSPH** {**ESC**} Presses SERVICES and selects Print Settings Page Header. If there is already a header,* Symphony *adds a space to it, otherwise* Symphony *starts*

```
       A          B         C        D        E         F
1  time1
2
3  timesub {RECALC time1}{CONTENTS time2,time1,9,120}
4          {S}PSPH {ESC}
5          ¦¦Printed on @ at
6  time2
7          ~QQQ
```

a new header by typing a space. Then, when it processes {ESC}, Symphony removes the header, whether it is just a space or the previous header with a space added on. The extra space character ensures that the macro will work whether or not a header already exists. Without the space, the {ESC} command might cause Symphony to back up one level in the menu.

　　¦¦ **Printed on @ at**　*Begins the new header line. The cell below,* time2, *completes the header line by entering the time.*

　　~QQQ　*Enters the header as a print setting and returns you to the worksheet.*

11. CENTERING LABELS

When *1-2-3* enters information into a cell via the /XL macro command, it left-justifies the entry. To center an entry made to the current cell, use the following code:

```
      A          B
1  \c        /XLEnter your last name: ~~
2            {EDIT}{HOME}{DEL}^~
```

When you run the macro, *1-2-3* prompts you to enter your last name. The program stores your response in the current cell and then centers the entry.

Gordon M. Lustila
Tolland, Conn.

Here's a variation that centers an entry made to a prespecified cell. A nice feature of this technique is that the pointer doesn't move from its current location to the cell containing the entry.

```
      A          B
1  \r        /XLEnter your last name: ~last~
2            /RLClast~
```

The macro stores the entry in last, *presses slash, selects Range Label Center, specifies* last *as the range of labels to center, and presses Return.*

12. EDITING DATABASE RECORDS

The Release 1A macro in cells B1..B2 of the following figure lets you update a database record:

```
       A         B          C         D
1  \e         {GOTO}crit~{?}~
2             /DQF{ERR}~
3
4             Serial #
5  crit
6
7  Serial # Description
8     87647 red helmet
9     12345 kickstand
10    57321 tube pump
11    66452 bike rack
12    51124 deflectors
```

The sample database is in range A7..B12, and the criterion is in B4..B5. To edit a record containing the serial number 12345, invoke the macro, enter the number 12345 when the macro pauses, then press Escape when the error message *Unrecognized key name {...}* appears in the bottom-left corner of the screen. The pointer remains on the first cell in the corresponding record (cell A9).

Jim Nancarrow
Maple Valley, Wash.

Release 2/2.01 users can edit a record found by the Query Find command. Use the LeftArrow or RightArrow key to move the cursor to the desired field. Then type the new entry (or press the EDIT key and edit the existing entry), and press Return. Press the DownArrow or UpArrow key to move the pointer to other records that match the criterion.

13. DATA CONVERSION

Many times the data we enter into our spreadsheet is not in the form we had planned when we designed our spreadsheet. Rather than making an intermediate calculation on a calculator or changing the data after it's entered, I use the following simple macro, which handles data conversion as I input the data:

```
       A         B          C
1  \c         {?}*factor{CALC}~
2             {DOWN}
3             /XG\c~
4
5  factor        0.01
```

Before invoking the macro, I enter the conversion factor into the cell named *factor*. If I use the conversion factor .01, I can enter in dollars and cents without a decimal. Other uses include time conversions (minutes to hours, hours to seconds, etc.), U.S. measurements to metric conversions, foreign currency translations, and temperature conversions (Celsius to Fahrenheit).

Richard Evans
Longwood, Fla.

14. BLANKING CELLS

Is there a macro that can erase duplicate numbers in a column, leaving the cell blank? The numbers are arranged in ascending order as follows:

	A
1	2
2	3
3	3
4	3
5	5
6	6
7	6
8	6
9	7

Frank S. Vorcilek
Westbrook, Maine

The following macro will erase one or more duplicate numbers:

	C	D
1	num1	
2	num2	
3		
4	\r	/C~num1~
5	skip	{DOWN}
6		/C~num2~
7		/XInum1<>num2~/XG\r~
8		/C~num1~/RE~
9		/XGskip~

Enter the labels as shown. To assign the labels in column C as range names for the adjacent cells of column D, press slash, select Range Name Labels Right, indicate range C1..C5, and press Return. To run the macro, position the pointer in cell A1 (the first number in the column), hold down the MACRO key, and press R. To stop *the macro after it processes the last number in the column, press the Break key. (On the IBM keyboard, hold down the Control key and press Break.)*

Here's how the macro works:

/C~num1~   *Copies the value in the current cell into* num1.

{DOWN}   *Moves the pointer down one cell to the next number in the column.*

/C~num2~   *Copies the value in the current cell into* num2.

/XInum1 < >num2~/XG\r~   *Tests whether the value in* num1 *is equal to the value in* num2. *If so, then 1-2-3 continues processing keystrokes after the first tilde in the same line. These instructions tell 1-2-3 to continue processing macro commands in the cell named* \r. *If the values in* num1 *and* num2 *are equal, 1-2-3 ignores the remaining instructions in this line and continues processing macro commands in the line below.*

/C~num1~/RE~   *Copies the value in the current cell into* num1, *then erases the current cell. This step is necessary to erase more than one duplicate of a number.*

/XGskip~   *Tells 1-2-3 to continue reading keystrokes in* skip *rather than in the first line of the macro. If 1-2-3 branched to the first line of the macro,* num1 *would receive a blank as a result of the /C command.*

15. INSERTING ROWS

Is it possible to write a macro that inserts a user-specified number of rows into the worksheet? The macro should prompt for the number of rows to insert, then insert the rows after row 10. I can't figure out how to turn the number of rows that I want to insert—for example, 105—into the label A11..A116, which specifies the range.

Mary Reno
Stoneham, Mass.

Using a self-modifying macro, you can insert a specified number of rows. Since you know the row number after which you want the rows inserted, your macro can add the number supplied by the user and thereby calculate the bottom of the insert range. The macro might look like the figure at the top of the next page.

This shows the entire macro in cells A1 through B8, although you can put it anywhere as long as the entire macro is above or below row 10. Once you've entered the macro into the worksheet, assign the labels shown in column A as range names for the cells to their right. Move the cursor to cell A1 and issue the Range name Labels Right command. Then press End Down Return. Start the macro by holding down the MACRO key and pressing R (check your 1-2-3 documentation for instructions on invoking macros). Here's how the macro works:

/RNChere~ ~   *Names the current cell* here. *This macro moves the cell pointer and edits the contents of another cell. This step marks the starting point of the cell pointer. When the macro finishes running, the cell pointer returns to this starting point.*

	A	B	C	D	E
1	\r	/RNChere~~			
2		{GOTO}rows~			
3		/XNNumber of rows to insert?~~			
4		{EDIT}+10{CALC}{HOME}'~			
5		/WIRa11...a			
6	rows				
7		~{GOTO}here~			
8		/RNDhere~			
9					
10	stuff				
11	stuff				

{GOTO}rows~   *Sends the cell pointer to the cell named* rows. *Rows, which is within the body of the macro, will ultimately contain the row number that is the bottom of the insert range.*

/XNNumber of rows to insert?~ ~   *Prompts you for the number of rows to insert and places your entry as a value into the current cell (*rows*).*

{EDIT} + 10{CALC}{HOME}'~   *Adds 10 to the value contained in* rows *and turns the result into a label so that the macro can use it later.*

/WIRa11..a   *Issues the Worksheet Insert Row command and starts indicating the insert range, omitting only the row number of the bottom of the range. By now that number is contained in* rows, *the next cell of the macro, and the macro processes it to complete the range reference.*

~{GOTO}here~   *Presses Return to complete the Worksheet Insert Row command, then sends the cell pointer back to the cell named* here, *which is the cell that was current when the macro started.*

/RNDhere~   *Deletes the range name* here.

16. LOCATING A COLUMN

Is it possible to write a macro that moves the cursor from one cell containing a label to another cell containing the same label? For example, we enter the pay period as a single-cell label that reads *JUL 1985*. The pointer should then move to the column headed with this label. Since we make room for the next month's data by inserting a new column, all the existing columns move to the right each month. Therefore, a simple {GOTO} command won't work.

George Trussell
Columbus, Ga.

Assign each column heading as the range name for the cell containing it or as the range name for the cell directly below it. When you insert a new column and enter a new column heading, use the Range Name Labels Down command to assign the new heading to the next cell down the column. If the cell into which you enter the pay period is pay, *the following macro will get you where you want to be:*

	A	B	C	D
9		/XLEnter pay period ˜pay˜		
10		/Cpay˜targ˜		
11		{GOTO}		
12	targ			
13		˜		
14				
15	pay			

Here's how the macro works:

/XLEnter pay period ˜pay˜ *Displays the prompt* Enter pay period *in the control panel. Whatever you type is stored as a label in the cell named* pay.

/Cpay˜targ˜ *Copies the contents of* pay *to the cell named* targ. Targ *is within the body of the macro and will be processed as part of the following* {GOTO} *command.*

{GOTO} *Presses the GOTO key. By now the next cell contains the pay period you entered in response to the prompt. This is processed as the target address for the GOTO command.*

˜ *Finishes the* {GOTO} *command by sending the cell pointer to the appropriate column.*

17. FILE-RETRIEVE COUNTER

Is there a macro that can track the number of times a worksheet file has been retrieved?

Steven A. Breth
Winrock International
Arlington, Va.

This macro will do the trick:

	A	B
1	\0	/DFcounter˜counter+1˜˜˜
2		/FS˜R
3		
4	counter	

Enter all of the labels as shown into an area of the worksheet that the user will not see. (In Release 1A, be careful not to expand the active area of the worksheet *significantly by putting this macro far away from the rest of the worksheet information.) To assign the labels \0 and* counter *as range names for the adjacent cells in the column to the right, position the cell pointer in the cell containing* \0, *select /Range Name Labels Right, and press End DownArrow Return. A macro named \0 will start automatically each time the worksheet file is retrieved. Here's how the macro works:*

/DFcounter ~ counter + 1 ~ ~ ~ *Increases the value in* counter *by 1 when the file is retrieved.*

/FS ~ R *Resaves the worksheet into a file on disk. (Note that this step doesn't work if you are now using Release 2/2.01 and the file was created in Release 1A.)*

18. PRINTING WORKSHEETS CONSECUTIVELY

I have several files on one disk, each containing a print macro. Could I create a "print" program that would invoke the individual print macros to print the worksheets consecutively?

Roger Allen
City of Holyoke
Holyoke, Massachusetts

Most of your work is already done. Modify the print macros in all but one worksheet by adding /File Retrieve as the last command sequence. If you have three files on the disk named FILE1, FILE2, and FILE3 respectively, the macro in FILE1 should end with the command /FRfile2 ~ , and the macro in FILE2 should end with the command /FRfile3 ~ . When you modify the macros, assign the range name \0 (backslash zero) as macro names for each of them before saving the worksheets. (The print macro in FILE3 need not contain a /File Retrieve command, though you should name it \0.) The macro name \0 means "start running automatically when the worksheet is loaded." Worksheets linked in this fashion can cause some trouble when you want to make changes to the data they contain. Since the macro takes over automatically when the worksheet is loaded, you have to stop it by pressing Control-Break (hold down the Control key and press Break) before it processes the File Retrieve command. Of course, you can prevent the macro from printing out unwanted copies of files by turning off your printer before you retrieve the file.

19. ADDING A FOOTER

Before printing a worksheet, I'd like to enter a label in the worksheet as the footer. How can I modify my print macro so that it enters this label as the footer setting?

Tom Brooks
Atlanta, Ga.

First assign the range name footer *to the cell in which you will enter the footer. Then add the following lines of code at the beginning of your print macro:*

	G	H
1	\p	{SERVICES}PSPFx{ESC}
2		{footer}~QQ

Make sure you assign the labels in column G as range names for the adjacent cells in column H.

When you're ready to print your worksheet, enter the footer into the cell named footer. *Then start the print macro by holding down the Macro key and pressing P. Here's what happens when* Symphony *processes the additional lines of code:*

{SERVICES}PSPFx{ESC} *Presses SERVICES and selects Print Settings Page Footer. When* Symphony *prompts for the footer, the macro enters the letter* x, *then presses Escape to clear the footer setting. Without this step,* Symphony *would add the new footer to the end of an existing one.*

{footer}~QQ *Calls* footer *as a subroutine, entering the label contained in* footer *as the footer setting, then presses Quit twice to return to the first level of the print menu.*

20. BEATING THE /GNU PAUSE — I

I've written a macro that updates some graphs on my *1-2-3* worksheet. The problem is that every time the macro processes a Graph Name Use command, I have to press a key to get it to continue. Is there any way around this? Also, how can I get a macro to start running automatically when a worksheet is loaded?

George Innis
Fort Collins, Colorado

If you use two monitors, one for text and the other for graphs, a macro will continue running after a Graph Name Use command. Using one monitor for both text and graphics, I know of only one way around the problem you describe—other than getting someone else to press the keys for you. Start by copying the drivers from your 1-2-3 System Disk onto a blank disk (or from your 1-2-3 directory into a "clean" directory if you are a hard-disk user). Mark this your Graphics Driver Set. Now create new drivers for your System Disk (or 1-2-3 directory) by following the instructions in the "Installing 1-2-3 Drivers" section of your 1-2-3 manual. Choose the Mono option for this new set. Once created, copy the new drivers to their own disk or directory marked Non-Graphics Drivers. When you wish to run 1-2-3 with graphics capability, copy your Graphics Driver Set onto your 1-2-3 System disk and run 1-2-3. When you wish to update your graphs without the annoying pauses for each Graph Name Use command, copy the Non-Graphics Drivers onto your System Disk before starting 1-2-3.

To get a macro to start running automatically when the worksheet is loaded, *name the macro \0 (backslash zero). If you want to start the macro a second time after the worksheet is loaded, give it a second name consisting of a backslash and letter combination. You cannot start a macro named \0 by pressing MACRO-0.*

21. BEATING THE /GNU PAUSE — II

I have written a macro that updates several graphs. It selects /Graph Name Use, redefines the graph ranges, and preserves the changes via the Graph Name Create command. To prevent the macro from pausing after each Graph Name Use command, I simply press the Spacebar several times after I start the macro—once for each graph being updated. I can update 15 graphs without having to sit and press the Spacebar whenever the macro pauses.

Jerry Blossom
Casper, Wyoming

This is a nice solution to the /Graph Name Use pause problem. The space characters are stored in your computer's keyboard buffer while the macro is running. One is removed from the buffer each time the macro tries to pause. Apparently, your computer has a 15-keystroke buffer. Some computers have more, others fewer, and for many computers you can obtain software that increases the size of your keyboard buffer. In any case, this solution is far more convenient than any alternative we know.

22. SPELLING CORRECTOR

Here's a macro that corrects letter-transposition errors in a DOC window:

	A	B
1	\t	{MENU}M~{RIGHT 2}~

For example, if I inadvertently type the word *this* as *thsi*, I position the cursor over the S, hold down the MACRO key, and press T. The macro transposes the S and I into their correct order.

Jesse J. Dean
The Equitable Financial Services
Rochester, Minn.

23. FORM-WINDOW MACROS

In the FORM window, I wanted to repeat a field entry from one record to the next, or to add 1 to the value from the corresponding field of the previous record.

Just as you did, I use formulas in the *Default* column of the Definition range. For this to work, I need to recalculate the Definition range each time I start a new record. Hence, I developed the following "insert" macro:

	D	E	F	G
1	\l	{WINDOWSOFF}{SWITCH}		
2		{RECALC entry_df}		
3		{SWITCH}{WINDOWSON}		
4		{PGDN}		

While working my database, rather than pressing the Insert key to enter a record, I simply press MACRO-L.

Donald G. Velcio, CPA
Brooklyn Heights, Ohio

This is an excellent idea, and you can make the macro even more efficient. Symphony's {RECALC} command recalculates a worksheet range no matter what environment you're using when the command processes. You can leave all the windowing acrobatics out of your macro and obtain identical results:

	D	E	F	G
1	\l	{RECALC entry_df}		
2		{INSERT}		

The technique also suggests an improvement on another macro:

	D	E	F	G
1	\c	{GET key}		
2		{IF key="{"}{{}{BRANCH \c}		
3		{RECALC main_df}		
4	key			
5		{BRANCH \c}		

This macro recalculates the Definition range each time you press a key, but it runs quickly and eliminates the screen flicker of the orginal macro. Thanks for the tip.

GROUP

4

Bugs and Debugging

1. WHAT IF YOUR MACRO DOESN'T WORK?

The strength of a macro can sometimes be its weakness; it does *exactly* what it is told to do. It cannot guess what you intend it to do. Thus, if there is an error in the macro, it will quit, complain (by beeping), or start writing macro code into your worksheet.

A macro can cause significant damage by writing over or erasing portions of your worksheet. For this reason it is a good practice to make a copy of your worksheet before you start testing your macros. If the worksheet is damaged — find the error, retrieve the copy, and then correct it. For the same reason it is wise not to have the cell pointer on the macro itself when you test it.

These are the most common errors when writing macros:

- Omitting a /, or switching it with \
- Omitting a ~
- Reversing a command — /WSC instead of /WCS
- Typing a superfluous space in a command (usually at the end of a line)
- Not assigning the correct macro range name; in *1-2-3*, the name must have a backslash plus a letter, or \0 in the case of an autoexecuting macro. In *Symphony*, a backslash followed by a number will also work, as will any other range name.
- Misspelling a {BRACKETED} command
- Misspelling or not assigning a range name
- Omitting a Quit to terminate a menu sequence

When a macro fails, inspect it first. This often exposes the problem, especially if you look at the portion of the macro where it failed.

If you still have problems, go back to basics. Perform the task manually, recording each keystroke as you go.

2. AN ALTERNATIVE TO STEP MODE

Using Step mode to debug hundreds of lines of macro code is tedious. An alternative is to embed {INDICATE} commands within the macro where you suspect a problem. Each {INDICATE} command causes the cell address of the macro statement being processed to appear in the message indicator at the top-right corner of the screen. For example, if you think your macro has a problem in the code running from C150 to C200, embed an {INDICATE} command in every tenth line — in cells C150, C160, and so on. If the macro statement in cell C150 is {GOTO}final~, modify it to read {INDICATE C150}{GOTO}final~. As soon as the macro malfunctions, press the Break key to stop it. Then check the indicator to determine where the error occurred. If the indicator reads C160, you know that range C160..C169 contains the offending code.

Cydnie Jones
New York, N.Y.

3. EDITING COMPLEX MACROS

While writing complex macros, it's often necessary to debug small portions of the larger macro. The one-line macro {DISPATCH @CELLPOINTER "address"} will start processing macro commands at the location of the cell pointer.

Be careful to use this macro only in situations when it won't produce unintended results. For example, if the macro is intended to work in a DOC window, starting the macro as described may not be possible or may cause unintended results.

Danny Lawrence
Brighton, Mass.

To start your macro running with any cell and from any point within Symphony, *modify the debugging macro to read {DISPATCH start}. Then in* start, *enter the cell address of the macro commands to process first. This debugging procedure is more useful to Release 1 users, since most of the Release 1.1 and Release 1.2 macro error messages display the cell address of the problematic line of code.*

4. INSERTING ROWS

I use the following macro to insert rows:

	A	B	C	D
1				
2	{MENU}IR{DOWN 3}~			

However, if I position the cell pointer in the cell containing the macro, cell A2, and then invoke it, the error message *Syntax error in macro key/range {...}* appears. If I move the macro to another row but still invoke it in column A, it works fine.

Laszlo Huszar
The Netherlands

This macro inserts three blank rows between the current row and the row above the current row. If you invoke the macro when the cell pointer lies in a row containing these instructions (or above them), the inserted rows move the macro downward on the worksheet. Using your example, the macro moves from cell A2 to cell A5. When it finishes inserting the rows, Symphony looks for more macro instructions immediately after the Insert Row command — in the cell that originally contained the macro. This cell no longer contains macro commands. The error message alerts you to the fact that the macro has been altered significantly enough that it may not have performed as intended.

Avoid problems by never asking a macro to insert rows above itself unless the window in which the rows are inserted is restricted to omit the macro instructions. Also, be sure your macro doesn't insert columns to the left of its own code or the same error will occur.

5. ERASING CELLS

On page 31 of your article on *1-2-3* utilities in the December 1985 issue, you describe the simplest utility you've ever seen. The utility erases the contents of the current cell. I believe my method is even better in that you don't need to create a macro. You simply strike the Spacebar once and press Return.

John Agee
Anchorage, Alaska

The technique you describe does delete the contents of the current cell, but it doesn't leave the cell empty. Cells "erased" this way actually contain two characters: a label prefix and a space character. If you include such a cell in a range used in the @COUNT function, you're likely to get inaccurate results. These cells behave differently from truly blank cells in database operations. Also, cells containing spaces can be confusing for people who rely on End-Arrow key combinations to move around on their worksheets. Cells containing spaces cause even more trouble in Release 2 since spaces have string values and aren't valid in most numeric formulas.

6. PROBLEMS WITH /XC

I recently came across a limitation of the /XC and /XR commands. When the /XClocation~ command tells *1-2-3* to continue reading keystrokes at the specified location, *1-2-3* remembers the absolute address of the /XC statement. When *1-2-3* then encounters the /XR command in the subroutine, it should return to the cell containing the /XC command to continue reading keystrokes.

However, if the subroutine instructs *1-2-3* to insert or delete rows above the /XC command, or insert or delete columns to the left of this statement, macro execution will not resume in the cell containing the /XC command—instead the macro resumes executing at the absolute address that originally contained this command. For example, assume that your macro begins in cell B3:

```
        A        B        C
1  hello!
2
3  \x       {HOME}hello!~
4           /XCinsert~
5           {HOME}goodbye!~
6
7  insert   /WIR{DOWN}~
8           /XR
```

The /XC statement in cell B4 branches to the subroutine *insert*. In the subroutine, the keystroke instructions /WIR will move the entire macro down two rows.

The /XC statement is now located in cell B6. However, when *1-2-3* encounters the /XR command, macro execution continues at cell B4, the original address of the /XC command. Since cell B4 is now blank, the macro stops. If cell B4 is not empty, all sorts of interesting things can happen, since *1-2-3* thinks it is at the next step of the macro.

Kevin Pribilsky

All releases of 1-2-3 behave this way. If your subroutines must insert or delete rows and columns in the worksheet to the left or above the main macro, use the /XG branching command rather than the /XC and /XR commands.

7. NO RECALCULATION WITH /XN AND /XL

I've noticed that the /XN and /XL commands do not cause *1-2-3* Release 1A to recalculate when they enter a value or number into a cell. Even worse, the *Calc* indicator is not turned on in manual recalculation. This might cause problems if you use a total or print out the worksheet immediately after running a macro containing /XN or /XL. The solution is to follow the /XN or /XL command with a {CALC} command in your macro.

John Predmore
Fairport, N.Y.

To speed up the macro, unless it must recalculate after each /XN and /XL command, include only one {CALC} as the final macro command.

The problem you describe is corrected in Release 2/2.01. When a Release 2 macro processes a /XN or /XL command, the worksheet automatically recalculates. If recalculation is set to manual, 1-2-3 illuminates the Calc *indicator.*

8. ERROR-TRAPPING IN LOOPS

The {ONERROR} statement in a {FOR} loop doesn't seem to work properly. We'd like *Symphony* to detect the error, display a message, then continue processing the loop. Instead it detects only the first error, displays the message, and stops. When we rewrite the macro using {BRANCH} statements, we can trap all the errors without trouble. Is there any way around this problem?

F. Mateo García
Iberia Lineas Aereas De Espana
Madrid, Spain

You've already discovered one way around the problem. When Symphony *detects an error, it clears all of its macro subroutine pointers, losing track of what it was processing when the error occurred. However, in some cases you can force* Symphony *to finish processing a {FOR} loop in spite of any errors.*

If you know where in the loop to expect an error, your error-trapping routine can include copies of the steps that are likely to be missed should the error occur. Alternatively, the error-trapping routine can call the original subroutine to repeat the steps that the macro missed on account of the error.

Let's see what happens when an error occurs while a macro is running. The following macro combines many copies of a small file named DUMMY into the current worksheet—not a particularly useful application other than to illustrate this technique. You indicate the number of copies to combine in the cell named targ, *then place the cell pointer in a clear area of the worksheet, cell G1, for example. When you start the macro, it combines a copy of DUMMY, moves the cell pointer down one page, combines a second copy of DUMMY, and so on, until the {FOR} loop has processed as many times as you indicated:*

	A	B	C	D
1	count			
2	targ			
3				
4	\m	{FOR count,1,targ,1,rout}		
5				
6	rout	{S}FCCEIFdummy~		
7		{PGDN}		

Before you can run the macro you must assign range names; point to cell A1, press MENU, select Range Name Labels Right, press DownArrow five times, and press Return. Then enter a value into targ *(cell B2). For this example, use a low value such as 3. If you're using a hard-disk system, assign A: as the default directory before you try this (press SERVICES and select File Directory, press Escape, type A:, and press Return).*

The macro fails if you run it without first putting a disk containing a file named DUMMY into the disk drive. Presumably, if you've made this mistake, you'd like the macro to pause and let you insert the appropriate disk, then continue where the error first occurred. The following is a macro that simulates this procedure:

	A	B	C	D	E	F
1	count					
2	targ	3				
3						
4	\m	{FOR count,1,targ,1,rout}				
5						
6	rout	{ONERROR oops}				
7		{S}FCCEIFdummy~				
8		{PGDN}				
9						
10	oops	{GETLABEL "Insert DUMMY disk; press Return",temp}				
11		{rout}				
12		{LET targ,targ-count}				
13		{BRANCH \m}				
14						
15	temp					

Rows 1 through 4 of the worksheet are identical to those of the last model, but I've modified the subroutine named rout *and added an error routine named* oops. *It starts with an* {ONERROR} *statement that tells* Symphony *to branch to the routine named* oops *should an error occur. Before you run the macro, assign range names; point to cell A10, press MENU, select Range Names Labels Right, then press PageDown Return. Here's how the macro works:*

{FOR count,1,targ,1,rout} *Starts the* {FOR} *loop. With the value 3 in the cell named* targ, *the loop processes three times.*

{ONERROR oops} *Begins error trapping. If an error occurs from here on,* Symphony *will lose track of the* {FOR} *loop and branch directly to the cell named* oops.

{S}FCCEIFdummy~ *Combines the entire file named DUMMY into the worksheet starting at the current position of the cell pointer. This is where an error is most likely to happen. If the disk drive is empty or the file doesn't exist,* Symphony *branches to* oops; *otherwise, it proceeds to the next cell.*

{PGDN} *Moves the cell pointer down one screen to make room for the next copy of DUMMY. After this step,* Symphony *increases the value of* count *and once again starts the subroutine, repeating the process until* count *is greater in value than* targ.

Here's how the error-trapping routine works:

{GETLABEL "Insert DUMMY disk; press Return",temp} *Displays the prompt* Insert DUMMY disk; press Return, *then stores in the cell named* temp *whatever you enter. This gives you an opportunity to put the correct disk in the data drive so that the macro doesn't repeat the error.*

{rout} *Calls the subroutine named* rout. *This is the same routine that the* {FOR} *statement was processing when the error occurred. That routine starts error trapping, tries to combine the file named DUMMY, then moves the cell pointer down one page. Assuming you have supplied the proper disk, the macro continues processing the next step of the error-trapping routine. If you haven't supplied a disk with DUMMY on it, the resulting error cancels the subroutine, transfers control to the cell named* oops, *and proceeds as described starting in the previous step.*

{LET targ,targ−count} *Places the value of* targ *minus* count *in the cell named* targ. *This is the difference between the number of loops the* {FOR} *statement was meant to process (*targ) *and the number that it had processed successfully before the error occurred (*count).

{BRANCH \m} *Restarts the macro. The macro processes the* {FOR} *command, resetting* count *to 1 and using the new value of* targ *to stop the loop.*

This technique doesn't work if your macro relies on the changing value of count *to generate unique results on each pass through the loop. The technique you described as having worked for you is better suited to that type of application.*

9. RECALCULATION BUG

Symphony Release 1.1 does not always recalculate correctly after attaching the Macro Library Manager. Here's the problem: I retrieve a file in which recalculation is set to manual in natural order. I attach the Macro Library Manager and load a macro that contains a {CALC} command. Instead of recalculating in natural order, the spreadsheet recalculates columnwise.

This only happens when the Macro Library Manager is initially attached. If I subsequently retrieve a worksheet, the recalculation takes place in the correct order. Furthermore, if I call up the worksheet and press CALC once before attaching the Macro Library Manager, subsequent recalculation is in natural order.

David Watkins
Goldman Sachs International Corp
London, England

Both the Lotus United Kingdom office and Lotus's U.S. headquarters confirmed this problem. Lotus Product Support in the United Kingdom told us that a macro in the Macro Library Manager that contains the {CALC} command works properly if you load the macro before you retrieve a file. However, if you retrieve the file first and then load the macro that contains the {CALC} command, you will have to invoke the macro four times to get it to work properly.

APPENDIX
1

1-2-3 RELEASE 2/2.01 AND SYMPHONY MACRO COMMANDS

Keyword	Action
{?}	Stops macro temporarily, letting user type, move the cell pointer, and access the menus; macro resumes when user presses Return.
{name arg1,arg2,...}	Calls a subroutine named *name*, optionally passing arguments for use by the subroutine.
{BEEP number}	Sounds one of four different tones
{BLANK range}	Erases the contents of a specified cell or range.
{BRANCH location}	Transfers macro flow of control to *location*.
{BREAKOFF} and {BREAKON}	Disables and enables the use of the Break key to stop a macro.
{CLOSE}	Closes a disk file that has been opened with the {OPEN} command.
{CONTENTS targ, source, width, format}	Copies the *source* cell to the *targ* cell as a label, optionally formatting the result using a particular column width and numeric display format.
{DEFINE location1: type1,location2: type2,...}	Specifies cells that will store arguments passed to a subroutine during a subroutine call.
{DISPATCH location}	Branches to destination named at *location*.

Keyword	Action
{FILESIZE cell}	Records in *cell* the number of bytes of a currently opened disk file.
{FOR counter,start, stop,step,routine}	Repeats the commands beginning in *routine* as many times as indicated by the values of *start, stop,* and *step*. This is called a FOR loop.
{FORBREAK }	Stops a FOR loop. Processing continues immediately after the last {FOR} command.
{GET cell}	Causes macro to pause until the user presses a key, then records the keystroke as a label in *cell*.
{GETLABEL prompt, cell}	Displays *prompt* in the control panel and stores the user's response as a label in *cell*.
{GETNUMBER prompt, cell}	Displays *prompt* in the control panel and stores the user's response as a value in *cell*.
{GETPOS cell}	Determines the current position in an opened file, and enters at *cell* a value representing that position.
{IF condition}	Processes subsequent commands in the cell holding the {IF} statement only when *condition* evaluates to true.
{INDICATE string}	Replaces the standard indicator message at the upper-right corner of the screen with characters specified by *string*. Omitting *string* restores the indicator's normal message.
{LET cell, value}	Places the value (numeric or string) of *value* into *cell*.
{LOOK cell}	Copies a single character from the keyboard buffer to *cell* without removing the character from the buffer.
{MENUBRANCH menumap}	Displays a customized menu whose instructions are found starting at *menumap*, then branches based on a user's selection.
{MENUCALL menumap}	Similar to {MENUBRANCH}, however, processes the menu instructions and their associated steps as a subroutine.

Keyword	Action
{ONERROR location, cell}	Causes flow of control to shift to *location* if an otherwise fatal error occurs. Optionally stores *1-2-3* or *Symphony*'s error message in *cell*.
{OPEN filename, mode}	Opens a disk file named *filename* for reading, writing, or both.
{PANELOFF}	Suppresses updating of the control panel while a macro is running.
{PANELON}	Restores redrawing of the control panel, canceling a {PANELOFF} command.
{PUT range, column, row}	Places a value (numeric or string) into the cell in *range* represented by the column and row offset represented by *column* and *row*.
{QUIT}	Stops the macro.
{READ bytes, cell}	Reads from an opened disk file the number of characters specified by *bytes*, and stores the characters as a string in *cell*.
{RECALC range, condition, count}	Recalculates *range* proceeding row by row.
{RECALCCOL range, condition, count}	Recalculates *range* proceeding column by column. For this and the previous command, *condition* is a condition to be met before recalculation finishes, and *count* is the maximum number of times *1-2-3* or *Symphony* should recalculate in trying to satisfy the condition. *Condition* and *count* are optional arguments.
{RESTART}	Stops all subroutines currently in progress; the macro continues with the next command, as though starting a new macro.
{RETURN}	Ends a subroutine call or {MENUCALL} subroutine; the macro continues with the command following the last subroutine call or {MENUCALL} command.
{SETPOS number}	Sets position in an opened disk file to the character represented by *number*.

Keyword	Action
{WAIT time}	Causes macro to pause until the computer's clock time matches *time*.
{WINDOWSOFF}	Suppresses redrawing of the windows while a macro is running.
{WINDOWSON}	Restores standard window redrawing, canceling a {WINDOWSOFF} command.
{WRITE string}	Copies characters represented by *string* into an opened disk file.
{WRITELN string}	Adds a carriage-return-line-feed sequence to *string* and writes the result in the opened disk file.

Symphony only:

Keyword	Action
{HANDSHAKE send, receive, timeout, cell}	Sends a string, *send*, to a remote computer, and waits *timeout* seconds to receive a string, *receive*. Optionally stores the response in *cell*.
{PHONE string}	Dials a telephone number represented by *string*. Abnegates the need to switch to a COMM window to phone a remote computer.

APPENDIX
2

SPECIAL KEY
INDICATORS

The special key indicators represent keys whose names defy single charac-ter descriptions. They appear below grouped by product. With the exception of *1-2-3* Release 1 and 1A users, you can include arguments in many of these keynames. The arguments indicate how many times your macro should press the named key. For example, {DOWN 3} means "Press the DownArrow key three times," and {CALC count} means "Press the CALC key as many times as represented by the value of the cell named *count*."

1-2-3 only:
  {QUERY}
  {TABLE}
  {GRAPH}
  {DEL}
  {NAME}

1-2-3 and *Symphony*:
  ~ (the return key)
  {EDIT}
  {ABS}
  {GOTO}
  {WINDOW}
  {CALC}
  {UP}
  {DOWN}
  {LEFT}
  {RIGHT}
  {HOME}
  {PGUP}
  {PGDN}
  {END}
  {ESC} or {ESCAPE}
  {BS} or {BACKSPACE}
  {DELETE}

Symphony and
1-2-3 Release 2 and 2.01:
  {INSERT}
  {BIGLEFT}
  {BIGRIGHT}
  {MENU}

Symphony only:
  {WHERE}
  {JUSTIFY}
  {SPLIT}
  {INDENT}
  {CENTER}
  {CAPTURE}
  {ERASE}
  {ZOOM}
  {DRAW}
  {SWITCH}
  {SERVICES}
  {TYPE}
  {BIGDOWN}
  {BIGUP}

Symphony Release 1.1/1.2 and
1-2-3 Release 2/2.01:
  {~}
  {{}
  {}}

INDEX